ENVIRONMENTAL REGULATIONS
AND CORPORATE STRATEGY

Environmental Regulations and Corporate Strategy

A NAFTA Perspective

Alan Rugman, John Kirton,
and Julie Soloway

UNIVERSITY PRESS

OXFORD
UNIVERSITY PRESS

Great Clarendon Street, Oxford OX2 6DP

Oxford University Press is a department of the University of Oxford.
It furthers the University's objective of excellence in research, scholarship,
and education by publishing worldwide in

Oxford New York

Athens Auckland Bangkok Bogotá Buenos Aires Calcutta
Cape Town Chennai Dar es Salaam Delhi Florence Hong Kong Istanbul
Karachi Kuala Lumpur Madrid Melbourne Mexico City Mumbai
Nairobi Paris São Paulo Singapore Taipei Tokyo Toronto Warsaw

with associated companies in Berlin Ibadan

Oxford is a registered trade mark of Oxford University Press
in the UK and in certain other countries

Published in the United States
by Oxford University Press Inc., New York

© Alan Rugman, John Kirton, Julie Soloway 1999

The moral rights of the authors have been asserted
Database right Oxford University Press (maker)

First published 1999

All rights reserved. No part of this publication may be reproduced,
stored in a retrieval system, or transmitted, in any form or by any means,
without the prior permission in writing of Oxford University Press,
or as expressly permitted by law, or under terms agreed with the appropriate
reprographics rights organizations. Enquiries concerning reproduction
outside the scope of the above should be sent to the Rights Department,
Oxford University Press, at the address above

You must not circulate this book in any other binding or cover
and you must impose this same condition on any acquirer

British Library Cataloguing in Publication Data

Data available

Library of Congress Cataloging in Publication Data

Rugman, Alan M.
Environmental regulations and corporate strategy: a NAFTA
perspective/Alan Rugman, John Kirton, and Julie Soloway.
p. cm.
Includes bibliographical references and index.
1. Environmenal law—North America. 2. Free trade—Environmental
aspects—North America. I. Kirton, John J. II. Soloway, Julie A.
III. Title.
KDZ670.R84 1999 341.7'62—dc21   99-24522
ISBN 0-19-829588-X

1 3 5 7 9 10 8 6 4 2

Typeset in Photina by
Cambrian Typesetters, Frimley, Surrey
Printed in Great Britain
on acid-free paper by
Biddles Ltd, Guildford & Kings Lynn

Preface and Acknowledgements

This book is the result of an intense collaboration among three scholars from several core public policy disciplines: Alan Rugman of management studies and economics; John Kirton of political science and international relations; and Julie Soloway of law and regulation. Our collaboration had its origins in our shared research interest arising from earlier work related to trade–environment issues. Alan Rugman's was inspired by his analyses of how protectionist firms in the United States captured the administration of the antidumping and countervailing duty process to deny Canadian firms the entry they needed to the market on which their corporate fortunes depended. John Kirton's arose from his study of the role of international institutions in the management of the Canada–US relationship and of how environmental considerations could best be inserted into the free trade agreements—NAFTA, the WTO, APEC, and the FTAA—that Canada, the United States, and Mexico were negotiating in the 1990s. Julie Soloway's emerged from her analysis of NAFTA's environmental effects and the quality of dispute settlement under international trade law within NAFTA and the WTO.

In all cases our scholarly interest was reinforced by our role as advisers to firms, governments, and international organizations on how managers and policymakers could act more effectively to meet the challenges of a rapidly changing world. Kirton and Rugman served as successive members of the government of Canada's International Trade Advisory Committee during the time the Canada–US Free Trade Agreement and NAFTA were being negotiated and implemented. They worked with Soloway on three major projects for the NAFTA Commission for Environmental Cooperation. Rugman and Kirton acted as consultants for major North American and international corporations, adding a sensitivity to the practical, policy-oriented implications of their analysis for business, government, and NGO practitioners.

These interests led us to initiate, in April of 1997, a three-year project on 'Trade, Environmental Regulations and Canadian Competitiveness', with the financial support of the Social Sciences and Humanities Research Council of Canada, through their programme on 'Managing for Global Competitiveness'. To assist this project we assembled an advisory group of senior individuals from the business, government, and NGO sectors: John Howard, Senior Vice-President, MacMillan Bloedel; David Winfield, Senior Vice-President, Northern Telecom; Someshwar Rao, Director, Industry Canada; Sarah Richardson, Trade–Environment Program Manager, Commission for Environmental Cooperation; Michael Cloghesy, Centre Patronal de l'Énvironnement du Quebec; and Ken Ogilvie, Executive Director, Pollution Probe. We are grateful to the SSHRC for their indispensable financial support under award 804-97-0005 and to the individuals on our advisory group for taking on this responsibility and for the assistance they have provided.

During our first year we produced an edited volume assembling and analysing the classic works on trade–environment issues, published nine articles and book chapters that provided a theoretical and empirical foundation for this volume, and presented five additional conference papers to test emerging arguments and enrich our thinking through scholarly dialogue in many disciplinary settings. We are grateful to the many individuals and organizations who facilitated this process.

We particularly appreciate the contribution of the several publications and individuals who provided permission for us to use portions and versions of previously published work as the basis for many of the chapters in this volume. These are *The Journal of World Trade* for the material in Chapter 2, *The Journal of Transnational Management Development* for the material in Chapter 3, *The American Review of Canadian Studies* and David Vogel for the material in Chapters 4 and 6, the University of Southern California's School of International Relations and *Columbia International Affairs Online* for the material in Chapter 5, Mario Shettino and David Vogel for the material in Chapter 9, and the Center for Strategic and International Studies in Washington, DC, Sidney Weintraub and Christopher Sands for the material in Chapter 10.

In researching and writing this book we benefited substantially from earlier work done under the auspices of two projects supported by the Commission for Environmental Cooperation: the 'NAFTA Environmental Effects Project' whose study on *NAFTA's Institutions: The Environmental Potential and Performance of the NAFTA Free Trade Commission and Related Bodies*, co-authored by John Kirton and Rafael Fernandez de Castro provided a research foundation for Chapter 5, and the 'Regulations as Barriers to Trade Project' whose report, co-authored by Alan Rugman, Mario Schettino, and David Vogel, similarly enriched Chapter 9.

We also wish to acknowledge with gratitude the contribution of our many colleagues who shaped our thinking on the trade–environment issues directly relevant to this book or who gave us valuable comments, criticisms, and information on the various chapters of our book as it passed from conception, through individual chapters, to an integrated whole. These include Alan Alexandroff, Werner Antweiler, Stephen Blank, Stephen Clarkson, Joseph D'Cruz, Alan Deardorff, Charles Doran, Lorraine Eden, Dan Esty, Raphael Fernandez de Castro, Robert Friedheim, Harriet Friedmann, Glen Fox, Michael Hawes, Walid Hejazi, Robert Howse, Joseph Jockel, Stephen Lamy, Alejandro Nadal, Virginia Maclaren, Armand de Mestral, Maureen Molot, Don Munton, Stephen Mumme, Sylvia Ostry, Ford Runge, Christopher Sands, Ed Safarian, Daniel Schwanen, Robert Stern, Christopher Stone, Dan Trefler, Michael Trebilcock, Alain Verbeke, Konrad Von Moltke, Leonard Waverman, Sidney Weintraub, and Duncan Wood. We are similarly grateful for the vital contribution of the anonymous reviewers of our initial SSHRC grant proposal, subsequent publications, and prospectus and manuscript for Oxford University Press.

Among the many individuals from outside the academy who provided exceptional assistance, we acknowledge the particular intellectual contribution of Denis Audet, John Audley, Jose Montemayor Dragonne, Jonathan Fried, Susan Hainsworth, Philip Hemmings, John Hueneman, Pierre Marc Johnson, Olga Ojeda, Suzanne Troje, David Van Hoogstratten, and John Weekes.

We further appreciate the assistance of those at the University of Toronto and Templeton College, Oxford University, who eased our task as we moved from grant application, through research and writing to publication. We received outstanding support from Mary Lynne Bratti, and Joan Golding and Rashida Chee-a-kwan of the University of Toronto's Centre for International Studies, Hilary Buttrick of its Rotman School of Management, Marilyn Laville of its International Relations Program, and Denise Edwards of Templeton College at Oxford University. We have a special debt to the Director of the Centre, Professor Louis Pauly, who generously provided the facilities for our research and hosted the 'NAFTA Seminar' which provided valuable commentary. We are also grateful to our dedicated research assistant, Cecilia Brain.

We owe much to our editor at Oxford University Press, David Musson, for rapidly identifying the value of this enterprise and guiding it, with enthusiasm and conviction, through to a speedy and trouble-free publication.

We finally wish to thank our partners and families. They not only graciously accepted the long hours we spent away from them while researching and writing this book, but also displayed the interest in, support for, and enthusiasm about the project that inspired us along the way. We dedicate it to them.

Alan Rugman, Oxford
John Kirton, Toronto
Julie Soloway, Toronto

31 August 1998

Permissions

Kirton, John, 'NAFTA's Commission for Environmental Cooperation and Canada–US Environmental Relations', *American Review of Canadian Studies*, 27(3) (Winter 1997): 459–86. Reprinted by permission of ARCS.

Kirton, John, 'NAFTA's Trade–Environment Institutions: Regional Impact, Hemispheric Potential'. Paper presented at the University of Southern California's Center for International Studies, *Columbia International Affairs Online*, 1997. Reprinted with permission of Columbia University Press.

Kirton, John, 'The Impact of Environmental Regulation on the North American Auto Industry Since NAFTA', in Sidney Weintraub and Christopher Sands (eds.), *The North American Auto Industry under NAFTA* (Washington, DC: CSIS, 1998). Reprinted by permission.

Rugman, Alan M., Kirton, John, and Soloway, Julie, 'NAFTA, Environmental Regulations, and Canadian Competitiveness', *Journal of World Trade*, 31(4) (August 1997): 129–44. Reprinted with the kind permission of Kluwer Law International.

Rugman, Alan M., and Soloway, Julie, (1997) 'Corporate Strategy and NAFTA when Environmental Regulations are Barriers to Trade', *Journal of Transnational Management Development*, 3(4) (1997): 231–51. Reprinted with permission of The Haworth Press Inc.

Soloway, Julie A., 'Environmental Trade Barriers Under NAFTA: The MMT Fuel Additives Controversy', *Minnesota Journal of Global Trade*, 8 (1) (Winter 1999): 55–95. Reprinted with permission.

Vogel, David, and Rugman, Alan M., 'Environmentally Related Trade Disputes between the United States and Canada', *American Review of Canadian Studies*, 27(2) (Summer 1997): 271–92. Reprinted by permission of ARCS.

Contents

List of Figures   x

List of Tables   x

Abbreviations   xi

1. Introduction   1

Part I: Economic and Corporate Strategy

2. The Analytic Framework of Capture   23
3. Corporate Strategy and Environmental Regulation: Corporate Strategy Perspectives   38
4. Corporate Strategy and Environmental Regulation: Baptist–Bootlegger Coalitions   53

Part II: Complex Institutional Responsiveness: NAFTA's Political Experience

5. Trade and Environment Institutions: The NAFTA Regime   75
6. Environmental Institutions in Action: The CEC   91
7. Firm Responses to Trade and Environment Regulation   114

Part III: Case Studies of Complex Institutional Responsiveness

8. MMT and Investment Dispute Settlement   139
9. The Agriculture Disputes   162
10. Trade and Environment Regimes in Operation: The North American Auto Industry   183

Part IV: Conclusions

11. Implications for Firm Strategy and Public Policy   211

References   241

Index   253

List of Figures

2.1	Competitiveness, trade, and the environment	27
3.1	The NAFTA environmental regulations across the member states	41
3.2	NAFTA, trade, and environmental regulations	51
7.1	The institutional deepening of the NAFTA regime	133

List of Tables

1.1	Interviewees by community	14
1.2	Interviewees by country	15
1.3	Interviewees by community and country	16
5.1	NAFTA's share of US and Canadian exports, 1994, 1990–1994	88
5.2	US exports over imports 1994 (1990–1994)	89
7.1	The conditions of complex institutional responsiveness	116
7.2	Corporate strategies under complex institutional responsiveness	118
7.3	Political strategies under complex institutional responsiveness	122
8.1	NAFTA Chapter 11 cases initiated	155
9.1	NAFTA agriculture cases	166
11.1	Cases of North American environmental regulatory protection	212–14
11.2	Preferred corporate and political strategies by level of internationalization of firm	228
11.3	Outcomes of North American regulatory protectionism by country and issue (post-NAFTA)	229
11.4	Outcomes of resolved cases of North American environmental regulatory protection (pre- and post-NAFTA)	231
11.5	Resolved cases of post-NAFTA North American environmental regulatory protection dealt with through the NAFTA institutions	233
11.6	Major EU trade and environment disputes	238
11.7	Major US–EU trade and environment disputes	239

Abbreviations

AD	Antidumping
AIT	Agreement on Internal Trade
AMEG	Mexican Association of Cattle Feeders
APEC	Asia-Pacific Economic Cooperation
APHIS	Animal and Plant Health Inspection Service
ASC	Automotive Standards Council
BECC	Border Environment Cooperation Commission
BRI	Brewers Retail Inc. (Canada)
CAADES	Confederacion de Asociaciones del Estado de Sinaloa
CAFE	Corporate Average Fuel Economy Standards
CAT	Committee on Agricultural Trade
CCME	Canadian Council of Ministers of the Environment
CEC	Commission for Environmental Cooperation
CEPA	Canadian Environmental Protection Act
CFBF	California Farm Bureau Federation
CLC	Commission for Labour Cooperation
CNPH	Confederacion de Nacional de Productores de Hortalizas
COFLI	Coalition for Fair Lumber Imports (US)
CPPI	Canadian Petroleum Products Institute
CSPS	Committee on Sanitary and Phytosanitary Standards
CSRM	Committee on Standards-Related Measures
CTE	Committee for Trade and Environment
CVD	countervailing duties
ENGO	environmental non-governmental organization
EPA	Environmental Protection Agency (US)
EU	European Union
FDA	Food and Drug Administration (US)
FDI	foreign direct investment
FTA	Free Trade Agreement (Canada–United States)
FTAA	Free Trade Agreement of the Americas
FTC	Free Trade Commission
GAC	Government Advisory Committee
GATT	General Agreement on Tariffs and Trade
IJC	International Joint Commission
ISO	International Standardization Organization
ITC	International Trade Commission (US)
JPAC	Joint Public Advisory Committee
LTSS I	Working Group on Vehicle Standards
LTSS V	Working Group on the Transportation of Dangerous Goods

MAI	Multilateral Agreement on Investment
MMT	methylcyclopentadienyl manganese tricarbonyl
MNC	multinational corporation
MNE	multinational enterprises
MVMA	Motor Vehicles Manufacturers Association
NAAEC	North American Agreement on Environmental Cooperation
NAC	National Advisory Committee
NACE	North American Commission on the Environment
NADBank	North American Development Bank
NAFEC	North American Fund for Environmental Cooperation
NAFTA	North American Free Trade Agreement
NAPPO	North American Plant Protection Organization
NAPRI	North American Pollutant Release Inventory
NGO	non-governmental organization
OBD	on-board diagnostic system
OECD	Organisation for Economic Cooperation and Development
OEM	original equipment manufacture
SAGAR	Mexican Ministry of Agriculture
SECOFI	Mexican Ministry of Commerce and Industry
SPS	Sanitary and Phytosanitary Standards
TWGP	Technical Working Group on Pesticides
UHT	ultra-high temperature
UNICITRAL	United Nations Commission for International Trade
USDA	United States Department of Agriculture
USMEF	US Meat Export Federation
USTR	United States Trade Representative
WTO	World Trade Organization

1
Introduction

Overview

Recent advances in trade liberalization and new forms of environmental regulation present both strategic opportunities and obstacles for firms engaged in international trade and investment. The elimination of the traditional border barriers of tariffs and quotas under multilateral and regional trade agreements has opened new markets abroad, but at the same time removed the major instrument some firms have used to protect themselves at home from international competition. Thus, firms and governments are aggressively seeking alternative and innovative strategies to keep open access to international markets, while maintaining shelter at home.

The classic strategy for securing shelter has been the capture of the administration of domestic regulation, including the new generation of environmental regulations, by domestic industry. The industries seeking shelter often form alliances with environmental groups and seek protection through the discriminatory application of national and local environmental regulation, at times in violation of internationally guaranteed national treatment provisions and other trade disciplines. However, the recent emergence of international trade and environment regimes with substantial powers for dispute settlement, management and prevention, and international regulatory convergence, give outward-looking firms new opportunities at the international level to challenge and circumvent this growing phenomenon. The broader array of corporate strategies which results has flourished in North America under the innovative trade and environment rules and institutions created by the North American Free Trade Agreement (NAFTA).

This study develops a model of complex institutional responsiveness and demonstrates how it identifies and guides firm strategy in this new era of opportunities for national regulatory capture and international institutional regulation. It applies this model within the context of North America and explores its implications for Europe and Asia by relating the NAFTA experience to that of other regional trade arrangements and the World Trade Organization (WTO). Drawing on the disciplines of management studies, economics, political science, and law, it examines 24 leading and 84 relevant cases of efforts by firms to benefit from, or defend against, such capture through the use of international institutions. The research is based on 230 confidential interviews with senior executives and officials in North American and European companies, national governments, environmental groups, and research centres. The study shows how innovative corporate strategies (of both a market-oriented and politically directed nature) have successfully opened international markets previously closed by national and local environmental regulations and by the 'green and greedy' coalitions of protectionists and environmentalists that can lie behind them. Using the firm as the unit of analysis, it identifies how five types of environmental regulations intersect with four different kinds of firms to yield specific strategies. Based on this analysis, it suggests how managers should approach, and how government officials should reform, the operation and architecture of the new trade and environment regimes at the regional and global level.

Context and Scope of the Study

As firms move to take advantage of newly opened international markets, they increasingly encounter what appear to them to be complex, opaque, and ever-changing environmental regulations which deny them easy and profitable access to the foreign markets they need to maintain competitiveness. Such regulations are particularly costly when they are designed, supported, and administered in a way that benefits powerful coalitions of competing protectionist industries, often operating in alliance with politically influential environmental groups.

The past decade has witnessed a sharp increase in the number of trade disputes arising from such environmental regulations and coalitions. Yet it has also seen the creation of new international institutions to resolve these disputes in ways that both open international markets and safeguard the environment. The major reduction in national border barriers to trade, due to NAFTA, the European Union (EU) and the Uruguay Round of the General Agreement on Tariffs and Trade (GATT), has increased the visibility, importance, and protectionist impact of regulatory standards at the local, national, and international level. At the same time, the increasing severity of, and public concern about, environmental degradation has led to a proliferation of new and innovative environmental regulations at all levels.

Trade–environment conflict is thus growing steadily throughout the world across a wide range of industries. The EU has denied market access to genetically modified maize produced in North America, a move that has jeopardized overall EU–US trade relations (TED 1996). The EU has since 1989 denied market access to hormone-treated beef from the United States and Canada, prompting acute controversy and ongoing trade disputes at the WTO. The US ban on tuna caught using a 'dolphin-unfriendly' process led to years of acrimony between Mexico and the United States. Similarly, the US ban on shrimps caught using a 'turtle-unfriendly' process has been the subject of a trade and environment dispute involving Malaysia, Thailand, Pakistan, and India. Disputes over discriminatory eco-labelling schemes imposed by Europe and

North America on timber products from less developed nations have been so severe as to warrant separate international treaty negotiations. In addition to the high political stakes that trade–environment controversies now create for governments lie major impacts on the corporate fortunes of firms, from the world's largest multinationals, to small domestic producers competing with imports from abroad.

Companies facing such regulatory conflicts and the barriers that create them have a limited array of corporate and political strategies at their disposal. They can adapt their products and production methods to meet such foreign regulations, or establish subsidiaries abroad that can better conform to foreign regulations. Politically, they can mobilize their home government to help them litigate in a foreign government's national trade law system, hire lobbyists to advance their interests, and form coalitions with foreign suppliers and customers to alter the regulatory barrier and its protectionist impact. In all cases, however, such strategies tend to be time-consuming, costly, and often unsuccessful, especially for firms from smaller countries whose corporate fortunes depend upon sales in the large triad markets of the United States, EU, and Japan.

The recent emergence of conditions of complex institutional responsiveness with strong international regimes for trade and environment at the core, opens a new array of possibilities. They offer dispute settlement mechanisms that allow firms to activate a more neutral, rules-based mechanism to challenge foreign environmental regulations that can erode legally guaranteed access to markets abroad. They present processes to manage and even prevent disputes without expensive and lengthy litigation. They enable firms to participate in a process of harmonizing national regulations in ways that open the wider international market to all firms within a free trade area. Finally, they enable firms to better understand the character of foreign regulations and form coalitions with other firms, environmental groups, and government agencies in order to constrain the discriminatory impact of these regulations, or to create favourable regulatory regimes on a multilateral scale. In short, these new trade and environment regimes allow firms to respond to the threat of environmental regulatory protectionism by mobilizing international institutions in complex ways to access the markets they would otherwise be denied.

This process of complex institutional responsiveness is currently flourishing within North America. Both large and medium size enterprises from the three countries (with distinctive regulatory systems) are seeking access to the entire NAFTA market place, in part to equip themselves for the intensified competition that they face on a global scale. NAFTA came into force in January 1994. It represents the world's most advanced international regime for balancing and integrating the rules and procedures for trade liberalization and environmental protection. The core NAFTA trade agreement has created three major, innovative trilateral dispute settlement mechanisms to cover antidumping and countervailing duty disputes, general disputes, and direct foreign investment disputes. Its accompanying North American Agreement on Environmental Cooperation (NAAEC) has created three surveillance and enforcement mechanisms to constrain national environmental regulatory activity in ways that affect trade. The 50 regional institutions created or catalysed by these agreements are managing and preventing disputes. This leads to convergence of national environmental regulations in ways that can redirect international trade. The work of such institutions has created many new fora in which firms can join with actors at home and abroad to influence NAFTA's processes of dispute settlement and management, regulatory convergence and environmental cooperation, and the national politics and market dynamics which lie behind.

How do and should firms respond to this complex array of international institutional arrangements and possibilities to enhance international market access and thus the overall competitiveness for which sales in foreign markets are often crucial? Under what conditions should they mobilize the regional NAFTA institutions, rather than market-based, national governmental, or broader multilateral processes? When, how, and in what combination should they rely on NAFTA's mechanisms for dispute settlement, regulatory convergence, or regional cooperation and coalition building? And how can their national governments best assist them in this process and shape the trade–environment regimes of the future for this purpose?

Such questions have arisen with increasing poignancy with the recent proliferation of trade and environment disputes within North America, and between it and its major global trading partners. This was first apparent in the decade prior to NAFTA, when there were many such disputes that imposed major costs on North American firms and on global firms seeking access to the North American (primarily the US) market place. Such disputes embraced many types of regulation and firms. Indeed, they occurred at all levels of regulation (subnational, national, and international) and affected a broad range of domestic and multinational firms. For example, the tuna–dolphin disputes of the early 1990s, concerning a US-imposed ban on the import of Mexican tuna which had been caught by 'dolphin-unfriendly' fishing practices, was eventually the subject of two GATT dispute settlement panels. In the early 1990s, a dispute arose in the pulp and paper sector concerning a California environmental regulation which imposed a minimum 50 per cent recycled fibre content on all newsprint. This regulation had a serious and adverse impact on British Columbia newsprint producers, who depended heavily on California as an export market and who were unable to locally source the requisite amount of recycled newsprint. This regulatory barrier was eventually solved through a number of shifts in the British Columbian producer's strategies. In 1992 the Canadian province of Ontario imposed a $0.10/bottle recycling tax on all aluminium beer cans, 90 per cent of which came from the United States. This issue, part of a larger ongoing dispute between the United States and Canada concerning beer distribution, was solved through bilateral negotiations between the two countries. These cases and the many similar ones in Europe and other regions beyond North America demonstrate the increasing potential for environmental regulation to have serious impacts on firm competitiveness and to spark trade tensions between NAFTA parties. They also reveal the limited array of classic strategies which firms had available and activated in response.

The advent of NAFTA promised to bring a sharp increase in the number of such disputes, as it added to the mix the very different, often opaque and rapidly changing system of environmental regulations in Mexico, while simultaneously removing barriers along its borders to firms from the United States and Canada. However, along with NAFTA came a new and innovative system of legal and political mechanisms for managing environmentally related trade disputes and doing so in ways that advanced trade liberalization while respecting environmental values. At the heart of the NAFTA trade agreement is its Chapter 19 provisions for the settlement of disputes regarding the national determination of antidumping and countervailing duties, and its Chapter 20 provisions to cover general disputes. NAFTA also brought to the world a novel set of rules and mechanisms under Chapter 11 for investment, a set that in many ways has served as a model for efforts to construct a Multilateral Agreement on Investment (MAI). More broadly, the NAFTA created a set of 50 intergovernmental institutions that provide a permanent political system for dealing in advance with such disputes, and thus controlling or avoiding the need to take them to formal litigation. At the side of NAFTA came an interlinked NAAEC. Its 'roving spotlight' provisions in Article 13 provided for secretariat-initiated investigation into matters of environmental concern throughout North America. Article 14/15 additionally offered a process by which the interested parties—firms, citizens, and environmental groups—could petition directly for an investigation into a country's alleged non-enforcement of its environmental laws. The NAAEC also contained the power, in Part V, for the United States and Mexico to impose trade sanctions on each other to punish the systematic non-enforcement of government environmental regulations.

How well has this new NAFTA system for managing environmentally related trade disputes operated? Has it represented a marked improvement over the available mechanisms and results of managing such disputes in the previous fifteen years? Has it diminished the number and severity of the disputes which have arisen, notwithstanding the newly opened borders and new Mexican regulatory system? Has it enabled the firms and countries of North America to avoid the cumbersome and conflictual process of the GATT/WTO and find superior solutions within North America? Has it adequately addressed not only the familiar environmentally related trade disputes but the new generation of associated conflicts arising from transborder investment? And has it equipped firms from and operating in all three NAFTA countries and outside firms from around the world with an effective instrument to solve

6   *Introduction*

or avoid such disputes and thus take full advantage of the entire NAFTA and ultimately global market place?

The Debate in the Literature

The existing literature has provided only a cursory and unsatisfying answer to these important questions. The general literature on international business–government relations in general, and in regard to trade–environment issues in particular, has not yet systematically and comprehensively explored how the rich strategic interaction between these two major kinds of actors on the international stage—firms and governments—are transformed when they take place in the presence of, and through, international institutions. The complexity introduced by the advent of international institutions that matter is compounded when, as in NAFTA, they involve firms, and the environmental groups with whom they compete and coalesce, directly in their processes and governance structure.

Several major works have provided some of the individual building blocks required to construct the more complex and comprehensive analytical framework needed to explore these new dynamics. Most generally, Stopford and Strange (1992) identified the need to put firm–government interactions and strategies at the centre of international relations analyses in the new, rapidly globalizing world of the 1990s, but were largely silent on how international institutions autonomously operated as a third actor in this mix. Reciprocally, those major works exploring the important impacts of international environmental regimes in the 1990s have failed to identify firms, and often other societal groups such as ENGOs as significant actors in their creation and operation. Oran Young (1994) and Ronald Mitchell (1994) demonstrate the importance of international institutions in effecting environmental outcomes independent of the activities of national governments, and point to the role of non-governmental actors in such institutions. But they do not deal with the strategic behaviour of firms within this setting nor the way firms can combine with ENGOs to use such international institutions and their regulations in protectionist or other ways for their advantage. Nor do Haas, Keohane, and Levy (1993) relate the general ineffectiveness of the international environmental institutions they explore to the strategic calculations of firms or ENGOs.

The general trade–environment literature similarly does not use the firm or regional institutional structure as the unit of analysis. Esty's (1994) landmark book on trade and environment provides a comprehensive and thoughtful summary of the trade–environment debate focusing on the GATT as the primary regime in operation. Consequently, he argues for multilateral institutional development as a means by which to solve most of the trade and environment problems raised. Trade experts Bhagwati and Hudec (1996) have focused on questions relating to harmonization of environmental regulations and regimes. Here, the viability of a harmonization strategy in areas where domestic regulations diverge and create trade impacts is assessed. However, this approach does not consider the impact of discriminatory environmental regulation at the firm level.

Vogel (1995) has drawn together an explanation of the formation of environmental policy and regulation, while at the same time considering the specific question of how international trade agreements can constrain the formation of trade-restricting environmental, health and safety regulation. He analyses these disputes from the perspective of the increased participation of the NGO sector in international trade policy as well as the overall effects of this dynamic on levels of environmental regulation. However, he too does not focus on the firm and its strategies as the central unit of analysis.

The theory of shelter, as developed by Rugman and Verbeke (1990), explores the extent to which the administration of trade remedies (such as antidumping and countervailing duties) has been captured by firms seeking shelter from international competition. This has been applied to environmental regulation in the context of the forestry industry in later work by Rugman (1995) and provides part of the theoretical basis for the present study. However, this work does not incorporate the dynamics involved with complex institutional responsiveness in trading regimes and the much broader array of alternative strategies now emerging for firms.

The extensive literature on NAFTA itself has focused on the creation and content of the regime and speculations about how it might operate in the future (Johnson and Beaulieu 1996; Rubin and Alexander 1996). There has been little work carefully examining the actual operation of the regime in practice (Weintraub 1997). There has been none doing so from the perspective of the firm in response to environmental regulation under NAFTA. In contrast, we argue that the NAFTA regime does operate in a particular and unrecognized way, not as solidified jurisprudence, but rather as soft law and an emergent political process, that gives firms a rich new array of opportunities and constraints.

Major Findings

This study thus makes a substantial contribution to the existing literature by providing the first systematic examination of how the management of trade–environment disputes in North America has been changed by the advent of the new NAFTA mechanisms and how firms have acted and benefited in response. We examine in detail the full set of trade–environment disputes between or among the United States, Canada, and Mexico from 1980 to the present. We explore as a baseline the processes and outcomes in the pre-NAFTA era when protectionist coalitions of the 'green and greedy' abounded and when firms in North America could look only to the distant GATT, the Canada–US Free Trade Agreement (FTA), the power of their national governments in bilateral diplomacy, or direct foreign investment for a solution. We examine the architecture and application of the new innovative NAFTA-created system for environmentally related dispute settlement, political management, and pre-emptive dispute avoidance.

We also identify how the operation and practice of this institutional regime opens up new strategic possibilities for North American firms to succeed in the regional and global market place. We consider from a corporate strategy perspective how firms have mobilized these opportunities to their advantage and how they may best do so in the future. Thus, the use of 'shelter'—the capture of administrative regulations for industry protection—and cost minimization as firm strategies requires innovative strategic responses on the part of the firms negatively impacted by such environmental regulatory protection.

Firms doing business in and from North America now do so under a fundamentally new set of conditions—those of complex institutional responsiveness. This world is one where environmental regulations are urged on and adopted by governments, where firms are becoming more international and integrated in their production, and where international institutions—notably those of NAFTA—are emerging to manage the relationships when environmental regulations and international business interact.

These new conditions have made life far more challenging for even the largest firms seeking to do business across international boundaries in North America, since environmental regulatory protection is more frequent, widespread, entrenched, complex, and costly. However, for firms wishing to improve competitiveness by reducing the costs created by shelter-seeking competitors, environmental groups, and governments, these new conditions of complex institutional responsiveness also offer a new array of widely used, and often successfully employed strategies. Both before and after the advent of NAFTA, firms at large have continued to follow their basic generic corporate strategies of cost minimization, differentiation, or niching. They have enjoyed only limited success in using such traditional corporate strategies as exemptionalism, 'pay and expand', and altered production. Now, some firms, particularly the larger multinationals, are employing the new corporate strategies made available by complex institutional responsiveness. For example, firms are moving to produce to the standards of the major export market, producing closer to the border, and under the guarantees of NAFTA's Chapter 11, switching from exporting to foreign direct investment. They are also moving, in tandem with NAFTA's dispute settlement processes, to use an alternative strategy of private sector market sharing.

In the face of rising environmental regulatory protection, firms are also moving to employ a broad array of political strategies. There is an increased use of traditional political instruments: litigation in the home or regulating foreign country; lobbying in both countries; creating broad coalitions; bilateral diplomatic intervention by the home government; offsetting subsidization by the home government; reciprocal retaliation; and, above all, convergent national adjustment. However, by far the most striking development has been the use of NAFTA's many innovative dispute settlement mechanisms and institutions to mount new political strategies. A review of the 84 cases of environmental regulatory protection examined in this book reveals a sharp increase in the use of international institutions, especially those at the regional level and those created or catalysed by the NAFTA regime. NAFTA's innovative Chapter 11 dispute settlement mechanism for investment has been heavily used, while the use of other NAFTA institutions has led to a sharp rise in dispute management and prevention. The operation of these institutions during NAFTA's first five years has engendered regulatory convergence through negotiated, rules-government mutual adjustment, transnational coalition formation, the creation of regional coalitions for multilateral standards setting, and private sector standardization. The selective use of the most appropriate of such political and corporate strategies, both new and old, has benefited the full range of firms—domestic producers competing with imports, home-based exporters, home-based multinationals, and transnational MNEs.

This analysis thus demonstrates that the NAFTA regime works to increase market access and enhance competitiveness, for firms from all the participating countries, while also helping to protect the natural environment as well. While the United States is the largest beneficiary, Canada and Mexico prevail to a substantially greater degree than their relative size would suggest. Moreover, in many dispute settlement cases, all three countries benefit. Canada and Mexico tend to succeed in sectors where they have relatively large industries, such as forestry and agriculture, respectively. The US automotive sector cases reflect its market dominance and scientific capability, but provide trade liberalizing and environmentally enhancing gains for all consumers. In cases of internationally initiated environmental protection, the ecological vulnerability of the United States to its North American neighbours and the presence of a robust regional institution—the Commission for Environmental Cooperation—lead to an almost perfect equality of outcome. Taken together, for North American firms and governments, the NAFTA institutions and rules are creating a new North American community in which firms and other stakeholders have direct access to the international regulatory institutions such that their interests and identities are merging into one.

Notwithstanding this impressive legacy of early achievement, there are several ways in which North American firms and governments can continue to build their community. Managers can use their NAFTA instruments to further develop, through cross-border business alliances and other means, the fully integrated production platforms they need to succeed in the global market place. They can also shape the global rules in ways that reward the distinctive interests and values that flourish in North America. Policymakers can further strengthen the NAFTA trade institutions and processes of trilateralism, by creating trilateral institutional capacity in rapidly changing sectors such as energy. They can also enhance the scientific capabilities, industry involvement, and financial capacity of the NAFTA institutions. Finally, policymakers

10 Introduction

can broaden NAFTA by including the other free trade partners of the United States, Canada, and Mexico. This book argues that constructing a North American community that continues to reward firms, governments, and the ecology in each participating country is a feasible outcome of current trends.

Beyond NAFTA

The relevance of the conclusions of this study is not limited to the North American context. Trade and environment disputes are a global problem. The results of this study thus offer general lessons with applicability well beyond the North American experience. Smaller countries around the world are increasingly dependent on access to the large, rich triad markets in order to sustain global competitiveness.

The challenge of overcoming environmental regulatory protectionism has long been a defining feature of North America where Canada has depended on its prosperity for access to the ten times larger US market. This dynamic has recently intensified with the advent of regional free trade agreements such as NAFTA which embrace smaller partners such as Mexico. Such challenges appear in regional free trade agreements throughout the world. Within the EU, even large, export-oriented countries, such as the United Kingdom and Germany, have come to depend on assured access to the full European market place to build the global scale they require. Rapidly developing countries, such as Greece and Spain, have also realized that this is the essence of their growth strategy. Likewise, in Asia, access to the Japanese market has long been critical to the success of the export-oriented 'tiger' economies, while Japan's own prosperity is coming to depend on access to the full North American and Asian market. Even the United States, with a largely closed domestic economy and one-third of its trade with its North American partners, is increasingly reliant on access to Europe and Asia, in addition to the full North American market place, for its prosperity. In short, pronounced trade liberalization and proliferating environmental regulation in an era of rampant globalization has rendered even the largest firms from the largest economies relatively vulnerable in the sense that they must now identify innovative and successful corporate strategies to deal with the environmental regulations that keep them from the foreign markets they need.

Analytic Framework

These conclusions and their relevance emerge from the development and application in this study of a model of complex institutional responsiveness. In this model, new economic, regulatory, and institutional conditions present a dense array of complex trade and environment rules and institutions, such as those embodied in NAFTA. These new rules produce a more complex set of calculations and opportunities for firms facing environmental regulatory barriers abroad. They do so by creating a more complex array of corporate and political strategies which rationally calculating firms use in appropriate circumstances.

Three questions capture the major dimensions of this dynamic:

1. How do new regional dispute settlement, management, and prevention mechanisms operate to affect market access and entry costs for firms and those of their competitors, customers, and suppliers?
2. To what extent are firms engaging in or promoting regulatory convergence as a response to the new trade–environment regime?
3. How do firms use the new regime to reduce transaction costs, build capacity, and form corporate and political alliances with customers, suppliers, non-governmental organizations (NGOs), and political actors in foreign jurisdictions to enhance their competitive advantage in the regional and global market place?

To examine the full array of complex responses firms use to cope with environmental regulatory protectionism under these new conditions, it is necessary to take account of a broad set of regulatory behaviour relating to the environment. Thus, in this volume we adopt a broad conception of 'regulation'. At its core, regulation consists of all action by federal and subfederal governments and their international institutions designed to control firms and other civil society actors by proscribing their behaviour through formal legislation, administrative action, informal guidance, or legitimation. It extends to the action regarding the operation of the standards setting system—the procedures for scientific testing, approval and certification through which government regulations are put into practice. It embraces compliance activity, including inspection and enforcement action. It further includes private sector standards setting activity by firms, their industry associations, or standards setting bodies on a sector-specific or economy-wide basis. Such action is often a substitute for, or done in anticipation of, formal government regulation, and may lead to the latter by being referenced in government regulation or procurement practices.

We also employ an equally broad conception of the 'environment' as a subject category for government regulatory activity. At its core lies all regulatory activity directed at moderating the impact of government or societal activity on the natural or physical environment—its air, water, land, and living things. Although such regulatory activity is taken with the conscious *intention* of affecting impacts on this environment, our definition includes all regulatory activity with an ecological *impact*, whether that impact was the primary motive or declared purpose of the regulation or whether such impacts were known and considered in advance. Our concept of the environment thus includes a broad array of safety, workplace, and consumer regulations, as many effects on the individuals and conditions of concern in such regulations are transmitted through processes in the natural or physical environment.

12   Introduction

Within the core of environmental regulations themselves, we include activity relating to product standards, production and processing methods, the inputs and ecological capital that production requires, and the waste and product disposal methods downstream. In short, in keeping with modern environmental thinking, our conception of environmental regulation embraces the full ecological footprint of the complete 'cradle-to-grave' product life cycle.

To structure our explanation, and undertake systematic analysis that sustains our conclusions, we focus on how firms have addressed environmental regulatory challenges in discrete issues. To do so we analyse the complete set of major trade or investment related environmental regulatory issues facing firms in North America since 1980 and we consider these issues at three levels of detail. Most broadly, our analysis is based on a wide array of 84 cases of environmental regulatory protection in North America from 1980 to the present. Listed in Table 11.1 in the concluding chapter, such cases are those which each involve both trade and environmental interests or implications, firms, NGOs, or governments from at least two of the three NAFTA members, and which are the subject of sustained intergovernmental or international institutional interaction. Together they embrace a wide array of primary, manufacturing, and service sectors, and cases where firms, NGOs, and governments take the initiative in generating the action that requires international action. Secondly, and more specifically, we focus on 24 leading cases where firms from North America have faced environmental regulatory barriers imposed by foreign federal or subfederal governments in North America. Finally, to explore the actual selection, skilful use, and success of various instruments of complex institutional responsiveness through careful process-tracing, we examine in detail three central cases, covering the fuels, agricultural, and automotive industries in the NAFTA era.

To conduct this analysis, it is important to span an array of industries that cover the spectrum of internationalization, ranging from those whose sales, market shares, profits, and inputs are domestic (and actually or potentially import competing), through those who are home-based exporters, to those who are home-based or ultimately transnational MNEs. To capture this spectrum, and incorporate important considerations of future trends and strategic aspirations as well as current conditions, this analysis avoids seductively precise but arbitrary definitions of when an individual firm passed the threshold from one category to another. Rather, analysis is concentrated on firms in the particular sectors that exemplify these key categories. For example, agriculture is a sector that is dominated by home-based exporters. This is especially the case in the United States where 30 per cent of the output of the sector is exported, compared to only 14 per cent of the US economy as a whole. Similarly, chemicals stands second only to the petroleum industry as the sector where US industry makes the largest investments overseas (James and Weidenbaum 1993: 52–4).

Introduction 13

Methodology

This framework of complex institutional responsiveness is applied to and tested against the evidence gathered through the use of two major research methods. First, an extensive programme of elite interview research was conducted. Second, a comprehensive review of existing survey research, published and primary works and documentation was undertaken.

The analysis is based primarily on a programme of 230 interviews conducted from the autumn of 1995 through to the summer of 1998. The interview programme involved a variety of interview methods, ranging from face-to-face interviews, telephone interviews, and small-group discussions, to formal individual reviews of draft text prepared by the authors. Of the 230 interviews, 179 consisted of direct interviews, and 51 of reviews of draft manuscript.

The 230 interviews were conducted in six waves, with each concentrating on a different facet of the research agenda. The first, taking place from the fall of 1995 to the spring of 1996, was designed to assess the broad range of NAFTA's environmental effects, through 58 interviews in the capitals of the three NAFTA countries. The second, conducted from the spring through the summer of 1996, focused on trade barriers, through 29 individual interviews concentrated in Canada and discussion in a small group exchange, with experts from all three NAFTA countries. The third, taking place from the summer of 1996 through the spring of 1997, consisted of 37 interviews with those involved in operating NAFTA's intergovernmental institutions in the three NAFTA capitals. The fourth, taking place in the autumn of 1997 and winter of 1998, focused on the trade impacts of regulatory heterogeneity, and included 35 individuals in Mexico City and Monterrey, Mexico. The fifth, taking place from the autumn of 1997 to the summer of 1998, included interviews and a small group session with 20 individuals dealing with the automotive industry from the United States and Canada. The sixth segment, which took place in spring 1997, was a review by 51 individuals from all three NAFTA countries of a draft of the material on NAFTA institutions.

The 179 direct interviews were overwhelmingly conducted by the authors themselves, on a face-to-face basis with the respondents. Each interview followed a semi-structured format, lasted on average one hour, and proceeded on a not-for-attribution basis. Notes were taken, from which interview transcripts were subsequently produced. Telephone interviews followed a similar format. Small group discussions, which included two sessions with a total of 20 individuals involved in the trade barriers and auto segments, allowed for a guided interchange over, respectively, a full day and a half day. This use of an interview instrument with an open-ended component, and the reliance on several different interview methods, was designed to increase the validity and reliability of the results and to allow for cross-cultural variation among respondents by country and professional community. To further enhance

14 Introduction

validity and reliability, several central individuals were interviewed on several occasions over the course of the three years.

As Table 1.1 indicates, interviewees were evenly divided between respondents from government and those from outside government. Of the 230 total, 48 per cent came from government, 24 per cent from business, 14 per cent from the research community, and 13 per cent from NGOs. The 179 direct interviews had a similar distribution, with a slightly heavier weighting for business and government respondents. Business respondents included those in firms, private sector associations such as Chambers of Commerce, and industry-specific associations. Governmental respondents encompassed a wide range of individuals from municipal, state/provincial, and federal governments, and from regional and multilateral intergovernmental organizations. NGOs contained those from the environmental community, supplemented by a few respondents from the broader consumer affairs community. Research respondents included lawyers in private practice, those in non-profit public policy bodies, and a few selected academic experts, usually with direct policy experience. Taken together this set allowed for a balanced distribution of information and perspectives from four different communities, encompassing in relatively balanced fashion both the government–non-government and trade–environment divides.

As Table 1.2 indicates, the respondents came equally from the three North American countries. Of the 230 total, 32 per cent came from the United

TABLE 1.1. *Interviewees by community*

Segment	Total number (%)	Business number (%)	NGO number (%)	Government number (%)	Research number (%)
NAFTA effects (1995–6)	58 (100)	16 (28)	11 (19)	26 (45)	5 (9)
Trade barriers (1996)	29 (100)	10 (34)	7 (24)	6 (21)	6 (21)
NAFTA institutions (1996–7)	37 (100)	∅ (∅)	∅ (∅)	37 (100)	∅ (∅)
Regulatory heterogeneity (1997–8)	35 (100)	16 (46)	1 (3)	13 (37)	5 (14)
Autos–fuels (1997–8)	20 (100)	8 (40)	1 (5)	10 (50)	1 (5)
Subtotal	179 (100)	50 (28)	20 (11)	92 (51)	17 (9)
Institutions review (1997)	51 (100)	6 (12)	11 (22)	19 (37)	15 (29)
GRAND TOTAL	230 (100)	56 (24)	31 (13)	111 (48)	32 (14)

Introduction 15

TABLE 1.2. *Interviewees by country*

Segment	Total number (%)	United States number (%)	Mexico number (%)	Canada number (%)
NAFTA effects (1995–6)	58 (100)	16 (28)	22 (38)	20 (34)
Trade barriers (1996)	29 (100)	3 (10)	3 (10)	23 (79)
NAFTA institutions (1996–7)	37 (100)	15 (41)	6 (16)	16 (43)
Regulatory heterogeneity (1997–8)	35 (100)	∅ (∅)	35 (100)	∅ (∅)
Auto–fuels (1997–8)	20 (100)	8 (40)	∅ (∅)	12 (60)
Subtotal	179 (100)	42 (23)	66 (37)	71 (40)
Institutions review (1997)	51 (100)	31 (61)	9 (18)	11 (22)
GRAND TOTAL	230 (100)	73 (32)	75 (33)	82 (36)

Note: Country defined by location of interview.

States, 33 per cent from Mexico, and 36 per cent from Canada (where, *inter alia*, the CEC headquarters is located). The distribution of the direct interviews was broadly balanced, with a slightly heavier weighting for respondents from Mexico and Canada. These distributions, defined by the country location where the interview or meeting took place, were very similar to those produced when country was categorized by the nationality of the interviewee, or the home base of his/her organization (when known).

As Table 1.3 indicates, there was a reasonable balance of respondents covering each of the four professional communities (business, NGO, government, and research) from each of the three NAFTA countries. The heavier emphasis on business respondents from Mexico and Canada is consistent with the core focus of this project on the regulatory barriers to entry faced by firms from smaller countries dependent for their global competitiveness on assured access to a large triad market. The emphasis on interviews with government officials from the United States reflects the importance of these officials in receiving, integrating, and resisting potentially protectionist pressures from US business and ENGOs acting individually or in alliance, in calculating broader and longer term US interests, and in forwarding the process of regulatory convergence on a regional or multilateral basis.

Interviewees came from all decisional levels, from the CEO to the working level. Interviews with CEOs came from the business and NGO communities.

16 Introduction

TABLE 1.3. *Interviewees by community and country*

Segment	Total number (% of total interviews)	United States number (% of total interviews)	Mexico number (% of total interviews)	Canada number (% of total interviews)
Business	56 (24)	7 (3)	26 (11)	23 (10)
NGO	31 (13)	9 (4)	11 (5)	11 (5)
Government	111 (48)	47 (20)	28 (12)	36 (16)
Research	32 (14)	10 (4)	10 (4)	12 (5)
GRAND TOTAL	230 (100)	73 (32)	75 (33)	82 (36)

Those with senior executives came from all four communities. Interviewees came primarily from senior and middle executive levels across all four communities. In many cases their verbal interview responses were supplemented by written reports and documents, some otherwise unavailable, that they provided on the activities of their organizations.

This structured interview base was enriched by several other research methods. The judgements in this study were importantly enhanced by the informal participant-observation involvement of the senior authors in several relevant forums, notably as members of the Canadian Government's International Trade Advisory Committee (Rugman and Kirton), in three major projects sponsored by the Commission for Environmental Cooperation (Kirton and Rugman), as Chair of the North American Environmental Standards Working Group (Kirton), and as a consultant to major Canadian-based multinational corporations (Rugman and Kirton). In addition, this study drew on the advice and judgement of an advisory network constructed for this project, composed of senior representatives from the government, business, and NGO community. It was also enriched by multistakeholder conferences and seminars held under the auspices of the CEC's NAFTA Environmental Effects project, direct observation of CEC Council at its 1996 meeting, and the presentation of preliminary results to scholarly and multistakeholder audiences in all three countries. In addition to the normally scholarly venues, these included conferences held under the auspices of the OECD, CEC, US Congressional Research Service, and the Center for Strategic and International Studies.

The project also benefited from access to the results and underlying data of several mailed and telephone surveys of firms and interview programmes conducted by others, including Stephen Blank and Stephen Krajewski, Lorraine Eden and Maureen Molot, the American Chamber of Commerce in Mexico, the Bank of Montreal, Rogelio Ramirez de la O, and Sidney Weintraub and Jan Gilbreath. The extent and quality of this material, and the generous access we had to it obviated the need to conduct an extensive mailed survey of firms for this project alone.

Introduction   17

Underlying this work was an extensive examination of published and primary works and documentation. This included comprehensive reviews of newsletters such as *Inside NAFTA, Inside U.S. Trade, America's Trade*, and the *International Trade Reporter*. Also used were materials issued (both published reports and on internet website material) by relevant international organizations, namely, the CEC; the NAFTA institutions; the GATT/WTO; the OECD; relevant NGOs, and with the foreign affairs, trade, and environment ministries of the three NAFTA countries. Extensive database research provided documentation and relevant literature, through a reliance on OECD Olis Online; Lexus/Nexus; Quicklaw; Westlaw, and World Trade Online. Extensive Internet research was also conducted, primarily with the assistance of Infoseek; Netscape and Microsoft Explorer.

Contents

The resulting analysis of how firms respond to environmental regulatory protectionism through the strategies of complex institutional responsiveness available in the NAFTA era is outlined in four parts. The first part, containing Chapters 2 through 4, provides the theoretical and empirical foundation for the book. Chapter 2 provides an overarching analytic framework relevant for the analysis of trade and the environment. It features a model consisting of a twenty-cell matrix created by multiplying the five levels of environmental regulation (ranging from municipal to international) that can affect four different types of firms (ranging from domestic to transnational MNEs). This chapter employs theoretical perspectives from the three disciplines of corporate strategy, law, and political science. Here the model is applied to North America and the NAFTA experience in the interaction of trade, environment, and firm competitiveness. To illustrate the framework, a case study examines the discriminatory restrictions that were imposed on the Canadian export of UHT milk to Puerto Rico in 1992 and were eventually the subject of an FTA dispute resolution panel. The case study further draws out some of the legal issues involved in litigating trade and environment disputes and provides an initial example of how North American firms are engaged in the process of complex institutional responsiveness.

Chapter 3 develops further the corporate strategy elements of the framework, through the application of the theory of shelter to environmental regulation. After a review of the theory's specific analytic elements, five environmentally related trade disputes are examined from the perspective of the injured firm. The chapter concludes that in all five cases, a shelter-based strategy is pursued on the part of the firms benefiting from the environmental regulation. Also identified are the coalitions that are formed between industry and environmental groups—the 'baptist–bootlegger' coalition which provides an initial indication that a protectionist agenda is being pursued.

Exactly how an environmental regulation becomes discriminatory, and how 'baptist–bootlegger' coalitions form and operate to this end, is the subject of Chapter 4. Here ten cases are discussed in order to explore the dynamics of regulatory capture, with a heavy emphasis on the operation of 'baptist–bootlegger' or 'green–greedy' coalitions, that is, coalitions of environmental non-governmental organizations and firms seeking to benefit from protectionist regulation. This concept was first introduced by Vogel (1995). The ten cases, from 1982 to 1996, give rise to a wide range of responses from firms facing a discriminatory environmental regulation. As the operative regime develops from the GATT to the FTA and ultimately to the much more complex NAFTA, so too do the complexity and inventiveness of the responses of firms in their strategic behaviour.

Part II, containing Chapters 5 through 7, takes up the NAFTA regime and potential firm responses to it. It thus identifies and analyses the array of available firm strategies that collectively constitute complex institutional responsiveness. Chapter 5 develops a new explanation of the operation of the environmentally relevant intergovernmental institutional structure created by the NAFTA regime. It finds that the NAFTA institutions with environmental responsibility have often been successful in assisting the market access and competitiveness of Canadian and Mexican firms by constraining US regulatory protectionism and engendering balanced, non-hegemonic regulatory convergence. This occurs in areas where US ecological vulnerability is high and where US export interests seek to protect their high and growing trade surplus in the regional market. The regime has also, and more powerfully, assisted US firms to grow in the full NAFTA market place, and firms from all three NAFTA countries to build the foundation and scale required to compete more successfully on a global basis.

Chapter 6 reviews in detail the NAFTA-created Commission for Environmental Cooperation, with a focus on its early operation and its potential for action. It employs regime analysis to identify where the work of the CEC could be most relevant and helpful in balancing the complex and diverse interests of civil society, firms, and government.

Chapter 7 examines the possible and actual effects that the NAFTA institutional process and the CEC have had on firms in all NAFTA countries. Following the regime analysis developed in the previous chapter, this chapter explores how firms can and do respond to these new institutions and dispute settlement mechanisms, both reactively by adjusting corporate and political strategies, and proactively to innovatively take advantage of them. This chapter also highlights the extent to which deepening integration raises new strategic challenges for firms, and requires far-reaching firm-level adjustments under NAFTA.

Part III of the book, containing Chapters 8–10, considers a number of detailed, critical case studies that assess the causes, content, and successes of strategies of complex institutional responsiveness.

Chapter 8 explores complex institutional responsiveness from the perspective of NAFTA's novel investor–state dispute settlement mechanism and the major cases that have been brought to that mechanism thus far. To date, there have been four cases initiated under this provision, three of which have had strong environmental aspects to them. The focus is on the first environmentally related case. It involves MMT, an octane-enhancing fuel additive which has been the subject of an intra-provincial and international trade ban in Canada. The case involves a complex group of actors from the oil industry, the auto industry, and the Canadian government departments responsible for trade and environment. The next two cases both involve US investments in Mexico in the waste disposal industry. In both of these cases, the US firms allege that the Mexican government's treatment of their investment has violated the provisions of NAFTA.

Chapter 9 focuses on agricultural disputes, an area which has been particularly vulnerable to the discriminatory use of health and safety regulations in both North America and Europe. Disputes abound in trade in fruits, vegetables, and meat products, most of which are dealt with at the official government level. This chapter demonstrates that the NAFTA institutional structure can be beneficial in the management and resolution of such disputes.

Chapter 10 explores the interaction between the NAFTA institutional structure and firm behaviour in the automotive sector. It highlights the impact of the NAFTA process in inducing firms to secure regulatory convergence, often on a private sector and broadly multilateral basis.

Part IV of the book contains Chapter 11, which offers general conclusions about how strategies of complex institutional responsiveness have been used successfully to overcome environmental regulatory protectionism in the NAFTA era. Based on the study of the NAFTA regime and the firm response to it, this chapter outlines the implications that doing business in the global market place will have for firm strategy, and suggests how trade environment regimes should be shaped to enhance both firm competitiveness and ecological quality in the future.

Part I
Economic and Corporate Strategy

2

The Analytic Framework of Capture

This chapter develops a general framework for the analysis of the relationship among trade liberalization regimes, environmental regulation, and firm competitiveness. Using NAFTA as an empirical testing ground, these relationships are explored from three different disciplinary perspectives. First, the issue is examined from a corporate strategy perspective, that is, an exploration of the problems facing, and responses of, firms subject to the administration of discriminatory environmental regulation, with specific reference to the theory of shelter. A twenty-cell matrix is used to describe how five different levels of environmental regulation can affect four various types of firms. Second, the legal implications of regulatory capture/shelter are explored to better understand the legal processes at play within NAFTA and the legal instruments firms have at their disposal. Specifically, both the national treatment obligations and the legal frameworks that govern environmentally related trade disputes are analysed. Third, political science perspectives are employed, such as the theory of complex interdependence and neo-liberal institutionalism, in order to illustrate how corporations and other stakeholders can influence regulatory processes, and how international regimes can constrain the protectionist regulatory actions of national governments.

These three perspectives are combined into a new and unified model relevant for the analysis of trade and the environment. The strength of this framework lies in the fact that it is not limited to NAFTA but can be extended to a wide variety of regional and global contexts that span all levels of environmental regulation and all types of firms, functioning within different trading regimes.

The North American Free Trade Agreement (NAFTA) is the first international trade agreement to incorporate environmental regulations (Globerman 1993). It does this in several provisions within the core NAFTA text but, above all, through the side agreement establishing the Commission for Environmental Cooperation (CEC). The institutional fabric of NAFTA, and the CEC in particular, is of great interest to researchers, since it provides an ongoing laboratory to examine propositions from the newly emerging field of trade and the environment (Rugman 1995). The work of the CEC is of great relevance for Canadian business as the CEC is a legally and institutionally powerful body charged with the review and harmonization of environmental regulations in North America (Richardson 1993; Munton and Kirton 1994; Johnson and Beaulieu 1996; Winham 1994; Kirton 1998).

The CEC will have an important impact on corporate strategy and Canadian competitiveness since, at the moment, many environmental regulations can be used as barriers to trade (Orme 1996). For example, it is well known that the key attraction of NAFTA for Canadian firms is market access to the United States, the world's largest, richest, and nearest market (Hart 1994). Yet, a variety of Canadian firms have had their access denied (or the price of entry increased) by US federal-level and/or state-level environmental regulations. Discriminatory US environmental regulations have affected firms in the forestry sector (newspaper recycling laws in California and other states), in agriculture (UHT milk restrictions, health inspections of meat and potatoes), in the fishery sector (lobster, salmon, and herring), and in other areas involving the automobile/petroleum sectors, and asbestos. Here, partial denial of full entry to the US market, and even the uncertainty about, or added transaction costs for ensuring access, can have an adverse effect on the sales of firms in these sectors, and thereby on Canadian competitiveness. In some instances Canadian-imposed environmental regulations have affected US businesses, such as the Ontario levy on beer cans and legislation restricting the export for disposal of PCB wastes. In this situation, there is little strategic impact on US competitiveness and such Canadian-imposed regulations seem to be irritants to bilateral trade and investment.

Canadian Market Access and US Environmental Regulations

For Canadian firms doing business in the United States, barriers to trade present managers with a serious problem. Despite the institutional provisions of the Canada–US Free Trade Agreement (FTA) and NAFTA, which have helped to foster economic integration, many regulations and standards remain subject to political influence, including the administration of environmental regulations (Kirton and Richardson 1992; Housman 1994). The CEC has the power to introduce dispute settlement procedures to avoid environmentally related trade disputes as well as to harmonize or promote convergence in national environmental regulations. The CEC could then render existing regulations and regulatory systems less diverse and more transparent, assist with NAFTA's dispute settlement mechanism, and potentially exercise its own powers of investigation and enforcement. The ability of the CEC to function in this way will depend in practice on its own priorities and professional capacity, and the relationship it establishes with national governments, NAFTA's other intergovernmental institutions, and societal constituencies. Moreover, the United States contains the world's largest and most politically active environmental movement, and its political and legal institutions are very open to influence from environmental non-governmental organizations (ENGOs), business, and other interested actors. Thus, the volume and impact of US environmental regulations affecting Canadian business will continue to grow, especially as a new generation of environmental regulatory approaches, such as voluntary standards set by industry, takes effect.

The Analytic Framework of Capture 25

An opportunity exists for Canadian-based firms to improve their access to the US market through the work of an institution whose mandate includes the avoidance of environmentally related trade disputes. In general, the work of the CEC, in conjunction with NAFTA's other institutions, will affect the access of Canadian firms to the US market in three major ways: (1) by constraining US environmental regulations with a protectionist impact; (2) by fostering convergence of environmental regulations that are conducive to the practices and capacities of Canadian as distinct from US firms; and (3) by undertaking programmes of environmental cooperation that support Canadian firms in the United States, in Mexico, and in international markets.

Of these, the first is the most critical. The CEC is charged with the examination of a number of issues in the area of trade and the environment, among them, the avoidance of environmentally related trade disputes. Article 10.6 of the NAAEC states that '[t]he Council shall cooperate with the NAFTA Free Trade Commission to achieve environmental goals and objectives of the NAFTA by: ... (c) contributing to the prevention or resolution of environment-related trade disputes by: ... (1) seeking to avoid disputes between the Parties.' This section of NAAEC gives the CEC Council (the three nations' environment ministers who head up the CEC) the mandate to identify, monitor, and even be proactively involved in the avoidance of environmentally related trade disputes. To date, the CEC has not investigated specific cases, but it has expressed interest by commissioning academic papers

NAFTA and Environmental Regulations

In one of the CEC papers, Vogel, Rugman, and Schettino (1997) classify twenty-four environmental regulations relevant to NAFTA and examine to what extent such regulations have been of benefit to domestic producers and have been trade barriers facing foreign suppliers. It is found that a number of conservation and recycling measures, along with health and safety inspections, can act as trade barriers, a point also made in Vogel (1995) and Rugman (1995). Such regulations can have serious detrimental effects on the competitiveness of Canadian industry, and can even result in a substitution of exports from Canada towards foreign direct investment in the United States (Rugman 1995).

The adoption of trade-restricting environmental regulations takes place despite the application of the 'national treatment' principle to trade and investment in NAFTA (Rugman 1994). Under the national treatment provisions of NAFTA, governments are not required to harmonize regulations but they are required to treat trading partners in a non-discriminatory manner (Rugman 1990). From a Canadian viewpoint, even when foreign and domestic firms are treated the same, there can still be a discriminatory impact on a foreign firm due to asymmetries in market access, with the ten times larger US market being a huge potential loss for Canadian-based firms (Rugman 1995). Indeed, the provisions of NAFTA apply to standards-related measures that may *directly* or *indirectly* affect trade in goods or services between the NAFTA signatories (Article 901). Thus far, however, the state-to-state dispute settlement provisions of NAFTA have not been used for such disputes (Kirton and Soloway 1996).

The 'capture' of the administration of environmental regulations by domestic producers parallels the capture of the administration of US countervailing duty (CVD) and antidumping (AD) laws, as documented in Rugman and Anderson (1987) and Rugman and Verbeke (1990). This was of particular concern to sectors such as forestry, steel, and agriculture. The Canadian concern about such denial of market access has had a detrimental impact on North American trade and led to the creation of the Chapter 19 dispute settlement panels in the FTA and NAFTA (Schwanen 1995). Environmental regulations have traditionally remained under the sovereignty of nations and had been exempted from multilateral trade treaties until NAFTA. The side agreement in NAFTA is the first international trade agreement to include the environment and, through the CEC, there is the potential to develop a mechanism by which to prevent or adjudicate environmentally related trade disputes. So far the CEC has not exercised this mandate but the door remains open for such action.

Toward a Theory of Trade and the Environment

Within the context of the institutional provisions of NAFTA, the matrix developed below can provide a better understanding of the linkages between trade and the environment and how these linkages can affect Canadian competitiveness. The field of trade and the environment is a new one, bringing together rather disparate literatures in economics, politics, law, management strategy, and the environment; there is a need to integrate these large literatures into a reasonable synthesis.

A new theory of trade and the environment can be based on Figure 2.1 which brings together five levels of trade-related environmental regulations and four types of corporations, yielding a total of 20 cases. While this matrix has been developed with NAFTA and its trade and environment issues in mind, it is conceivable that the matrix may be generalized to other institutional frameworks, such as environmental regulations in the EU.

Trade-related environmental regulations can be imposed at five levels of government authority:

(1) multilateral rules established under the General Agreement on Tariffs and Trade (GATT) and World Trade Organization (WTO);
(2) regional-level rules, such as in the European Union (EU) and in NAFTA;
(3) national-level rules, such as federal laws in Canada and in the United States;
(4) sub-national rules, such as state and provincial laws;
(5) municipal or local regulations, in cases where these are not under provincial or state jurisdiction.

Level of environmental regulations

Type of corporation	Multilateral (GATT/WTO)	Regional (EU/NAFTA)	National	Sub-national (State/province)	Municipal
Domestic firms	1	2	3	4	5
Home-based exporter	6	7	8	9	10
Home-based MNE	11	12	13	14	15
Transnational (decentralized) MNE	16	17	18	19	20

Fig. 2.1. Competitiveness, trade, and the environment

These five levels of government may or may not be able to harmonize such environmental regulations, achieve mutual recognition of environmental regulations, or even agree on minimum standards of such regulations. At present there is great diversity in both regulations and standards established by governments and the manner in which private-sector firms react to them (Kirton and Richardson 1992; Kirton et al. 1996). Moreover, despite extensive ongoing interaction on environmental and trade issues, including that between Canadian provinces and US states, there are relatively few instances where formal, harmonized regimes have emerged (Munton and Kirton 1994, 1996).

The concept of trade today needs to be refined in this manner, since the majority of the world's trade is conducted by large multinational enterprises (MNEs). Using public data on foreign direct investment (FDI) and trade, Rugman (1988) has demonstrated that over half of the world's trade is conducted by the 500 largest MNEs and that 80 per cent of this trade is conducted by triad MNEs. Moreover in the case of the Canada–US relationship, a full 40 per cent of trade takes place between different components of the same corporation and a further 30 per cent takes place between firms associated through strategic alliance, joint ventures or licensing agreements (Weintraub 1994; Rugman 1990; Hart 1994). Thus, trade and the environment really means the MNE and the environment.

There are four basic types of companies affected by environmental regulations:

(1) domestic firms (which do not engage in foreign trade);
(2) a home based firm which does some exporting;
(3) a home-based MNE which does FDI and trade;
(4) a decentralized 'transnational' MNE with FDI and trade.

These four categories of firms are discussed in Rugman and Hodgetts (1995) and in Rugman and D'Cruz (forthcoming).

With the two axes of Figure 2.1 linking trade and the environment, the issue of competitiveness is captured within each of the 20 cells of the matrix. For example, a Canadian forestry firm in row 2 (a home-based exporter) or row 3 (an MNE) can be affected by five different types of environmental regulations. These are: the GATT/WTO multilateral rules of non-discrimination and national treatment; NAFTA regime procedures carried out by the CEC; Canadian federal-level environmental policy; provincial policies, as in British Columbia and Ontario affecting domestic and foreign firms; and even municipal regulations concerning waste disposal, chemical discharge in waters, use of land, etc. The three softwood lumber CVD cases of the last twelve years are in cells 8 and 13, reflecting the administration of US CVD law at federal level. A newsprint firm, however, is also potentially affected by state-level newspaper recycling laws (in cells 9 and 14). The MNE in cell 14 has more strategic options than an exporting firm in cell 9. For example, the MNE can switch modes of market access from exporting to foreign direct investment in a swifter and more efficient manner than purely home-based firms.

In terms of political science issues, one key aspect to be considered is the role of host-country managers in gathering intelligence about, and intervening in, legal systems and US judicial processes. They could engage local counsel and lobby relevant industry associations. Here an MNE in cells 13 and 14 can pass on such insights to strategic decision-makers at home, whereas an exporting firm has far less host-country information or intervention/lobbying opportunities (cells 8 and 9), apart from those provided by its distributors and customers (Gotlieb 1984, 1991; Doran and Sokolsky 1984). But perhaps the best positioned firm is a transnational firm, with strategic autonomy from its host-country managers who may be able to lobby directly as domestic citizens and keep open access; these cases of 'national responsiveness' are in cells 18 and 19 (Bartlett and Ghoshal 1989). Here a theory of how Canadian corporations and other stakeholders can influence the US regulatory process can be based on the theory of complex interdependence developed by Keohane and Nye (1989) and the particular role of MNEs in this process, as outlined by Nye (1974) and Leyton-Brown (1974).

This new type of theory of trade and the environment can help to resolve such strategic issues. Each of the 20 cells of Figure 2.1 can be investigated as separate cases and then cross-linkages can be found between them. For example, in the softwood lumber CVD, the manner in which US business subnational actors have lobbied at the federal level (using US Senators such as Hatfield, Packwood, and Bacchus) and influenced CVD decisions can be investigated. These issues link a cluster of cells such as 8, 9, 13, 14, and also potentially 7 and 12, when NAFTA dispute settlement procedures are included. If the WTO were to improve on the GATT subsidies code, then cells 6, 11, and 16 would also be involved. Purely domestic firms (usually small and medium-sized firms) in row 1 will not be affected directly by such international rules (although they could be competing in their home market with subsidized foreign firms, yielding an indirect effect). This research examines the interaction between the cells, in order to illustrate the manner in which trade and investment affects Canadian competitiveness.

In order to provide comparisons and contrasts with the US–Canadian experience, it is worthwhile to consider environmental regulations from other areas, especially the EU. The EU has perhaps the most advanced institutional structure in the form of 'eco-labels', labels attesting to the environmental friendliness of a producer, as reported by Vogel (1995). The possible use of eco-labels as barriers to trade affecting Canadian firms can be assessed using the framework of Figure 2.1, for example the impacts range across cells 2, 7, 12, and 17.

The theoretical model can also incorporate key aspects of the theory of shelter (Rugman and Verbeke 1990, 1994). Shelter theory can be applied formally to environmental regulations as trade barriers rather than the earlier application to the administration of US CVD and AD laws. This will require an understanding of the CEC and other NAFTA institutions, market access, lobbying behaviour, corporate adjustment, and success or failure in overcoming green protectionism. In short, analysis using Figure 2.1 can demonstrate how political and corporate strategies work and it can offer suggestions about recommendations for public policy and private sector strategies to improve Canadian competitiveness as environmental issues assume increasing importance.

The corporate strategy and the environment approach of Michael Porter can also be incorporated in the matrix of Figure 2.1. Porter and van der Linde (1995) argue that it is good policy for a government to pass strict environmental regulations. Then firms based in that country (usually the United States) will have to develop new core competencies in environmentally sensitive manufacturing. Eventually, these firms can go abroad and use their strong home base as a staging ground to beat other less environmentally sensitive firms in global markets. This policy starts in cells 8 and 13 of Figure 2.1 and it may then spread into cells 7, 12, 6, 11 (if regional and multilateral organizations eventually enhance their environmental rules). The Porter policy presumes that other countries will not 'compete' by inconveniently raising their own domestic environmental regulations too soon (before the US-based firms have geared up at home) and that the regional and multilateral organizations also follow along, rather than initiate new environmental regulations. Thus, it is a matter of timing. If the US government is a first mover, it can spur US-based firms to be the first 'green' MNEs and their environmental credentials should help them beat out competitor firms on the world stage, once the world stage also becomes green.

The problem, from a Canadian perspective, with the Porter hypothesis is that it is difficult to think of any sector where it could be applied. Virtually all

Canada's MNEs sell far more abroad than at home. The average ratio of foreign to total sales for Canada's largest 20 MNEs is over 70 per cent (Rugman 1990). Thus, if the Canadian government were to impose tight new environmental regulations Canadian-based MNEs would have to invest and restructure for a market which takes a minority of their sales. These firms would prefer to adapt their manufacturing to suit the environmental regulations of their major customers abroad (especially when the big market for Canadian firms is the United States). In short, as far as Canadian competitiveness is concerned, the Porter hypothesis is completely wrong. By forcing Canadian-based firms to take on board stronger, new environmental regulations, the Canadian government will actually reduce the international competitiveness of such firms as it changes their strategic focus from their major markets and makes them inward-looking instead of outward-looking. These points were first developed in Rugman (1995) and explored within the context of the Canadian forest products sector and associated environmental regulations. This, again, is an example of cells 8 and 13 in Figure 2.1.

The NAFTA Legal Framework and Environmental Regulations

In this section we examine the legal framework of NAFTA in detail as an example of the manner in which environmental regulations can be used for protectionist ends. Although NAFTA recognizes the need to limit standards and other technical barriers to trade that may be used by a member state for protectionist means, the legal framework of NAFTA makes it very difficult for individual investors and companies to win an environmentally related dispute. Chapter 9 of NAFTA defines the rights and obligations of each NAFTA member in the setting of standards-related measures so as not to unduly interfere with trade objectives. This is captured by column 2 of the matrix in Figure 2.1, and also in the first column insofar as the NAFTA legal provisions are consistent with those in the GATT.

An environmental standard that violates the national treatment rules against discrimination may be permitted if it meets the conditions set out in the standards setting provisions of NAFTA. Parties to NAFTA have the right to adopt standards-related measures at the level of protection they deem appropriate, including measures which relate to the protection of the environment (broadly defined to include human, animal, and plant life and health). Parties further have the right to restrict trade in goods or services that do not comply with those measures. However, under NAFTA, trade-restrictive environmental standards are subject to certain legal disciplines. Chapter 9 of NAFTA sets out a number of limitations on the extent to which member countries may enact environmental standards with trade-restricting effects. The language found in Chapter 9 follows and largely builds on the FTA and the work of the GATT in the area of technical barriers to trade.

The following questions outline five steps which can be used to analyse whether a trade-restricting environmental measure would be permitted under NAFTA. These questions are adapted from the text of Chapter 9 of NAFTA. They incorporate the three-step test developed by Condon in an earlier interpretation of Chapter 9 (Condon 1994).

(1) Does the standard violate the principle of non-discrimination (national treatment)?
(2) Does the standard *relate to* environmental protection (broadly defined)?
(3) Does the standard create an *unnecessary obstacle* to trade?
(4) Does the standard support the pursuit of a *legitimate environmental objective*?
(5) If a trade restriction is necessary, has the *least trade-restrictive measure* been chosen?

If an environmental standard can meet the above criteria, then it would not be found contrary to NAFTA. Regulations found to be inconsistent with NAFTA can be challenged under Chapter 20 which covers state-to-state dispute settlement, or, in the case of an investment of a NAFTA member, under Chapter 11 which covers investor–state dispute settlement. While there has been no NAFTA panel to date that has considered these issues (Kirton and Soloway 1996), previous decisions of similar provisions under the GATT and the FTA offer some guidance in the interpretation of the italicized provisions above. The GATT is of direct relevance as Article XX of the GATT is incorporated into Chapter 9 of NAFTA through Article 2101(1).

The NAFTA regulations dealing with standards can potentially affect all companies who export within North America, leaving the dispute settlement mechanisms as a last resort for companies who believe their NAFTA guaranteed rights have been impaired. Indeed, companies would have to persuade their national governments to take on their cause to have a panel consider such issues under Chapter 20. This, of course, is a largely political process involving issues in cells 2, 7, 12, and 17 of the matrix in Figure 2.1, with potential linkages (under GATT) to cells 1, 6, 11, and 16. To obtain standing for Chapter 11 dispute settlement, the aggrieved company must have an investment affected by the environmental standard in the country whose regulations they seek to challenge.

Beyond the remote chance of dispute settlement, and probably of more practical benefit to companies, is the NAFTA created institutional structure which is designed to address these issues at a government to government level before they escalate into full trade disputes. This consists of over 50 trilateral government committees, sub-committees, and working groups equipped to deal with the micro-level issues arising between NAFTA parties. The private sector is actively involved in making representations of their concerns on these committees and working groups (Kirton and Fernandez de Castro 1997). The action here is in cells 7, 12, and 17 of Figure 2.1, and it is here that the legal framework of NAFTA can have important effects.

It is helpful to consider in more detail the five-part test presented above. This will demonstrate that the legal provisions of NAFTA cannot adequately address corporate concerns about the denial of market access due to discriminatory use of environmental regulations.

1. Does the standard violate the principle of non-discrimination (national treatment)? National treatment is explicitly required in Chapter 9 (Article 904(3)), that is, all standards must treat all member countries equally in setting environmental standards. It is *only* the environmental regulation which violates national treatment that is potentially challengeable. Such a finding was held in the lobster case, where an FTA panel considered whether the application of domestic US minimum size requirements violated the national treatment obligations guaranteed to Canada (Condon 1994). The panel found that the regulation was not discriminatory, as it treated Canadian and US lobsters equally. This case falls into cells 8 and 7 in Figure 2.1.

2. Does the standard *relate to* environmental protection (broadly defined)? To be exempt from the requirement of non-discrimination, a standard must relate to one of the enumerated categories of environmental protection set out in Article 904(1). Is the trade-restrictive standard directly connected with a legitimate environmental programme, or has it been implemented to protect domestic industry from competition? GATT and FTA jurisprudence give guidance in the interpretation of what the term 'relating to' actually means in practice. GATT and FTA panels have interpreted standards which 'relate to' environmental protection to essentially mean standards whose purpose is 'primarily aimed at' environmental protection (Trebilcock and Howse 1995). Under this test, measures which impose an undue burden on trade without a corresponding environmental benefit should be revealed as protectionist in nature and contrary to NAFTA.

The herring and salmon case decided by a GATT panel in 1988 (Vogel 1995) is an example of these legal provisions in cells 7 and 6 of Figure 2.1. In the herring and salmon case, the Panel considered whether a conservation measure was 'primarily aimed at conservation of an exhaustible natural resource'. The measure in question was a Canadian law requiring that herring and salmon caught in Canadian waters be processed in Canada before export. The panel found that such a measure went beyond what was necessary for conservation purposes and the measure was therefore not 'primarily aimed at' conservation.

3. Does the standard create an *unnecessary obstacle* to trade? Article 904(4) prevents the adoption of standards-related measures that create an unnecessary obstacle to trade. Article 904(4) further states that an unnecessary obstacle to trade will not be inferred where the measure's demonstrable purpose is to achieve a legitimate objective and the measure does not exclude goods of other NAFTA countries that meet that objective. Whether a trade barrier is necessary depends on, *inter alia*, whether the trade restriction is the most effective means

available to achieve the standard's environmental goal and that there are no equally effective and reasonable means of achieving the environmental goal without restricting trade (Trebilcock and Howse 1995). As there is wide latitude in the interpretation of these letters, this provision has been described as ineffectual and one which a carefully drafted environmental regulation could easily navigate around (Johnson and Beaulieu 1996). Thus, exporters who are seeking to challenge what they believe to be an unfair environmental regulation are not likely to succeed on these grounds.

4. Does the standard support the pursuit of a *legitimate environmental objective*? Article 915 defines a legitimate objective as one which includes 'the protection of human, animal or plant life or health, the environment or consumers, including matters relating to quality and identifiability of goods or services and sustainable development . . . *but does not include the protection of domestic production*' (emphasis added). This fairly open-ended definition of a legitimate environmental objective is balanced by a prohibition of protectionist measures. The language used here represents a change from the comparable article in the FTA, which used the term 'legitimate *domestic* objective'. This would seem to imply that both domestic and extra-territorial environmental policies may be pursued (Condon 1994). This solved, at least for North America, the ongoing controversy in international trade law of whether trade restrictions could appropriately be used for environmental policies which extend beyond the jurisdiction of a member country. This issue was best characterized by the US–Mexico tuna–dolphin disputes pre-dating NAFTA, which are issues in cells 8, 13, 6, and 11 of Figure 2.1. The US–Mexico tuna–dolphin case involved the extra-territorial application of a conservation measure. The United States banned tuna imports from Mexico because of the high dolphin mortality rate associated with the manner in which Mexicans caught tuna. A GATT Panel found, in this instance, that a country could not justify trade restrictions for conservation purposes outside its own jurisdiction.

5. If a trade restriction is necessary, has the *least trade-restrictive measure* been chosen? NAFTA does not contain a 'least trade-restrictive requirement' such as exists under GATT Article XX. However, one has been interpreted as being implied in NAFTA (Condon 1994). This requirement asks whether a country has chosen the least trade-restrictive alternative in the creation of an environmental standard to achieve an environmental goal. If there is a way of achieving an environmental goal that is less trade restrictive, that method must be employed.

From this discussion of the legal framework of NAFTA, we conclude that the NAFTA disciplines on technical barriers to trade do not pose much of a threat to the abuse of environmental measures. The legal disciplines on trade-restricting measures afford a wide degree of latitude in enacting environmental regulations. NAFTA members who believe that they have been adversely affected by such regulation will bear the onus of demonstrating non-compliance by another NAFTA party. Given these considerations, if there is a reasonable connection between a trade-restricting standard and an environmental objective, it is unlikely to be found contrary to NAFTA. To further investigate the implications of the legal framework of NAFTA for corporate strategy, we now turn to a specific case study.

A Case Study: UHT Milk

The problems facing exporters created by environmental provisions is best illustrated by the examination of an actual case, the export of UHT (ultra-high temperature) milk from Quebec to Puerto Rico, which was the fifth Chapter 18 case decided under the FTA. It was the only panel decision on the issue of sanitary and phytosanitary standards. Although sanitary and phytosanitary standards are covered by Chapter 7, the legal disciplines are similar to Chapter 9. As such, this case raises key issues and provides insight into how future determinations may be dealt with under NAFTA. This is a case study of a cell 8 issue in Figure 2.1 as affected by legal and institutional procedures in cell 7.

In an effort to increase milk sales, Puerto Rico changed its milk standards in 1987. To that end, the Puerto Rican Department of Health and Agriculture adopted new regulations and entered into interagency agreements designed to improve the quality of milk production. The new procedures provided for a mandatory licensing process to ensure compliance with health and safety requirements. This would then allow milk and milk products produced in Puerto Rico to be shipped throughout the United States. Prior to the adoption of the new standards, Lactel, a milk company based in Point Claire, Quebec, had sold UHT milk in Puerto Rico for fourteen years. Despite its long-standing and problem-free presence in the Puerto Rican market, UHT milk from Quebec did not comply with the new regulations and therefore could not obtain a licence. In order to comply with the new regulations, either the Canadian and Quebec governments would have to harmonize the relevant legislation with that of the United States or Lactel would have to obtain certification of equivalency. Lactel wished to establish equivalency because harmonization between Canada and the United States was not an option at that time. However, for a number of reasons, the United States would not conduct an equivalency study and UHT milk from Quebec was denied entry into Puerto Rico on 31 December 1991. Despite repeated attempts by the Canadian government at the diplomatic and bureaucratic level to be afforded an opportunity to demonstrate equivalency of Quebec's milk sanitation standards, Puerto Rico continued to prohibit imports of Quebec UHT milk. In the fall of 1992, Canada requested that a dispute resolution panel be struck under Chapter 18 of the FTA.

At the FTA panel, Canada argued that the United States had violated the FTA on four main points. First, Canada argued that Puerto Rico's licensing requirements violated Article XI of the GATT (as incorporated in the FTA) which prohibits quantitative restrictions. In the alternative, Canada submitted that the licensing requirements violated the national treatment provisions of the GATT found in Article III (as incorporated in the FTA) as Quebec UHT milk was treated less favourably than milk produced in the United States. Second, Canada submitted that the refusal of the United States to issue a licence for the sale of Quebec UHT milk was a disguised restriction on trade and therefore not justifiable under GATT's exception relating to the protection of health found in Article XX(b). Third, Canada argued that the United States failed in its obligation to facilitate agricultural trade by introducing technical standards that were essentially a disguised restriction on trade, without providing for an equivalency study. Fourth, Canada submitted that it had been denied its reasonably expected benefits negotiated under the FTA which 'upset the previously existing competitive relationship between domestic and imported products' (Davey 1996: 59).

The United States rebutted the Canadian submissions by stating that the licensing requirements were an internal health and safety measure undertaken within their sovereignty and were equally applicable to domestic and foreign milk producers. Accordingly, neither Article XI nor Article III of GATT applied. The United States submitted that in the event it had breached the FTA, the GATT Article XX exception applied. The United States also argued that the obligation to facilitate agricultural trade was of a 'best efforts' nature only. The United States further argued that it was reasonable to upgrade its milk standards, therefore Canada had not been denied any of its expected benefits under the FTA.

The FTA panel agreed with most of the arguments put forth by the United States. It concluded that Article XI did not apply as the licensing requirements were an internal measure, rather than a quantitative restriction. The panel further found that the obligation to facilitate trade was of a 'best efforts' nature only. The panel did not view the milk regulations as a disguised restriction on trade. In Canada's favour, the panel noted that the efforts among government officials to establish equivalency were unsatisfactory and that Canada's reasonably expected benefits under the FTA had been denied, although not by the fault of the United States. The panel recommended that an equivalency study be undertaken within two months in order to allow UHT milk from Quebec to re-enter the Puerto Rican market.

In late 1995, two years after the panel report, an equivalency study was completed and UHT milk from Quebec was permitted to enter the Puerto Rican market. The UHT case highlights the problems for corporate strategy in the current North American trade and environment framework. From the viewpoint of Lactel, the Quebec exporter in cell 7 of Figure 2.1, the trade liberalization guaranteed is rendered essentially meaningless. The fact that the panel found that there was nullification and impairment of NAFTA benefits is not in itself helpful, as it is not accompanied by an adequate remedy. The recommended two months for the conduct of the equivalency test were not met. Lactel's market share and corresponding advantages have been lost, and will not be easily regained in the new competitive environment in Puerto Rico. This environmental regulation served as a barrier to trade.

Our conclusion is that the product should not have been banned before the opportunity to prove equivalency was afforded to Lactel. The equivalency principles were not given adequate weight or merit in the decision. This case also illustrates the failure of the FTA/NAFTA committees and subcommittees to adequately address the problem of arbitrary changes to corporate strategy. Dispute avoidance through the work of the committees and working groups forms part of NAFTA policy, since NAFTA allows for the establishment of a number of ad hoc and standing committees. Articles 723 allows for consultations in Working Groups on sanitary and phytosanitary measures to take the place of regular consultations under Article 2007 in the process leading up to formal dispute settlement under Chapter 20 (Commission for Environmental Cooperation 1996a).

Although the UHT milk case was legally resolved, Figure 2.1 shows that the amount of time and money involved for a cell 7 company to enforce its guaranteed rights in cell 8 can be prohibitive, leading to an unsatisfactory outcome. In terms of corporate strategy, this would force an exporting firm, such as Lactel, to consider acquisition of a conforming plant or production itself in the United States (i.e. becoming an MNE) in order to ensure market access. The repercussions of such environmentally related changes on corporate strategy and competitiveness are only beginning to be considered in research on trade and the environment.

Conclusions

Further multidisciplinary research is needed to develop a theory of trade and the environment. This theory should be based primarily on the literature relating to corporate strategy, particularly to the theory of shelter as it explains corporate strategic responses to trade-related environmental regulations. It should also be informed by theories of political science which shed light on how various actors (firms, ENGOs, lobbyists) can influence the environmental regulatory process. Such an approach would help develop a theoretical grounding for deeper analysis of the intersection between trade and the environment and offer an opportunity for institutions such as the CEC to further its mandate.

The UHT case illustrates the complexity of the issues involved in a trade and environment dispute. Once the administration of environmental regulations can be captured by domestic industries who stand to gain from the protectionist effects of such regulation, then foreign firms are required to make a strategic response. NAFTA's current legal and institutional framework, which broadly guarantees national treatment, has made great gains in terms of including environmental considerations in a trade agreement. However, the five-part test to establish whether an environmental regulation is protectionist in nature remains inadequate to combat shelter-based environmental regulations. This can have devastating impacts on a firm whose business is substantially reliant on foreign sales, such as exports.

Firms from smaller countries are increasingly finding the access to the large triad markets they need for global competitive success imperilled by the proliferation of environmental regulations. In the North American case, the advent of the North American Free Trade Agreement in 1994 brought both a major opening of the US market to firms from Canada and Mexico, but also a set of potentially powerful environmental provisions and institutions that could inhibit the use of national and subfederal environmental regulations with protectionist impacts. This complex institutional addition to the prevailing multilateral and domestic regulatory structures offered all types of firms, from domestic and home based exporters to home based MNEs and transnational MNEs, a new instrument to combat regulatory protectionism. Their potential value is shown by the fact that the classic five legal tests which a national or subfederal environmental regulation must meet if it is to survive a challenge as being a protectionist measure under NAFTA's Chapter 9 on standards demonstrate that the straight legal application of the trade agreement's dispute settlements provisions is likely to be an inadequate instrument in protecting exporting firms from protectionist barriers. The case of UHT milk, adjudicated under the FTA, further suggests that this inadequacy will prevail in the sanitary and phytosanitary area as well as the general standard provisions of NAFTA itself, as the standard trade dispute settlement mechanism does not operate with sufficient strength in imposing remedies or speed in ensuring national compliance to preserve a firm's market access. Yet under NAFTA, exporting firms now have available to them more than the classic corporate strategies which include: withdrawal from the export market, alteration of production processes, and securing production facilities in the foreign market. They also have more than legal dispute adjudication and the political strategy of bilateral home government diplomacy. They now have the new institutional options of using the broad array of NAFTA institutions for purposes of timely, low-cost dispute avoidance and management.

3

Corporate Strategy and Environmental Regulation: Corporate Strategy Perspectives

The preceding chapter developed a framework of twenty different cases where five different governmental levels of environmental regulation interact with four different levels of internationally exposed and involved firms. The resulting twenty cells where the challenge of environmental regulatory protection arises permit different strategic responses on the part of firms affected by those regulations. This chapter explains and documents some of the varying corporate strategic responses firms have available and employ, in order to develop this framework into an explanatory tool.

The focus here is the North American market place, where firms in the United States and Canada have sought to prevent firms located in the other NAFTA countries from gaining market access through the 'capture' of the administration of environmental regulation. Five cases are examined in an effort to discern whether such cases constitute part of a shelter-based strategy by the firm. This is done through an examination of the various corporate and government players involved in each case and the alliances they have formed with environmental groups. The way in which firms have adjusted their strategies to take account of these barriers are identified. Responses range from the aggrieved firm establishing a presence through foreign direct investment in the market from which they are denied access to intensive lobbying on the part of that firm.

This analysis also illustrates the diversity in the range of sectors where these disputes can erupt and the severe impact that such trade-restricting environmental regulation can impose. Such disputes can occur over a similarly diverse range of environmental regulations, notably, as explored here, the broad classifications of: conservation; packaging and labelling requirements; and health and safety regulations. The five cases span the pre- and post-NAFTA period. They vary in the degree to which they employ the new complex instruments of NAFTA (or alternatively the FTA or the GATT), as a means by which to successfully combat the discriminatory application of domestic environmental regulation. In many of these cases, we will argue later in the book, these affected firms may have been better off by mobilizing NAFTA's international institutions in more complex ways than they did to secure the markets they were denied.

If the state of California enacts a newspaper recycling law which requires 50 per cent recycled fibre in newsprint, this could have a dramatic effect on Canadian forest product firms exporting newsprint to the US market (over 90 per cent of Canadian newsprint production is exported, mainly to the United States and European Union). For perfectly valid environmental reasons, the California law now requires that a newsprint producer use the 'urban forest' of recycled newsprint more than the traditional source of fibre supply in the forests of British Columbia (BC). The logistical costs of transporting used newsprint back to the BC mills are prohibitively high (even at recent prices for used newspapers). Therefore, to stay in business, Canadian newsprint producers would be forced to build large de-inking plants in California near large urban concentrations such as Los Angeles. This would require switching from the export of newsprint to foreign direct investment (ownership) of California-based newsprint production. Thus, the US regulations can have the potential to impose major strategic management choices on a Canadian (or Mexican) firm compared to a domestic US firm, which simply makes an internal US-regional relocation decision.

The strategic choices of non-US firms (and their efficiency and competitiveness) are affected by NAFTA's rules, regulations, and procedures. Indeed, in terms of strategic management decision-making, it is conceivable that US rival firms (in forest products, for example) would seek to 'capture' the process by which relevant US-environmental regulations are enforced and new laws imposed, in order to use them in a discriminatory manner against Canadian (or Mexican) competitors. This type of corporate behaviour has been analysed as part of the theory of 'shelter' (Rugman and Verbeke 1990). The domestic environmental regulation leads to a new entry barrier imposed on foreigners, and this has the potential to deny firms access to the large US market necessary for an efficient global strategy. The use of corporate strategy and its relationship to environmental issues has been explored in Rugman (1995). This work also examines the issue of subsidies, market access, and the Canadian forest products industry.

The extent to which firms from Canada and Mexico can be denied entry to the US market based on this discriminatory use of 'domestic' environmental regulations is investigated in this chapter. Senior managers and industry analysts have been consulted and interviewed in order to gain knowledge about potentially vulnerable Canadian and Mexican industries. This research builds upon the work of David Vogel (1995) and Vogel and Rugman (1997).

This environmental issue is related to the issue of the use of subsidies and US trade remedy laws, where the latter have been used as barriers to entry. The manner in which US domestic firms have captured their administration at the US International Trade Commission and Commerce Department is well known to legal scholars, economists, and trade negotiators. The concern about the loss of market access was a major driver for the Canada–US Free Trade Agreement (FTA) and NAFTA. The issue of the covert influence of US firms on

40   *Economic and Corporate Strategy*

the administration of countervailing duties and antidumping laws has been investigated by numerous writers, including Rugman and Anderson (1987). In this chapter, the body of work in corporate strategy is applied to NAFTA and its environmental provisions, with a particular focus on five recent cases: Ontario beer cans; ultra-high temperature (UHT) milk; agriculture border inspections; PCBs; and MMT. In each case, we attempt to elaborate the framework by examining a number of criteria that can be used to evaluate whether the environmental regulation is being administered for 'shelter'.

We use NAFTA as a setting for this analysis, as it provides a new set of rules which governs not only trade but the interaction of trade and environmental regulation. NAFTA provides an institutional structure which addresses issues relating to environment and trade 'frictions', through its over 50 trinational committees, sub-committees, and working groups (Kirton and Fernandez de Castro 1997). NAFTA also offers a legal framework which potentially limits the extent to which environmental regulations with a trade-restricting effect can be enforced by the NAFTA parties. NAFTA's dispute settlement mechanism provides a means by which to challenge such regulations (Rugman, Kirton, and Soloway 1997*a*).

A Classification of Environmental Cases under NAFTA

Figure 3.1 provides a simple descriptive classification of over twenty environmentally related disputes which have arisen under the FTA and NAFTA. The figure is arranged in three columns representing the three member countries of NAFTA, and in three rows representing a classification of type of environmental regulations. The three types are: (1) conservation; (2) packaging and labelling; and (3) health and safety regulations, especially inspection.

This set of twenty-five cases is examined in much greater detail in a study by Vogel and Rugman (1997). Here five of these cases will be analysed independently of the framework in the larger study and the focus will be mainly upon the United States and Canada, apart from one Mexico–United States agricultural border inspection issue. Most of the US–Mexican cases involve such disputes over agricultural products subject to health and safety inspections. Despite NAFTA, many of these inspections often appear to occur in an arbitrary manner and are correlated with lobbying activities by US domestic producers who are losing US market share to Mexican producers (Vogel, Rugman, and Schettino 1997). These five cases are italicized in Figure 3.1.

In this chapter, the issues of agriculture border inspections and UHT milk are taken as comparable US–Canadian agricultural cases. In both of these cases, the United States has initiated measures which restrict Canadian imports. To balance these cases, two Canadian-imposed barriers to trade are discussed: the PCB export ban and the legislation affecting MMT (defined later). Finally, the case of Ontario beer cans is studied as a parallel to the California newsprint recycling case discussed earlier. The conservation cases (tuna/dolphin, lobster,

Type of regulation	Geographic source of barrier		
	US	Canada	Mexico
Conservation	Tuna–Dolphin Lobsters Shrimps	Salmon/herring (2 cases) Forestry-stumpage	
Packaging and labelling	California recycling	**Ontario beer cans**	
Health and safety	Asbestos Avocados Beef **Blueberries** Mangoes Papaya **Potatoes** Tomatoes Trucking **UHT milk** Vanilla Wheat	**MMT auto emissions** **PCB export ban**	Christmas trees Meat

Fig. 3.1. The NAFTA environmental regulations across member states

etc.) have been analysed separately in Vogel (1995). The cases in Figure 3.1 are updated and re-evaluated in Vogel and Rugman (1997).

Case 1: Ontario's Tax on Aluminium Beer Cans

In 1992 a trade dispute erupted between Canada and the United States over a 10 cents per can recycling tax imposed by the Ontario government on aluminium beer cans. The United States claimed that this tax was discriminatory, as US beer is exported and sold in Canada in aluminium cans, while over 80 per cent of Canadian beer is sold in bottles. The United States further claimed that this was an attempt to protect Canadian beer from the competition of cheaper US beer. The tax applied only to beer cans; it did not apply to soft drink, juice, or other aluminium beverage containers.

US beer exports to Ontario are about US $30 million annually whereas US beer imports from Ontario are much greater, at US $170 million. Canadian firms (Molson and Labatt) are much more vulnerable to US trade actions than are the US beer exporters to Canada, such as Stroh and Helleman, as they are more dependent on access to the US market.

The recycling tax was one battle in a larger war between Canada and the United States concerning restrictive provincial regulations on pricing and distribution. In Ontario, as in all provinces across Canada, beer is sold through

Brewers Retail Inc. (BRI), a government monopoly distribution scheme. A General Agreement on Tariffs and Trade (GATT) panel was struck in 1988 pursuant to a US complaint about monopoly distribution and pricing, which ruled largely in favour of the United States. Canada did not comply with this ruling, claiming that the monopoly distribution scheme was an issue falling under the exclusive jurisdiction of the provinces. In a follow-up 1992 GATT panel, in which many of the same issues were reconsidered, the United States again claimed that the provincial monopolies 'maintained listing and delisting practices for imported beer, limited the access of imported beer to points of sale, restricted the private delivery of imported beer to points of sale, levied import mark-ups on beer and imposed minimum price requirements on beer inconsistently with [the GATT]' (GATT Panel Report 1993). The Panel ruled in favour of the United States, finding that Canada had violated its national treatment obligations to the United States.

On the issue of the recycling tax, which (from 1989 to 1992) was 5 cents per bottle, the Panel did not find that the taxes themselves were inconsistent with the GATT, but rather the absence of a deposit/return system for those cans was inconsistent with the GATT. While domestic beer companies had established a deposit/return scheme for bottles and cans at the BRI outlets, this scheme was not available for use for the return of US beer cans, and the creation of a separate, parallel scheme was prohibitively expensive (GATT Panel Report 1993).

After the release of the GATT panel decision in April 1992, Ontario doubled the recycling tax to 10 cents per can. This tax increased the retail price of US beer, along with additional duties imposed, from $19.83 to $24.35 per case (French 1993). A final agreement was reached between the parties in August 1993 which did not rescind the tax, but improved access for US firms to BRI outlets in Ontario. It also lifted a 50 per cent retaliatory duty levied on beer shipped from Ontario to the United States and a 50 per cent Canadian duty imposed on some US beer exports to Ontario.

The Ontario government claimed that the levy was not imposed as a protectionist measure. Rather, the tax was part of its 'recycle, reuse, and reduce' environmental action plan. It has argued that glass bottles were more environmentally efficient, since they can be reused an average of 15–18 times, use less energy and create less pollution than aluminium recycling, and are less likely to end up as garbage in landfills. Ontario further claimed that without the additional tax, the province's extensive recycling efforts would be undermined, as consumers would switch to less expensive imported beer sold in aluminium cans which would in turn force Canadian brewers to switch to cans as well.

Two US firms, Anheuser-Busch and Strohs, raised a number of questions regarding the environmental effectiveness of the levy. First, the fact that Ontario has not subjected all aluminium cans (i.e. soft drink, juice, and food) to such a tax raises concerns about the purpose of the legislation, which fails to capture the majority of aluminium cans used by consumers. Second, it takes more energy to move heavy and voluminous bottles than to move a similar volume capacity of cans from the United States to Canada. Third, there were claims that the weight of bottle caps from bottles destined for landfills comprises more than 12 per cent of aluminium not recycled. These efforts were supported by Canada's largest aluminium producer, Alcan, who began a vigorous campaign in opposition to the tax which included a full page advertisement in Canada's largest newspapers (French 1993). Alcan claimed that the tax had resulted in increased costs to the consumer and the loss of hundreds of jobs in Ontario.

Environmental groups took the side of the Ontario government and aligned themselves with the Canadian beer industry. They viewed the tax as part of a broader issue on how the NAFTA partners will 'negotiate away' valid environmental regulations when they conflict with NAFTA trade obligations. The environmental groups sought to have the beer tax excluded from any negotiations on beer and warned of the dangers of undermining the environmental policies of the United States' trading partners.

While nothing in FTA/NAFTA prevents parties from setting their own environmental regulations, they are prevented from using such regulations as disguised barriers to trade. The Canadian beer industry was vulnerable to competition from US beer, and Canadian beer firms were dependent on market access to the United States. This 'green tax' was arguably part of a strategy to retain their market share in Ontario, after they had lost on a number of pricing and distribution issues before the GATT.

Case 2: Puerto Rico Ban on UHT Milk from Quebec

In 1992 Canada initiated an action against the United States under Chapter 18 of the FTA regarding new milk standards adopted by the Puerto Rican government. Despite a fourteen-year history of trouble-free exports to Puerto Rico, UHT milk from Quebec produced by Lactel Inc. was denied entry into Puerto Rico on the basis that it did not comply with the requisite health and safety standards. The Canadian government claimed that this new-found health and safety standard was a restriction on trade and an outright violation of the FTA. The US government claimed that it was free to set its own health and safety standards, and that its obligations under the FTA did not diminish that freedom.

The origins of the dispute go back to 1987, when Puerto Rico changed its milk standards to align itself with the rest of the United States. This was done in an effort to gain access to the US market, thereby increasing milk sales. To that end, the Puerto Rican Department of Health and Agriculture adopted new regulations and entered into interagency agreements designed to improve the quality of milk production. The new procedures provided for a mandatory licensing process to ensure compliance with health and safety requirements.

This meant that milk could not be sold in Puerto Rico without a licence. Puerto Rico wanted to be able to ship its milk and milk products throughout the United States, which would now be permitted under the new regulatory scheme. Despite Lactel's long-standing presence in the Puerto Rican market, UHT milk from Quebec did not comply with the new regulations and it was consequently unable to obtain a licence.

A licence could be obtained by Lactel in two ways. One, the Canadian government could adopt exactly the same processing and inspection regulations as the United States. This was not feasible as Canada already had in place a sophisticated and effective federal–provincial legal framework governing milk production which could not be readily changed. Milk sanitation is not a problem in Canada. Furthermore, adopting the US regulations would impose significant capital costs on firms, requiring Lactel to reconfigure its production plant in order to comply 'to the letter' with US regulations. The second way to obtain a licence was for Lactel to obtain a certificate of equivalency from the United States Food and Drug Administration (FDA) attesting that milk standards in Quebec provide the same degree of protection as the Puerto Rican standards. NAFTA Article 714 provides that parties should 'to the greatest extent practicable' pursue the equivalence of health and safety standards without reducing the level of protection. Lactel applied for equivalency, but for a number of reasons, the United States stalled this process and ultimately refused to conduct the equivalency study necessary for certification. UHT milk from Quebec was denied entry into Puerto Rico on 31 December 1991.

Despite repeated attempts by the Canadian government at diplomatic and bureaucratic levels to be afforded an opportunity to demonstrate equivalency of Quebec's milk sanitation standards, Puerto Rico continued to prohibit imports of Quebec UHT milk. NAFTA's institutional structure provides for the establishment of working groups to facilitate trade in agriculture (Kirton and Fernandez de Castro 1997). A bilateral 'UHT subcommittee' was established to examine the issue, under the auspices of the trilateral FTA Technical Working Group on Dairy, Fruit, Vegetable, and Egg Inspection, but was ultimately unsuccessful in resolving the issue. In the autumn of 1992, Canada submitted a formal request for dispute resolution pursuant to Chapter 18 of the FTA.

The findings of this FTA panel in 1993 offered mixed results. The panel did not view the milk regulations as a disguised restriction on trade and found that the obligation to pursue equivalency was of a 'best efforts' nature only. However, the panel noted that the efforts among government officials to establish equivalency were unsatisfactory and that Canada's reasonably expected benefits under the FTA had been denied, although not by the fault of the United States. This essentially meant that it was reasonable for Canada, after fourteen years of exports, to have been granted equivalency status. At the same time, however, the Panel did not find any wrongdoing on the part of the United States, nor did if find that the United States had acted in bad faith. The panel recommended that an equivalency study be undertaken within two months in order to allow UHT milk from Quebec to re-enter the Puerto Rican market.

The issue was finally resolved in 1995 when a joint study by agriculture officials from Canada and the United States concluded that the Quebec and US system of UHT milk production were equivalent and, on 25 October 1995, Quebec exports to Puerto Rico were again permitted. From 1977 to 1981, Lactel held 100 per cent of the Puerto Rican UHT milk market. Between 1982 and 1985, market share fluctuated between 25.3 and 88.4 per cent and continued to have significant market presence until the ban was imposed in 1991. Although market access was ultimately the desired result for Lactel, it is really a case of 'too little, too late'. Lactel had been denied market entry for over three years, after which time it found it almost impossible to regain its market share and corresponding advantages. It was not until late 1995, a full two years after the Panel report and four years after the imposition of the ban, that the equivalency study was completed and UHT milk from Quebec was permitted to enter the Puerto Rico market. In effect, the regulation excluded Lactel from the market.

The UHT case has demonstrated that there is no adequate remedy for a small foreign producer adversely affected by health and safety regulations under NAFTA. Neither the dispute resolution process nor the mechanisms provided by NAFTA's institutional structure were helpful to the Canadian firm in maintaining its market access to the United States as guaranteed under NAFTA. Lactel's market in Puerto Rico eroded over the three to four years it took to complete the NAFTA legal process and alternative Puerto Rican suppliers benefited from this discriminatory environmental regulation.

Case 3: US Inspection of Canadian Potatoes and Blueberries

Potatoes

In December 1995 and January 1996 the United States Department of Agriculture dramatically increased the number of inspections of Canadian potatoes entering Maine, and it rejected several truckloads of potatoes. The increased border inspections were attributed to lobbying by Maine potato growers, whose 1995 crop was a failure (Vogel and Rugman 1997). Canadian potatoes from nearby New Brunswick and Prince Edward Island filled the market shortage. Usually US officials rely on work undertaken by Canadian inspectors to grade and classify potatoes exported to the United States. It is unusual for US inspectors to repeat the process. On 15 December 1995 New Brunswick agriculture minister Doug Tyler called on the federal government to take action to offset Maine's increased inspections of Canadian potatoes. It was alleged that Maine potato growers were really concerned about issues relating to income stabilization rather than Canadian potatoes. To resolve the dispute, in January 1996, Canadian agriculture minister Ralph Goodale hired additional Canadian inspectors of US potatoes. In 1994 the United States exported more potatoes to Canada (253,000 tonnes) than it imported (179,000 tonnes).

The potato issue is not settled. In May 1997 the United States Department of Agriculture (USDA) issued a notice limiting potato tuber and plant imports from Newfoundland and parts of Central BC in order to prevent the introduction of disease and insect pests into the United States. However, in its notice, USDA claimed that the impact on trade was likely to be minimal as Canada currently limits intraprovincial movement in potatoes from this region for the same reason.

Blueberries

In October 1991 shipments of frozen blueberries destined for Oregon were prevented from entering the United States. They were either stopped at the border and sent back to Nova Scotia or were detained pending further testing. Wild blueberries are the most valuable crop for Nova Scotia. In 1991 the Nova Scotia blueberry crop was valued at over Can. $15 million. The next biggest crop was apples, valued at just over Can. $10 million (Sutton 1993). Only 5 per cent of the blueberry crop is consumed locally, the rest is frozen and exported to Europe (75 per cent) and the United States (20 per cent). There are two companies in Nova Scotia who have the facilities to freeze blueberries, Cobi Foods, Inc. and Oxford Frozen Foods Limited (Sutton 1993).

Dimethoate is a pesticide used on Nova Scotian blueberries in order to control insects and pests which destroy blueberry crops. It is used on a variety of crops in both Canada and the United States, but must be registered for use on specific crops (Sutton 1993). Dimethoate is not registered for use on blueberries in the United States, although it is registered for use on US grapes, citrus, nut crops, melons, and other vegetables. Since the United States has a zero tolerance for dimethoate, and trace amounts of the pesticide were found on the Nova Scotia blueberries, they were not in compliance with the US regulations. The processing firms were forced to cover the extra costs associated with the return freight and additional inspections.

In an effort to avoid border inspection problems again, Nova Scotian growers began to use an alternative pesticide, imidian, as a replacement for dimethoate. Imidian is registered for use in both Canada and the United States. However, it is significantly more expensive at Can. $10 per acre compared to the cost of dimethoate at only Can. $2 per acre. Imidian is also more costly to apply, as it requires the use of special equipment, while dimethoate requires no such special application equipment (Sutton 1993). Consequently, the United States' refusal to accept Nova Scotian blueberries with dimethoate, a pesticide allowed on other US fruit, imposed severe discriminatory financial penalties on both the Nova Scotian blueberry growers and processors.

Sutton (1993) makes the point that the blueberry dispute is an example of the power imbalance between Canada and the United States which the FTA did little to adjust in terms of a fairer trading relationship. In fact, the provisions in the FTA which deal with mutual recognition and harmonization of standards did not prevent the apparently capricious actions of the United States. Nova Scotia blueberries suffered further reputational damage. This was evidenced by new concerns about product quality on the part of its European customers as a result of the incident.

In the case of potatoes from BC and Newfoundland, the evidence does not seem to support a claim that the regulations are being used for shelter, although additional research on trade impacts would be required. This underscores the role that scientific evidence must play in trade disputes, and the evaluation of whether an environmental regulation is created in order to shelter a domestic producer from foreign competition (Soloway 1997). The discretionary and capricious use of border inspection measures illustrated in the New Brunswick/PEI and Maine dispute reveals a more suspect agenda on the part of producers in the United States.

Such a problem also lies behind the six US–Mexican agriculture disputes in Figure 3.1. One example is the Mexican avocado, which has been excluded from the US market for over eighty years because of Mexican plant pests such as the avocado seed weevil, stem borer, and seed moth. Proposals to allow Mexican avocados into the United States have traditionally met opposition from California growers, represented by the California Farm Bureau Federation (CFBF) who have voiced concerns that the Mexican pests pose a threat to California's US $251 million avocado industry.

Despite CFBF opposition, the ban on Mexican avocados was partially lifted recently, after a comprehensive study concerning the risk of infestation posed by them. Selected growers of Mexican avocados are now permitted to export avocados in the California 'off' season (November to February) to a limited number of states.

Case 4: Canadian Ban on Exports of PCBs

On 20 November 1995 former Canadian environment minister, Sheila Copps, issued an interim order banning the export of polychlorinated biphenyl (PCB) waste. This prevented Canadian exports of PCBs to US-based disposal plants. The ban was partially lifted under former Environment Minister Sergio Marchi in February 1997. It will allow the export of PCBs destined for destruction or incineration, but continues to prohibit PCB exports destined for landfill sites.

The reason provided by Minister Copps for the ban was concern over inadequate disposal standards at many of the US waste disposal facilities. This order followed a November 1995 decision by the US Environmental Protection Agency (EPA) to allow, on a selective basis, the import of PCBs for destruction in the United States. Prior to the EPA decision, PCB imports had been restricted

48 *Economic and Corporate Strategy*

since 1980, providing protection for Canadian waste disposal facilities (Vogel and Rugman 1997).

There have been claims that the ban was imposed for protectionist reasons. S. D. Myers, an Ohio-based waste disposal company and Waste Management Inc. of Oak Brook, Ill., objected to the ban on the grounds that it reduces its business by diverting Canadian PCB waste from central Canada to the only alternative PCB waste disposal incinerator in Swan Hills, Alberta, owned by Chem-Security Inc. This would force firms in central Canada to incur an additional 40 per cent in transportation costs and prevent them from using the less expensive US facilities. Canadian businesses and local governments argued that they would face up to Can. $200 million in increased costs to clean up their PCB stockpiles. The province of Ontario has 116,000 tonnes of PCB wastes stored in 1,700 different locations. Industry would thus prefer to ship the waste for destruction to nearby US locations, rather than to Alberta.

A legal challenge to the Copps interim order was initiated in December 1995 by Canadian firms with PCB wastes, including a group of Quebec industries and an Ontario waste disposal transportation company (Vogel and Rugman 1997). These parties alleged that the interim order was a violation of the Canadian Environmental Protection Act (CEPA), which grants the Minister extraordinary powers only in the event of an emergency threat to human health. Officials in Environment Canada advised Minister Copps that the interim order was not justified, as the export of PCBs to the United States did not pose a significant danger to the environment or to human health. In documents filed by federal officials in response to the December 1995 action, it was also alleged that the interim order would violate NAFTA, as it was an export ban imposed as a barrier to trade (Vogel and Rugman 1997).

Chem-Security of Alberta allegedly lobbied for the PCB export ban, providing evidence of a shelter-seeking strategy. Additional companies who benefited were Bovar Inc. located in Calgary, Alberta and Cintec Inc. located in Montreal. These companies have additionally complained that with the partial lifting of the ban, they are forced into a situation of competing with US companies with less stringent standards.

Case 5: The MMT Gasoline Additives Issue

The Canadian government has recently passed a bill banning all international and intraprovincial trade in the fuel additive MMT (methylcyclopentadienyl manganese tricarbonyl). MMT is an octane-enhancing fuel additive, introduced in 1997 as a replacement for lead. The ban in MMT is the culmination of an ongoing battle between two major sectors of the Canadian economy: auto manufacturers and petroleum producers. At its most basic level, auto manufacturers support a ban on MMT, as they claim it reduces the efficacy of the new generation of pollution control equipment they have developed in response to increasingly stringent emission standards. Petroleum producers, who blend MMT with gasoline in their refineries, oppose a ban on MMT, as they claim that they will be forced to undertake significant capital expenditures to reconfigure their plants for alternative fuel additives. The auto manufacturers can claim victory in the MMT battle, but the war is not over. At the heart of this issue is the question of which industry will bear the future costs of producing the technology to meet the ongoing demand for emissions reduction (Soloway 1999).

An initiative of Environment Canada, the ban on MMT was justified for three reasons. First was the protection of the health of Canadians. Second was the goal of 'positive and progressive harmonization' of North American fuel standards. The third reason was to protect jobs and consumers from adverse economic impacts, due to increased engineering costs for auto companies (Soloway 1999). When examined in this context, Bill C-29, a ban on trade for environmental purposes, seems to be legislation designed for both environmental and economic protection. MMT itself was not banned as a toxic substance under, for example, CEPA. Only its movement across borders has been prohibited.

The Motor Vehicles Manufacturers Association (MVMA) represents all 21 motor vehicle manufacturers in Canada. They have lobbied intensively for the removal of MMT for gasoline, arguing that their pollution control devices required by law will malfunction with the use of MMT and impose severe costs in warranty repairs and re-engineering in order to correct the problem. They further argue that they have invested over Can. $4 billion jointly to develop pollution control devices in direct response to government regulations. The MVMA states that they simply do not have the required technology to meet current emission standards with MMT in gasoline.

At the same time as banning MMT, Environment Canada is also supporting the use of alternative 'green' fuel additives, namely ethanol, which is made from corn. Environment Canada has stated one of the benefits of the ban was to help the fledgling ethanol industry, which has received substantial subsidies from the Canadian government. The ethanol industry has also been involved in lobbying for the use of greener fuel additives, although on a much smaller scale than the MVMA.

Over fifty environmental groups representing millions of citizens throughout North America have banded together to form massive coalitions in Canada and the United States to support the ban on MMT (Soloway 1999). They believe it is harmful to the public health for two reasons: (1) it is a harmful and dangerous 'neurotoxin' emitted from autos directly into the environment with negative human health impacts and (2) it causes increased emissions by harming the autos' onboard pollution monitoring equipment. The environmental groups have also formed a coalition with the auto industry in the effort to ban MMT.

The Canadian Petroleum Products Institute (CPPI) has strenuously opposed a ban on MMT. They allege that the ban contravenes several provisions of

50   *Economic and Corporate Strategy*

NAFTA and will result in over Can. $100 million in increased costs to the industry in capital cost adjustments. They further argue that a ban on MMT will result in increased consumer costs, as MMT is the least expensive fuel additive available. Ethyl Corp., the sole North American producer of MMT has launched a challenge under Investment provisions (Chapter 11) of NAFTA, alleging, *inter alia*, it contravenes the national treatment provisions of NAFTA.

Given the framework presented at the start of this chapter, it is not readily apparent who is seeking shelter through the use of an environmental regulation. In this complex issue, arguably the auto industry, which is seeking to protect its $4 billion investment in emissions control technology, is benefiting from an environmental regulation imposed for reasons beyond strictly environmental considerations. Additionally, the ethanol industry will also derive 'shelter' benefits from a ban on MMT.

Shelter and Environmental Regulations

In this chapter we can analyse each of the five cases by looking for a 'baptist–bootlegger' coalition (Vogel 1995). In the US prohibition era, baptists were opposed to alcoholic consumption on moral grounds while bootleggers actually benefited from prohibition by the production and sale of illegal alcoholic beverages. Similarly, today there is often a coalition formed between domestic environmental groups in favour of environmental regulations on public good grounds and domestic producers who recognize an opportunity to impose entry barriers against rival foreign producers. The latter trade barriers occur only when the environmental regulations are administered in a discriminatory manner, that is, by an effective denial of the national treatment provisions which are available to most traders under the NAFTA (Rugman 1995). National treatment can be denied directly by, for example, a regulation which expressly treats a foreign producer differently from a domestic producer. More subtle, however, are those regulations which appear to be non-discriminatory, but which in effect operate in a discriminatory manner against foreign producers. These are the focus of the case studies. In all of the cases examined, we found some evidence of a baptist–bootlegger coalition. This is a form of shelter.

It is useful to consider a modification of Figure 3.1, as shown in Figure 3.2. This builds upon a separate theoretical framework developed by Rugman and Verbeke (1994). On the horizontal axis, the locus of environmental regulations, that is, the place where such regulations are in effect, is reported across three geographical levels: trilateral (meaning across all three countries in NAFTA); national (meaning within one of the three member countries of NAFTA); and sub-national (meaning within one internal region of the three member countries of NAFTA, such as a state or province). For example, agriculture measures imposed by the United States at the border would be placed in the first column as such measures could apply throughout North America. In contrast, the

Corporate Strategy Perspectives 51

Type of regulation	Locus of regulation		
	Trilateral	National	Sub-national
Environmentally-based	1 Agri: phyto-sanitary standards Technical standards Health standards	3 Asbestos ban Tuna–Dolphin	5 California recycling
Shelter-based	2 Avocados **Blueberries** Cherries Mangoes **Potatoes** Tomatoes **UHT milk** Vanilla Trucking inspections	4 **MMT auto emissions** **PCB export ban** Salmon/herring Softwood lumber CVD	6 **Ontario beer cans**

Fig. 3.2. NAFTA, trade, and environmental regulations

California newsprint recycling measure operates only within the State of California, thereby placing it in the third column. On the vertical axis two types of regulations are defined: environmentally based and shelter-based. As noted earlier, the theory of shelter is explained in Rugman and Verbeke (1990). A shelter-based regulation is defined as an environmental regulation 'captured' in its administration by a domestic industry lobby which desires to use the regulation as a discriminatory entry barrier against a foreign competitor.

Based on the analysis of the five cases in this chapter, it is apparent that in all of the cases, the environmental regulations have moved to the lower half of Figure 3.2, i.e. into the shelter-based categories. (We do not include all of the cases of Figure 3.1 in Figure 3.2.) The sub-national case of Ontario beer cans is arguably a discriminatory measure, even more so than the California newsprint recycling (which Canadian forestry firms feel would put it also into area 6). The PCB export barrier is in area 5; it benefits the Alberta producer at the expense of US producers. Finally, the UHT milk and the potato and blueberry cases are in area 2, due to the evidence of domestic pressure for increased tightness in the administration of health codes and in inspection procedures. The MMT case has also moved into the shelter-based part of the figure. Although the evidence here is mixed, there are arguably still two Canadian industries (autos and ethanol) seeking the administration of an environmental regulation for economic reasons.

Conclusions

In this chapter we explored a previously underdeveloped aspect of corporate strategy for US and Canadian trading firms: how to manage the link between environmental regulations and trade barriers. These firms are affected by a growing number of domestic environmental regulations which can have the ultimate impact of creating barriers to entry against foreign companies. It was found that sometimes domestic firms can influence the administrative process by which environmental laws and regulations are imposed and that their actions are part of a corporate shelter-seeking strategy. The five recent cases discussed here are representative of the set of over twenty environmental disputes which have arisen in the first three years of NAFTA.

The overall conclusion of this chapter is that few environmental regulations will exist independently of business lobbying. Wherever there is a 'baptist'-like environmentalist reason for a regulation, there is also a 'bootlegger' domestic industry ready to benefit from the regulation. In Vogel (1995) the baptist–bootlegger metaphor has been examined at length and applied to a set of environmental regulations. In this chapter, additional evidence has been found of the close relationship between environmentalists and domestic producers seeking shelter through protection. Despite the best intentions of environmentalists, the administration of environmental regulations in North America can be subject to domestic corporate lobbying. The use of such shelter-seeking strategies by domestic firms at the expense of foreign rival producers is inefficient, as are all types of protection.

Do firms use domestic environmental regulations as part of a strategy of capture to protect themselves from the imports of foreign competitors? The five cases examined in this chapter, including those involving conservation, packaging and labelling, and health and safety regulations, show that environmental regulations with protectionist impact are a prevalent barrier to business, both for Canadian firms seeking to export to the United States, but also for US firms seeking to export to Canada. Although it is difficult to discern the details of a conscious strategy by firms to capture domestic environmental regulations for their own protectionist impact, the frequency of protectionist benefits from such regulations and the presence of coalitions of domestic firms and environmental groups supporting them point to how widespread and severe environmental regulatory protectionism can be. Although several of the five cases extended into the NAFTA era, in only one case—Ethyl's Chapter 11 claim with respect to the ban in MMT—were the new NAFTA institutional mechanisms used to help resolve the dispute, making the corporate costs and political management of these disputes much more costly than they could have been.

4

Corporate Strategy and Environmental Regulation: Baptist–Bootlegger Coalitions

This chapter extends the analysis of environmental regulatory protectionism from corporate strategy to the operation of the 'baptist–bootlegger' coalitions, and how such coalitions offer an initial indication that the government has enacted a trade-restricting environmental regulation for the protection of industry interests rather than environmental interests. Here a list of criteria are presented that illustrate a means by which to distinguish between the more benign situation of when an environmental regulation affects the relative costs of producers (as all such regulations do) and those environmental regulations that develop into cross-border issues. The institutional challenge is thus to use and develop the NAFTA institutions in such a way as to enable governments to distinguish between legitimate and inappropriate trade-restricting environmental regulations.

Here ten cases are explored, starting as far back as 1982 and going to the present. This provides a historical perspective of the problem of trade–environment disputes and highlights the new institutional opportunities of the NAFTA era. The cases of UHT milk, Ontario beer cans, the fuel additive MMT, and the disposal of hazardous PCBs are revisited to highlight the dynamics of 'baptist–bootlegger' coalition formation and operation, and supplemented by four additional fisheries cases between Canada and the United States, softwood lumber, and California newspaper content requirements.

These cases reveal that the degree to which the affected parties actually use the institutional structure of the international trade regime as a means by which to offset negative impacts varies widely. Some of the early fisheries cases demonstrate the willingness of parties to lobby their governments to establish panels under the GATT and eventually the FTA after it came into force. Here firms and their governments rely on a legal strategy—using the specific provisions of trade agreements which prohibit violations of national treatment and the imposition of quantitative restrictions, save for certain exceptions. The interpretation of these seemingly fine legal points help to define how effectively the regime operates in practice. The softwood lumber case illustrates the more rare case of 'environmental subsidies' where NAFTA's Chapter 19 panel, which deals with issues relating to subsidies and countervailing duties only and not environmental questions, was used. In this case, a number of other political strategies were used in tandem on both sides of the border.

In the case of MMT, other companies like Ethyl Inc. have begun to actively engage the NAFTA dispute settlement mechanisms on a number of different levels. The degree of complex institutional responsiveness in evidence thus expands with the advent and the development of the NAFTA regime. All of these cases demonstrate the opportunities and possibilities for firms to understand, assess, and actively employ a trade regime's institutional mechanisms as a necessary tool in a successful international business strategy.

This chapter explores ten environmentally related trade disputes that have arisen between the United States and Canada. They fall into three broad categories: conservation regulations, recycling policies, and industrial goods and processes. Six of them involve complaints by the United States against Canada and four involve Canadian allegations. We are interested in finding out if the use of environmental regulations can become non-tariff barriers to trade. These ten cases reveal the broad range of regional and national environmental regulations that have become the focus of trade conflicts between these two countries.

Virtually every environmental regulation affects the relative costs and opportunities of producers. For such a regulation to have an impact on the rules governing trade, three additional factors are required. First, one or more of the producers adversely affected by the regulation must be located in another country. Second, those producers must turn to the political system to apply pressure to challenge the regulation which adversely affects them. Third, the aggrieved producer must claim that the foreign regulation which adversely affects them violates the terms of an international trade agreement or treaty.

It is the existence of a foreign, politically mobilized stakeholder which transforms a national or regional regulatory standard or policy into a trade issue. But while every regulation which is challenged as an alleged non-tariff barrier clearly disadvantages foreign producers, this may or may not be the reason why it was adopted. In some cases, there may be little or no gain to domestic producers, while in others, pressures from domestic producers may be the primary reason why the regulation was approved. However, the fact that a regulation confers a competitive advantage on a domestic producer does not by itself demonstrate that this domestic regulation is illegitimate, as it may nonetheless serve a legitimate public purpose. And in fact, many trade disputes may stem from differences in national regulatory priorities and policies. Distinguishing between legitimate and inappropriate regulations that disadvantage foreign producers is an important and ongoing challenge for governments which have entered into agreements to liberalize trade.

In this chapter we analyse each of the ten cases by looking for a 'baptist–bootlegger' coalition (Vogel 1995). In the US prohibition era, Baptists were opposed to alcoholic consumption on moral grounds, while bootleggers actually benefited from prohibition by the production and sale of illegal alcoholic beverages.

Similarly, today there is often a coalition formed between domestic environmental groups in favour of environmental regulations on public good grounds and domestic producers who recognize an opportunity to erect entry barriers against rival foreign producers. The latter trade barriers occur only when the environmental regulations are administered in a discriminatory manner, that is by an effective denial of the national treatment provisions which are available to most traders under the North American Free Trade Agreement (Rugman 1995). National treatment can be denied directly by, for example, a regulation which expressly treats a foreign producer differently from a domestic producer. More subtle, however, are those regulations which appear to be non-discriminatory, but which in effect operate in a discriminatory manner against foreign producers. These are the focus of the case studies. In all but one of the following ten cases examined, we find evidence of such a baptist–bootlegger coalition.

Case 1: Prohibition of Imports of Tuna and Tuna Products from Canada (GATT decision, 1982)

In 1979 Canada seized 19 US tuna boats fishing inside Canada's 200-mile fisheries zone (both this and the following two cases are discussed in detail in US Congress 1994: 87–8; see also Manard 1992: 400–4). The United States, acting under the 1976 Fishery Conservation and Management Act, retaliated by prohibiting the entry of all tuna and tuna products from Canada. Although the embargo was subsequently lifted following the two nations' signing of a treaty on Pacific coast albacore tuna, Canada asked that a GATT dispute settlement panel address the legality of the US embargo.

The Panel rendered its decision in 1982 agreeing with the United States that tuna stocks did constitute 'an exhaustible natural resource' whose trade could be restricted under GATT's Article XX. However, the Panel also ruled that this Article did not apply because the United States had not imposed identical or similar restrictions on domestic tuna consumption or production. Accordingly, under the GATT the US action constituted an impermissible 'quantitative restriction' on trade.

Case 2: Measures Affecting Exports of Unprocessed Herring and Salmon (GATT decision, 1988)

In 1988 a second dispute over conservation policies between the United States and Canada went before the GATT. Canada, as part of its effort to improve the conservation and management of its fisheries, had prohibited the export of unprocessed herring, and pink and sockeye salmon. Canada contended that these prohibitions were necessary to prevent the export of unprocessed herring and salmon that did not meet its national quality standards for these fish. The United States complained to the GATT on the grounds that the

Canadian export restriction was discriminatory: by treating fish caught for domestic consumption differently from fish intended for export.

The dispute panel ruled against Canada on similar grounds to the previous dispute between the two countries. Canada's export ban was ruled to be inconsistent with its obligations under the GATT because it had not placed similar limits on the domestic consumption of these fish. Moreover, Canada had not limited access to herring and salmon supplies, in general, but only to certain unprocessed salmon and herring. Accordingly, 'there was no link between conservation of these species and the export prohibition.' The panel noted that 'the purpose of including Article XX in the General Agreement was not to create a loophole for discriminatory or protectionist trade policy measures, but to insure that GATT rules would not hinder conservation policies' (GATT 1992: 26).

Case 3: Canada's Landing Requirement for Pacific Coast Salmon and Herring (FTA decision, 1989)

Following the adoption of the 1988 GATT panel's report on Canadian fish exports, Canada revoked its regulations prohibiting the export of unprocessed herring and salmon. However, Canada also imposed new regulations requiring that five species of salmon as well as all commercial harvest of roe herring caught in waters off Canada's west coast be first brought ashore at a licensed fish landing station in British Columbia for biological sampling. Following sampling, the fish could be exported. Canadian officials argued that this requirement was necessary in order to enable them to promote the conservation of these important species, which were being depleted due to inadequate fisheries management. The United States complained that although the new regulations on their face did not directly affect exports, their clear *effect* was discriminatory, since the burden of compliance fell exclusively on exporters (see US Congress 1994 and Valiante and Muldoon 1990: 253–4). By contrast, fish purchased by Canadian processors would be landed in Canada in any event. Accordingly, the United States argued that the Canadian requirement was an export restriction due to 'the extra time and expense US buyers must incur in landing and unloading, as well as dockage fees and product deterioration' (Runge 1990: 56). US officials went on to argue that the law's real purpose was to protect British Columbia's fish processing industry from US competition, since fresh fish has to be processed as soon as it is brought ashore. In sum, they contended that 'the Canadian landing requirement was an environmental policy acting as a disguised restriction on international trade' (ibid).

After consultations between the two nations failed to resolve the dispute, the United States had the choice of seeking settlement under either the GATT or the FTA. The United States chose the FTA. Whichever venue the United States had chosen, the legal basis of the United States' complaint would have been identical, since the relevant provisions of the GATT had been incorporated into the FTA.

The dispute panel determined that the Canadian regulation, while ostensibly an internal measure, was in fact a trade restriction, since it imposed a 'materially greater commercial burden on exports than domestic sales'. According to the panel, 'the cost of complying with the landing requirement would be more than an insignificant expense for those buyers who would have otherwise shipped directly from the fishing grounds to a landing site in the United States' (quoted in ibid. 57).

The second issue addressed by the panel was whether or not the Canadian rule was justified by the 'exception' clause of Article XX of the GATT, which also had been incorporated into the FTA. Drawing upon the criteria established by the GATT ruling on Canada's export ban, the panel argued that for Article XX to be applicable, the *primary* aim of the trade restriction had to be conservation. The panel concluded that this was not the case, since it was highly unlikely that Canada would have imposed the same requirements 'if its own nationals had to bear the actual costs of the measure' (ibid.).

Moreover, the landing requirement failed the 'proportionality test', since Canada could have achieved the same conservation objectives by exempting a portion of the catch from the landing requirement. The panel specifically suggested that allowing between 10 and 20 per cent of the fish catch to be exported directly would not adversely affect Canada's conservation programme. The reaction of the two governments to the panel ruling suggested the depth of their differences over this commercial dispute. Canada's Department of International Trade, Fisheries and Oceans issued a press release that accepted the panel's report, but added that it had 'found that a landing requirement is a legitimate conservation measure' (Lewington 1989: B4). US officials, in turn, offered a rather different interpretation. Noting that the panel members had suggested an alternative to the landing requirement, they complained that Canada had read 'the findings in the narrowest way possible to maximize protection for west coast interests' (ibid.).

Officials from both nations were troubled by the resulting impasse. A US official predicted that the dispute 'could have adverse effects for the FTA', while his Canadian counterpart acknowledged that the dispute over the meaning of the panel's ruling did not augur well for the future of an agreement whose purpose was to liberalize trade (ibid. B1).

Following additional negotiations both sides announced a compromise agreement: 75 per cent of the catch must be first landed in Canada, while the remaining 25 per cent could be directly exported. The United States regarded this outcome as satisfactory, but it upset both the government and fisheries processing industry of British Columbia. British Columbia's International Business Minister predicted that 'this decision will have negative impacts on this important resource and the industry that supports it' (Drohan 1989: B1).

The executive director of the Fisheries Council of British Columbia complained that 'what the panel decision actually does is strike down a legitimate resource conservation scheme and recommend substitution of an expensive, loophole-laden, unmanageable dual reporting scheme' (quoted in Shrybman 1991: 8). A Canadian environmental lawyer concluded that 'the salmon and herring case illustrates that in a contest between environmental and trade objectives, the former is not likely to come out the winner,' adding that 'the implications of this precedent for other conservation programs are very serious' (ibid. 101).

Case 4: Lobsters from Canada (FTA decision, 1990)

The following year another trade dispute broke out between the two countries over fishing rules, this one was brought by Canada against the United States. In order to conserve its domestic lobster stocks, the United States had limited the harvesting and marketing of lobsters below a certain size. However, the mixing of smaller Canadian lobsters with US lobsters had made it difficult for US officials to enforce this restriction.

In addition, a number of US lobster fishermen complained that the federal size requirement put them at a competitive disadvantage vis-à-vis their Canadian competitors. Accordingly, in 1989 the United States amended the Magnuson Act to make it unlawful 'to ship, transport, offer for sale, sell, or purchase, in interstate or foreign commerce, any whole live lobster . . . at a size below that specified by the Act' (quoted in Manard 1992: 409). This restriction applied to all lobsters, regardless of where they were originally harvested.

This legislation significantly limited the exports of mature Canadian lobsters to the United States. Canada argued that due to the different temperature of Canadian waters, Canadian lobsters reach sexual maturity at a smaller size and that because the ban on the importation of smaller sized lobsters affected only Canadian imports, the size limitation was, in effect, a 'trade restriction which the United States is attempting to disguise as conservation measure' (von Moltke 1993: 122).

According to Canadian officials, nearly one-third of Canadian lobster exports were affected by the prohibition, resulting in an annual loss of 40 million dollars. The United States countered that the minimum size requirement was an internal measure that applied equally to domestic and foreign lobsters, not a border measure targeted at imports. And because it treated Canadian and US lobsters alike, it was consistent with the GATT principle of national treatment.

In a divided (3–2) vote, the panel upheld the US position on the grounds that the minimum size provisions enacted by the United States were 'primarily aimed' at the conservation of US lobsters (Manard 1992: 410). The minority opinion, however took strong issue with this conclusion, arguing that the United States should have been required to demonstrate that its legitimate conservation objectives could not have been met by alternative measures, such as the special labelling of Canadian small lobsters.

The minority report also reviewed the legislative history of the amendment to the Magnuson Act. While it found a number of statements that underscored the conservation rationale for the lobster size restriction, it also found evidence that another important purpose of the legislation was to remedy the fact that 'US lobster fishermen were at a competitive disadvantage because they were subject to more stringent conservation regulations than the Canadians' (Roht-Arriaza 1992: 70). The minority report concluded that the United States 'had not made their case strongly enough to lead ... to the conclusion that the measures were primarily aimed at conservation' (ibid.).

By contrast, the majority opinion acknowledged that although the Magnuson Act was in part motivated by perceptions of 'unfairness' on the part of US lobster fishermen, this did not render the US size restriction illegitimate; on the contrary, they explicitly acknowledged the legitimacy of these perceptions. Neither the majority nor the minority report chose to address the Canadian claim that its lobsters reached sexual maturity at a smaller size than US lobsters because of differences in water temperature.

Case 5: Ultra-High Temperature Milk (UHT) from Quebec

In 1992 Canada initiated an action against the United States under Chapter 18 of the FTA regarding UHT milk from Quebec.[1] After fourteen years of trouble-free exports to Puerto Rico, UHT milk from Quebec produced by Lactel Inc. had been denied entry on the basis that it did not comply with the requisite health and safety standards. The Canadian government claimed that this new-found health and safety standard was a sham, and was more properly characterized as a barrier to trade and an outright violation of the FTA. The US government claimed that it was free to set its own health and safety standards, and that its obligations under the FTA did not diminish that freedom.

In an effort to increase milk sales, Puerto Rico changed its milk standards and harmonized them with the rest of the United States in 1989. It required that all milk imported into Puerto Rico either comply with specific processing requirements or have been processed under substantially similar regulations and be inspected by a state official certified by the US Food and Drug Administration (FDA). Because compliance with the specific processing requirements would mean that the Quebec company would have to make substantial adjustments to its business, it decided to apply for equivalency status. For a number of reasons, the US FDA refused to conduct an equivalency study, even after repeated negotiations and consultations among diplomats and relevant government officials. A UHT Subcommittee was established under the bilateral Technical Working Group on Dairy, Fruit, Vegetable, and Egg Inspection.[2] The issue culminated in an exchange of letters between the Canadian Minister of International Trade and the Acting US Trade

Representative. All of these efforts were ultimately unsuccessful and UHT milk produced in Quebec was excluded from the Puerto Rico market on 31 December 1991, and Canada initiated formal dispute settlement proceedings under NAFTA.

The Panel offered mixed results. It found that Canada had experienced non-violation nullification and impairment of its reasonably expected benefits under the FTA. This essentially meant that it was reasonable for Canada, after fourteen years of exports, to have been granted at least equivalency status. But the Panel did not find any wrongdoing on the part of the United States and did not find that it had acted in bad faith. The Panel ordered that equivalency studies be undertaken within a reasonable period.

From 1977 to 1981, Lactel held 100 per cent of the Puerto Rico UHT milk market. Between 1982 and 1985, market share fluctuated between 25.3 and 88.4 per cent. It was not until late in 1995,[3] a full two years after the Panel report and four years after the imposition of the ban, that the equivalency study was completed and UHT milk from Quebec was permitted to enter the Puerto Rico market.[4] Although this is the desired result, it is arguably a case of 'too little, too late'. Lactel had been denied market entry for three years, after which time it found it almost impossible to regain its market share and corresponding advantages.[5] In effect, the regulation acted to exclude Lactel from the market. Essentially, this UHT case has demonstrated that there is no adequate remedy for a foreign producer adversely affected by health and safety regulations under NAFTA.

Case 6: Softwood Lumber (FTA decision, 1994)

Another long-standing trade dispute between the United States and Canada involves the forestry industry. US lumber producers have long claimed that Canadian provinces have been subsidizing the production of softwood lumber and that this represents an unfair competitive advantage.

In 1986 the United States Commerce Department responded to a lawsuit brought by US forestry producers and issued a preliminary determination that assessed the alleged subsidy to Canadian lumber producers at 15 per cent. The Canadian government imposed a 15 per cent tax on exports of lumber by signing a Memorandum of Understanding (MOU) with the United States on 30 December 1986 (Hart, Dymond, and Robertson 1995). This allowed Canadians to keep the money that would otherwise be paid to the US Customs.

This export tax arrangement was written into the 1989 FTA. One of its provisions allowed the tax to be phased out as the provinces increased their stumpage rates. Stumpage is the price paid by Canadian producers for the use of timber on provincially owned lands. By 1991 the BC government had increased its stumpage charges by over 15 per cent and the export tax had been reduced to zero. British Columbia accounts for over two-thirds of all lumber exports to the United States. The second largest producer, Quebec, had also increased its forest charges and its export tax was 3 per cent.

In September 1991 the federal and provincial governments in Canada suspended the export tax MOU. They argued that the provinces were now taxing the Canadian industry at the 15 per cent rate determined by the United States in 1986. However, the US Coalition for Fair Lumber Imports (COFLI) lobbied for a new investigation. In March 1992 the United States imposed a provisional duty of 14.48 per cent. This was imposed in two parts: 6.25 per cent due to the stumpage 'subsidy' and 8.23 per cent due to the BC log export ban (Anderson 1995).

In the US ruling, released on 15 May 1992, the penalties were reduced to 6.51 per cent. The stumpage subsidy was reduced to 2.91 per cent and the log export subsidy to 3.6 per cent. Canadian companies selling lumber to the United States had to continue to post bonds until the 1994 appeals processes under the FTA and NAFTA were resolved. In July 1992 the US International Trade Commission (ITC) ruled that Canadian subsidies had caused injury to US producers. The Canadian government appealed this decision to a dispute settlement panel under Chapter 19 of the FTA. The dispute was resolved in 1994, overturning both the ITC and the US Department of Commerce decisions. Chapter 19 dispute settlement panels are limited to questions of material injury and environmental issues are generally *ultra vires* of such questions.

In 1994 a sum of one billion Canadian dollars was repaid to Canadian lumber exporters, following the FTA ruling. As a response to persistent political pressures from large US lumber growers in the south-east, the Canadian federal government eventually proposed to increase its taxes on exports of Canadian softwood lumber (McKenna, Fagan, and Lush 1996: B1–B2). In February 1996 Canadian and US officials reached an agreement cutting Canadian exports of softwood lumber by more than 10 per cent. Specifically, BC imposed quotas on shipments to the United States. In exchange, the US industry committed to refrain from initiating any countervail actions for five years (Lush 1996: B1).

Case 7: US State Newspaper Content Requirements

During the 1980s, approximately one-third of US state governments enacted recycling laws to encourage the use of recovered materials in newsprint in order to reduce their urban landfill problem. These laws required that certain types of pulp and paper consumed in the state contain a minimum recycled content. According to the Conference Board of Canada, '(f)rom the viewpoint of the Canadian pulp and paper industry, [US recycling legislation] is a . . . disguised non-tariff barrier to trade because Canada does not have the supply of recycled fibre to maintain market share in the United States.' Canada's largest pulp and paper firm specifically urged the Canadian government to challenge US newspaper recycling laws 'as a ploy of US newsprint producers seeking to gain competitive advantage' (quoted in Shrybman 1991).

A Canadian lawyer has noted that the US state laws would probably pass GATT, and thus FTA, scrutiny because they neither applied to processes nor discriminated on the basis of national origin. However, he also noted that the recycling-content laws had imposed a real hardship on the Canadian pulp and paper industry.

> Canadian producers are finding that this law or policy, depending on the proximity of the state in question, has had a major impact on their ability to meet the recycled content of the product . . . they may have to import into Canada used newsprint from the United States, de-ink it in Canada (a very toxic process) and then recycle it for export back to the United States . . . effectively add[ing] another leg of transportation and cost to the production of newsprint. (Thomas 1992: 390)

By substantially increasing the costs of supplying paper to the US market, the US newsprint recycling requirement had resulted in a decline in the Canadian share of the US newsprint market of between 4 and 8 per cent (ibid.).

Twenty-one out of the twenty-five states that are mainly supplied by Canadian producers have adopted recycled-content regulations; however, six of the twenty-five states that are mainly supplied by US producers also imposed similar regulations (Romain 1993: 9). The US recycled-content legislation is imposed on only two paper grades: newsprint and directory papers. Some Canadians have complained the reason these two paper grades were singled out was due to the fact that the main suppliers of these two grades were Canadian and that the entire purpose of the regulations was to exclude Canadian suppliers from the US market (ibid.).

The recycled-content rules have recently been extended in the United States to 'Green Government Procurement' paper products which must now contain 50 per cent recycled material and 20 per cent post-consumer waste. The US government only accounts for about 2 per cent of the total US paper consumption and thus this rule will not have a major impact on Canadian producers. However, it may well create the potential for EPA guidelines that will affect the demand for recycled content in virtually all grades of paper sold in the United States. Canadian producers would be substantially affected if state governments and the private sector followed these guidelines. Tradable recycled-content credits have been proposed by ENGOs in order to give producers more flexibility in the application of recycled-content rules.

While US environmentalists, as well as US firms involved in the recycling business, strongly defended US recycling laws, these laws have been criticized by Canadians on environmental grounds. Most obviously, some contend that these laws have impaired the Canadian environment, since the de-inking process creates a great deal of sludge. More fundamentally, the US recycling requirement, like many eco-labelling schemes, is based on an end-product analysis of environmental impact. For example, the environmental impact of paper production is affected not only by the amount of virgin wood used but also by the cleanliness of the manufacturing process, including the amount of chlorine bleaching. It can also be influenced by the quality of forest management. Yet the latter two dimensions are not addressed by recycled-content standards.

Case 8: Ontario Beer Can Tax (1993)

In 1992 another trade dispute emerged between the United States and Canada over a sub-national recycling regulation, this time with US producers challenging a Canadian regulation. Like the lumber and fisheries disputes, this long-standing issue has as much to do with market access as with environmental standards.

This particular conflict dates from the mid-1980s, when the United States and the European Community complained about Canadian restrictions on the sale of imported beer in the province of Ontario. Following unsuccessful negotiations, the EC and the United States called for the convening of a GATT dispute panel. In 1988 the panel ruled against Canada; however, Canada did not comply on the grounds that the import restrictions were a matter for provincial authorities. Accordingly, the United States filed a second complaint with the GATT. In October 1991 the GATT ruled that Canada had failed to comply with its earlier ruling.

A tentative agreement was reached in the spring of 1992. However, the following week Ontario announced a doubling of the tax on aluminium cans to $.10 a can. This tax increased the retail price of US beer, all of which was sold in aluminium cans, from $19.83 to $24.35 per case.

The Province of Ontario described the levy as a 'green tax' whose purpose was to encourage the use of refillable bottles. Provincial officials contended that glass bottles are more environmentally efficient, since they can be used an average of 15–18 times and they are less likely to end up in garbage cans and landfills. Ontario further claimed that without the additional tax, the province's extensive recycling efforts would be undermined as consumers would switch to less expensive imported beer sold in aluminium cans which would in turn force Canadian brewers, virtually all of whom used bottles, to switch to cans as well. According to a Canadian official: 'ten cents seems to be the correct level to make it an effective incentive to change consumer behaviour' (Rusk 1992: B3).

US beer companies, along with US trade associations representing aluminium and can manufacturers, claimed that the Ontario tax was a 'protectionist weapon' disguised as an environmental regulation, since virtually all (80 per cent) Canadian beer was sold in bottles, while virtually all beer imported from the United States was sold in cans (Dunne and Simon 1992: 5). As further evidence of the protectionist intent behind the Canadian action, they noted that Ontario had only taxed non-refillable alcohol containers, not canned soft drinks or food. One commentator noted, 'Ontario [has] impose[d] a ten cent tax on beer *cans*, but not on beer bottles, which Canadian producers

64   *Economic and Corporate Strategy*

predominately use. There could be a reasonable environmental distinction between cans and bottles. But if so, why does Ontario's tax *not* apply to cans of soft drinks, juice, soup etc.?' (Charnovitz 1992: 219). The beer can tax has also been criticized on environmental grounds. According to one study, the recyclable aluminium can and the refillable glass bottle are both 'environmentally efficient and essentially indistinguishable' (Bougie 1993: A15). Moreover, more than 80 per cent of beer cans are in fact recycled. In addition, the United States claimed that it consumes more energy to move bottles—which are both larger in volume and heavier—than it does to move a similar number of cans. Aluminium cans consume no more energy to produce than the washing, transportation, and refilling of bottles.

Ontario responded that US brewers could avoid the tax by switching to 'environmentally friendly' bottles. US brewers replied that the extra weight made bottles too expensive to ship. The position of the Province of Ontario was strongly backed by Canadian environmental organizations. A lawyer with the Canadian Environmental Law Association argued that 'the United States has to play by our rules . . . the US system should not be imposed on us, when ours is more environmentally sound' (Rusk 1992). However, a columnist for the *Toronto Star* agreed with the United States, describing the tax as 'a smoke screen for protectionism' (quoted in 'Beer Blast' 1992: A14).

In July 1992 the United States imposed a 50 per cent *ad valorem* tax on beer from Ontario, though this was due to the continuing impasse over the broader issue of market access rather than to the beer can tax. On 5 August 1993 a comprehensive settlement was reached that removed a variety of barriers to exports of US beer and the United States rescinded its tax. According to one columnist, the United States did not want to force the Canadians to rescind an environmental regulation, especially in light of the upcoming debate over the environmental impact of NAFTA, and Ontario's beer can tax was allowed to stand (Bradsher 1993: D1).

Case 9: Canadian Ban on MMT

The Canadian Parliament recently passed a law banning international and interprovincial trade in MMT.[6] MMT is an octane-enhancing fuel additive. It was introduced in 1977 as a replacement for lead. In a recent statement before a Senate Standing Committee on Energy, Environment and Natural Resources considering the legislation, Environment Minister Sergio Marchi cited three rationales for the ban in trade of MMT.[7]

The first justification cited was the 'health of Canadians and their environment'. MMT is alleged to harm new and improved pollution control devices in autos. As vehicle emissions are a major contributor to poor air quality, the inability to control emissions will exacerbate this problem. Additionally, MMT itself which is present in vehicle emissions is believed by many environmental organizations to be a neurotoxin, with especially harmful effects experienced by children.[8] Second, Marchi justifies the ban on the 'issue of fuels in the larger North American context'. He argues that fuel and emission control technologies should be treated as part of an integrated system to reduce motor vehicle emissions, which would entail harmonization of fuel standards between Canada and the United States. This would allow motor vehicles built with emission controls to work across the continent.[9] Third, Marchi cites the issue of 'economic impact'. Marchi acknowledges the cost to oil refiners in capital costs adjustments to be $115 million initially plus an additional $50 million in yearly operating costs. However, he claims that this amount is far outweighed by a yearly $1.5 billion savings in health costs.

Various stakeholders have been active in the debate leading up to the passage of the legislation. The Canadian Petroleum Producers Institute (CPPI) are firmly against a ban in MMT because of the costs involved in making changes to their refinery operations. The Motor Vehicles Manufacturers Association (MVMA) represents all 21 motor vehicle manufacturers in Canada and Canada's auto dealers are firm supporters of the ban, believing that its pollution control devices would malfunction with the use of MMT and impose severe costs in warranty repairs and re-engineering in order to correct this problem (see McKenna 1996b and Keenan 1996: B6). The MVMA formed a coalition with the environmental groups who opposed the bill on public health grounds. Whether this coalition is sufficient to form a baptist–bootlegger alliance referred to in the introduction of this paper remains to be seen, as there is no clear foreign winner or loser. However, it has been alleged that the real issue at stake here is whether the auto industry or the petroleum industry will bear the cost of developing the technology to meet increasingly stringent demands for reduced pollution. The MMT issue is just the first in a number of similar fuel additive disputes (sulphur, benzene) that are currently in progress.[10] Until now, the MVMA has argued that it has primarily been autos that have met this challenge and they need the cooperation of the petroleum industry to continue.

It is not clear why a ban in trade was chosen, rather than a general prohibition of MMT. The ban in trade has been highly contentious and is the subject of a number of alleged breaches of NAFTA. Ethyl Corp., based in Virginia, is the sole North American producer of MMT. It distributes MMT in Canada through its subsidiary Ethyl Canada, Inc. Ethyl Corp. has recently launched a NAFTA Chapter 11 dispute against the Canadian government for breach of its obligations to foreign investors guaranteed under NAFTA. Essentially, Ethyl Corp. is alleging that the ban in intraprovincial trade in MMT violates national treatment obligations by treating foreign-owned producers worse than Canadian producers of MMT. Although there are currently no producers of MMT, it is plausible that Canadian firms could manufacture MMT in each province separately, without violating the law. It was further alleged by Ethyl Corp. that the actions by the Canadian government (1) constitute a measure tantamount to expropriation and (2) violate the performance requirement provisions of NAFTA.[11]

66   Economic and Corporate Strategy

Additional trade implications are a potential NAFTA challenge under Chapter 20, NAFTA's state-to-state dispute settlement mechanism.[12] The Alberta government has also stated that the proposed bill violates Canada's Internal Trade Agreement (McKenna 1997: B8).

Case 10: Canadian Ban on Exports of PCBs

On 20 November 1995, former Canadian environment minister, Sheila Copps, issued an interim order banning the export of polychlorinated biphenyl (PCB) waste. This order banned Canadian exports of PCBs to US-based disposal plants.[13] The ban was partially lifted under Environment Minister Sergio Marchi in February 1996. Exports of PCBs destined for destruction or incineration will be permitted, while PCB exports destined for landfill sites will not (McKenna 1996c: B3).

The ban was imposed out of concern over inadequate disposal standards at many of the US waste disposal facilities, although there have been claims that the ban was imposed for protectionist reasons. S. D. Myers, an Ohio-based waste disposal company and Waste Management Inc. of Oak Brook, Ill. both claim that the ban has had an adverse effect on its business, as it forced Canadian industry to ship its PCB waste from central Canada to the major Canadian PCB-destruction facility located in Swan Hills, Alberta. Instead of shipping PCBs to the much closer waste disposal sites in the United States, Canadian firms located in eastern or central Canada were forced to incur an additional 40 per cent in transportation costs to send their PCBs for destruction across the country to Alberta (McKenna and Feschuk 1996: B1), costing Canadian industry more than $300 million (Corcoran 1996b: B2). Apart from the extra transportation expenses, the cost of destroying PCB waste in the United States is reported to be approximately half that of Canada.[14] Canada has 50,000 tonnes of PCBs in waste or in storage, so this issue was highly contentious at the time of the ban.

Prior to 1979, US companies were allowed to import PCBs for waste disposal. From 1980 to 1995 the US Environmental Protection Agency (EPA) restricted permit imports of PCBs, with some exceptions on a case-by-case basis. On 15 November 1995 the EPA relaxed the import ban on S. D. Myers after it found that the company had satisfied the standards specified in a new US regulatory framework for the disposal of PCBs and that imports of PCBs would not result in an unreasonable risk of injury. The director of EPA's enforcement indicated that other US firms could also request permission to import PCBs.[15]

The interim order was further criticized as a violation of Canada's Environmental Protection Act, which permits such orders to be issued only in the event of an emergency threat to human health. A legal challenge to the Copps interim order was initiated in December 1995 by Canadian firms with PCB wastes, including a group of Quebec industries and an Ontario waste disposal transportation company (Freeman 1995: A11). A number of parties claimed that the export of PCBs to the United States did not pose a significant danger to the environment or to human health and that the order violated the terms of NAFTA, as it was an export ban and as such a barrier to trade.[16] The main benefactor of the protectionist nature of the ban are Canadian waste disposal firms, among them: Bovar Inc. located in Calgary, Alberta; Chem-Security, located in Swan Hills, Alberta; and Cintec Inc. located in Montreal. These companies have complained that with the partial lifting of the ban, they are forced into a situation of competing with US companies with less stringent standards (McKenna 1996b: B3).

Conclusion

In nine of the ten cases reviewed here it has been found that an environmental regulation was used as an indirect trade barrier. The only exception is the MMT case which is really a dispute between the petroleum industry and the auto manufacturers. In all nine of the other cases a domestic 'bootlegger' industry can be identified as benefiting from the environmentally based trade barrier placed in the path of its foreign rival. The actual political process by which domestic producer interests and environmental non-government organizations may or may not have formed coalitions was not explored in this chapter and is the agenda for ongoing research. However, these cases demonstrate the existence of strong baptist–bootlegger interests, even in the otherwise tranquil waters of United States–Canadian economic relations.

In general, the above cases illustrate that there are opportunities for firms to use environmentally related trade barriers at international, national, and subnational level. Trade-related environmental measures can arise in at least two ways: (1) by imposing discriminatory policies against imports as part of the environmental regulation; (2) by enforcing product standards that either completely restrict or place a significantly higher cost burden on foreign producers. As a result, environmental trade policies and regulations can be manipulated unilaterally to offset the public goods objectives and competitive effects of governments' environmental policies. The result is a shelter-based environmental regulation, which is defined as an environmental regulation 'captured' in its administration by a domestic industry lobby which desires to use the regulation as a discriminatory entry barrier against a foreign competitor (Rugman and Verbeke 1990).

Nine of the ten cases analysed clearly illustrate that shelter-based regulations were imposed as disguised environmental regulations to protect the home market from foreign competition. These cases include: US restrictions on Canadian imports in the cases of lobster, softwood lumber, newsprint, and UHT milk and Canadian restrictions on US business in the cases of tuna, herring and salmon (2 cases), beer cans, and PCBs. The remaining case, MMT, is based on environmental regulations in which there is no clear domestic producer who benefits at the expense of a prohibited importer.

For the purpose of summarizing this chapter, it is useful to look more closely at the analysis supporting these conclusions. The lobster, and the two salmon/herring cases illustrate protectionism disguised as a conservation measure. The salmon/herring cases illustrate the use of conservation measures which have the effect of impeding international trade. Here, Canada discriminated against US fishing producers and buyers by forcing landing and unloading requirements on them, which proved to be an extremely costly and time-consuming trade barrier. In softwood lumber, the US industry has attempted for at least fifteen years to keep out Canadian imports, even resorting to invalid environmental allegations concerning alleged subsidies.

The case of UHT milk demonstrated that the United States initiated measures meant to restrict Canadian exports to Puerto Rico by trying to make Canada conform to US methods of milk production and inspection. UHT milk was an unusual case in that the imposed environmental regulation discriminated against Quebec milk producers, in favour of Puerto Rican or US milk producers who benefited from the trade restriction.

The PCB export ban benefits Quebec and Alberta waste disposal plants at the expense of US producers, a case of trade protectionism disguised as an environmental concern. The sub-national case of Ontario beer cans is unquestionably another example of a discriminatory measure. The United States disputed Ontario's environmental levy, alleging that it had imposed discriminatory and protectionist provincial restrictions on aluminium beer cans imported to Ontario.

Finally, the MMT case spans the Canadian and US border and pits auto makers against the petroleum industry in both countries. There is no evidence at present that a 'domestic' environmental trade barrier would benefit Canada and discriminate against US opponents of the ban because there are no Canadian producers of MMT. The MMT case is one of the few environmental and trade disputes that does not illustrate a shelter-based regulation disguised as an environmentally based barrier to trade.

The case of softwood lumber offers an example of how the resolution of trade disputes with an environmental dimension can escalate beyond the sphere of the trade regime itself into the political arena. The softwood lumber agreement of 1996, negotiated outside of the framework of NAFTA, is currently showing signs of strain. The BC government, in response to the demands of industry faced with a shrinking Asian export market, has lowered the stumpage fees. The current dispute between the United States and Canada involves the issue of whether such a move is consistent with the terms of the agreement, as well as other tariff classification issues (Inside US Trade 1998).

This dynamic—the resolution of trade issues beyond the NAFTA trade regime itself—has also played out in the case of Pacific salmon, the subject of long-standing controversy between the United States and Canada. Both countries are currently negotiating the renewal of the Pacific Salmon Treaty, which governs the management and conservation of the Pacific fisheries stocks. Such treaties are negotiated to deal with the difficult question of what share of the total allowable catch each nation's industry will be entitled to. Such treaties provide a negotiating framework to deal with difficult and often very scientific issues relating to conservation and resource management. Although the negotiation of such treaties can arouse intense and political controversy, they will and should reduce the use of discriminatory environmental regulations in the future.

Business and environmental coalitions are being forged as one strategy to reduce rather than reinforce or create the restrictive impact of environmental regulation. A Canadian logging company, MacMillan Bloedel, had formerly been the target of a heavy campaign on the part of the globally active environmental group Greenpeace for its clear-cutting of old-growth forests. In a shrinking and highly competitive market, MacMillan Bloedel has allegedly found a balance between 'politics, social values and the corporate bottom line' in response to the pressures of potential boycotting by European customers and the threat of discriminatory eco-labelling of products that use logs from ancient forests (Matas and Lush 1998). Instead of clear-cutting forests, they have now adopted a method called 'niche logging'—a move lauded by Greenpeace. Increasingly concerned about the threat of environment and trade disputes, global firms are thus forging new alliances with environmental groups rather than confrontation (Greenpeace 1998).

Some of these North American cases are paralleled by similar incidences in the EU. For example, the Danish bottles' case parallels the Ontario beer case in many respects. It involved the legality of Danish recycling provisions which required that all beer and soft drinks be sold in returnable containers that could be refilled. Firms denied market access complained to the European Commission, after which Denmark was persuaded to allow each firm a quota of non-compliance containers which they could import into Denmark as long as a deposit and return scheme was established. The European Commission found this regulation to violate the Treaty of Rome—a finding subsequently upheld by the European Court of Justice (ECJ). The ECJ found that although the deposit and return system was 'necessary' for Denmark's chosen level of environmental protection, the quantitative restriction was not, as the 'least trade-restrictive' alternative had not been used (Trebilcock and Howse 1998). The implications of this decision on the ability of firms to take advantage of protectionist environmental regulation are unclear. In one sense, the ECJ allowed a high degree of deference to a Member State's choice of environmental regulation even when discriminatory. Yet at the same time, the ECJ found that the regulation violated the Treaty of Rome because it was not the least trade-restrictive alternative available to Denmark (Walker 1993).

The ECJ seemed to limit the extent to which countries may enact trade-restricting product specification measures in the German Beer Purity case. Here, Germany passed a regulation that required only specific ingredients be used to produce beer, in order to be labelled as such. The specific ingredients were those used in traditional beer production. However, the ECJ stated that such regulations are not permitted 'to crystallize given consumer habits so as to consolidate an advantage by national industries concerned to comply with them' (Walker 1993).

70   Economic and Corporate Strategy

One important comparative point is that the institutional capacity of the EU to consider the legality of trade-restricting environmental regulation in a legally binding permanent supranational institution, reveals important differences in the two systems. For example, the European system makes adjudication of such disputes easier in the sense that a large part of the political element is removed and the focus is purely legal, rather than political, as is the case when ad hoc panels are established at the behest of national governments. Accordingly, the Ontario beer case found its solution beyond the legal dispute settlement mechanisms within North America.

NOTES

1. *In the Matter of: Puerto Rico Regulations on the Import, Distribution and Sale of U.H.T. Milk from Quebec*, USA-93-1807-01, 3 June 1993. Ultra-high temperature (hereinafter UHT) milk is produced by heating milk to 138° Celsius for a minimum of two seconds. The milk is then cooled and packaged in hermetically sealed boxes. UHT milk has a shelf life of between six and twelve months at room temperature.
2. The FTA (and subsequently NAFTA) established a number of committees, subcommittees, and technical working groups to facilitate the implementation of trade commitments.
3. Interview with Agriculture Canada official, 22 May 1997.
4. Part of the reason this process was so time-consuming was that the UHT milk from Quebec issue had been tied to the larger issue of trade in fluid milk between Canada and the United States. The resolution arrived at by Canada and the United States included: (1) a declaration of equivalency for UHT milk from Quebec, and (2) an equivalency process for all fluid milk shipped between the United States and Canada. From a trade law perspective, it is highly questionable whether these two issues should have been tied for their resolution. Interview with Agriculture Canada official, 22 May 1997.
5. Interview with Agriculture Canada official, 19 Apr. 1996.
6. Bill C-29, The Manganese-Based Fuel Additives Act 1996. MMT is an acronym for methylcyclopentadienyl manganese tricarbonyl.
7. Speech delivered by the Honourable Sergio Marchi, PC, MP, Minister of the Environment, *Statement to the Senate Standing Committee on Energy, Environment and Natural Resources on Bill C-29: The Manganese-Based Fuel Additives Act*, 20 Feb. 1997.
8. Many of the adverse health effects of MMT are believed to be similar to those of lead, such as symptoms similar to Parkinson's Disease. Although MMT does reduce vehicle emissions of nitrous oxides, it increases the emission of volatile organic compounds, one of the leading precursors to smog. See Statement of Karen Florini, Senior Attorney, Environmental Defense Fund, 10 Apr. 1996.
9. MMT had been banned in the United States for 17 years by the Environmental Protection Agency (EPA). The EPA ban was recently overturned on a point of administrative law so its use is no longer prohibited. However, 15 of the major US petroleum companies have voluntarily refrained from using MMT pending EPA health testing results. The State of California, a leader in emission control legislation, presently bans the use of MMT in fuel.

Baptist–Bootlegger Coalitions   71

10. Industry representatives, government officials, and environmentalists met recently to consider how to remove or reduce sulphur emissions from gasoline (see Corcoran (1996a: B2).
11. 'Canadian MMT Bill Heads to Senate, Closer to Chapter 11 Complaint', *Inside NAFTA*, 8 Jan. 1997.
12. 'U.S. May Challenge Canada via NAFTA in MMT Case, Ex-Negotiator says', *Inside NAFTA*, 29 Nov. 1995, and 'Company May Press U.S. for NAFTA Challenge on Canadian Fuel Bill', 15 Nov. 1995.
13. PCB waste is found mostly in oils formerly used as coolants in electric equipment and industrial hydraulic fluids.
14. The cost of incineration at Swan Hills, Alberta, has been as high as $4,500 per tonne compared to $2,400 per tonne in the United States. Much of the savings is due to lower transportation costs. See also Corcoran 1996b.
15. *Inside EPA*, 'EPA Decision to Ease Ban on PCB Imports Draws Fire from Staff', 3 Nov. 1995, 10.
16. Environment Canada justified the export ban by the Basel Convention on the Control of Transboundary Movements of Hazardous Wastes and their Disposal (the 'Basel Convention'), which obligates its signatories to dispose of hazardous wastes within their own borders. However, the United States has not ratified the Basel Convention, so it is unlikely that its restrictions would prevail over those of NAFTA. Moreover, under the Agreement between the Government of Canada and the Government of the United States of America Concerning the Transboundary Movement of Hazardous Waste (the 'Canada–US Transboundary Agreement'), Canada is under a positive obligation to permit the export of PCBs. In addition, according to Article 11 of the Basel Convention, 'the provisions of this Convention shall not affect transboundary movements which take place pursuant to such agreements, provided that such agreements are compatible with the environmental management of hazardous wastes and other wastes as required by this Convention.' Thus, the Basel Convention does contemplate the existence of bilateral arrangements for trade in waste between OECD countries where facilities are adequate. Under Article 104, where there is an inconsistency between NAFTA and certain international agreements, including the Basel Convention, and the Canada–US Transboundary Agreement, the latter prevails provided that Canada chooses the alternative that is least inconsistent with NAFTA, if it has a choice among equally effective and reasonably available means of complying with its treaty obligations. Thus, according to the terms of the Basel Convention, Canada has an obligation to permit the exports of PCBs to the United States and the interim order may have been in contravention of Canada's obligations under NAFTA.

PART II

Complex Institutional Responsiveness

NAFTA's Political Experience

5
Trade and Environment Institutions: The NAFTA Regime

Trade agreements, with their legally based dispute settlement mechanisms, have developed into a core element of corporate strategic behaviour. As argued in the preceding chapters, NAFTA has made a major advance in the arena of dispute settlement, largely because of its Chapter 11 provisions. This investor–state dispute settlement mechanism allows foreign nationals and corporations themselves to bring an action against a government for breach of a treaty obligation, while NAAEC's Articles 14–15 similarly allow firms to initiate actions over a government's alleged failure to enforce its environmental regulations.

But well-constructed trade agreements do much more than settle disputes. Rather, they have the capacity for dispute avoidance and prevention before the stage where conflicts escalate into litigation. They have rules and institutions that deal not only with the application of environmental regulation but with the ongoing operation of regulatory systems and the shaping of the actual content of the regulations that firms face. In short, institutions can provide companies with knowledge about foreign regulations as well as the ways in which foreign regulatory systems work, such as information regarding testing, certification, and accreditation. They can assist countries in creating modern and effective regulatory systems. And they can produce a convergence of national and sub-national regulations on a broader regional and multilateral level.

Most observers looking comparatively at the world's major trading agreements and their potential to combat present and prospective environmental regulatory protectionism offer only a limited assessment of the capacity of NAFTA's trade–environment regime to fulfil this array of functions (Steinberg 1997; Abbott 1996; Esty and Gerardin 1997). To them, the exemplar regime is the highly integrated European Union, with its capacity for binding supranational adjudication on the part of the European Court of Justice and its legal and institutional framework which provides an effective balance between the free movement of goods and the protection of the environment.

At the other end of the spectrum stand weaker trade agreements in terms of institutional capacity, such as the WTO. Its Committee for Trade and the Environment (CTE), established with high expectations in 1995, has largely failed. When the CTE issued its report in November 1996 at the Singapore Ministerial, it became clear that almost 'two years of inter-governmental deliberations had yielded little output' (Charnovitz 1997: 342). The Organisation for

Economic Cooperation and Development (OECD), while conducting useful work in dispute prevention and convergence, is largely a forum for research and discussion, rather than for international negotiation and lawmaking. Asia-Pacific Economic Cooperation (APEC), despite its deadline for free trade across the Asia-Pacific region by 2010/2020, has produced few results thus far in the area of trade and the environment, despite the fact that all three NAFTA members are APEC members. Its rotating secretariat and emphasis on consultative cooperation rather than binding legal commitments make it a poor contender for an extensive legal structure (Rugman and Soloway 1997). The nascent FTAA has similarly produced few results to date (Kirton 1998). Only the Canada–Chilean trade agreement has adopted the NAFTA model to some extent and implied that a CEC-type institution will be established in the near future.

Most observers put NAFTA in the middle of this spectrum, while placing it towards the lightly institutionalized end (Steinberg 1997; Vogel 1995). However, a careful review of NAFTA's actual performance, based on the first five years of its operation, suggest that NAFTA has been a much more effective regime than these early comparative analyses suggest. This is especially true if one looks beyond the actual cases that have been taken before actual dispute settlement panels but examines more broadly incidences of dispute management, regional capacity building, and regulatory convergence.

This record thus indicates that international institutions, even lightly developed ones such as NAFTA, do make a difference. The NAFTA regime has been successful in dispute avoidance, transparency creation, and capacity building through the work of its 50 intergovernmental committees, subcommittees, and working groups which deal with issues between the parties as they arise. They have helped, for example, to render accessible Mexico's sometimes opaque and sometimes non-existent system of sanitary and phytosanitary standards. In some cases, such as the transportation of dangerous goods and pesticides, the committees have achieved regulatory convergence. Moreover, this is not a case where there is a hegemonic imposition of the United States' will over that of its weaker NAFTA partners. Nor is it a case of powerful trade interests dictating local environmental preferences. Rather it is a case of mutual adjustment between three countries and the trade–environment communities in ways that both open markets and raise environmental standards to meet the challenges of the next millennium.

Nor have the NAFTA institutions operated as another governmental incubator of green and greedy coalitions to pursue protectionist strategies. Rather they have fostered business and ENGO coalitions such that their energies have been redirected in ways that are both trade liberalizing and environmentally friendly. In doing so, they have opened the institutional arena to business to pursue a broader range of new and more complex environmentally oriented export and investment strategies.

Introduction

The coming into force of the NAFTA and its side agreements on 1 January 1994 produced major legal and institutional changes in the traditional economic and environmental relationship among the United States, Mexico, and Canada. The core NAFTA text and accompanying North American Agreement on Environmental Cooperation (NAEEC) gave North America and the world an innovative trade–environment regime that accorded environmental principles a more equal and integrated place than ever before. It transformed three, at times distant, bilateral relationships, with virtually no regular and permanent intergovernmental connections, into a multifaceted, trilateral relationship spawning an emergent regional community. Moreover, it brought regional international organization to North America. The informal, binational, diplomatic processes of old were supplemented by bodies—for the environment, labour, and (prospectively) trade—with single secretariats, budgets, headquarters, and governing charters. Taken together, these changes heralded a fundamental transformation in the dominant regime for regional North American governance.

Yet whether these NAFTA-created novelties in legal principles, rules, and institutions represent a genuine case of regime change in practice, and one which fosters trade and investment while limiting the scope for environmental regulation to impose protectionist barriers, depends critically on how effective this new NAFTA trade–environment regime is in operation. Some scholarly observers and NAFTA's many critics, focusing only on NAFTA's new dedicated environmental institution, the Commission for Environmental Cooperation (CEC), argue the regime has done little to fulfil what they see as its core purpose of ensuring the effective enforcement of national environmental regulations (Mumme and Duncan 1996; Public Citizen 1995). Such conclusions are consistent with analyses of the intense, often special Canada–US relationship which have pointed to the limited effectiveness historically of bilateral institutions, in what should be an easy domain for liberal-institutionalist processes to unfold (Swanson 1978; Spencer, Kirton, and Nossal 1982). They are also compatible with the judgements of those examining multilateral 'institutions for the earth', who conclude that very little environmental change has come as a result of international institutional activity (Haas, Keohane, and Levy 1993; Keohane and Levy 1996).

Yet other assessments are more favourable to the basic precepts of liberal-institutionalist theory, by pointing to the autonomous importance of these new international institutions. Some see the capacity and early record of the Commission for Environmental Cooperation itself as heralding an institution with considerable potential (Munton and Kirton 1994; Johnson and Beaulieu 1996; Abbott 1996; Audley 1997). Still others view the broader array of NAFTA trade institutions as engendering effective environmental cooperation among the parties in several instances, and promising to constrain national and subfederal environmental regulations that serve as barriers to trade (Kirton and Fernandez de Castro 1997; Kirton 1997a; Weintraub 1997; Rugman, Kirton, and Soloway 1997b). Providing general support to this perspective are those instances in the multilateral realm where the rules of environmental regimes have made a distinct difference in national government behaviour (Mitchell 1994).

This chapter argues that during its first four years in operation, NAFTA's trade–environment regime, through its environmentally relevant trade institutions, has effectively encouraged communication, capacity building, and compliance, constrained national regulatory protectionism, engendered a trade-facilitating, high-level regional convergence of national environmental regulations, and served as an incubator and a foundation for regional cooperation in broader international fora. The impact of vastly superior US power and leadership remains evident (Steinberg 1997). But this impact is at a structural and sectoral level, for such action has been most advanced in areas where US export interests in the region are most acute. Moreover the autonomous force of the regime in rendering the preferences of the three countries and those of the trade and environmental communities more equal is evident in the broadly balanced pattern of interaction and outcomes, in several areas. Indeed, performance is most advanced in those areas, notably the chemicals sector. Here, the otherwise predominant US power is offset by the ecological vulnerability of the United States to its NAFTA partners, the presence of a multilateral regime 'nest' to facilitate cooperation, and the insulation of government actors from direct, concentrated industry pressure.

NAFTA as a Trade–Environment Regime

The NAFTA trade and environment agreements and institutions constitute a robust, if nascent, regional 'regime', where a regime is initially defined in its classic conception as a set of 'explicit or implicit principles, norms, rules and decisionmaking procedures around which actors' expectations converge in a given area of international politics' (Krasner 1983). Here regimes are usefully conceived of more broadly as 'institutions', a concept which embraces classic regimes, but adds bureaucratic organizations, and informal conventions. Institutions thus consist of 'persistent and connected sets of rules and practices that prescribe behavioural roles, constrain activity, and shape expectations' (Haas, Keohane, and Levy 1993: 4–5). Regimes and institutions are employed here, in conventional fashion, as intervening variables which mitigate the impact of differences in member countries' and policy communities' capabilities and interests to constrain the otherwise self-interested unilateral behaviour of their dominant members (Keohane and Nye 1977; Keohane 1984).

Regime theory has been criticized for paying insufficient attention to how powerful countries, notably the United States, disproportionally shape and benefit from the apparent public good which a regime represents (Strange 1996). This criticism is of particular force when regime theory is applied to the 'hard' case of North America, where profound disparity in capability abounds. In conventional cross-national terms, the United States, in overall economic weight, is ten times larger than Canada and almost twenty times larger than Mexico. Equally important, in transgovernmental and transnational terms, on a region-wide basis, at the national and sub-national levels, a historically separate, long established, and powerful trade policy community confronts a more recent, less capable environmental community (Young 1994: 25–6). It is thus not surprising that a comparative study of the negotiation and implementation of trade–environment rules in the NAFTA, WTO, and EU concludes that such environmentally enhancing rules develop more quickly and stringently as rich, 'green' countries use their market access power (through coercion and compensation) to secure their interests vis-à-vis a smaller, weaker set of developing countries. This dynamic, alongside deepening integration, leads ENGOs in the rich green countries to demand such rules (Steinberg 1997). This analysis of the creation and content, and prospectively the operation, of the NAFTA trade–environment regime thus argues that it represents and codifies the particular preferences of a predominant United States and the very powerful environmental NGO community within it.

The NAFTA trade–environment regime's effectiveness in practice, however, depends on its ability to offset this profound disparity in order to engender balanced trilateral and trade–environment cooperation and capacity building. It also depends on its ability to constrain the propensity of the powerful United States and its national and subfederal governments to adopt environmental regulations with protectionist effect, to promote regional regulatory convergence through mutual adjustment; and to engender regional cooperation in multilateral forums. Of particular interest is the potential for the regime to constrain the ability of US industries and environmental groups to form coalitions of the 'green and greedy' that seek and secure environmental regulation to serve their protectionist self-interest (Vogel 1995; Oye and Maxwell 1994; Vogel and Rugman 1997).

Analytically, the autonomous impact of the NAFTA trade–environment regime can be assessed by examining both behavioural processes and substantive outcomes against the initial preferences and underlying interests of both the three member countries and those of the region-wide trade and environment communities. The behavioural dimension examines the three countries' actions, through the institutions, to fulfil the regime's non-discretionary and permissive mandates through trilateral interaction and openness, equal initiation of proposals, and full flexibility and equality on the coalitions that form and prevail. The substantive dimension explores how institutional outcomes equally reflect the initial preferences or underlying interests of all the three countries, give equal weight to the claims of trade and the environment, and most broadly, reflect the core principles of sustainable development as articulated in the principles, norms, and rules of the NAFTA and NAAEC. The regime is considered effective to the extent that trilateral, and trade environment, interaction and equality, rather than US and trade actors/interests or green/greedy coalitions prevail. The regime is also considered effective to the

80   *Complex Institutional Responsiveness*

extent that differences among the three countries are superseded by those between region-wide trade and environment communities. In this analysis it is ultimately important to differentiate between the interests of the US as a country and the environmental interests of the North American region.

NAFTA's Trade Institutions in Operation

A review of the environmentally relevant principles, norms, and rules embedded in the core NAFTA trade text reveals that the agreement did bring a major change in the prevailing trade–environment framework within North America, as well as by global standards. NAFTA's principles, norms, and rules changed the prevailing trade–environment framework in two significant ways. First, NAFTA affirmed the value of trade–environment equality and integration. Second, it expanded the force of environmental protection, while maintaining trade openness at the regional level (Munton and Kirton 1994; Housman 1994; Rugman and Kirton 1999; Audley 1997). However the NAFTA regime's specific decision-making procedures, as operationalized in the institutions that interpret and implement the rules, have given less emphasis to this embedded normative structure. Even so, among the 50 trilateral trade institutions from the ministerial to the working level that NAFTA created or catalysed, the dozen with direct environmental responsibility have in several cases had a clear impact. They have fostered a regular, balanced, trilateral communication, confidence and capacity building, high-level regulatory convergence, and regional cooperation in multilateral forums that tempers the autonomous actions of US and trade actors, including their ability to impose environmental regulations with protectionist impact.

From an environmental perspective, NAFTA marked a sharp departure from the FTA (which had minimal environmental provisions), from earlier Canada–US agreements for environmental cooperation (which only tangentially addressed economic affairs) and from the prevailing trade–environment regime in the GATT and WTO, or the soon to be conceived Asia-Pacific Economic Cooperation (APEC) and Free Trade Agreement of the Americas (FTAA) (Rugman and Kirton with Soloway 1998; Rugman and Soloway 1997; Abbott 1996). The core NAFTA trade text began, in its preamble, by specifying that the purpose of the trade agreement was, *inter alia*, to proactively 'promote sustainable development', and to 'strengthen the development and enforcement of environmental laws and regulations', as well as undertaking 'economic activities in a manner consistent with environmental protection and conservation' (Canada 1992). NAFTA also specified that its trade and economic provisions would not override members' obligations to the world's major multilateral environmental agreements—covering trade in endangered species, ozone depleting substances, and hazardous waste movement.

This deference to the concerns of the global ecology over the continental economy was reinforced by NAFTA's detailed commitments. Most notably

Chapter 7, on sanitary and phytosanitary standards, enabled each NAFTA country to set the level of environmental protection it considered appropriate. Chapter 9 conferred a similar right for standards measures generally. In both cases, however, these rights were disciplined by the requirement for more transparent and justifiable risk assessment procedures to avoid the use of trade-restricting environmental standards. Chapter 11's Article 1114 prohibited a country from lowering environmental standards or their enforcement in order to increase or maintain investment in its territory, and mandated intergovernmental discussions in the event of non-compliance. Equally importantly, the core NAFTA text gave many of the specific trilateral institutions it created mandatory powers to interpret, implement, and extend specific responsibilities for environmental action. In some instances, notably dangerous goods transportation and automotive emissions, it identified a precise timetable and target for action. It also offered permissive mandates for some of these institutions to act on specified environmental subjects should they so wish. More generally, the mandates of other bodies, such as agriculture, dealt with issues of such clear environmental relevance that they too had the mandate to operate in environmentally enhancing ways, given the text of NAFTA's preamble.

The environmental regulatory impact of NAFTA's 50 trade institutions depended overwhelmingly on the performance of six particular bodies. The first two, which regulated regional activity in the field of chemicals (as well as packaging and transportation) were the Land Transportation Subcommittee's Working Group on the Transportation of Dangerous Goods, and the Trilateral Working Group on Pesticides (a joint creation of the Committee on Standards and the Committee on Sanitary and Phytosanitary Standards). The second two, regulating agriculture, were the Committee on Agricultural Trade and the Committee on Sanitary and Phytosanitary Standards. The third, regulating the automotive sector in its operating and manufacturing segments, respectively, were the Land Transportation Subcommittee, and the Automotive Standards Council (both of which were subcommittees of the Committee on Standards-Related Measures).

A review of the performance of NAFTA's environmentally relevant institutions over the first three years of operation shows several patterns (Kirton and Fernandez de Castro 1997). First, after a slow start, there has been since 1996 a sharp takeoff in the activities of these bodies, with virtually all now having established their procedures, structures, priorities, and work plans. Regular trilateral interaction is now a reality. Second, there has been a notable institutional proliferation. The 26 bodies created by the initial NAFTA text have now doubled in number and new trilateral bodies with an environmental relevance have emerged within and outside the NAFTA structure across a broad array of issue areas. Third, there has been a trend towards balanced and open trilateral cooperation, as Mexico has become a fuller partner in the problem-solving spirit that has (amidst the inevitable differences of interest and hard bargaining) long characterized the Canada–US relationship. Fourth, there has been a wide variation in performance. Some bodies, such as those for the Transportation of Dangerous Goods and for Pesticides, have rapidly generated high-level convergence of standards through mutual adjustment, while others, notably the Automotive Standards Council and Subcommittee on Land Transportation, have been slow to act. Finally, at the ministerial level and elsewhere, NAFTA's trade institutions and the Commission for Environmental Cooperation have done little to interact with each other to produce an integrated, balanced, and thus stable trade–environment regime.

More specifically, NAFTA institutional activity has had four effects on capacity building, communication, regulatory convergence, and broader regional cooperation: (1) it is encouraging and assisting Mexico to introduce environmental regulations where none existed before; (2) it is leading to an understanding of legitimate geographic and environmentally based differences in standards (e.g. Mexico testing for automotive emissions at a higher altitude than does the United States); (3) it is identifying areas where Mexico has higher and different standards than the United States, and incorporating an array of such features from all three countries into a common approach; (4) it is aimed at developing common North American positions in broader international fora, both to shape the broader regime to meet specific North American interests (and thus benefit North American firms) or to ensure broad multilateral harmonization as a value in its own right.

NAFTA's 'enforcement' or dispute settlement mechanisms have also operated in ways that have constrained national environmental regulations with protectionist effect, without inhibiting the emergence of high-level regional standards. Throughout the ongoing NAFTA debate, environmental and other critics of the Agreement had raised concerns about how effectively the new textual commitments to the environment would be implemented. Concern focused on the NAFTA dispute settlement process that was based almost entirely on trade expertise, with limited provisions for the incorporation of environmental sensitivity, science, and non-governmental groups (Orbuch and Singer 1995). Yet in the limited experience thus far, NAFTA's three major dispute settlement mechanisms (in Chapter 19 on antidumping, subsidies, and countervail; Chapter 20 on general disputes; and Chapter 11 on investment disputes) have had a neutral or slightly constraining effect on national-level regulations with protectionist impact.

With three exceptions, these mechanisms have not been mobilized during their first four years against national or sub-national regulations with environmental implications, as virtually no cases with a clearly environmental character have been brought before these NAFTA mechanisms. It is still too soon to definitively determine, even based on FTA precedents, whether the presence of the NAFTA mechanism is having a deterrent effect on the passage or use of environmental regulations with protectionist impact. Yet the paucity of such cases suggests that North American industry is unable to identify any clear protectionist impact of national or subfederal environmental regulation.

The three exceptional cases have all arisen under NAFTA's novel investment mechanism. The first case, MMT, involved a US firm complaining under Chapter 11 about Canadian regulatory action using trade restrictions for environmental purposes by banning the importation and interprovincial trade of the environmentally harmful gas additive MMT (Rugman and Soloway 1998; Soloway 1999). It is not yet clear how NAFTA's Chapter 11 process will treat the case. In the interim, even though independent court action in the United States has temporarily made the use of MMT legal in the United States, about 80 per cent of the US industry is voluntarily refusing to use the MMT additive, pending a final legal determination. The second case entering a Chapter 11 process involves a US-owned firm (Metalclad) operating in the hazardous waste business in Mexico, complaining that a Mexican state government is refusing to allow its new site to open, on the grounds it does not meet zoning, environmental, and building regulations. The third case involves a US-owned firm operating in Mexico's waste disposal business which is charging that actions by municipal authorities have prevented it from carrying on business after a significant capital investment in new facilities. (Most recently, there are signs that a US-owned waste management company, USA Waste, is seeking US $60 million from the Mexican government for the alleged breach of a contract for street cleaning and landfill development in Acapulco.) In the three cases filed thus far, and in the prospective USA Waste case, it is US multinationals in the oil and environmental services industries, respectively, using the NAFTA mechanism to ensure access to the Canadian and Mexican market. American investment interests are thus far the dominant, indeed exclusive players, in taking advantage of the NAFTA Chapter 11 mechanism. But in only one case, MMT, is the US company claim one which challenges national environmental regulations. In the other three cases, all involving Mexico, a successful challenge would see the NAFTA mechanism used to promote the interests not only of US multinationals but also of the local Mexican ecology. There are thus good initial grounds for concluding that the NAFTA Chapter 11 dispute settlement mechanism is operating to the advantage of US multinationals and against traditional local regulatory protectionism, but also, and more importantly, in favour of the local ecology and environmentally enhancing transborder investment, technology, and management. The potential for the joint gains that sustainable development promises, and that NAFTA established as a governing ideal, are clearly being enhanced by the operation of the regime in its early years.

Because NAFTA's environmental regime emphasized the effective enforcement of national regulations, it has thus far delivered less international regulatory convergence than the European Union, where international harmonization formed the focus of the regime (Esty and Geradin 1997). Yet the NAFTA environmental regime and institutions have created a clear bias towards regional convergence. This is best conceived of as a dynamic process unfolding in discrete, if partially overlapping, stages: (1) communication among actors to lower transactions costs and thus enhance market access and environmental learning; (2) capacity building to develop modern regulatory systems in partner countries; and (3) convergence of regulations towards a common system and state. The NAFTA regime in its first three years has produced through this process considerable convergence in environmental regulations, despite the three countries' disparity in overall capabilities and initial diversity in economic and regulatory development.

The breadth of subjects covered by the 50 NAFTA institutions and the activities with which they deal (many of which are in subfederal jurisdiction) suggest that the NAFTA institutions will have an ever stronger constraining effect in the future on state-level environmental regulatory protectionism, and produce greater region-wide regulatory convergence. The existing trend is towards convergence at higher levels of environmental regulation. Only in the case of pesticides are there concerns that the NAFTA process is causing the higher (in this case Canadian) national standards to be lessened.

Across the six institutions where NAFTA's work on environmentally related regulations is concentrated, however, there has been a wide variation in the degree of convergence sought and secured, the level of environmental standards aimed at and achieved, and the trilateral rather than bilateral or unilateral character of the bargaining and outcome. The Working Group on the Transportation of Dangerous Goods (LTSS V) and the Technical Working Group on Pesticides (TWGP) stand as successful cases of rapid, high, and balanced convergence based on a broadly multilateral rather than US national standards. In sharp contrast, much less of the convergence specified as a goal in NAFTA has occurred in the Working Group on Vehicle Standards (LTSS I) and the Automotive Standards Council (ASC) where US and trade/industry preferences have largely prevailed. The Committee on Sanitary and Phytosanitary Standards (CSPS), and the Committee on Agricultural Trade (CAT) have a mixed record, with the latter moving to address regional interests in broader multinational forums.

This variation across the six cases reflects the impact of six factors. The first, causing extensive, balanced, high-level regulatory convergence, is the visible, concentrated, and obvious transborder character of the environmental harm and resulting ecological vulnerability of the United States. An accident involving the transportation of dangerous goods is likely to attract publicity, and damage political and corporate reputations and resources, in contrast to less visible, long-term, diffusely impacting automotive emissions or pollution prevention measures. Moreover sprayed pesticides flowing by air or water from Mexico into the United States are more likely to galvanize political pressure and action from geographically concentrated constituencies than are the more subtle issues dealt with by the CSPS. The direct ecological vulnerability of the United States to threats emanating from partner jurisdictions, especially Mexico, creates an effective chemical 'intervulnerability' and a powerful incentive for action (Doran 1984). This is a process of 'dynamic intervulnerability' as NAFTA's trade provisions increase transportation and truck travel in particular through the United States and with it the threat of chemical spills from trucks (more than rail cars or sea tankers) on US soil. A full 80 per cent of US–Mexican and 60 per cent of US–Canadian freight is carried by trucks, with 40 per cent of all US exports to Mexico flowing through Texas highways and roadways, and moves to create more Canada–Mexico road corridors are under way (Fry 1997). In the particular case of pesticides, US ecological vulnerability to Mexico (and the domestic political need of President Clinton for an additional Congressional vote to secure NAFTA's passage) placed pesticides prominently on the agenda of the NAFTA institutions. Even then, the three national governments (and the institutions themselves) retained wide latitude in determining how the issue would be processed and resolved. Here the US administration used the NAFTA institutions to deflect local (in this case Texan) demands for punitive national action.

A second cause of high-level regulatory convergence is the presence of a 'nested regime' in the broader international system that fosters a nonhegemonic framework for regional action. This dynamic corresponds to the logic and preferences of multilateralists and globally oriented multinationals who fear the costs of closed regional trade liberalization agreements (Aggarwal 1983) Work on the transportation of dangerous goods, where harmonization has proceeded fastest and furthest, is explicitly grounded in, and guided by, the established regime of the broader United Nations Economic Commission for Europe. The successful case of pesticides has the similarly multilateral OECD as its nest. Automotive emissions activity lacks a similarly strong multilateral nest. In the partially successful agricultural cases, the three North American countries look abroad primarily to advance regional interests in the formation of the still nascent and non-Eurocentric regimes forming in the FTAA, APEC, and the WTO.

A third cause is the insulation of the NAFTA institutions from direct, undiluted corporate influence. LTSS V on dangerous goods transportation contains only national government officials, while the TWGP incorporates a broad array of stakeholders, including both industry and ENGOs. In contrast, the ASC relies on a national industry advisory committee in Canada, the Automotive Advisory Council, to serve as its working group.

A fourth, but less salient, factor is the functional need to harmonize standards to reap NAFTA's trade gains. Thus, transportation operations have seen rapid action as trade requires road transportation which enhances the probability of chemical spills. In contrast, in automotive emissions, the trade barriers and incentives are less apparent. Yet the cognate area of trucking standards, where Texas refused to open the border to Mexican trucks by the NAFTA-specified deadline, and where Mexico granted Canada early and privileged access to the Mexican market, shows that industry-rewarding functionalism or 'engrenage' is by itself not enough. It also reveals politically motivated preferential action by NAFTA's two lesser powers to offset the gains otherwise available to the much larger United States.

A fifth factor is the cost to powerful industries of the high-level harmonized standards. Dangerous goods work has proceeded rapidly on creating a regional emergency response guide for small packages. But progress has been slow for large containers, halogenated organic chlorides (where the chemical-producing industry is seeking to shift the cost to the railroads by requiring super-strong tanker cars), and hazardous waste shipment (where the Canadian government was seeking to protect the commercial prospects of an Alberta disposal plant). In contrast, in the case of pesticides, action is spurred by the prospect that a single standard and test covering the entire region would facilitate trade by lowering costs (in money and time) to government and industry as well as lead to improved environmental protection.

A sixth factor is the support of MNEs who are most likely to be able to afford and benefit from a single, ultimately global system, and their relative influence over dispersed transportation interests and subfederal governments with a poor record of harmonizing on their own. In the case of dangerous goods transportation, officials in large national governments and large MNEs have a joint interest in preventing provincialism, with the transaction costs such autonomous regulatory activity brings. Particularly in Canada, NAFTA is seen to provide an institutional instrument to engender an interprovincial uniformity that could not be secured in the pre-NAFTA years. However there are limits to MNE-driven multilateralism as an explanation. The case of automotive emissions reveals the reluctance of a large, concentrated, US-owned industry (despite its high degree of North American integration and transnational character) to subject itself to a trilateral dialogue dominated by government officials. This is particularly true when such officials are from departments other than the industry and commerce sector, where the auto industry has traditionally received sympathetic hearing. Behind these national bureaucratic factors lie others—notably the difficulty the automotive industry has experienced in coming to an accommodation with the oil industry, and the automotive industry's continuing preference, despite occasional disappointments, for voluntary standardization at less than government-envisaged levels (Kirton 1997b).

There are few signs that the environmental achievements of the NAFTA institutions have come at the expense of trade liberalization values, through the promotion of national or regional protectionism rather than a broad multilateral regime. The absence of regional convergence in the failed cases is, on the whole, not driven by US coalitions of environmentalists and firms insisting on unilateral autonomy and thus national environmental regulatory protectionism. Such coalitions might be expected to form to resist regional regimes which constrain their freedom to secure the national or subfederal-level regulations they desire to protect the home market for local firms (De Sombre 1995; Vogel 1995; Vogel and Rugman 1997). Yet, with the exception of pesticides, environmentalists are notable in their absence across the spectrum of NAFTA economic institutional activity. They are also absent from behind-the-border bargaining in the cases, such as autos, where environmental regulatory convergence was not achieved.

There have not as yet emerged regional coalitions seeking to use the NAFTA institutions to gain environmental rules for the North American region at the expense of outside firms seeking to export into North America. Nor have such coalitions emerged in support of North American firms wishing to develop the critical regional mass to penetrate markets outside. Their general absence is apparent in the early preferences of members of the North American Trilateral Standardization Forum, the private-sector driven trilateral body that liaises with the government-only Committee on Standards-Related Measures (CSRM), meeting immediately before CSRM meetings. The Forum's Mexican members, representing an economy with 85 per cent of its trade concentrated on the US market on average, have some tendency to prefer distinctive regional standards, as do smaller, domestically oriented US firms with few export interests. Yet Mexican members have displayed an initial affinity for cooperating with Canada, and a distrust of solutions embracing the United States. Canadian members come from an economy where 38 per cent of GDP comes from goods and services exports, where 81 per cent of merchandise exports go to the United States and where Canadian factories produce more for the export than the domestic market (Fry 1997). But for reasons of diversification and a multilateralist ideology, they have displayed a general preference not for US-based regional standards but for a single multilateral regime of 'one standard, one test, one mark'. The US members, coming from a country that sends only one-third of its exports to Canada and Mexico, rationally prefer multilaterally compatible regional standardization. This rational multilateral preference is reinforced by Mexico's reluctance to accord US firms privileged access to their markets. Taken together, then, there are several grounds for concluding that NAFTA's economic institutions, without US hegemony or 'coalitions of the green and greedy' behind them, are leading to a balanced, trade-facilitating, high-level convergence of environmental regulations. This occurs most strongly in cases where the environmental damage is direct and visible and the resulting ecological vulnerability of the United States high, where there is a multilateral nest, and where the institutions are insulated from industry influence and the costs to industry low. The ecological vulnerability that offsets superior US and trade community capability, multilateral institutions and ideology, and the insulation of state actors from singular industry influence through the NAFTA institutions generates balanced regional regulatory convergence.

Yet there remains evidence of predominant US power and interest exercising its impact at a second, more structural level. The NAFTA institutions have succeeded in producing successful, rapid, high-level convergence of environmental regulations in areas (dangerous goods transportation and pesticides) where the chemical industry is most involved. They have failed to do so where the interests of the automotive industry are at stake. (The agriculture bodies stand as mixed cases.) Consistent with this pattern is a model of 'secure the regional export market' for competitive US business interests, rather than one which emphasizes the protectionist influence of US firms or the transaction-cost need of US-based multinationals with regionally integrated production systems to secure a single regional standard.

As Table 5.1 indicates, high-level regulatory convergence through NAFTA's institutions arises where the NAFTA market has expanded most for the home-based exports of the US industry most affected from 1990 to 1994 (row 2). Canadian and Mexican interests matter much less. As Table 5.2 shows, success comes most in sectors in which the relevant US industry has, more specifically, an export surplus with: (1) its NAFTA partners; (2) with both NAFTA partners (and hence an incentive to harmonize on a trilateral basis); (3) where those surpluses are increasing from 1990 to 1994 (as NAFTA takes hold in anticipation and action); and (4) where the regional surplus is a large portion of US industry's global surplus. There is thus a fusion between the export interests of competitive US industries in the NAFTA market place, and the high-level environmental regulatory convergence that will lower their transaction costs and ease their access to sustain their success.

TABLE 5.1. *NAFTA's share of US and Canadian exports, 1994, 1990–1994 (%)*

	Chemicals	Agriculture	Autos
1. NAFTA share of US exports 1994	26.6	24.0	34.2
2. NAFTA share of US exports 1990–94	4.6	4.5	1.7
3. NAFTA share of Canadian exports 1994	80.1	55.4	96
4. NAFTA share of Canadian exports 1990–94	10	14	1.8
5. NAFTA share of Canadian–US Exports 1994	53.4	39.7	65
6. NAFTA share of Canadian–US Exports 1990–4	7.3	9.3	1.8

TABLE 5.2. *US exports over imports 1994 (1990–1994) (US $ millions)*

	Chemicals (2)	Agriculture (2)	Automative (2)
Canada	2,413 (+954)	–375 (–286)	–1,879 (–3,448)
Mexico	3,283 (+1,682)	128 (+972)	–4,323 (–2,621)
NAFTA	5,695 (+2,636)	–247 (+686)	–6,202 (–6,069)
World	16,122	6,789	–82,091
NAFTA as % World	35%	–3.6%	7.6%

The impact of NAFTA's trade environment regime should be assessed in the first instance by examining the content and effect of its environmentally related rules, and the mandate and structure of its institutions. The next stage is to analyse the actual operation of the trade and environment institutions created to give effect to, and expand, those specified principles, norms, and rules. Among the 50 trilateral intergovernmental institutions created or catalysed by NAFTA, those with the most direct environmental responsibility during their first four years have had a mixed record in fostering regular, balanced, trilateral communication, capacity building, effective dispute settlement, high-level regulatory convergence, and regional cooperation in multilateral forums and dispute management. The work of the NAFTA dispute settlement mechanisms thus far suggests that the innovative Chapter 11 process on investment has been an important instrument for assisting US MNCs to secure access to the Mexican and Canadian markets by challenging national environmentally related regulations. However, they have operated in ways that are, on the whole, environmentally enhancing. The successful performance of the NAFTA bodies dealing with chemicals, in contrast to the poor performance of those in the automotive field and the mixed performance of those in agriculture, points to the partial success of NAFTA's trade–environment regime in constraining US regulatory protectionism and engendering balanced, non-hegemonic regulatory convergence. This process is most advanced: (1) where there is visible ecological intervulnerability between the United States and its neighbours; (2) where a multilateral nest exists; (3) where there is government insulation from societal pressures; (4) where there is a strong, direct functional need to harmonize; (5) where the cost to powerful industries is low; (6) where there exists support from MNCs and the regional export interests of US industry.

In short, NAFTA's intergovernmental institutions matter. They promote the competitiveness of North American firms by assisting them in overcoming information, resource, and regulatory barriers at the national and local level, and by strengthening their ability to create a more favourable regulatory regime in key markets outside the region. This is done in ways that are demonstrably environmentally enhancing and that thus further equip North American firms to capture the more environmentally sensitive and global market place of the future.

Thus, the relative success of the first half-decade of NAFTA's institutional structure in balancing trade and environment concerns offers lessons for other global trade agreements. In particular, it offers opportunities for high, balanced regulatory convergence without the high, hierarchical degree of integration required by an EU-style regime. The FTAA, currently being negotiated, is, and will continue to be, influenced by the NAFTA institutional structure. Although some critics view NAFTA's regionalist focus as a 'second-best strategy', or alternatively as a potential 'stumbling block' towards the ultimate goal of a multilateral regime (Charnovitz 1997: 376), such a view denies the value and functional reality of the NAFTA model and experience over the last half-decade.

6
Environmental Institutions in Action: The CEC

Arguably the most innovative feature of the NAFTA trade–environment regime came not from the environmental provisions and institutions contained within the trade agreement itself, but in the separate environmental agreement that accompanied, and was critically linked to, the trade agreement. The accompanying North American Agreement on Environmental Cooperation (NAAEC), and the Commission for Environmental Cooperation (CEC) which it created, represent a unique approach to building an international trade–environment regime, and one which has become a model and referent for future regional and multilateral trade liberalization agreements. The NAAEC endowed the CEC with significant new mandatory and permissive powers for environmental surveillance-enforcement, environmental cooperation, and trade–environment integration. It further created an innovative institutional structure composed of a ministerial-level Council, a single regional Secretariat located in Montreal, and a Joint Public Advisory Committee (JPAC) to involve business, environmental non-governmental organizations (ENGOs), and other stakeholders.

During its first three and a half years in operation, the CEC in its enforcement-surveillance and environmental cooperation functions had an autonomous impact in improving environmental quality in North America, in ways that facilitated trade, constrained national and sub-national regulatory protectionism, and promoted regional regulatory convergence at a high environmental level, to the benefit of industry and citizens in all three countries. But in contrast to the principles, norms, and rules embedded in the NAAEC, the CEC had very little impact in directly promoting the integration and equality of the trade and environment communities. This failure, and the further setbacks the CEC suffered in 1997–8, have rendered it unable thus far to realize its full potential to promote the competitive strategies and interests of North American industry.

The advent of the NAFTA on 1 January 1994, its accompanying North American Agreement on Environmental Cooperation (NAAEC), and resulting Commission for Environmental Cooperation (CEC) brought a potentially major change in the historic pattern of Canada–US environmental governance. In the first instance, NAFTA and NAAEC promised to transform a hitherto almost exclusively bilateral relationship into a new trilateral community, by making many issues, processes, and institutions that flourished along the

49th parallel the subject of a new, overarching, trilateral structure (Spencer, Kirton, and Nossal 1982; Swanson 1978). Second, the new CEC, with its single, well-staffed Secretariat and potentially far-reaching powers, provided a new, institutionalized regional centre of political activity for an 'informal' relationship long dependent on ad hoc, transgovernmental problem-solving by functional specialists on each side of the border (Fox, Hero, and Nye 1976). Third, the new CEC was endowed with a comprehensive mandate embracing the full range of environmental issues, and was assigned important trade-related responsibilities. The NAFTA–NAAEC regime thus took the Canada–US environmental relationship into a more integrated, mutually supportive, but potentially conflictual connection with economic subjects, logics, and communities at the centre of the Canada–US relationship in the 1990s (Kirton 1994, 1993). Indeed, the trilateral character, institutional strength, and broad mandate of the CEC suggested that the Canada–US environmental relationship would now importantly and increasingly depend upon how this new, innovative institution would operate in practice.

More than three years after the CEC came into existence, there remains considerable disagreement about its overall potential and actual performance. The first and largest group of observers are the sceptical critics. They argued, during the initial NAFTA debate from 1990 to 1993, that the prospective CEC was inadequate to offset the environmentally destructive effects that NAFTA's far-reaching trade and investment liberalization would bring in throughout North America, particularly in Mexico. Assessments of the CEC's early operation by non-governmental organizations (NGOs) remained critical (Public Citizen 1995). Scholarly observers assert that the CEC is in a weak position and might contribute to effective transboundary environmental management only insofar as its often reluctant or suspicious member governments will support it (Mumme and Duncan 1996). More recently, among the many reviews that accompanied the July 1997 Congressionally mandated Presidential report on NAFTA's performance, there is a widespread view that NAFTA's environmental legacy and the CEC itself have been a disappointment (USTR 1997). The primary concerns are: (1) that the CEC and its companion US–Mexican bilateral institutions, the Border Environmental Cooperation Commission (BECC) and the North American Development Bank (NADBank) have insufficient funds to address the large need for new environmental infrastructure; (2) that the CEC has processed few complaints about its member countries' failure to adequately enforce their environmental laws; and (3) that citizens and ENGOs relative to private sector investors have limited access to NAFTA's institutions (Council on Hemispheric Affairs 1997; Economic Policy Institute 1997; Lustig 1997).

A second group of observers are contingent optimists (Johnson and Beaulieu 1996; Abbott 1996). They judge that the positive environmental impact of the CEC depends on a host of ever-changing factors in its internal organization and broader environment. These internal factors include proper staffing for the Secretariat itself, and its technical expertise, analytic quality, and independent verification of information supplied by governments. The critical factors in the CEC's relationship with national governments are adequate funding levels, the independence of the CEC and its Secretariat, the quality of ministerial participation, the commitment of the parties to the CEC, and the legitimacy of the ministerial Council's recommendations in the view of domestic environmental agencies. Also central are several factors allowing the CEC to develop a supportive constituency beyond national governments, notably, the quality of appointees to the CEC's innovative Joint Public Advisory Committee (JPAC), the latter's relationship to the Council and Secretariat, the links established with the broader environmental community, and the openness, transparency, and proactiveness of the CEC structure.

A third group looks to the CEC with even greater expectation. These integrative enthusiasts suggest that the establishment of the CEC marked a substantial move towards organizational and procedural supranational governance by creating a new centre of political activity and legitimacy in North America (Munton and Kirton 1994; Kirton and Fernandez de Castro 1997; USTR 1997; Weintraub 1997; Sweeney 1997; CEC 1997a). They acknowledge that the CEC's effectiveness will be contingent on robust resources, respected and skilled staff, and the composition of its advisory body. It will also depend on a location in a major centre to allow access to media, scientists, and ENGOs, essential resources for the institution to acquire the scientific credibility, public visibility, and citizen scrutiny necessary to influence the environmental activities of otherwise distracted, cost-conscious member governments. Yet they point to its ability, amidst difficult political circumstances, to attract skilled staff, initiate major and popular programmes of trilateral environmental cooperation, engage on important trade and economic issues, and push the limits of initiative and independence to the point where national governments are uncomfortable on particular matters but still broadly supportive.

This study joins the debate by analysing the composition, operation, and impact of the CEC during its first, formative four years and the changes it has brought to the prevailing regime for Canada–United States environmental governance. It argues that although the CEC was a US-initiated institution accepted with considerable reluctance by Canada and especially Mexico, it has in its early years survived formidable political and financial obstacles, to emerge as a permanent, legitimate, comprehensively active, and increasingly effective centre of North American governance. While its initial compliance concerns and cooperative actions have been focused on Mexico, it is now beginning to have a real impact on environmental activities between and within the United States and Canada, and build a strong rules-based regime that constrains the actions of the member governments. Moreover, it is both deepening its societal and governmental roots and broadening its relevance beyond the North American community to the expanded partnership now being forged with Chile, and prospective members of the Free Trade Agreement of the Americas (FTAA). Although member governments are moving to exert increasingly widespread and detailed intergovernmental control over the Secretariat's operations, this itself is a sign of the professional success, political influence, and broad public and stakeholder support that the institution has developed.

The NAFTA–NAAEC Negotiations

The origins of the CEC can be traced most broadly to the increasing intensity, severity, and scientific and public recognition of trilateral environmental interdependencies and problems in the North American region during the 1990s. Migratory species such as the Monarch butterfly, grey whale, and 250 bird species travelled among or shared a common habitat in Canada, the United States, and Mexico. Pesticides and pollutants banned in Canada and the United States but still legal in Mexico appeared in the Great Lakes, while some feared that US firms might be exporting hazardous wastes to the less regulated environment of Mexico. While these ecological interdependencies within the North American region may themselves have warranted a trilateral body for environmental cooperation, it was the prospect of NAFTA and its extensive trade and investment liberalization that spurred widespread demands for immediate action. The prospect arose that increased trade, investment, and resulting growth would create further stress on environmentally fragile areas, such as the *maquiladoras* in northern Mexico, or the transportation corridors that carried NAFTA trade from Canada, through the United States to Mexico (Rugman 1994; Kirton et al. 1996; Kirton and Soloway 1996). Many were aroused by Ross Perot's charge that Mexico's lesser capacity for effective environmental enforcement would lead US and Canadian industries to be 'sucked' down to 'pollution havens' in Mexico. They would then be free, under NAFTA's rules, to invest and operate as nationals and export their goods barrier-free back into the United States and Canada. Additionally, specialists on environmental–economy linkages, empowered by the epistemology of sustainable development highlighted by the 1992 United Nations Conference on Environment and Development at Rio, pointed to the many ways in which trade and environment concerns were integrally related and could be made mutually reinforcing (Rugman and Kirton 1999; Rugman, Kirton, and Soloway 1997a, 1997b; Vogel and Rugman 1997; Kirton and Richardson 1992).

The emergence of the CEC, and with it a trilateral, supranational, comprehensive regime for Canada–US environmental governance, began with the negotiation of the initial NAFTA (Richardson 1992, 1993; Housman 1994). This process started with a trilateral summit declaration on 9 February 1991, and was concluded by the three governments' trade ministers in Washington,

DC on 12 August 1992. From an environmental perspective, the NAFTA they produced marked a sharp departure from the Canada–US Free Trade Agreement (FTA), which had minimal environmental provisions, and from earlier Canada–US agreements for environmental cooperation, which had addressed only tangentially economic affairs. For NAFTA began, in its preamble, by specifying that the purpose of the trade agreement was, *inter alia*, to 'promote sustainable development', and to 'strengthen the development of environmental laws and regulations'. Moreover, the parties pledged to undertake their 'economic activities in a manner consistent with environmental protection and conservation' (Canada 1992). NAFTA also specified that in cases where its trade and economic provisions conflicted with the obligations of the world's major multilateral environmental agreements—notably the 1973 Convention on Trade in Endangered Species, the 1987 Montreal Protocol on Ozone Depletion, and the 1989 Basel Convention on Hazardous Waste Movement—the latter would prevail. This deference to the concerns of the global ecology over the continental economy was reinforced by the detailed treatment of ecological considerations in many of the more important chapters of the NAFTA text. Chapter 7, on sanitary and phytosanitary standards, enables each NAFTA country to set the level of environmental protection it considers appropriate for agricultural goods. Chapter 9 confers a similar right for standards measures more generally. Chapter 11's Article 1114 prohibits a country from lowering environmental standards or their enforcement in order to increase or maintain investment in its territory. Yet NAFTA's critics raised important questions as to how effectively the new textual commitments would and could be implemented through a NAFTA dispute settlement process that was based almost entirely on trade expertise, with limited provisions for the incorporation of environmental sensitivity, science, and non-governmental groups.

By 17 September 1992 these and other concerns led the environment ministers from Canada, the United States, and Mexico, meeting in Washington, DC, to announce the initiation of negotiations to design an environmental accord to NAFTA and an accompanying trilateral institution (then known as the North American Commission on the Environment, or NACE). The importance of generating a strong environmental side agreement and institution was underscored when Bill Clinton, during his campaign for the presidency, declared on 4 October 1992 his support for a strong North American Commission on the Environment, and repeated his commitment upon his election in November. Capturing the support of American ENGOs was important both for Clinton's electoral success and for the eventual legislative passage of the Republican-initiated NAFTA. Led by the National Wildlife Federation, major American environmental organizations pressed on a number of issues as the price for their support of NAFTA. They wanted an agreement and institution that would lead to an upward harmonization of standards and enforcement in Mexico to US levels; allow for ample public participation and transparency in advice, deliberation, and reporting; and permit the use of trade sanctions to enforce compliance by the parties with their domestic and international environmental obligations. Their core concern was that Mexico's general inability, or apparent unwillingness, to actually enforce its often high national environmental standards would lead to environmental degradation that would harm Americans across the border, inspire US and other industries to locate in Mexico to avoid high compliance costs in the United States, and thus generate political pressure to lower environmental standards and compliance costs to save industry and jobs back home.

These demands inspired resistance from Americans, centred in the Republican Party and business community, who feared that 'their' original NAFTA would now be encumbered by trade sanctions that would contradict its core trade-liberalizing purposes. This would further lead to a large, expensive new trilateral bureaucracy with extensive powers of enforcement and regulation over the private sector. Most Canadians also felt that the introduction of trade sanctions would provide an opportunity for protectionist forces in the United States to overwhelm the legally-guaranteed free access to the US market that Canada already enjoyed under the FTA. This would thus do major economic damage to the export-dependent Canadian economy, for little, if any, environmental gain in Mexico. Sovereignty-sensitive Mexico also felt improvements in its environmental performance depended not on wealth-reducing trade sanctions or threats, but on the economic, technological, and fiscal resources that trade and investment liberalization would bring, supplemented by direct programmes of environmental cooperation.

The North American Agreement on Environmental Cooperation

After a full year of negotiation, led by trade officials, the three countries on 13 September 1993 concluded a final North American Agreement on Environmental Cooperation (Winham 1994). Although the US government had succeeded only partly in securing its initial desire for a powerful, independent body equipped with trade sanctions, the result represented a major advance for institutionalized sustainable development in North America (Canada 1993). Its preamble and objectives, stated in Part I, expressed a commitment to the goals of sustainable development and the 1972 Stockholm and 1992 Rio conferences, and placed a new emphasis on public participation and transparency. Part II listed the general obligations of the parties (in reporting, emergency preparedness, education, science and technology, environmental assessment, and economic instruments), their commitment to high and continuously improving levels of environmental protection, the prompt publication and serious enforcement of environmental laws and regulations, the rights of private persons, and the transparency of domestic legal processes. Part III defined the composition, powers, and procedures of the new CEC. Part

IV set forth the obligation of each party for the prior notification of proposed or actual environmental measures and the prompt provision of relevant information. Part V dealt with the resolution of disputes, through the stages of consultation, initiation of procedures, request for and composition of an arbitral panel, rules of procedure and participation, the preparation of initial and final reports, the implementation of the reports, and the suspension of benefits in the event of non-compliance. Part VI provided general definitions, while Part VII dealt with the coming into force, amendments and accession to, and withdrawal from, the agreement.

As a document designed to allow each of the three governments to mobilize and maintain the support necessary to secure legislative and electoral approval for NAFTA, the agreement was a remarkable success. It allows each country to set and alter its own environmental policies and procedures, but obliges each to provide high levels of protection, to strive for continuous improvements, to promptly publish proposed measures, and to offer where possible advance notification and opportunities for comment. It mandates a process aimed at developing greater compatibility of environmental technical regulations, standards, and conformity assessment procedures, without reducing levels of environmental protection. And it obliges each country to effectively enforce its environmental laws and regulations through national government action, and to ensure that its domestic legal system allows 'interested persons' to pursue alleged violations.

At the core of the agreement is a well-crafted compromise over the critical issue of international enforcement. In cases where one party is alleged to have a persistent pattern of failure to effectively enforce its domestic environmental laws over economic activity involved in or affecting North American trade, international action is possible. Here, when a party initiates a complaint against another party for such a failure, the CEC's ministerial-level Council can establish an international arbitral panel to report, provide a remedial action plan, and, if necessary, levy monetary fines. These fines are limited to US $20 million for any single assessment in the first year, and no more than .007 per cent of the annual total trade in goods between the parties thereafter, with the fines being given to the Commission for use in environmental remediation in the violating country. In the event that such fines are not paid, the agreement gives the United States the ultimate power to impose trade sanctions on Mexico, and vice versa, in the event of a 'persistent pattern' of domestic non-compliance and enforcement. Canada succeeded in avoiding such a threat by allowing its international compliance obligations to be enforced through its domestic judicial process.

Together, the package promised to maintain the scope for economic gain, minimize the potential for protectionist distortions, and raise the record of actual environmental compliance and performance in Mexico, Canada, and the United States. International trade-restricting action for environmental purposes is limited to cases of a persistent pattern of environmental non-compliance. It comes at the end of a long process of government-initiated complaint, consultation, arbitration by an expert panel, creation of an implementation plan, and relatively modest monetary fines. Moreover the threat of trade sanction applies to only two of the three NAFTA parties, and leaves the world's largest two-way trading relationship—that across the Canada–US border—untouched. At the same time, environmentalists have secured a layered network of voluntary compliance, fines, and ultimately trade and domestic judicial remedies to ensure compliance, with the revenues raised devoted directly to correcting the environmental offence.

The agreement also injected significant additional environmental sensitivity and expertise into the trade dispute settlement mechanisms of the NAFTA itself. Article 10.6 directs that the Council 'shall cooperate with the NAFTA Free Trade Commission' to achieve that agreement's environmental purposes, by receiving comments from ENGOs, by assisting in Article 1114 consultations over alleged 'pollution-haven' investment encouragement, by making recommendations and identifying experts for all NAFTA bodies, and, most broadly, by 'considering on an ongoing basis the environmental effects of the NAFTA'. Although this is a formidable array of mandatory functions, the initiative for accomplishing such enhanced environmental activity in the trade arena still rests substantially with the NAFTA Free Trade Commission (FTC), and the trade policy community that controls it.

Beyond environmental standards, enforcement, and the settlement of trade disputes lay the tasks of environmental cooperation. The agreement, in Article 2, mandates the parties, with respect to their own territory, to report on the state of the environment, develop environmental emergency preparedness measures, promote education, scientific research, technology development, and economic instruments, and assess environmental impacts. It specifies that the Council 'shall' promote and facilitate environmental cooperation, exchange of information, technical cooperation, and develop recommendations for public access to information, appropriate limits for specific pollutants, and environmental impact assessment of projects with transborder effects (Article 10.3–5, 7). It also specifies that the Council 'may' consider and develop recommendations on nineteen specific subjects, including those aimed at strengthening the role of environmental considerations in national and trilateral economic activity. Under Article 9 of the NAAEC, the Council, as CEC's governing body, oversees all CEC operations.

With such a broad array of standards setting, enforcement, trade dispute, and environmental cooperation functions, of both a mandatory and discretionary kind, the effect of the agreement depended critically on the resources made available to, and the operation of the new CEC. This body was deliberately born as a minimum framework or platform, to be developed and shaped as environmental demands and political pressures evolved in future years. Yet in its essential architecture the new body represented a major advance on previous, all bilateral, environmentally relevant institutions on the North American continent.

The CEC Structure

The CEC has a threefold institutional structure: a ministerial-level Council as the governing body; a single Secretariat (located in Montreal) for technical, administrative, and operational support; and a 15-member multi-stakeholder Joint Public Advisory Committee (JPAC) to advise the Council on any matter within the scope of the Agreement. There also exists provision for a National Advisory Committee (NAC) and a Government Advisory Committee (GAC) within each of the three countries. Finally, under NAAEC Article 9.5(a), the CEC's Council may establish standing committees, working groups, or expert groups as it deems appropriate.

The Council

At the institutional apex stands the 'Council', which is, at a minimum, an annual meeting of the cabinet-level or 'equivalent representatives' of the three countries. It should not, like so many Canada–US joint ministerial committees before it, wither away due to lack of interest or political changes at the top of national governments. While it is possible that it may be relegated to junior cabinet ministers or other functionaries (including political appointees along the lines of the International Joint Commission (ICJ)), the 'equivalent representatives' provision enables an expansion to include additional ministers from the economic as well as natural resource and environmental domains, or even a linkage to meetings of leaders themselves.

Affirming the single character of the CEC's Council, and endowing it with genuine if modest supranational characteristics, are the provision for two-thirds majority voting among the three country participants on several important procedural issues. Although the Council will normally operate by consensus, and thus empower each of the three countries with a veto, the Council moves from pure national control to supranational constraint in several areas. Most notably the national veto is removed as only a two-thirds majority is required to instruct the Secretariat to prepare a factual record on allegations of non-compliance made by non-governmental organizations (Article 15.2); to make the final factual record public (Article 15.7); to make a factual record available to the JPAC (Article 16.7); to prevent the Secretariat requesting information from a party (Article 21.2); to make public Council recommendations to parties about the resolution of a dispute (Article 23.4); and to convene an arbitral panel to consider an alleged persistent pattern of enforcement failure (Article 24.1). In addition, in areas where the Secretariat takes the initiative, the individual national veto is also removed, as the Council must mobilize a two-thirds majority vote to reject appointments to the Secretariat proposed by the Executive Director (Article 11.3), and to prevent the Secretariat from preparing a report 'on any other environmental matter related to the co-operative functions of this Agreement' (excluding cases of alleged non-enforcement) (Article 13.1).

For a United States which has long resisted international organizational constraints on its sovereign prerogatives, and for a United States–Canadian relationship that has long avoided formal international organization, the NAFTA institutions represent a significant departure. These provisions allowed for the possibility that a future US government deemed unsympathetic to environmental concerns (as during President Reagan's first term) could itself be outvoted by a Canadian–Mexican majority. They were primarily motivated, however, by a desire to remove a Mexican government veto over the effective environmental enforcement of national environmental laws and to ensure the open decision-making cherished by US ENGOs. Such a scenario is politically conceivable if such a Canadian–Mexican majority were supported by significant ENGOs, publics, and legislators in the United States. However, it is more likely that any prospective Canadian–Mexican majority would be exercised in the direction of supporting national prerogatives and governmental discretion, given the even greater sensitivity about sovereignty and the less-developed network of ENGOs in the two smaller NAFTA countries. It is also likely that all three governments will accept an implicit mutual non-aggression pact, and be reluctant to launch enforcement investigations against one another for fear that their partners will retaliate by launching similarly embarrassing investigations against them. Finally, any government that feels itself consistently outvoted or otherwise discriminated against retains the ability to curtail the operation of the CEC by reducing or withholding financial support. The agreement specifies that each party shall contribute an unspecified but equal share of the annual budget of the Commission 'subject to the availability of appropriated funds in accordance with the Party's legal procedures' (Article 43).

In practice, the operation of the Council has indicated that the CEC is being given the active ministerial-level support and guidance it requires, is manifesting the first signs of procedural supranationalism, and is moving towards the balanced trilateralism that reduces the prospects of the body being, as in 1992–3, a project and instrument of the United States. The Council moved swiftly into operation, holding its first meeting on 23 March 1994, in Washington, DC. The second was held in October 1995, in Oaxaca, Mexico, the third in July 1996 in Toronto, and the fourth in June 1997 in Pittsburgh. Thus, in contrast to their trade ministerial colleagues on NAFTA's Free Trade Commission (who missed their annual meeting in 1996), the environment ministers have met annually for the first four years. Only for their June 1997 meeting in Pittsburgh did a Canadian election and an imminent vote on environmental protection in the US Congress lead Canada's Minister of the Environment and the US EPA Administrator, respectively, to send substitutes.

By the time of its third ministerial Council meeting, held in Toronto on 31 July–1 August 1996, there were signs that the Council was beginning to take an aggressive approach on the ambitious question of integrating and balancing environment and trade concerns. The Council placed the task of forging an equal, integrated trade–environment linkage in the interests of sustainable development at the forefront of the CEC's priorities. Canadian environment minister Sergio Marchi personally pledged that trade liberalization remain linked to environmental cooperation. EPA Administrator Carol Browner included trade among her priorities for a more focused CEC agenda. Mexican environment secretary Julia Carabias noted that trade problems could not be allowed to place pressures on projects at the expense of the environment. The JPAC also called for more attention to the trade–environment issue. The Council concluded by calling, in its communiqué, for a meeting with NAFTA's trade ministers to discuss shared concerns (CEC 1996b). Most importantly, the Council recognized the expansive, extra-regional implications of their trade–environment work. Looking ahead to a Canada–Chile bilateral free trade agreement and subsequent Chilean accession to NAFTA, representatives from Chile participated as observers in the public meetings (but not in camera Council session). Some Council ministers underscored the importance of the CEC in ensuring North American solidarity in the councils of the world. All three ministers agreed in their final communiqué on the need to contribute to the trade–environment debate in the World Trade Organization (WTO) in the lead-up to its ministerial meeting in December 1996.

The Ministers at Toronto also stressed their desire for a more focused agenda. Their approval of new priorities meant a budget reallocation of US $1.5 million (of the US $9 million annual budget) with US $0.5 coming from administrative expenses and US $1 million from programme areas. It was left to the Secretariat to determine what was to be cut. Over the following year, the Secretariat responded to the Council's direction by almost halving the number of projects, from 26 in 1996 to only 15 in 1997. The CEC's Strategic Programme thus came to concentrate on five areas: environmental conservation; environmental protection; environment, trade, and economy; enforcement cooperation and law; and information and public outreach (CEC 1997b).

In the year following Toronto, there were also clear signs that a more balanced, trilateral partnership was beginning to emerge. These patterns were evident in the CEC's actions regarding environmental compliance. At Toronto, the CEC Council authorized, with public unanimity, a factual investigation of the actions of the Mexican authorities in constructing a pier and supporting port infrastructure in Cozumel allegedly without adequate environmental assessment. Such a decision was strongly resisted, at all levels, in Mexico, whose representatives argued that construction had taken place before the NAFTA and NAAEC took effect. In contrast, requests by American NGOs for similar actions against the US government had previously been rejected. Although there were good legal grounds for so doing, there arose an appearance that the CEC's investigatory powers were being deployed exclusively against Mexico.

A review of the overall record, however, indicates that the CEC investigatory mechanisms have acquired substantial trilateral balance. As of July 1997, two Secretariat Article 13 reports (which the Council could stop by a two-thirds vote within thirty days) had been completed. While the first, concerning the death of birds at the Silva Reservoir, focused on Mexico, the report found no evidence that Mexico's poor environmental practices were responsible for the deaths. The second report, dealing with the long-range transport of air pollutants, equally embraced all three countries.

The Article 14–15 process, which allows any NGO, business, or person to complain that a party is failing to enforce its environmental laws, has also become balanced. In its first three years, the Secretariat received ten such submissions, of which three dealt with the United States, two with Mexico, and five with Canada. In its first year, both cases came from the United States, and were terminated by the Secretariat on the grounds that the CEC lacked the legal authority to proceed. Of the four cases filed in 1996, the Secretariat terminated the two dealing with Canada, converted the one dealing with the United States into an Article 13 inquiry, and proceeded with the Mexican Cozumel case, with a report expected in August 1997. Of the four cases (three Canadian and one Mexican) submitted in the first half of 1997, the CEC is proceeding with one, dealing with hydroelectric dams in British Columbia. Canada thus seems likely to join Mexico as the subject of Article 14–15 scrutiny. While the United States appears to be the great beneficiary, having escaped CEC investigation thus far despite its active array of ENGOs, it must be recalled that the Article 14–15 process remains critically dependent on the actual enforcement performance of governments within each country, in relation to the real but restricted legal powers invested in the CEC.

In the broader, more policy-sensitive area, of trade–environment linkages, however, trilateralism has been slower to emerge. A de facto United States–Canadian partnership within the CEC was evident at the Council meeting in Toronto, where the United States and Canada were visibly more enthusiastic and ambitious than Mexico in their conception of the CEC's trade and environment work. Mexican caution continued to be apparent in the following year, over the CEC's project to develop a framework to monitor NAFTA's Environmental Effects (DePalma 1997).

The Secretariat

The CEC marks the advent not only of trilateralization but also of genuine international organization in North America. For the CEC Secretariat is not an assemblage of national sections periodically coming together as a joint institution (as with the IJC), nor a co-located and integrated command headquarters (as with the North American Aerospace Defence Command) but a single permanent trilateral organization. It features an overall Executive Director, a common bureaucratic staff (the Secretariat) in one location (in Montreal). Although the Council is a small body that will rely overwhelmingly and overtly on consensus decision-making, the presence of a permanent Secretariat, aided by JPAC, and the numerous requirements for publicity will ensure that the CEC does not easily become the full captive of national governments. The Secretariat is to be and has been recruited on the basis of merit, not to receive instructions from any external authority other than the Council, and to issue a public report on the activities under the agreement, including the state of the environment in the territories of the parties. It also has considerable investigatory powers. It can under Article 13 initiate investigations on any matter within its very comprehensive workplan or related to its cooperative function and these investigations can be stopped only if two of the three Council members object within 30 days. It also, under Article 14–15, decides which complaints of non-enforcement from societal actors it will recommend to the Council for action, in the form of the preparation of a factual record.

The Secretariat is mandated to provide technical, administrative, and operational support to the Council and to committees and groups established by the Council. There are about 50 full-time employees. A budget of US $9,942,000 was approved for 1997, contributed equally to by the members (CEC 1997b: 91). Although this makes the CEC Secretariat much larger than its sister NAFTA institutions, the Commission for Labor Cooperation (CLC) in Dallas and the Secretariat of the FTC which was established in Mexico City in autumn 1997, its budget remains substantially smaller than was initially envisaged. Indeed, Congress in its NAFTA implementing legislation authorized an initial US contribution of US $5 million for fiscal year 1995, in anticipation of an overall CEC budget of US $15 million by that time (US 1994: 25). The need for expanded funding has been enhanced by the major expansion of CEC activities since 1994, and by the diversion of US $1,600,000 (in 1997) to fund a responsive North American Fund for Environmental Cooperation established by the Council in 1995. Yet Mexico and Canada, beleaguered by the 1994–5 economic crisis and the 1995 severe reductions to Environment Canada's budgets, respectively, have been unwilling to authorize an increase thus far.

In establishing its organization and mounting its operations, the CEC has moved faster than the other NAFTA-related organizations, in part because it was the first to select the Secretariat's Executive Director. The professional background of its three senior officials, in government service, legal practice, and the management of a scientifically-oriented ENGO, reinforce the Secretariat's ability to acquire the credibility it requires among its many constituencies.

The autonomous political impact of the Secretariat is limited by the fact that it is formally assigned no policy advisory responsibilities, and is designed primarily as an international public utility to lower transaction costs among the parties for arranging meetings, preparing and translating documents, implementing Council decisions, and receiving complaints. But, in addition to its scientific and legal expertise regarding the Article 13 and 14–15 processes, it has available and has effectively employed several instruments of influence. One is the scientific credibility it has commanded and the broader support base and epistemic community it is fostering through the many expert groups, study teams, and consultations it has created during its first three years. The second is its contribution to concrete progress on environmental priorities of governments and publics, such as its role in creating regional action plans to reduce and perhaps eventually eliminate from North America harmful pesticides and chemicals, notably PCBs, DDT, chlorodane, and, prospectively, human-caused releases of mercury (CEC 1997*d*).

A third area flows from the Secretariat's development of a modern, common, and harmonized statistical base for measuring the environmental performance of the three parties. This apparently technical activity has long represented a core part of the real political power that international organizations can deploy (Strange 1996). A Secretariat report comparing pollutant releases across North American industry, released in July 1997, attracted widespread media attention for its central finding that the US jurisdictions of Texas and Tennessee, and Canada's largest province, Ontario, have the worst environment performance, based on 1994 data (CEC 1997*c*). Mexico, lacking the data required for its inclusion in the study, escaped critical attention. The Secretariat's display of relatively autonomous statistical power was thus further evidence of the move to trilateral balance, rather than a use of international organization for the benefit of the most powerful United States.

The autonomy of the Secretariat can be evaluated only in the context of the trend for national governments to become much more frequently engaged, in much more detail, with the Secretariat's operation, in the intervals between the annual ministerial meetings of the Council itself. The CEC soon created an intergovernmental body of Alternative Representatives or 'Alternates' to the ministers, at the Assistant Secretary-level, to manage the work of the CEC and its Secretariat. The Alternates now meet monthly, in person or by conference call, with the pace of their meetings growing from two in 1994 and five in 1995 to 11 in 1996. They are assisted by a lower-level General Standing Committee, which meets twice as frequently (for example 21 times in 1995 and 24 times in 1996, not including participation at the project level) (CEC 1997*a*).

A further sign of the intergovernmentalization of the CEC, from its potential architecture as an autonomous Secretariat receiving instructions only annually from the ministerial-level Council, is the emergence of several Working Groups to provide direction and assistance in specific programme or project areas. Such Working Groups have currently emerged to deal with the conservation of North American birds, the sound management of chemicals, transboundary environmental impact assessment, environmental enforcement and compliance, wildlife enforcement, and, by late 1997, trade and environment. In addition, CEC project teams are instructed to work with intergovernmental bodies such as the trilateral Committee for Wildlife and Ecosystem Conservation and Management, the Technical Working Group on Pesticides, and a team of experts drawn from governments on new approaches for improving environmental performance (CEC 1997*b*).

It is tempting, but premature to identify this trend as indicating in all or most cases an intergovernmental 'capture' or 'micromanagement' of an otherwise autonomous CEC by national governments. Despite the practical burdens it places on limited Secretariat resources, such detailed governmental engagement can, at least over time, lead to greater understanding of, and support for Secretariat activities within national governments. Government resources can supplement those of the CEC to permit a more ambitious programme than would otherwise be possible. Government officials can learn and adjust as well as instruct and direct. A healthy tension between governmental and Secretariat perspectives on the same issue can lead to policy improvement and innovation. More complex coalitions may emerge, with the Secretariat entering as a fourth actor to break deadlocks among the three governments. And because two such intergovernmentalized processes, for birds and new approaches for improving environmental compliance, include NGOs and business as part of the process, more complex coalitions and broader support may emerge. At a minimum, the intensification of governmental interest in the Secretariat's detailed activities is eloquent testimony to the present and potential influence and political relevance the body has acquired.

JPAC

The CEC structure also contains, as its third major component, an innovative, 15-member Joint Public Advisory Committee, conceived as a single trinational body rather than three national sections meeting together. Its role is to ensure citizens of the three countries contribute strongly to the efficient execution of the CEC work and mandate. JPAC is to meet at least once a year, at the time of the regular session of the Council, which is obliged under Article 8.4 to hold a public meeting. It may also convene at its members' discretion. The JPAC may advise the Council on any matter within the scope of the agreement. It is entitled to review the Commission's annual programme, budget, report, and any Secretariat reports on other environmental matters. It can also provide technical information to the Secretariat.

These requirements, and the public participation and reporting provisions elsewhere in the NAAEC, make it possible for the CEC to become an important centre of political activity, agenda setting, and legitimacy on North American environmental matters, in ways that the national governments will find it difficult to ignore. Its prospects for so doing were heightened by the composition of the initial appointments to JPAC, which included strong representation from the business community, as well as the ENGO, and aboriginal communities.

Moreover, JPAC has proven to be very active. By June 1997 JPAC had met 14 times, four of which were in connection with the annual Council. JPAC provided advice to the Council seven times in 1995 and ten times in 1996 on a wide range of issues, as well as receiving instructions from the Council on how JPAC activities should be focused.

JPAC's members have proven to be ambitious in their conception of the CEC's agenda and work programme, and strongly supportive of the involvement of the CEC in trade–environment issues. Equally importantly, in 1996 and 1997 a total of 805 individuals had attended JPAC consultations, with 240 coming from NGOs, 162 from industry, 219 from government, and 184 in their individual capacity (CEC 1997a: 23). JPAC has thus done much to broaden, in number of actors and multisectoral breadth, the base of CEC engagement and support.

In addition to the trinational JPAC, each member country was empowered by the NAAEC to create a National Advisory Committee (NAC) that advises their Commission member on CEC matters. The United States established its 14-member NAC in September 1995. Canada created its 6-member NAC in August 1996. Mexico followed a different model, assigning its NAC responsibilities to the six senior members of its five regional sustainable development councils that together comprise its National Consultative Committee for Sustainable Development. There is also a parallel structure of Government Advisory Committees (GACs) within each country. It remains to be seen whether these NACs and GACs will provide deeper support for the CEC within each country, provide a further drain on limited CEC resources, or serve as vehicles of intergovernmental capture.

The CEC–NAFTA Institutions Relationship

Of particular importance in determining the effectiveness of the CEC is the ambitiousness, intensity, and influence with which it addresses the broad, vital economic dimensions of its mandate and pursues its overall sustainable development objectives. Here a critical challenge is the relationship the CEC develops with the NAFTA Trade Commission, both at the level of its ministerial Council, and with the 50 or so official-level bodies created or inspired by the NAFTA agreements (Kirton and Fernandez de Castro 1997; Weintraub 1997). This is especially true in regard to those two dozen or so Trade Commission and other trilateral, intergovernmental economic bodies with explicit environmentally related provisions or direct environmental impacts within their mandate.

The relationship between the CEC and NAFTA's economic institutions is just beginning to develop, with both bodies at the ministerial level recognizing the importance of the interconnected agendas, asking for a joint meeting, but proving unable thus far to mount such an event. At its first meeting in 1994 NAFTA's FTC reviewed its relationship with the CEC and agreed to try to meet in 1994 with its CEC ministerial counterpart to achieve the highest possible level of coordination. At its 1995 meeting, the trade ministers again discussed the relationship among the three NAFTA Commissions. At the initiative of Canada's Roy Maclaren, who chaired the meeting, they asked for a report from their ministerial counterparts in the CEC Council on how the environmental agreement and CEC workplan was in support of the NAFTA. The request arose from a feeling in some areas of the trade community that the CEC Secretariat, under its Executive Director, was becoming too independent of governments. In general though, the trade ministers were not particularly suspicious of the CEC. During the first few years of NAFTA, the CEC's ministers had had little relationship with the trade ministers and trade policy. Their request stemmed not from a real concern, but a recognition that the institutions established by the accompanying agreements were enjoined to be supportive of NAFTA. The trade ministers wished to know how their environmental colleagues interpreted NAFTA's Article 104, the legal clause which deals with the relationship of the accompanying agreements to NAFTA. They asked for a report to determine if the CEC and CLC had the same perspective as the FTC on the interpretation of NAFTA's Chapter 1 objectives as specified in Article 102. The trade ministers wished their environmental colleagues to explain how they were putting the relevant clause in their agreement into operation. As part of this process, the trade policy community asked what elements of the CEC work programme related to NAFTA, recognizing that the CEC's ministers, belonging to a free-standing institution, were free to pursue their own interpretation of the agreement. The trade ministers also asked for a report from the CEC Council on how the environmental agreement was supporting NAFTA.

At their 1996 meeting in Toronto, the CEC ministers reciprocated the interest and invitation. They asked for a joint meeting with their trade counterparts to review North America's experience in trade and environment policy integration. By the summer of 1997, however, no such joint ministerial gathering had taken place.

At the official level, there was also very little early contact between the CEC and those involved in NAFTA's economic institutions. The CEC itself had moved from the start to implement in an ambitious fashion all of its trade-related responsibilites. Indeed, it placed the trade and environment link at the centre of its organizational culture and priorities, taking as its mission statement the following charge: 'The CEC facilitates cooperation and public participation to foster conservation, protection and enhancement of the North American environment for the benefit of present and future generations, in the context of increasing economic, trade and social links between Canada, Mexico and the United States' (CEC 1997b: 101). Yet a trade–environment dialogue proved slow to emerge.

In part the early isolation of the two communities flowed from the preoccupation of each with developing its own institutions, priorities, and work programmes, and the slow start which each has experienced in varying degrees. In part it derived from the absence within the trade community of a single trinational Secretariat able to mount a dialogue at the Secretariat level with the CEC. And it also stemmed from the absence within each national capital of a single NAFTA coordinative centre with an overview of the activities of all the Trade Commission and other trilateral institutions and able to mount a trade–environment dialogue at the national level.

In such a situation, it was easy for a lack of communication to breed a lack of awareness of cooperative opportunities and an absence of trust. Yet even in those early years members of the trade community could identify several ways in which the CEC's work was or could be of benefit. More generally, there was a considerable understanding of the way environmentally enhancing cooperation could assist the trade and industry community by providing a single set of rules that made trade easier and less expensive, by producing a single testing system that reduced costs to all three federal governments, and by supporting distinctively North American interests in broader regional forums.

More recently, the trade–environment dialogue has been strengthened, as co-ordinative centres and consultative processes have developed within the respective national capitals. Contributing to this national-level dialogue, and raising it to the international level, was the emergence in the late spring of 1997 of a forum within which trade and environment officials from the three countries engaged with the experts in the CEC's study team on NAFTA's environmental effects. Although this development was a sign of the potential importance of the CEC's work on NAFTA's trade impact, the emergence of a truly integrated and balanced trade–environment engagement depended critically on the relationship the CEC Secretariat would forge with its FTC counterpart, when the latter established its single Secretariat in late 1997.

Deepening and Broadening

The growing strength of the CEC during its first three and a half years is also evident in the broadening and deepening of the institution. During the negotiations, Canada had crafted an accession clause that envisaged the NAFTA, NAAEC, and CEC admitting additional members, and from countries not necessarily restricted to the Western Hemisphere. The prospect of a rapid broadening decreased when the US Congress refused to give President Clinton the fast track authority necessary to negotiate Chilean accession. The stalemate continued after the 1996 presidential election as the Republican majority appeared reluctant to offer the authority for a parallel environmental and labour accord that the administration insisted was vital. Canada proceeded to negotiate its own, bilateral but NAFTA-compatible free trade agreement with Chile. In the first half of these negotiations, the Canadians were not insisting on provisions comparable to those of the NAAEC. But the advent of a new trade minister in Canada resulted in such a demand being added to the Canadian list. Thus, the bilateral Canada–Chilean agreement, announced in November 1996, represented the first real broadening of the NAAEC model, and thus the relevance of the CEC. It remains to be seen whether the momentum will continue through the quadrilateralization of NAFTA during the second Clinton administration, and the extension of the NAAEC provisions into the free trade processes under way in the FTAA and the APEC. The May 1997 identification by APEC trade ministers of the environmental products and services industry as an early candidate for liberalization suggests that the APEC process may be ripe for a trade–environment integration that it has refused to take up to date.

On both trade–environment and more environmentally specific subjects, much of the CEC's work has come to be conducted with a conscious focus on how it can influence broader international forums, either as a means of asserting distinctive North American regional interests within them, or leading to the construction of a more multilateral regime. Such ambitions are clearly evident in the CEC's desire to display leadership on the reduction and phase-out of chemicals of global concern, to have its North American Pollutant Release Inventory serve as a model for other areas of the world, to encourage trade–economic–environmental compatibility between North America and other trading regimes, and to increase environmental technology exports to the Americas (CEC 1997b).

There are also some limited signs that an institutional deepening of the NAAEC is underway. As an estimated 75 per cent of the responsibility for environmental protection in Canada rests with provincial governments, it is important, both for the application of the CEC's enforcement powers and politically for the legitimacy its acquires, for Canadian provincial governments to accede to the agreement. Alberta did so at an early stage. Quebec, where the CEC headquarters is housed, did so in the summer of 1996. Other interested jurisdictions, such as Manitoba and Nova Scotia, have been deterred by the practical cost of reviewing and revising their existing environmental laws. However Canada's remaining provinces, including dominant Ontario and British Columbia, show few signs of wishing to accede. And the CEC is not reported as being involved in any of the 103 linkages between Canadian provinces and US states on environmental matters operating in 1995 nor in the 649 such linkages covering all issue areas in the same year (Munton and Kirton 1996; Kirton and Munton 1996).

Conclusion

In conclusion, during its first three years the CEC has made substantial progress in adding to environmental governance, a trilateral rather than bilateral regime, a de facto supranational rather than merely international process, and a single centre with a comprehensive mandate embracing trade and economic concerns. Its moves in these directions, while still limited, acquire significance in the context of the formidable obstacles the nascent institution has faced. In the first instance, the CEC, and the broader NAFTA environmental regime was the product less of any fundamental enduring commitment to environmental values on the part of the three governments in North America, than of a temporary need of a Republican and then Democratic President to secure sufficient domestic support to ensure legislative passage of a historic free trade agreement. Slow growth rates and persistent employment insecurity, particularly in Canada, and a strong emphasis on fiscal reduction have meant a major decrease in environmental priorities and budgets since the peak of the Rio conference in June 1992.

Thus, it is hardly surprising that three and a half years after the CEC was founded, there remains little of the widespread enthusiasm and energetic, often unrestrained, optimism that surrounded its birth. The genuine innovations within the NAFTA–NAAEC–CEC architecture, in bringing trilateralism and regional international organization to North America and a more integrated, balanced trade environment regime to the world could not be realized rapidly and robustly in practice as the moment of political creation passed into routine operation focused on complex environmental challenges. Nor were the rhetorically appealing promises made by President Clinton and his American allies to ensure NAFTA's passage capable of being quickly fulfilled, especially amidst the Mexican economic crisis of 1995 and the severe reduction in environmental budgets of governments in the United States and Canada from 1994 onward. Yet against the century-long established pattern of Canada–US environmental governance, as well as historic US–Mexican suspicion and Canadian–Mexican benign mutual ignorance, there are clear grounds to move beyond contingent optimism about the CEC's autonomous contribution into a confident if cautious form of integrative enthusiasm.

It is clear that during its first three and a half years the CEC has brought trilateralism in an intense and permanent way to North America and to Canada–US environmental governance. The regular annual ministerial-level meetings of the Council, the creation of dozens of intergovernmental Working Groups and experts groups, and numerous consultations through JPAC have, along with the Secretariat and JPAC, created a dense, multi-layered web of new trilateral activity. This new activity has embraced national politicians, civil servants, influential societal actors, and individual citizens. In the realm of enforcement, the initiation of Article 13 and 14–15 investigations, and the absence of Article 23–24 intergovernmental enforcement actions and sanctions show that from the start, the CEC has not been an instrument for the United States to single out Mexico. The United States has thus not benefited from a poorer partner forced to pay the price for American political preferences and economic interests. And in the area of environmental cooperation, through the power of statistical comparison and publicity, the July 1997 North American Pollutant Release Inventory (NAPRI) report and the public reaction to it suggests that it is the United States and Canada that are being singled out and constrained. Only in the core, increasingly high policy area of trade and economic linkages does US enthusiasm and Canadian commitment meet a Mexican caution, exacerbated by the severe economic crisis experienced in the latter country in 1995.

It is also clear that the CEC has emerged as a respected, professional, and effective organization, with its Secretariat making skilful use of its limited resources to exercise autonomous influence to which occasionally reluctant or resistant national governments adjust. The professional staff in the Secretariat have succeeded in engaging a broad constituency of experts in the CEC's work, which, together with JPAC consultations, have increased the visibility and credibility of, and supporting constituency for the CEC's increasingly focused but still comprehensive work. Although there is a growing need for expanded funding, the CEC has maintained its funding levels in the face of severe budgetary reductions within national environmental agencies. In the realm of enforcement, the Lake Silva and Cozumel cases in particular, and the broader pattern of Article 13 and 14–15 activities indicate that the often hidden influence of procedural supranationalism, through the two-thirds majority voting provisions and powers of Secretariat initiation and legal screening, is proving effective. The Secretariat's use of autonomous scientific and statistical power was evident in the case of NAPRI. Although the absence of intergovernmental enforcement action points to a mutual non-aggression pact that has disappointed some, the limited time that has passed, the severe economic crisis in Mexico in 1995, and the very cooperative capacity building and deterrent powers of the CEC make it likely that any persistent pattern of non-enforcement by national governments has lessened since 1993. And the intensification of intergovernmental engagement is evidence both of the Secretariat's growing demonstrated and potential usefulness and influence, and of its relevance as a forum for building a constituency as well as being captured and constrained.

It is also firmly evident that the CEC is acquiring a more expansive relevance by fostering more integrated and balanced trade–environment decision-making, by seeking to broaden its influence to other jurisdictions, and by very slowly deepening the engagement of subfederal governments within North America in its activities. It has moved quickly, comprehensively and aggressively on its trade–environment responsibilities, reached a balanced standoff at the ministerial level with its FTC counterpart, and is beginning to engage intensively with the government trade community within national capitals and through a new CEC forum for trade and environment officials. The prospect of dialogue at the inter-Secretariat level has moved closer with plans for the autumn 1997 creation of the FTC. The CEC has involved Chile in its activities, and consciously designed its activities to achieve results in broader multilateral fora. Also it is slowly beginning to engage North American state and provincial governments, through the accession of some Canadian provincial governments to its Agreement.

Taken together, the CEC's first three and a half years have been a crucial time of initial testing, growth, and development, made all the more difficult by the lingering euphoria of the birth experience and the political assault on environmentalism in the United States and Canada in the mid-1990s. But through this difficult period the CEC has not only survived but thrived. Its

112 *Complex Institutional Responsiveness*

advocates and analysts alike can anticipate strengthened grounds for their understandably sober enthusiasm to grow in the years ahead.

As the CEC moved through the fourth and into its fifth year of operation, it was sobriety rather than enthusiasm that dominated the assessment of the CEC. The slow emergence of the CEC as an autonomous regional regime promoting sustainable development continued, as its record in surveillance-enforcement and environmental cooperation demonstrates. Yet powerful resistance from national governments emasculated the CEC's modest moves in forwarding trade–environment integration and equality, threatened to destroy the professional capacity and reputation of the Secretariat, and called into question the willingness of the three governments to respect the NAAEC they had signed a few years earlier. The unprecedentedly severe setbacks of 1997–8 flowed not only from the traditional sources of resistance in Mexico's trade ministry and the industries allied with them. They came also from new assaults by industry sector's departments in national governments in all three countries, and from the political weakness of trade liberalizers and environmental protectors in the United States operating amidst a pervasive, populist antipathy towards NAFTA in that country. Such setbacks added new complexities to the calculations of a corporate community that was just beginning to acquire confidence that the CEC could be a useful component of their corporate strategy, and that was starting to acquire competence in making the CEC mechanisms work for them.

As the CEC approached its fifth anniversary, the patterns set in its first three and a half years continued most clearly in the area of surveillance-enforcement. A third Article 13 case, initiated in the autumn of 1997, concerned the protection of the San Pedro Conservation area along Arizona's border with Mexico, a key riparian area which migratory birds used as a resting stop every winter. By placing the United States and Mexico under scrutiny in a case involving a core trilateral ecological intervulnerability (given that the birds migrated in part from Canada), the case furthered the non-hegemonic and pro-environment impact of the CEC.

Similarly, the six new Article 14–15 cases filed in 1997–8 showed a steadily escalating use of the CEC process, which had attracted only ten such cases in the CEC's first full three and a half years of operation. Of these six cases, three were filed against Mexico, two against Canada, and one against the United States, a pattern which shows an equalization of scrutiny, if one with a continuing hegemonic bias. Of the six cases, however, only one as of July 1998 was judged worthy by the Secretariat to be sent forward for a response from the Canadian government.

There were similar incremental advances in the realm of environmental cooperation. Perhaps the most notable was the CEC Secretariat's role in creating regional action plans to reduce and eventually eliminate harmful pesticides and chemicals, notably DDT, PCBs, chlorodane, and, prospectively, human-caused releases of mercury (CEC 1997d). Differences in substantive preferences were evident, as participants sponsored by the CEC Secretariat sought a full elimination of such chemicals while those from the governmental community sought a substantial reduction. The equalization of outcomes across the preferences of the three countries was evident.

Yet in the realm of trade–environment integration, the modest advances of the early years were in danger of being destroyed. Although the NAAEC specified a mandatory obligation for the CEC to assess on an ongoing basis NAFTA's environmental effects, pressure from Mexico's trade ministry succeeded in denying funding for the implementing project for the first half of 1997, and denying it adequate funding to proceed with new work in 1998.

These setbacks came amidst the autumn 1997 denial by the US Congress of the fast track authority President Clinton needed to negotiate the FTAA, the reluctance of many US ENGOs to support fast track without a guarantee that an environment side accord would be negotiated as part of any trade agreement, and a pervasive antipathy among many US Congressmen, interest groups, and their supporters towards NAFTA. Public opinion polls indicated majority support among the US public for NAFTA and the gains for US business flowing from the Agreement were impressive. Consequently, the defeat of fast track and the broader reversal for the CEC can be seen as a policy-level case where the new coalition of the internationally oriented US business community and those US ENGOs, conscious of an inherent ecological intervulnerability, temporarily failed to prevail. It also suggested that US business as a whole was still in the early stages of discovering how the new NAFTA institutions and a strong CEC could serve as an innovative instrument to advance their corporate economic and ecological concerns.

7
Firm Responses to Trade and Environment Regulation

Traditionally, environmental regulatory barriers have posed a specific set of threats which restrict the strategies of firms engaged in international business. The classic threat is from foreign environmental regulations that deny access to the large, lucrative export markets. Such regulatory barriers have been particularly formidable when they moved to ever higher levels, were backed by powerful coalitions of protectionist industries and environmental groups in the foreign market, and administered by a trade dispute system in large national governments over which outside firms from smaller countries had little control. In such situations, as the UHT case indicates, the time and expense of litigation and lobbying, even with the full support of one's home government, could be an enormous competitive disadvantage for a firm. The major alternative response, available primarily to those large firms with vast resources and long time horizons, was to produce at home to meet the stringent regulations in the large, Vogel-type 'California' export market (Vogel 1995), calculating that these high and ever-rising regulations would keep one's competitors, foreign and domestic, at bay.

Today, however, firms face a much more complex situation. Environmental regulations are proliferating at the local, national, and international levels. They are expanding from product to production/processing and distribution/disposal phases, and intensifying conflict among industries in different sectors. At the same time, the advent of internationally integrated production systems is making such local and national regulatory borders increasingly costly, as firms build a larger base enabling them to compete on a fully global scale. This is true even as the rise of multinational production and international business alliances allows firms more readily to produce and exert influence within once closed foreign markets. Finally, to help manage these new intersections of opening markets and compounding environmental regulations, there has arisen a new array of trade liberalization agreements, led by NAFTA, with new rules for trade–environment integration and new institutions to ensure that the values of both environmental protectors and trade liberalizers are simultaneously enhanced.

The more complex regulatory and competitive environment, and the array of international institutions which govern it, presents firms with new obstacles and opportunities in their response to business challenges abroad. This chapter outlines the expanded array of corporate and political strategies which firms now have available in this complex institutional environment, and identifies how firms at different stages of internationalization are best able to benefit from particular instruments within this menu. The chapter thus begins by identifying the key factors that have changed the regulatory, business, and international institutional environment facing firms—the new conditions of complex institutional responsiveness. It then discusses the new corporate strategies firms now have available, and the new repertoire of political strategies that the new institutional complexity opens for them. It concludes by analysing which of these new corporate and political strategies are likely to be most appealing to, and hence adopted by, firms, from domestic producers through to transnational firms at different levels of internationalization. In doing so it provides an analytical foundation for the case studies, in the next section, which will offer detailed tests of which strategies are being employed by different types of firms, and what competitive success they have fostered. The final section of the volume deals directly with how different types of firms can combine the new instruments of corporate and political strategy together to enhance their competitive success.

The New Environment for Complex Institutional Responsiveness

Traditionally, all but the largest firms operating as monopolies or oligopolies in relatively closed markets have needed to be responsive to challenges from competing firms and their home governments abroad. But now, virtually all firms have been forced to respond to such international competition. As Table 7.1 notes, the widespread demise of closed regimes, along with major multilateral and regional trade liberalization during the 1990s, has opened up a world market. In seeking to enhance their competitiveness in this far more international arena, firms face new complexities in regulatory, production, and international institutional conditions.

The first set of complexities arises from the behind-the-border defences of environmental regulations and standards, which the reduction of border tariffs and quotas have rendered more visible and valuable as protectionist devices. The recent era of rising environmental consciousness has added new complexity to the traditional environmental regulatory barriers firms face in foreign markets, and at home as well. Mass public concern with environmental protection has fuelled ever more stringent and rapidly changing regulations, with more flexible enforcement schedules, tradeoffs between target levels and deadlines, compliance assistance for firms, and, under the precautionary principle, more flexible standards for scientific proof. Sub-national governments have begun to adopt a rapidly changing array of local regulations, fragmenting such previously large markets as the United States and raising the costs of producing for sale across it. A new generation of multilateral environmental agreements has established an additional set of regulations at the international level, and often incorporated trade-restrictive measures to enforce compliance with them.

At all levels, from the local to the international, regulation has come to focus not only on the characteristics of products entering a market but on the

TABLE 7.1. *The conditions of complex institutional responsiveness*

Background conditions
1. Trade and investment liberalization
2. Technological speed and spread

Government conditions
1. Mass public environmental concern
2. New generation environmental regulations
3. Subfederal regulatory fragmentation
4. Multilateral environmental regulations with trade restrictions
5. Process/production and distribution/disposal regulations
6. Extended liability and reputational costs
7. Total systems regulation and intersectoral coordination

Business conditions
1. Integrated production with just-in-time inventory
2. International business alliances
3. Global markets and competition

International institutional conditions
1. International trade–environment institutions
2. Empowered secretariats
3. Direct firm/ENGO access and participation

methods by which they are produced, processed, distributed, and disposed of anywhere in the world and all along the value chain. The traditional focus on product characteristics has thus been joined, in a cradle-to-grave vision, by regulatory action over the entire product cycle, from production and processing methods, to waste reduction and product disposability. Firm reputations and liabilities can now be strongly affected by the practices of their suppliers and partners. And the emergence of a total systems approach to environmental protectionism has intensified the clash among once separated industries, such as autos and oil, about who could and should best bear the additional environmentally enhancing costs. This maze of multilevel, rapidly changing, ever more stringent, and far-reaching regulation imposes major costs on those firms unable to respond before their competitors to the harsh demands of this new environmental regulatory world.

Accompanying these developments in the arena of environmental regulation are similarly far-reaching changes in the world of international business. The advent of internationally integrated production and just-in-time inventory processes means firms need to be able to import and export freely and without interruption across international boundaries. This requirement compounds the costs which even minor regulatory detours or delays can impose, and simultaneously generates new incentives for convergent or at least compatible environmental regulations across jurisdictions. The result is a new corporate 'intervulnerability', as the production systems of even large firms in large countries can be crippled if they are denied, by environmental regulatory action on a local or national basis, the irreplaceable critical inputs from abroad they need to maintain production and market share. Moreover, the expansion in multinational enterprise and international business alliances has further increased the cost of national regulatory protectionism and reinforced the pressure for compatible production standards (Dunning 1993; Rugman 1996). Finally, the advent of competition on a global scale, often from firms of much larger size, has underscored the need for a large protected home (or now multi-country regional) market to amortize fixed costs and build the required minimum scale.

Governing this clash between the world of more complex environmental regulations and global competitive pressures over the past decade is a third new development—the advent of potent international institutions with trade and environment responsibilities. Even those as lightly institutionalized as the FTA provide a new international centre, beyond national trade law systems, where firms can make a case that they have been denied market access by unjustifiable environmental regulatory protectionism. When, as with NAFTA, such institutions are accompanied by strong powers, institutions, and organizations that embrace both trade and the environment, they can provide a common forum and reference point for trade–environment communities to interact and their conflicts to be settled. And if, as in NAFTA, they provide for the direct participation of firms and environmental groups, as well as governments, from all participating countries, they can foster the development of complex transnational coalitions, and an emergent sense of common interests vis-à-vis the outside world.

New Possibilities for Corporate Strategic Response

The more heavily and innovatively regulated, internationalized, and institutionalized world of the 1990s presents firms not only with complex new obstacles. It also offers them new opportunities, in both their corporate and political strategies, to circumvent potential barriers and increase their competitiveness on a larger scale. Of initial interest are the vastly expanded array of corporate responses that firms, following a strict business logic, can now employ.

Traditional Strategies

Traditionally, firms facing the classic challenge of environmental regulatory protectionism in their major export market abroad have had a limited array of often unsuccessful strategies to employ. As Table 7.2 indicates, the first, often instinctive response, was to secure from the foreign regulatory authority a certificate of equivalency or another form of ad hoc exemption for a specific

TABLE 7.2. *Corporate strategies under complex institutional responsiveness*

Traditional strategies
1. Ad hoc exemptionalism
2. Domestic withdrawal
3. Pay and expand
4. Product or production alteration
5. Product alternatives
6. Export market diversification

New strategies
1. Produce to high environmental standards for a protected domestic market (Porter)
2. Produce to the high environmental standards in dominant export market (Vogel)
3. Relocate production to the border of an export market
4. Produce as a domestic input into unrestricted domestic goods
5. Open conforming production facilities in the foreign market
6. Private sector market sharing

shipment or product. Such a response of ad hoc exemptionalism was tried unsuccessfully by Lactel, at an early stage of the UHT case.

A second response, attractive when the foreign regulations were fully prohibitive for market entry, was to withdraw to the domestic market and seek replacement customers at home. Such a strategy of domestic withdrawal was an appealing second best option for smaller firms with a large domestic market, and for firms with products at early stages of the product cycle where domestic demand could be expected to rapidly expand.

A third response, attractive to firms which wished to preserve their export market, was to pay the incremental cost of the foreign regulation, hoping that by expanding production through foreign sales they could lower their unit costs and restore net profitability in their foreign sale. Such a response was attractive where the cost of the foreign regulation was modest rather than prohibitive, potentially transitory (while undergoing further scientific testing, for example), and where the export market was rapidly growing and serviced by few competing firms at home or abroad. In sunrise sectors, where the regulation stemmed from early government regulatory authority backed by few national producing industries and allied NGOs, such a strategy could prove to be a successful one over the longer run. This strategy was followed on the part of the US beer producers in the Ontario beer case. Rather than withdraw from the Ontario market, they simply 'endured' the additional 10 cent cost per can, while negotiating a whole host of additional access issues with the Ontario government.

A fourth strategy was to alter one's product or even production standard to meet the foreign regulation of the moment. This was an attractive option where the costs of the adaptation was low (perhaps restricted to a single low value input), where firms were installing new capacity in a product line dedicated to the export market and segmented from the rest of the firms' production capacity, and when the foreign market offered high profitability, a high percentage of the firms' sales, and confidence that the existing regulation would last for a long time (over the course of which incremental costs of adjustment could be amortized). Such a strategy of product/production alteration was evident in the case of New Brunswick blueberries, where the Canadian producer switched from the use of the pesticide dimethoate to that of higher cost but still affordable imidian, in an effort to meet the US regulation.

A fifth strategy was to shift to the production of alternative, even closely allied products, that did not face the specific regulatory restriction. This was particularly attractive when the abandoned product, relative to the alternative, was a mature, low value added product whose market share might be in a state of long-term decline. It was also attractive when the foreign regulatory barrier was highly product specific, and difficult to change or expand. This strategy of product alternatives was employed, successfully for a few years, by Canadian producers in the softwood lumber case, as they circumvented restrictions on their exports of 2 × 4s to the US market by drilling holes in them to create a new product for unrestricted export—drilled studs.

A sixth traditional strategy was market diversification—shifting sales to an alternative export market where the regulatory barrier did not exist. This was particularly attractive to mature export-capable firms able easily to overcome barriers of distance and language, to seek new customers in less or differently regulated markets. It was a real option when these alternative export markets were not likely to rapidly raise their regulations, or do so in a way that was different from that of the firms' home government. The diversion of newsprint exports from California to Asia was a strategy considered on the part of the BC forestry firms when they were denied access to the California market.

These traditional strategies were essentially reactive rather than proactive—they responded to the introduction by foreign governments of new or different environmental regulations. Although they depended on a calculation of how those and related regulations were likely to change in the foreign government, in other export markets and at home, the dominant assumption was that a foreign government would act without catalysing a sequence of strategic moves by other players. This would include other governments with regulatory powers, and firms and NGOs wishing to adopt or circumvent successful techniques. These traditional strategies are thus poorly suited to the new world of rapidly changing environmental regulation and strategic regulatory protectionism, extensive internationalization of business, and strong international institutions to constrain national regulations and create international regulations of their own.

New Strategies

Conditions of complex institutional responsiveness offer a much broader array of strategies. These strategies take account both of the new regulatory, competitive, and institutional processes at work, and the dynamic pace of technology which lies behind. They require firms to plan proactively over long time horizons, to calculate the second and subsequent order responses to their moves, and to consider the reactions of multiple actors, including firms, governments, NGOs, and international institutions, operating at home and abroad.

The first of these new strategies, developed in the work of Michael Porter (1990), is to readily accept and produce at home to the highest environmental standards in one's domestic market, in order to have the unique first mover advantage in export markets which are calculated to be moving to ever higher levels of environmental regulation (Porter and van der Linde 1995). Such a strategy, however, is available only to relatively large firms who can afford the initial additional costs, who have long time horizons, who can use their green production as an advantage at home among consumers to capture the domestic market and secure the required scale, and who have a large unfragmented national market to allow the minimum required scale (Rugman 1995). They are also appealing when the level rather than the form of regulation is at issue, when there is a single future standard that is probable and widely accepted, when regulations rise by a unilinear rather than leapfrogging process, and when technology-forcing innovation is likely.

The second strategy, suggested in the work of David Vogel, goes beyond producing to high levels at home to prepare for an uncertain future market abroad to directly produce to meet the high environmental regulations prevailing in the largest export market (Vogel 1995). This is the strategy that takes advantage of the 'California effect', under which German automotive producers at home and abroad met the higher environmental standards in their large California market, confident that the environmentally pioneering California regulations would eventually be adopted throughout the United States and in key markets around the world. Such a strategy offers strong first mover advantages in a world where markets, and higher environmental regulations, are becoming global. It involves significant risks, however, when several subfederal jurisdictions and countries are seeking to become the global environmental pioneer and when their differing regulatory approaches threaten to fragment the prospective global and existing national market place. Such uncertainty can be compounded, as under NAFTA, when the easy trade and investment access to jurisdictions with lower levels of environmental regulation and enforcement create a fear that there may not be a future upward movement, but rather a regulatory chill that freezes the current regime or even a regulatory race to the bottom.

A third strategy is to move production facilities closer geographically to an export market, in order to minimize the transportation costs, and to better absorb the temporary border delays that environmental regulations sometimes cause. This strategy is attractive to home-based exporters from countries such as Canada and Mexico vis-à-vis the United States, where a firm's home country is contiguous to the major export market and to the major consumers within it. Its logic is seen in the many operations that have opened and expanded, both before and after NAFTA, in the maquiladoras along Mexico's northern border. It was a potential strategy available to Canadian newsprint producers faced with the task of transporting recycled newsprint from major urban centres in California and elsewhere in the United States back for recycling in Canada (Rugman 1995). It has similar potential in cases, such as for US producers in the Ontario beer case, where transport costs imposed by recycling schemes constitute a significant cost of doing business. It is also attractive where just-in-time inventory methods are in use, and where there are additional advantages, for learning and marketing purposes, in being geographically proximate to customers.

A fourth strategy is to transform oneself from a home-based exporter into a domestic producer, by abandoning the newly closed export market and selling one's product as an input to another domestic producer whose products are free to enter the foreign market. This is the strategy pursued by Canada's leading steel producer, Stelco, when its steel exports to the United States were hit with a succession of antidumping duties. It diverted its product to supplying Canadian auto parts manufactures such as Magna who were free to ship to the United States. Here US protectionist action had the unintended effect of inducing a successful 'further processing' industrial strategy in Canada.

A fifth strategy is to transform oneself from a home-based exporter into a home-based multinational enterprise by opening production facilities in the country whose market is now closed to exports by the environmental regulation. NAFTA's investment guarantees allow firms to adopt this strategy with much greater assurance than before. This strategy is attractive in cases, such as the recycling cases, where geographic proximity is an advantage, and where the costs of a greenfield or takeover investment, including those of regulatory compliance, are not onerous. The process fostered by the use of this strategy is the opposite of the widespread fear of regulatory refugees closing facilities in high-cost environmental sanctuaries for relocation in pollution havens where environmental regulations and thus business costs are lower. Under this strategy firms move, but to jurisdictions with higher environmental regulations. It is likely to be most evident where countries employ environmental regulations that are easy and inexpensive for domestic firms, but difficult and costly for foreign firms, to meet.

A sixth strategy is when firms from both the importing and exporting country make an agreement regarding minimum prices in exchange for the withdrawal of antidumping actions or harassment through discriminatory environmental regulation. Such agreements exist outside the NAFTA institutional process. This has been especially prevalent in the agriculture sector, where in the case of Mexican tomatoes exports to Florida, such an agreement was made. The Florida tomato producers agreed to withdraw their antidumping actions and cease harassment over environmental and packaging standards in exchange for voluntary export quotas and minimum price floors on the part of the Mexican tomato producers.

New Possibilities for Strategic Political Response

In addition to their business-based strategies, firms have long possessed a repertoire of political strategies to employ in combating environmental regulatory protectionism abroad. On occasion, they have been able to mobilize the power of governments, and those who influence government action, to shape the content and application of regulations to their advantage, rather than just comply with those regulations. As with their corporate strategies, their array of available political strategies has been significantly expanded by the advent of the conditions under which complex institutional responsiveness can flourish.

Traditional Instruments

Traditionally, as shown in Table 7.3, the first response of firms faced with regulatory protectionism has been litigation. This requires mobilizing the power of one's home government to take up one's case and be an advocate in the national trade law system of the country imposing the regulation. For example, in the UHT case, Lactel mobilized the home, Canadian government at

TABLE 7.3. *Political strategies under complex institutional responsiveness*

Traditional instruments
1. Litigation through home government in the foreign national trade law system
2. Lobbying in the political system of the blocking party
3. Coalition creation with suppliers and customers in blocking country
4. Bilateral diplomacy through home government
5. Home government subsidization to offset costs
6. Retaliation with reciprocal home government measures
7. Convergent national adjustment

New instruments
1. International institutional dispute settlement
2. International institutional dispute prevention and management
3. International institutional communication and capacity building
4. International institutional regulatory convergence
5. Transnational coalition formation
6. Multilaterally oriented coalition building
7. International private sector standardization

the official and diplomatic level to help it secure a certificate of equivalency for its product. This is essentially a passive strategy, in which the firm and its government are responding to the procedures and schedule of the foreign national trade law system. As the experience of Lactel in the UHT milk case illustrates, the strategy of litigation, even when successful, can take so long, and involve such expense, that serious competitive damage is done. More costly still is the fear, born by repeated experiences of such 'process protectionism' against the firms' products, that future exports will be blocked to the point that the firm is deterred from pursuing future exports.

A second political strategy is lobbying, with the aim of inducing the foreign government to allow such discretion as its national trade law system exists to provide at least an exemption in such a case. Such a claim can often best be made by one's home government, as an exercise in 'exemptionalism' (Kawasaki 1998; Barry 1980; Cuff and Granastein 1972). Firms can reinforce their capacity to pursue such a strategy by retaining local legal counsel with political access in the foreign country, or by maintaining permanent corporate representation in the foreign capital (Gotlieb 1984). Here home-based MNEs have an advantage over home-based exporters in that they can employ their host country managers to gather intelligence about, and intervene as nationals in the legal and related political processes of the regulating government.

A third, more active strategy is coalition building—constructing and activating a broad coalition of interest groups within the regulating country and in third countries to secure a modification or suspension of the objectionable regulation. For example, in the softwood lumber case, and earlier related cases such as shakes and shingles (Rugman and Anderson 1987), Canadian firms mobilized the US consumers' interests. This included the US Homebuilders Associations (to whom the product was sold), those financing the US housing purchases, and consumers wishing to purchase homes. All of these groups had a vested interest in the low input prices and easy availability of Canadian lumber. Reciprocally, in the Ontario Beer case, Alcan (as a Canadian supplier to US firms exporting their beer in aluminium cans into the Ontario market) was mobilized against the Ontario environmental regulation. Transnational MNEs, with a presence in many countries, are often best positioned to employ this strategy as they can more easily mobilize third-party governments to join an intervention against the regulating government.

A fourth strategy is high level diplomacy. This involves mobilizing one's home government, at the leader, ministerial, or senior official level, to pursue the case on an intergovernmental basis, and perhaps link it to other issues in an overall bilateral relationship. Such a strategy is reinforced by the finding that in the Canada–US relationship, Canada tends to prevail in issues dealt with at the Summit level and linked to the overall state of the relationship (Nye 1974). Such a strategy can be pursued as a matter of segmented problem solving in the special relationship, an approach pursued with the joint Canada–US study by agricultural officials in 1995 in the UHT case. Or it can be done as a matter of pure intergovernmental bargaining. For example, in the softwood lumber case, following its failed arbitration through the FTA, including two Extraordinary Challenge Committees, the two national governments negotiated outside the trade law system to arrive at the 1996 Softwood Lumber Agreement with its own dispute settlement procedures.

A fifth strategy, attractive when the foreign government will not easily adjust, is subsidization—seeking a subsidy from one's home government to meet the cost of the foreign environmental regulation. This strategy is a variant of that employed by the Canadian government in August 1971 to help defend Canadian industry affected by the US government's unilateral imposition of a 10 per cent surcharge on all dutiable goods entering the United States (Sakurada 1998). It does raise the danger that such 'generally available' subsidies will trigger further countervailing duty action by the regulating governments. This is especially true in the case of the United States, where such duties are imposed on the gross amount of the foreign subsidy rather than the net difference between foreign subsidies and US subsidies to its home firms (Rugman and Anderson 1987). However, the successful use of environmental subsidies, for example, by the Alberta government to its beef-processing industry, and the opening to legitimize green subsidies in the WTO and modern regional trade agreements, can make this an appealing strategy. This is especially true when the size of the required subsidies is not large, when one's home government has an available fiscal surplus, and where there is a legitimate case for infant industry, automatically sunsetted subsidization (as with a one-time grant for environmental facilities for new plant construction).

A sixth strategy is retaliation—having one's home government impose mirror image regulatory restrictions of equal or greater magnitude on the imports from the country practising the initial regulatory protectionism. The use of this strategy is evident in the counter-retaliations over potato inspections along the Maine–New Brunswick border and in countless other similar cases between the United States and Canada. It is likely to be efficacious when the counter-retaliation is carefully targeted against politically consequential constituencies in the other country, or where the market share of the imports and thus leverage of the retaliating country is larger than that of its rival.

A seventh strategy is one of convergent national adjustment, that is, where firms intervene with their home government to adjust its national regulations unilaterally to correspond with those of a major foreign government to which the firms export. This is essentially a strategy of acquiescence, based on a calculation that a single international regulatory regime regardless of content is more beneficial through the reduction of transaction costs than nationally diverse systems of whatever character. This strategy stands in contrast to Porter production, where a firm seeks high home government regulation in advance of those foreign markets, and in contrast to Vogel where a firm seeks to meet foreign government standards in advance of its own home government. Convergent national adjustment represents the most rapid way of securing simultaneously an identity of foreign and home standards. Convergent national adjustment was the strategy pursued by Canadian auto manufacturers in demanding that the Canadian government change its regulations with respect to MMT in gasoline to conform to the United States standard which did not allow MMT. This strategy rationally appeals to MNCs for whom international transaction costs can constitute a primary regulatory barrier.

Whatever strategy, or blend and sequence of such traditional strategies is employed, all are heavily dependent for their use and success on the willingness of one's home government to take up the case of a single firm, to pursue it effectively with a foreign government and within a foreign country. Such dependence on one's home government can be a problem. At home, a firm might be too small and politically inconsequential to secure home government support, by virtue of its size, number of employees, regional location (where the governing party does not have a strong support base), campaign contribution record, or image and status as not being a national champion. Firms may not be able to mobilize sector-wide coalitions of other firms at home if the latter perceive that they can secure a competitive advantage from avoiding collective action (e.g. if they are less dependent upon exports to the regulating country's market). Domestic public opinion may make it difficult for a national government to vigorously pursue a national firm's cause, as indicated by the case of aboriginal leghold traps or the east coast seal hunt (the conduct of which offended domestic animal rights and environmental groups).

Looking abroad, a government may have limited leverage with a much larger foreign government, particularly at times of cool overall relations. And the interests of a particular firm might be traded off for higher political issues or to maintain good overall relations with a foreign government.

New Instruments

The new political instruments and strategies available under complex institutional responsiveness circumvent many of these obstacles. They are far less dependent for their use and success on the will, skill, and size of a firm's home national government. They still involve political action, but focus more directly on using other political forums and actors, particularly those of and opened by the new array of international institutions. Whereas the old strategies (rooted in mobilization by national governments) contain a bias towards entering into and escalating intergovernmental conflict, the new strategies (based in international institutions) begin with the rules-based third-party treatment of firm–government conflict and contain a built-in bias towards ever stronger forms of transborder cooperative action. They begin with the settlement of conflicts, and move into conflict management and prevention and ultimately into common action against larger outside challenges.

The first of these new political strategies is International Dispute Settlement. This involves taking one's dispute directly to the new NAFTA network of dispute settlement mechanisms. Like their FTA predecessors, they offer a rules-governed international forum with specific mechanisms for antidumping and countervailing duties cases (Chapter 19), and for general disputes (Chapter 20). Yet, unlike the FTA, they also offer, under Chapter 11, two mechanisms for investment disputes, and under the NAAEC, three mechanisms (Chapter 13, 14–15, and Part V) for dealing with environmental disputes. Most innovatively, two of these six mechanisms—NAFTA's Chapter 11 and NAAEC's Article 14–15—allow firms direct access to initiate and pursue cases, without involving their home government. The NAAEC's Article 13 enables firms to lobby the CEC Secretariat directly to initiate an investigation. The early widespread use of Chapter 11 for environmental cases, and that environmental cases constitute virtually all of the Chapter 11 cases to date, plus the absence of environmentally related cases among those dealt with by the more FTA-like Chapter 19 and 20 mechanisms shows the importance of this right of direct firm access. Furthermore, the widespread use of NAAEC's Article 13 and 14–15 cases, and the lack of any action under Part V (which requires government to government action) underscores the point. Firms and their competitors are no longer hostages to home governments. They can now move to redress national and local environmental regulatory protectionism directly at the international level.

The second of the new political strategies is dispute management and prevention. The mandate and the work of the NAFTA institutions and the CEC provide an incentive and capacity to deal with disputes before they automatically proceed to expensive and visible litigation through dispute settlement. Through the role of the ministerial councils and their subordinate official-level institutions and stand-alone Secretariats, disputes can be politically managed in ways that prevent them from escalating into major intergovernmental conflicts, or from arousing domestic political pressures that would further impede transborder trade. These institutions also have the power to act to prevent such disputes from arising in the first place. This capacity has proven its value already, specifically in regard to major regulatory protectionist issues relating to safety, notably in the US–Mexican trucking area. The role of the NAFTA coordinators, and since 1998, the NAFTA Deputy Ministers forum, has substantially reinforced this capacity for dispute management and prevention.

A third strategy, which extends the impetus for dispute prevention from conflict avoidance into the realm of actual cooperation, is the use of the NAFTA institutions for communication and capacity building. Through the NAFTA institutions, firms can learn about the regulations, certification procedures and accreditation, and regulatory development systems in other countries. Firms also have a NAFTA guaranteed right to comment on draft regulations and thus shape their content. NAFTA's institutions encourage firms to build regulatory capacity in partner countries, thereby ensuring that foreign regulations are similar to home country ones in the consistency and predictability of their application. Such capacity building can also aid foreign suppliers and the general business infrastructure. In both cases, the development of personal networks with those in partner's national regulatory systems can do much to alleviate misunderstanding, build trust, and lower the costs of commerce.

A fourth strategy is regulatory convergence—using the NAFTA institutions to have national and local regulations move over time to become more compatible or similar. There are many ways this harmonization process can take place, from mutual recognition of national standards, through minimum standards and procedures (such as accrediting test labs in the other country), to the negotiation and acceptance of common standards (Esty and Gerardin 1997). Such a process is easier to undertake and complete in areas of new regulatory activity, where no partner country has existing regulations and the interests that lie behind. It can vary in the level of the common standards aimed at (high versus low), the dynamics of movement (negotiated versus incremental; hegemonic versus mutual adjustment), the form (labelling, product, process, or disposal standards), the scope (regional versus multilateral), and the speed (including differential phase-ins).

A fifth strategy, facilitated by the NAFTA institutions, is to form transnational coalitions to secure the convergent regulations one favours. Because the NAFTA institutions bring together firms, ENGOs, and other stakeholders from all participating countries in their work, they ease the task of assembling transnational coalitions to overcome national obstacles backed by weaker, national firm coalitions. Broader coalitions can also widen the range of benefits available. Over time, this process can lead firms and their governments to redefine their interests, and to formulate business strategies in fully regional terms.

A sixth strategy is to engage in multilaterally oriented coalition building. This involves constructing coalitions across all communities and countries within the region to create a stronger North American constituency, aimed at securing the broader multilateral standards that favour North American industry interests. This strategy has been evident in the activities of firms in the chemicals industry.

A seventh and final strategy is to engage in regional harmonization, with or without a multilateral orientation, outside of the NAFTA institutions or even non-NAFTA intergovernmental forums. Such international, voluntary, private sector, standardization can be seen in the activities of the automotive industry, for whom the work of the relevant NAFTA institutions is distinctly secondary. It can also be seen, outside of the environmental domain, in the activity of the North American steel industry. Forty-eight steel firms have formed a region-wide association and have begun to act against the threat of low-cost steel flowing into North America from currency-weak Asia and Russia.

The Impact of the NAFTA Institutions on Firm Behaviour

An expanded array of corporate and political strategies available under conditions of NAFTA's complex institutional responsiveness has been documented.

128   *Complex Institutional Responsiveness*

Which are those likely to be, under rational calculation, most appealing to different types of firms? The advent of free trade agreements such as NAFTA, with strong trade and investment liberalization provisions, plus a thick network of institutions for shaping regulations and managing disputes, offers firms a new arsenal of opportunities and instruments to maintain and enhance competitiveness. These environmentally related institutions have thus far operated effectively to facilitate the access of Canadian and Mexican firms to the US market, and that of US firms to their partners' markets. They have also served to augment the ability of North American firms to penetrate global markets, and to enhance the North American environment at the same time. But among the many new instruments the NAFTA regime offers, how do domestic firms, home-based exporters, home-based MNEs, and transnational MNEs choose those particular instruments most appropriate to their overall size and operational scope? The basic rationale for particular instruments to be employed by these different types of firms is as follows.

In the first instance, domestic firms can take advantage of the new NAFTA institutional network in several ways. Most directly, small domestic firms can benefit from the direct contracting practices of the CEC itself. The CEC has allocated its modest budget with strict attention to equal disbursements among the three member government contributors, often through the formula of contracting enterprises from the three countries to work together on a particular project. Such certification by an international organization and development of a network of affiliates in the other two NAFTA countries, even at a very modest level, increases the export readiness of small domestic firms, helps to transform them into home-based exporters, and gives them an international network of firms with which they might supply or form cooperative alliances in the future. For small, domestic firms such a lowering of transaction costs and provision of a de facto guarantee of international governmental approval can be of considerable value.

The work of the NAFTA institutions more generally, particularly through its involvement of firms, has a substantial effect in bringing larger domestic firms and home-based exporters into contact, not merely with foreign distributors and customers, but with similar firms or potential competitors. From such concentrated contact can flow a greater sense of export opportunities, familiarity with local regulations, and the identification of local lobbying affiliates. It can also breed the trust and information required to forge larger strategic alliances that can help transform such firms into home-based MNEs, facilitate the sharing of industry best practices (including the adoption of environmental management systems), and foster a shared interest in working towards region-wide regulatory convergence.

NAFTA can assist home-based exporters in another way. Such trade agreements, by opening vastly larger markets with different, and in the case of Mexico at times less stringent, regulations give formerly domestic producers and their home country much larger markets for their existing products, and thus the resources and skills to meet the intensifying regulatory demands from abroad. At a minimum, NAFTA's trade liberalization provisions mean firms could find new markets abroad (Mexico) where their products meet the regulatory requirements, and thus insulate themselves from and reinforce their ability to compete with regulatory protectionism in a single large market such as the United States. NAFTA thus offers home-based exporters fully focused on the United States the strategy of export diversification.

NAFTA's trade liberalization provisions, and its innovative guarantees for foreign direct investment make it easier for firms to move production abroad, to service the former export markets, and the former home market. NAFTA thus gives home-based exporters the option of becoming home-based MNEs, at least on a regional scale. They can move existing and new production to lower cost jurisdictions such as Mexico to offset the higher costs of meeting the regulations required to export into the US market. Or they can move into the US market itself, and thereby better learn about and lobby for the national and sub-national regulations they can meet. In doing so, they place, as NAFTA's critics correctly identify, a market-based check on excessive enthusiasm for national environmental regulatory protectionism, especially the form that could harm firms in the global market place.

In addition, the NAFTA Agreements' environmental provisions and institutional mechanisms give firms a much enhanced array of possibilities. High and costly environmental regulations at home can force firms to look for investment locations abroad, where other production costs could be higher, distance from high value markets greater, and access to those markets more uncertain. In such a situation, of particular interest to experienced home-based exporters with several foreign markets and to home-based MNEs are those CEC programmes directly focused on corporate contributions to environmental enhancement, notably the development and spread of voluntary environmental management systems such as ISO 14000, and support for pooling environmental technologies of proven value in Mexico to enhance their export into the Americas as a whole. Their participation with ENGOs in such fora can also lead to shared interests both in sustainable development opportunities, or in green protectionism at a regional rather than the national or sub-national level where baptist–bootlegger coalitions predominantly form.

By far the most important impact of the NAFTA institutions, especially for the home based MNEs that dominate North American trade and investment, is their work in: (1) constraining the emergence and use of green protectionist regulations by national, subfederal, and local governments within the NAFTA community; (2) facilitating regulatory convergence across the region; and (3) fostering a single North American regional voice to combat such protectionism in external regions such as the EU and build a broader, more open multilateral regime.

A substantial number of the environmentally related trade disputes in the region (affecting domestic firms, home-based exporters, and home-based

MNEs), especially prior to NAFTA, arose from state and provincial regulations (Vogel and Rugman 1997). While such cases have thus far concentrated on agricultural and natural resource industries, pressures for state-level automotive emission standards (beyond California) and automotive inspection and maintenance programmes threaten to bring such subfederal regulatory escalation and proliferation to the manufacturing industries at the heart of the NAFTA economy.

For home-based exporters and MNEs it is often the uniformity, stability, and form rather than the level of regulation which is the central interest. Although MNEs are conventionally thought to be in favour of regulatory diversity across countries (so that they can exploit their comparative advantage by relocating to produce for export to global markets from the locations where their costs are the lowest), in practice it is costly to shift production to such locations. Moreover the high degree of intracorporate trade and management integration provides further incentives for firms to favour stable or slowly changing uniformity over rapidly changing diversity.

The NAFTA regime and institutions, in practice, have not led to a downward harmonization that has forced subfederal entities to reduce their environmental standards, where they are higher than the national or international norm (Kirton 1998; Orbuch and Singer 1995). Although allegations of a deterrent 'chill effect' persist (by which the NAFTA disciplines and institutions prevent subfederal entities from further increases and thus differentiation in their environmental regulations), the record of dispute settlement thus far suggests the incentives are otherwise. For while the CEC has acted against subfederal jurisdictions (such as British Columbia) for the alleged non-enforcement of existing environmental regulations, the NAFTA dispute settlement mechanisms have not yet moved against those seeking to set environmental regulations higher (apart from the MMT case in process against the Canadian federal government). In the British Columbia case, which is really a case concerning government-owned BC Hydro, it may be a public utility whose commercial interests are harmed, to the benefit of its private sector competitors. The NAFTA institutions and the CEC thus assist home-based exporters and MNEs with their most costly market access problem of subfederal regulatory proliferation, with little cost to existing levels of regulatory protection and some benefit against those states and provinces tempted to relax environmental enforcement.

It is here that the NAFTA institutions, implementing the NAFTA rules on standards, have been most effective. By bringing NAFTA disciplines to many areas of state and provincial regulatory activity, while restricting the direct participation of state and provincial officials in them, the NAFTA institutions in their composition and practice create a bias in favour of standards that are trade friendly, national, and regional in application (Orbuch and Singer 1995).

More generally, the NAFTA rules and institutions have assisted home-based exporters and MNEs from NAFTA's two smaller countries with the major threat they face, namely loss of market access to the United States. With unilateral environmental regulatory action by the national government of the United States, entrenched in a 'baptist–bootlegger' coalition, there is the threat of denial of access to the large and vital US market to firms who must export their products there to survive. The most analytically clear instances arise where the US government has embedded in its national laws trade sanctions against foreign firms allegedly not abiding by the practices prescribed in US regulations.

These cases follow a standard pattern, in which, first, US environmentalists seek and secure a higher US environmental standard (or support an international one). Second, US industry resists its imposition on US industry (or demands its imposition on external competitors from foreign countries). Third, a 'green and greedy' coalition is formed to secure unilateral trade sanctions as an enforcement mechanism. Fourth, the industry proceeds with its environmental partners to seek the internationalization of this standard (De Sombre 1995). Such a process, which might be termed the 'Washington effect', explained earlier in the chapter, as distinct from the 'California effect' (Vogel 1995), opens up two major strategies for foreign firms. The first is proactively forging alliances with US firms in the first stage to prevent such national environmental regulations from coming into force (or doing so in such a way that exempts Canadian firms from the application) and thus provide privileged access into the US market.

The second is to pre-emptively create an international standard (at or near the higher US level or acceptable to the dominant US industry–environmental–government alliance) before the damaging threat of unilateral sanctions emerges. The presence of a three-country regional forum, in which the US government feels comfortable, and with effective institutions to devise, implement, and enforce such standards, is a major asset, particularly to home-based exporters in Canada and Mexico. It helps to speed up the second strategy, given the slowness of the broad multilateral process and the latter's anti-environmental bias arising from the large number of developing countries exercising a drag effect.

A successful execution of this strategy is represented by the particular embedding of trade sanctions in the NAAEC regime (under Part V), and the use of the investigatory and enforcement powers of the NAFTA institutions and CEC. Here the trade sanctions weapon is in effect 'captured' by, and its use contained within, the international institution. It reduces the likelihood of US unilateral power by binding the United States to a rules-governed process that makes the threat of its use much less severe and thus less commercially damaging to outsiders. Because governments (and their environmental agencies) and not industry must trigger the use of NAAEC's Part V, its operation, if ever activated, is likely to have a pro-environmental bias, and not serve as an instrument for protectionist harassment.

The differential treatment of Canada and Mexico in the Part V regime (with

Canada but not Mexico subject to trade sanctions) admits of several interpretations. At the governmental level these include Canada's greater environmental reputation, the diffuse thrust of the Canada–US special relationship and the existing market access provisions of FTA. There is also a rational incentive for the United States not to subject itself to the threat of trade sanctions from its largest and most integrated export market, Canada, where so many US-owned and based MNEs operate.

At the firm level, the high degree of intrafirm integration between Canada and the United States provides MNEs with a strong incentive to eliminate potential trade sanctions that might impede their production systems. At the same time, the presence of a sanctionist regime (through fines, trade penalties, or domestic court action), has an impact in inhibiting US firms from lowering the effective environmental regulatory burden in their prized domestic market and reaping the rewards which may ensue. It is thus a victory for Canadian and Mexican domestic firms subject to US import competition, and home-based exporters (competing against domestic US rivals in the US market) at the expense of their US equivalents, while having an essentially neutral effect on US, Canadian, and Mexican home-based MNEs.

Looking ahead, the greatest value of NAFTA's environmentally related institutions will come in altering the interests of their governments and firms, and enhancing their capacity to advance common North American interests in broader multilateral forums. The trend towards broadly multilateral standardization will primarily benefit US MNEs whose broadly dispersed international markets and production create an overwhelming interest in a single, high-level environmental standard worldwide. The trend towards a regional caucus and common North American standards, distinct from that of the rest of the world, will primarily benefit Canadian and Mexican MNEs and exporters, as their major markets and production sites are primarily located in the United States and North America itself.

Yet several factors suggest that regionally distinct standards (perhaps extended from the NAFTA three to Chile and Latin America) will be the domain in which the largest convergence of industry and environmental interests is found. It is here, on a regional rather than global basis, that the ecological challenges are often most distinct, the environmental interdependencies most intense, and the capability-equalizing environmental vulnerabilities of the United States the greatest and most visible. With the United States becoming a more internationally open economy, and its internationalization increasingly concentrating on Canada and Mexico, smaller domestic and exporting firms in the United States will come to share this interest in region-specific commonality. Their Mexican and Canadian equivalents will share this interest.

The NAFTA regime thus suggests that North American firms have thus far been slow to take advantage of NAFTA's environmentally relevant institutions to foster the high-level, region-specific standards they will increasingly

Firm Responses to Regulation   133

require, especially as NAFTA's tariff phase-out proceeds. Moreover, they have been slow to identify the conditions under which 'green and greedy' coalitions in the United States can be induced, through proactive political intervention, to turn away from state and national level environmental regulatory protectionism, to solve their ecological and competitiveness concerns at the regional level, and to secure the support of their governments in this quest.

The degree of North American integration—a key condition of complex institutional responsiveness—has an important impact in determining how firms at different levels of internationalization work through the NAFTA institutions to produce regional environmental communication and capacity building, regulatory convergence, and multilaterally oriented capacity building.

All of the cases of NAFTA-based institutional regime deepening can be positioned in Figure 7.1. In Figure 7.1, the horizontal axis represents the degree of trilateral cooperation and regulatory convergence in the NAFTA-based institutions; either low or high. The degree of regulatory convergence is assessed across the three member countries of NAFTA through examination of a set of regulations. The measure of regulatory convergence depends on an assessment of factors such as the degree, speed, form, level, and scope of the NAFTA-based regulatory convergence experienced to date. For example, scope includes whether the regional regulations have plurilateral or multilateral coverage.

The vertical axis of Figure 7.1 represents the extent of North American integration; either low or high. The factors affecting integration include sets of economic and political parameters. The economics-related factors include the level and share of trade and investment, by sector and member country. It also includes the extent of a common infrastructure and the nature of business/sectoral lobbies. Political factors include: the specific language of the NAFTA text; the related institutional (bureaucratic) capacity to administer the legal text of NAFTA; the extent to which there is a 'nested' regime, i.e. how a NAFTA-based regulation relates to a multilateral one; the nature and strength

Extent of North American integration	Institutional-based degree of regulatory convergence	
	LOW	HIGH
HIGH	1 ASC (autos) MMT	3 Pesticides Dangerous goods
LOW	2 SPS Local services	4 CAT

Fig. 7.1. The institutional deepening of the NAFTA regime

134 *Complex Institutional Responsiveness*

of sub-national levels of decision-making; and the extent of ENGO lobbying activity.

The cases in Cell 3 represent the readily understandable instances in which a high degree of North American integration, recently enhanced by NAFTA, have led the NAFTA institutions to generate a high degree of trilateral cooperations and regulatory convergence. Examples are pesticides, the regime in dangerous goods, and the work of the Committee on Standards-Related Measures (CSRM) and the CEC itself.

Cell 2 displays the converse, where low integration co-exists with low NAFTA-based cooperation and convergence. Examples are local services and sanitary and phytosanitary standards (SPS) at present.

The cases in Cell 1, where high integration co-exists with low NAFTA-based cooperation and convergence, point to the role of alternative mechanisms, such as voluntary industry standards, but also to missed opportunities for firms to embed such arrangements in a more certain intergovernmental, institutional framework. Examples include the Automotive Standards Council (ASC) and MMT cases. Also here would be most of the integrated manufacturing sectors such as autos, oil and gas, and electricity (unless the BC Hydro case is effective and moves to Cell 3).

Finally, the cases in Cell 4 indicate how governments, through the NAFTA institutions, can take the lead in prodding the three countries to mount a stronger voice abroad, and perhaps in time more successfully to reduce barriers to trade within the region and at home. An example is the Committee on Agricultural Trade (CAT). Also here would be the Commission for Labor Cooperation (CLC), and possibly SPS in the future.

Conclusions

As firms operate in a more complex environmental regulatory system, they are faced with numerous challenges and opportunities. Firms at all levels need to take account of the new environment for complex institutional responsiveness, that is, careful strategic planning is required in order to navigate around these challenges and make the most of these competitive opportunities. Traditional corporate and political strategies available prior to the advent of the major multilateral and regional trade liberalization initiatives are no longer the most effective course of action. They tend to be reactive rather than proactive, and fail to take account of the realities in which firms must operate today where business is internationalized, environmental regulation is rapidly changing, and a new international institutional structure exists.

Conditions of complex institutional responsiveness offer a much broader array of both corporate and political strategies, which take account of the new regulatory, competitive, and institutional processes at work. In the case of NAFTA, its new set of international institutions charged with trade and environment responsibilities has provided multiple opportunities for firms which they are beginning to utilize. The NAFTA institutions have had particular success in constraining the emergence of 'green' protection at all levels of regulation, facilitating regulatory convergence, and developing a North American 'voice' to combat protection beyond its borders and influence the development of standards in international bodies.

The degree of North American integration on a sectoral basis as represented by trade, investment, and institutional capacity to administer NAFTA and other criteria is set against the degree of institutional-based regulatory convergence in Figure 7.1. In the future, sectors positioned in Cell 3 where there is a high degree of both region-wide integration and institutional-based regulatory convergence will be best poised to take advantage of the new environment for complex institutional responsiveness.

The array of corporate and political strategies discussed in this chapter can be generalized beyond the North American experience. The shifts from traditional to new corporate and political strategies are relevant for firms operating under the GATT/WTO, the EU, FTAA, and to some extent APEC. Where the conditions for complex institutional responsiveness are present (as they are embodied in NAFTA), there is a rational incentive on the part of firms to use the new, rather than old, strategies of complex institutional responsiveness.

Of course, the conditions of complex institutional responsiveness do not currently exist in all parts of the world. Not all jurisdictions have demonstrated mass public environmental concern, nor have they embraced a new generation of environmental regulation. And not all trading arrangements have created the necessary international institutional conditions. Across the APEC economies, for example, there has not been a consistent development of environmental regulatory frameworks. Nor have the requisite institutions been created. In contrast, within the EU, the conditions of complex institutional responsiveness are largely present. The WTO and the FTAA (as it currently stands) lies in between these two poles.

But complex institutional responsiveness is not the fate of North American and European firms only. Rather, it is expected that the conditions of complex institutional responsiveness will develop and gain momentum over time. And thus one can expect that firms will embrace these strategies as new institutions develop, as environmental concern becomes more pressing and the conduct of business becomes ever more international.

Part III
Case Studies of Complex Institutional Responsiveness

8
MMT and Investment Dispute Settlement

The new conditions of complex institutional responsiveness in general, and the new network of NAFTA institutions in particular, offer firms of different scale and scope a rich array of specific incentives for overcoming national and local environmental regulatory protectionism in critical foreign markets and thus for enhancing their overall competitiveness. To what extent have these new opportunities actually been identified and employed by firms? With what skill have they been implemented? And what success have they enjoyed? In short, are the rational incentives offered by the new conditions of complex institutional responsiveness a powerful predictor of, and explanation for, actual firm behaviour?

To address these questions, and test the logic outlined in the previous chapter, this chapter, along with the following two chapters, conducts detailed case studies of three particular environmental regulatory issues that have involved industries from the three North American countries and that have engaged in varying degrees and ways NAFTA's environmentally related institutions. The first is the case of MMT, an apparently environmentally harmful automobile fuel additive whose importation was banned by the Canadian government, leading its US-owned exporter into and distributor within Canada to activate NAFTA's Chapter 11 investment dispute settlement mechanism. The second is the case of agriculture, where disputes over the often discriminatory application of sanitary and phytosanitary standards have restricted trade throughout North America and beyond. The third is the case of the automotive industry, with a particular focus on efforts to reduce vehicle emissions on the part of original equipment manufacturers, fuel suppliers, and those involved in operational inspection and maintenance.

Together, a detailed exploration of these three cases allows a careful, disciplined process tracing and test of how complex institutional responsiveness is practised—how firms actually employ the NAFTA institutions and other instruments, as a matter of corporate and political strategy, to overcome, reduce, and circumvent environmental regulatory protectionism and thereby enhance competitiveness. These three cases embrace all four types of firms at their different levels of internationalization. The agricultural case centres on domestic producers faced with competition from imports, and often competing with small home-based exporters seeking to take advantage of the newly opened NAFTA market place. The MMT case deals with a US home-based exporter and multinational, Ethyl Corporation. And the automotive case has at its core the US-owned big three automakers and their major suppliers who are transnational MNEs operating on a global scale.

140 *Case Studies*

These three cases also allow an in-depth examination of various clusters of the new corporate and political strategies which conditions of complex institutional responsiveness allow. The MMT case explored in this chapter deals with dispute settlement, focused on the use of the innovative NAFTA Chapter 11 investment provisions. The agricultural case treated in Chapter 9 centres on dispute management and prevention, and the related contribution of processes of communication, capacity building, and regulatory convergence. The automotive case examined in Chapter 10 deals with regulatory convergence and cooperation in broader multilateral fora, with an emphasis on how voluntary private sector standardization can supplement or even supplant the work of NAFTA's regional intergovernmental institutions.

As these cases are still in progress, it is difficult to make definitive judgements about the ultimate success of the strategies employed by firms in each instance. But it is possible to make tentative, interim judgements about how the advent of the NAFTA institutions and the use of new instruments has furthered or retarded firms' interests relative to their experience before the conditions of complex institutional responsiveness arose. The agricultural case marks the clearest advance over the pre-NAFTA regime, despite continuing controversy over specific crops such as tomatoes and avocados. The MMT case has given a US firm an instrument previously unavailable, although the ultimate outcome of its use remains uncertain. In the automotive case, success is far less evident, as the NAFTA institutions and private sector standardization have thus far been inadequate to meet the new proliferation of regulatory diversity and uncertainty within North America, the need for automotive–oil industry coordination, and the severe challenges of the global market-place beyond. In all cases, however, there are strong signs that firms are moving aggressively and with some success to practise the particular strategies of complex institutional responsiveness most appropriate to the conditions they face.

The MMT Case: Introduction

In 1997 the Canadian government passed a bill banning all international and intraprovincial trade in the fuel additive MMT.[1] The ban in MMT arose from an ongoing battle between two major sectors of the Canadian economy: auto manufacturers and petroleum producers. Auto manufacturers support a ban in MMT on the grounds that it reduces the efficacy of the new generation of pollution control equipment in automobiles developed in response to increasingly stringent emission standards. Petroleum producers, who blend MMT with gasoline in their refineries, oppose a ban in MMT, on the grounds that they will be forced to undertake significant capital expenditures to reconfigure their plants for alternative fuel additives. At the heart of the issue is the question of which industry will bear the future costs of producing the technology to meet the ongoing demand for emissions reduction. Beyond the parties engaged in the dispute, the outcome of this case will have far-reaching implications for the future of NAFTA's Chapter 11.

An initiative of Environment Canada, the ban in MMT was justified by the Department on three grounds.[2] First and foremost was the protection of the health of Canadians. Second was the goal of 'positive and progressive harmonization' of North American fuel standards. The third reason for the ban in MMT was to protect jobs and consumers from adverse economic impacts, due to increased engineering costs for auto companies. Bill C-29, a ban in trade for environmental purposes, thus appeared to be legislation designed for both environmental and economic protection. MMT itself was not banned as a toxic substance under, for example, the Canadian Environmental Protection Act (CEPA) suggesting there were doubts about the scientific certainty of its environmental harm.[3] Only its movement across both national and provincial borders has been prohibited.

The issues and stakes raised by the MMT case are especially salient in the larger context of an integrated North American market place. As economies become more interdependent throughout the international trading system, environmental, health, and safety regulations can have profound impacts on international trade and investment (Vogel 1997). There is growing concern that firms and their governments are attempting to fill the 'protection gap' left by falling border barriers with the discriminatory application of environmental regulation.[4] The MMT case was regarded by its producers as an especially severe form of environmental regulatory protectionism, as with one regulatory change, it eliminated Ethyl's entire export market in Canada and rendered virtually valueless its Canadian plant and operations. The ban has a major impact on a US-owned firm, Ethyl Corporation, which exported MMT products from its plant in Richmond, Virginia, and mixed them into a final product at its fully owned plant in Sarnia, Ontario. Prior to NAFTA, faced with this incident of environmental regulation with a protectionist impact, Ethyl would have had few options. But NAFTA gave it a new instrument to use as the centrepiece of its more complex, and thus far successful, strategy. Using its right of direct access to a new international forum, it invoked NAFTA's Chapter 11 investment dispute settlement mechanism.

This chapter examines Ethyl's actions in the case of MMT and its implications for the analysis of trade-restrictive environmental regulation under conditions of complex institutional responsiveness. The following section highlights the context of the case. The third section offers a brief history and technical background of the MMT issue in both Canada and the United States. The fourth section outlines and evaluates the positions of the different stakeholders involved on an issue-by-issue basis. The fifth section looks at how the international institutional dispute settlement mechanisms have been used and the sixth section examines the degree to which the tools of complex institutional responsiveness have been engaged for MMT and other Chapter 11 cases. The final section offers some conclusions.

The North American Context of MMT

The case of MMT, with its many players pursuing separate agendas, engages the theory of complex institutional responsiveness on a number of different levels. First, there is a recent and pressing public concern over air quality in Canada, as indicated by a large NGO population (consumer groups, environmental groups, medical groups, labour groups, etc.) active on this issue. This has encouraged government action and has brought pressure to bear on the auto and oil industries. There is additionally the threat of environmental regulatory fragmentation, as different jurisdictions throughout North America have addressed air quality issues in varying ways, both at the national and sub-national levels. For example, the state of California has among the strictest regulations concerning air emissions within North America. This has created issues for the auto industry, which operates throughout North America as a fully integrated single market, in order to remain competitive. Its technology must thus keep pace with the increasing demand for lower emissions as well as meet the varying jurisdictional requirements. To this end, the auto industry has pursued an aggressive strategy of international regulatory convergence, as discussed in Chapter 10. The fate of the auto sector has obvious implications for the oil sector—they must necessarily produce a complementary fuel product to keep pace with such multiple demands. Which industry will bear what proportion of these costs of high-level harmonization is at issue in the present case. At the same time, NAFTA has provided a new institutional structure that has the potential to resolve such issues.

Thus, the case of MMT reveals two industries that have put in practice several corporate and political strategies, both traditional and new, in dealing with this issue. In this case, the limits of the market place have led the auto industry to resist corporate strategies which focus on product alteration/product alternatives or developing technology to meet the requisite standards, while continuing to use MMT in fuels. Instead, they have fought a more direct fight. They sought an outright ban on a particular product, using a combination of the traditional and new political strategies of complex institutional responsiveness. The auto industry has aligned with the NGO community in their efforts to ban the use of MMT, creating a powerful North American wide transnational coalition. They have lobbied heavily within Canadian, and in some instances US, national and sub-national governmental agencies responsible for environmental standards. They are represented by their trade associations within the relevant NAFTA institutions.

In response to what they perceive as protectionist action, the oil industry, particularly Ethyl, has engaged a number of political strategies simultaneously. This was done in response to the ban but also in anticipation of it. They are pursuing litigation strategies within the NAFTA dispute settlement system, Canada's Internal Trade Agreement, and within the Canadian domestic legal system. This chapter explores those strategies in further detail and evaluates their success to date.

History and Technical Background

MMT stands for methylcyclopentadienyl manganese tricarbonyl. It is an organometallic compound used as an octane enhancer in gasoline.[5] Ethyl Corporation of Richmond, Virginia, developed MMT in 1953 and is currently its sole manufacturer in North America. It is marketed under the trade name HiTEC©3000. Ethyl has a blending plant in Corunna, Ontario, which imports MMT and then sells it to Canadian refiners for addition to their gasoline (Standing Committee 1997). Ethyl is a multinational company with plants located in four countries and offices located in thirteen countries. Ethyl Corp. produces a range of fuel and lubricant additives and its 1997 net sales were in excess of US $1 billion. Expanding the sales of MMT, a technology-based firm specific advantage, is a key part of Ethyl's corporate strategy. The market for MMT is increasing, as it is a substitute for lead in gasoline, which is being phased out globally for environmental reasons.[6]

There are three central claims surrounding MMT, each of which will be more fully explored in the following section. The first claim is that MMT poses a significant and serious health hazard through the release of toxic manganese oxides directly into the environment through tailpipe emissions. There is significant controversy about what level of manganese oxide in the atmosphere is an acceptable level for human health. The second claim is that MMT increases overall auto emissions, particularly in smog forming particulates. Third, it is alleged that MMT causes auto emission control systems to malfunction, resulting in increased emissions of hydrocarbons and carbon monoxide and corresponding adverse health and environmental impacts (Standing Committee 1997).

MMT in Canada

MMT has been widely used in Canadian gasoline since 1977, when it was introduced as a replacement for lead (Environment Canada 1996b). The first initiative to have MMT removed from gasoline was in October 1990, in the form of a Private Member's Bill which was never enacted into law. The bill was introduced surrounding increasing environmental concerns about fuel additives and the introduction of 'cleaner substitutes'.[7] Former Environment Minister Sheila Copps next attempted a ban in MMT through the introduction in May 1995 of Bill C-94. It died on the order paper in February 1996 (McKenna 1996a). It was reintroduced in the House of Commons by then Environment Minister Sergio Marchi as Bill C-29. A Standing Senate Committee on Energy, the Environment and Natural Resources convened to consider Bill C-29 in February 1997. The ban on MMT passed its third reading in the Canadian Parliament on 25 April 1997 and came into force on 24 June 1997.

MMT in the United States[8]

MMT was progressively banned from use in the United States between 1977 and 1995 (the same year the Canadian government first acted). Since 1977, producers of fuel additives are required to obtain a waiver from the US Environmental Protection Agency (EPA) for their use. Ethyl applied for such a waiver in 1978, 1981, 1990, and 1991.[9] Each request was denied by EPA, as Ethyl's request failed to meet the conditions of s. 211(f)(4) of the US Clean Air Act[10] which requires the applicant to establish that the fuel additive will not cause or contribute to the failure of an emission control device.[11]

The EPA justified the denial of Ethyl's application on the grounds of insufficient data being made available and required additional tests to be undertaken in each instance. Ethyl appealed the January 1991 EPA waiver denial to the US Court of Appeals for the District of Columbia Circuit. In April 1993 the US Court of Appeal remanded Ethyl's waiver application for reconsideration by the EPA. In July 1994, however, the EPA denied Ethyl's waiver application again. Although Ethyl had demonstrated that use of MMT did not 'cause or contribute to a failure of any emission control or device',[12] the EPA later found that there was 'a reasonable basis for concern regarding the potential adverse effects of public health which could result from emissions of manganese particulates associated with MMT use'.[13] Ethyl then appealed this decision to the US Court of Appeals which ruled in Ethyl's favour.[14] The Court found that the EPA had exceeded its statutory authority under s. 211(f)(4) of the US Clean Air Act. A waiver application can be granted or denied only on the criterion of whether the fuel additive 'will cause or contribute to a failure of any emission control device or system'. The section does not contemplate the denial of a waiver based on public health effect. Accordingly, EPA granted a waiver for MMT on 17 July 1995.[15] Although MMT is now a legal fuel additive in the United States, its use is not widespread. Presently, US gasoline companies representing over 70 per cent of gasoline produced in the United States are not using MMT (Environmental Defense Fund 1996a).[16]

Stakeholder Positions

In both the United States and Canada, a number of powerful stakeholders have been involved in the MMT dispute. The following section outlines the claims of these actors on the relevant issues, illustrating how each one fits into the strategies of the key players. First the environmental claims are analysed examining both the direct and indirect effects of MMT. On this issue, the NGO community and the auto firms are closely aligned and transnational coalitions have been established throughout Canada and the United States. This strategy has been successful to the degree it has mobilized widespread public support for the removal of MMT from gasoline and inextricably linked it to the high-profile issue of air quality and airborne neurotoxins. To do this, it has relied on an arsenal of scientific evidence and testimony. This strategy, however, was rendered less effective by the fact that so much scientific uncertainty surrounds the issue of whether, or the extent to which, MMT harms human health. Second, the protected industry claims are examined. The ethanol industry produces a substitute product for MMT and thus stands to gain much from its restriction. They have received subsidies from the Canadian government and this alliance is examined, along with the validity of their environmental claims.

The Environmental Claims

1. Direct Effects: MMT Pollution   There has been a considerable effort on the part of the environmental non governmental organization (ENGO) community, both in Canada and the United States, to have MMT banned as a fuel additive. Large coalitions have formed in both Canada and the United States.[17] The coalition in the United States, led by the Environmental Defense Fund, claims to represent 37 environmental, medical, senior citizens, consumer, and religious groups with more than 14 million members throughout the United States and Canada.[18] Environmental groups are concerned about the toxic effects of airborne manganese at high levels.[19] Manganese is emitted from autos in very fine particles and then enters the lungs. Adults can usually metabolize manganese if it is eaten in food, but when manganese is absorbed into the lungs, it accumulates in the body. At high levels of exposure, manganese settles primarily in the brain, causing neurological impairments with symptoms similar to Parkinson's disease.[20] Studies have suggested that manganese has an effect on behavioural characteristics and learning ability in children.[21] ENGOs are also concerned that the public health impacts of the longer-term, lower dose exposures resulting from MMT use cannot be adequately assessed, as there is a lack of scientific data. Accordingly, the ENGO community believes that there are sufficient indications of harmful effects to justify a ban on MMT, just as had been the case with lead in gasoline. This is an application of the precautionary principle, which states that action may be taken before the scientific evidence is exhaustive and conclusive, in order that the public is not used as 'guinea pigs' (Environmental Defense Fund 1996c). Besides the impacts related to airborne manganese, it is alleged that MMT also increases smog through its disabling effects on auto control emissions equipment and catalytic converters, thereby causing related respiratory problems.[22] Although the ENGOs concede that there is some reduction in nitrous oxide (NOx) emissions through the use of MMT, such a benefit is judged to be minimal and far outweighed by the potential harms.

On the other side of this debate, Ethyl claims that there are 'important environmental and economic benefits associated with MMT'.[23] Ethyl contends that MMT is not harmful to the environment. On the contrary, Ethyl argues that MMT can reduce smog-related nitrogen emissions by up to 20 per cent as

146 *Case Studies*

well as reducing carbon-dioxide emissions. Furthermore, MMT conserves energy by reducing crude oil consumption, resulting in savings of up to $500 million a year to refiners.

These conclusions were challenged in a study commissioned by the Motor Vehicles Manufacturers Association (MVMA), the results of which contradicted Ethyl's findings. This study questioned the 'scientific rigour' of the experiments and found that the improvements in NOx emissions were considerably overestimated (Abraham and Lawless 1995). The Senate Standing Committee considered the issue of whether MMT in gasoline posed a threat to the health of Canadians and found that it did not (Standing Committee 1997). Despite the evidence introduced by ENGOs which supported the allegation that MMT is a dangerous neurotoxin, the Senate Committee based this conclusion on a 1995 Health Canada risk assessment of the health implications of MMT. It found that MMT did not pose a risk to health.[24]

It is difficult to ascertain the degree of health risk posed by the use of MMT in gasoline, given the wide divergence of scientific evidence on this topic. It is significant to note that MMT has not passed the thresholds required in order to be banned as a toxic substance under the CEPA. Article 34 of CEPA would allow a ban on MMT as a 'toxic substance'. This would require Health Canada to declare it as such, an action which has not been taken due to a lack of supporting evidence. Articles 46 and 47 of CEPA would permit a ban on MMT if there is clear evidence that it would impair the functioning of vehicle equipment. The 'precautionary principle' approach is not included in this section; a fairly high hurdle is imposed which requires scientific evidence to be definitive.[25] Environment Canada decided not proceed by this route because of the inconclusive and contradictory evidence on whether MMT did indeed impair the functioning of vehicle equipment.[26]

2. Indirect Effects: MMT and Autos The Canadian Vehicle Manufacturers Association (CVMA) has consistently supported a ban on MMT since the early 1990s. The CVMA, which represents all twenty-two manufacturers who supply automobiles to the Canadian market, has done extensive testing and research on the effects of MMT on automobiles. It claims that MMT leaves residues in the auto systems which have an adverse effect on oxygen sensors and catalytic converters and are responsible for spark plug misfire. As the vehicle manufacturers have anticipated the new generation of emissions standards, the majority of 1996 vehicles for sale in Canada meet 1996 US federal emission requirements. A central element of these is the On-board Diagnostic System (OBD II), which will be mandatory beginning in 1998. MMT residues affect the monitoring of the catalysts and malfunction indicator lights which identifies to drivers emissions-related problems in vehicles. This has led to an increase in warranty claims and corresponding costs which are passed along to the consumer. Some manufacturers have gone so far as to write exclusions from liability into their warranties if MMT gasoline is used.[27] Manufacturers are further threatening to withdraw the industry-standard 100,000 kilometre warranty if MMT is not removed from gasoline.[28] This would have an enormous impact on Canadian consumers.

Moreover, the CVMA notes that pollution-reducing technology to date has focused on vehicle hardware, rather than gasoline formulation. The CVMA argues that it is necessary to improve gasoline formulation as well, in order to attain the standards for better ambient air quality demanded by the public (MVMA 1995).

Members of the CVMA have invested over $4 billion in research and development to meet the new emissions standards which remove up to 98 per cent of hydrocarbons, carbon monoxide, and nitrogen oxide from exhaust emissions. This technology is at risk of becoming ineffective with the use of MMT. Such technology is developed for one North American market through joint venture research of the major auto firms. The US emission standards, while undergoing revisions, are currently more stringent than Canadian ones. However, different technology cannot be developed for different jurisdictions; it must be viable for the whole continent, which would further support the auto industry's goal of a harmonized gasoline standard. The CVMA contends that it is impossible to meet the demand for reduced air emissions while MMT is in gasoline. It argues that the various stakeholders must pull together to solve the pollution problem. Such a team effort requires the efforts of consumers, fuel suppliers, maintenance providers, and the government in order to continue to minimize environmental impacts (ibid. 13).

In response to these claims, the Canadian Petroleum Products Institute (CPPI) commissioned a study to consider the effects of MMT on vehicle emission monitoring systems. The study involved testing 206 vehicles with an aggregate mileage of 11.4 million kilometres.[29] The study did not find evidence of any negative effect on 180 of 185 test vehicles. The remaining five had either problems not related to the use of MMT, and one had a faulty spark plug.[30] Additional testing conducted by Ethyl Corp. has found that MMT had no effect on OBD II or any other vehicle equipment.[31]

In its review of Bill C-29, the Senate Standing Committee considered the question of whether MMT did indeed cause OBD malfunctioning. The Committee noted how diametrically opposed the evidence presented was. However, it concluded that in light of the precautionary principle, Bill C-29 was a responsible, prudent course of action on the part of the federal government.[32]

Given this divergent and highly technical evidence, it is difficult to evaluate the extent to which MMT does in fact harm emission control systems. Admittedly, on the part of the auto industry, the real concern is whether a North American industry standard will emerge in automobiles, fuel and hardware which will allow them to best capitalize on their sunk costs in technology development. One North American standard in one North American market will further allow them to leverage costs and achieve scale economies. In that sense, the consequences of losing this battle could have detrimental economic impacts on them.

The Protected Industry Claim

Environment Canada introduced Bill C-29 as part of a 'Clean Air Agenda' designed to improve air quality.[33] The agenda gives priority to 'new car emission standards, new fuel efficiency rules and new encouragement for alternative fuels'. This item originated from a set of recommendations by the Canadian Council of Ministers of the Environment (CCME) Task Force on Cleaner Vehicles and Fuels (CCME 1995a). The recommendations were developed through a consultative process which included representatives from ENGOs and industry among others (CCME 1995b). The first recommendation of this report was the upward harmonization of vehicle emission standards with the United States (CCME 1995a). The second recommendation encouraged the development of alternative fuels and vehicles (CCME 1995a). The fifth recommendation established maximum sulphur content for low-sulphur diesel fuels (CCME 1995a). The sixth recommendation established maximum amounts of toxic chemicals which contribute to air pollution and ozone depletion: benzene, aromatics, olefins, and sulphur (CCME 1995a). The report concluded that by following these recommendations, there would be significant reductions in fine particulate matter, ozone, and toxic emissions. Corresponding health benefits would accrue to Canadians over the next twenty-three years: mortality would be reduced by up to 4,400; chronic bronchitis by up to 29,600; and cancer by up to 60 cases. The report further claimed that the economic benefits could reach $31 billion over the same time period.[34]

The report did not directly address the issue of MMT in gasoline, but did so indirectly through the support of stricter standards and specific ceilings on pollution-causing chemicals. The levels of emissions supported by this report could not be met by the current automobile technology and fuel containing MMT. The report also highlights the fact that MMT issue is really part of a larger framework in which fuel formulations are coming under increasing scrutiny, in particular other fuel additives such as benzene and sulphur. Environment Canada has initiated action on all of these recommendations.

In furtherance of these recommendations and the Clean Air Agenda, the issue of alternative fuel additives has moved into the spotlight. Ethanol, produced primarily from corn, is a more expensive and cleaner alternative to MMT. The ethanol industry claims that the use of ethanol in gasoline will result in a 25–30 per cent reduction in emissions of carbon monoxide and an unspecified reduction in particulate matter, air toxics, and ozone.[35] Unlike fossil fuels which release greenhouse gases into the atmosphere when utilized, ethanol is produced from renewable biological feedstocks such as grain. It is also alleged that the use of ethanol as a fuel additive will benefit the economy as well. This is due to the fact that increased ethanol production will provide a new market for agricultural products, which will make farming more economically viable. These economic benefits will ripple outward—leading to increased employment and increased opportunities for farming to transportation and manufacturing.

The industry further argues that prices will fall as production increases and economies of scale are achieved. There are currently four ethanol plants in Canada. Commercial Alcohol has two plants, one recently built in Chatham, Ontario, and the other in Tiverton, Ontario. There are also plants in Saskatchewan and Manitoba. Among the economic claims of the plant in Chatham, Ontario, are the creation of 400 direct and indirect jobs, a new market for 15 million bushels of locally produced corn annually, and additional economic activity from trucking maintenance and supplies required for the plant. Commercial Alcohol has also stated that its product contains over 75 per cent Canadian content. Its press release also cited a number of additional Canadian suppliers which had substantial contracts in place at the time the Chatham plant was built (RFA 1997).

Environment Canada has provided financial support to Canada's fledgling ethanol industry[36] and further has justified the ban on the basis that it will provide an opportunity for ethanol as well as other fuel substitutes (Environment Canada 1996a). This would be consistent, according to Environment Canada, with a national policy to support the domestic production and use of renewable fuels (ibid.).

This suggests that the ban on MMT was not undertaken for purely health reasons, but to provide 'shelter' for a domestic 'infant industry' competing with a mature US-owned industry producing and importing into Canada.[37] This brings into question the motivations of the Canadian government in passing Bill C-29. There is a strong agriculture lobby, pressing for protection and assistance, to which the government appears responsive (Corcoran 1996c: B2). Vogel has found a similar political economy of ethanol in the United States, where a powerful farm lobby exists. He notes that it has historically been a heavily subsidized and protected industry not for its environmental benefits, which are dubious, but in order to increase farm income and reduce US dependence on imported oil.

The Canadian Petroleum Products Institute (CPPI), which represents all major oil producers in Canada, has raised concerns about the environmental claims of the ethanol industry. The CPPI argues that a full environmental lifecycle analysis (i.e. from the growth of corn to the burning of the fuel) must be undertaken to really evaluate its environmental benefits.[38] Vogel notes that ethanol is not clearly more environmentally friendly than its alternatives. He cites a study undertaken by the National Academy of Sciences in the United States which found that the use of gasohol would reduce carbon-monoxide emissions by 25 per cent but correspondingly increase hydrocarbons by as much as 50 per cent and nitrogen oxide by 15 per cent (Vogel 1997: 114). The

150   *Case Studies*

study also found that ozone pollution (smog) may increase due to the fast evaporation rate of ethanol and thus concluded that its use will not necessarily increase air quality, and very well may be detrimental (Vogel 1997, quoting Bovard 1995: 24–8).

The CPPI is particularly concerned about how this issue is resolved because of the other octane enhancers (sulphur, benzene) which will be considered under the Clean Air Agenda. It is alleged that the cost of cutting sulphur from gasoline would be high for oil refineries. A recent draft report by a joint committee of industry and government examined the health and economic benefits of reducing sulphur pollution from cars and trucks. It estimated that the cost of removing sulphur from their gasoline to the level of California benchmark would cost an initial investment of $1.8 billion plus millions annually in operating costs.[39]

MMT and International Institutional Dispute Settlement

Ethyl Corp. has put forth a number of claims that the Canadian regulation of MMT violates several sections of NAFTA. It has actively sought redress under NAFTA's state-to-state dispute settlement procedures (Chapter 20) and NAFTA's investor–state dispute settlement mechanism (Chapter 11).[40] The Chapter 20 dispute has not proceeded to arbitration to date, but the Chapter 11 case was settled before full adjudication by an international arbitral panel. In the Canadian domestic courts, Ethyl Corp. has additionally alleged that the regulation is unconstitutional as it amounts to 'an unwarranted intrusion into an area of provincial jurisdiction' (McKenna 1997: B8). Additionally, the recent victory of the governments of Alberta, Saskatchewan, and Quebec over the federal government in a dispute under the Agreement on Internal Trade (AIT) is examined.

NAFTA's Chapter 11

Chapter 11 of NAFTA provides rules for the resolution of investor–state disputes through arbitral panels. Companies or individuals from a NAFTA country who are investors in another NAFTA country can initiate a claim against the government of the host country if they believe that their rights under the specific provisions of Chapter 11 of NAFTA have been breached (Eklund 1992). Thus, Chapter 11 does not provide an expansive list of grounds on which to bring an action, unlike the state-to-state dispute settlement mechanism, Chapter 20, where the breach of almost any provision it actionable. Although a number of cases have been initiated under Chapter 11, no other case has resulted in the establishment of a dispute settlement panel to date.

In September 1996 Ethyl Corp. filed a $251 million (US) claim against the Canadian federal government, on behalf of its investment in Canada, namely Ethyl Canada Inc. (Americas Trade 1997*a*: 9). The Ethyl case has gone the furthest in using the provisions of Chapter 11—a panel was established in late 1997 under the rules provided by the United Nations Commission for International Trade (UNCITRAL).[41]

Ethyl claimed that Bill C-29 is inconsistent with three provisions of NAFTA: national treatment, performance requirements, and NAFTA expropriation provisions.[42] National treatment requires non-discriminatory treatment between foreign and domestic firms.[42] Bill C-29 does not explicitly prohibit the sale of Canadian-made MMT, it just prohibits its movement. By prohibiting its movement, however, it prevents the sale of foreign-made MMT in Canada. Thus, hypothetically, Ontario-made MMT could be legally produced and sold within the province. However, as previously noted, only one producer—Ethyl Corp.—holds the patent and produces MMT in North America. Ethyl made the case that Bill C-29 violates NAFTA's national treatment provisions because it discriminates against Ethyl Canada and Ethyl Corporation because MMT can still be produced and used locally (Standing Committee 1997). National treatment provisions are further breached because, since there is no difference between MMT produced in a province or in the United States, Bill C-29 could confer an unfair advantage to Canadian-based investors selling the same product, as opposed to non-Canadian based investors (ibid.).

Under NAFTA Chapter 11, governments are prohibited from imposing performance requirements, that is, imposing additional demands on a firm as a condition of an investment in a NAFTA country.[44] Ethyl Inc. contends that its subsidiary, Ethyl Canada, is required to purchase Canadian-made MMT in order to remain in the MMT distribution business. In this way, Bill C-29 imposes performance requirements on Ethyl Canada. It violates NAFTA prohibition on performance requirements, by requiring the purchase of local goods.[45] In order to retain its presence in the Canadian market, it will be required to purchase Canadian-made MMT. As there is no manufacturer of MMT presently in Canada, Ethyl would thus be required to build manufacturing and blending plants in each province or territory of Canada.

Finally, Ethyl Corp. argues that Bill C-29 is tantamount to expropriation under NAFTA, as Ethyl Canada's business has been terminated with the ban. Such expropriation, according to NAFTA, requires compensation (Standing Committee 1997). Specifically, Ethyl Corp. is alleging a loss in value in its manufacturing plant, a decline in future sales, and damage to its corporate reputation (Sforza and Valliantos 1997).

Arguments were also presented at the Standing Senate Committee that Bill C-29 was not contrary to NAFTA, as Canada has the right to pursue the type and degree of environmental protection it desires and that Canada is further permitted to adopt a precautionary stance on MMT. It was further argued that concern about the national treatment issue is unfounded for two reasons. First, since there currently exists no Canadian facility which produces MMT, Bill C-29 does not discriminate in favour of domestic production and second, the obligation to provide national treatment does not encompass situations

152 *Case Studies*

where a separate domestic industry may receive tangential benefits such as ethanol.[46] It was further argued that an adverse impact of a bona fide regulation does not constitute expropriation under Chapter 11.[47]

In July 1998 a settlement was reached outside the panel process where the Canadian government agreed to pay Ethyl Corp. $19.3 million (for costs and lost profit) and repeal the ban on MMT (McCarthy 1998*b*: A3). The Canadian government announced that there was no evidence that MMT was harmful in low amounts to human health (ibid.). The government further stated that the auto industry had failed to make the case that MMT damaged their on-board diagnostic systems (ibid.). This was a major victory for Ethyl Corp., who now plan to use the repealed ban as a part of their worldwide marketing strategy for MMT (ibid.).

NAFTA's Chapter 20

An additional option for Ethyl was to persuade the US government to initiate dispute settlement procedures with the Canadian government under NAFTA's Chapter 20. There is currently no Chapter 20 claim in progress. Chapter 20 of NAFTA provides a mechanism for state-to-state dispute settlement (Kirton and Soloway 1996), which can be used for 'any actual or proposed measure or any other matter that it considers might affect the operation of NAFTA'.[48] In order for a Chapter 20 case to be initiated, the United States Trade Representative (USTR) would have to take up Ethyl's case against the Canadian government. Given the position of EPA on MMT, it is unlikely that the Clinton Administration will take up this issue.[49] Despite the low likelihood that a Chapter 20 panel will be actually established, a case has been established that Bill C-29 is contrary to NAFTA. Concerned about the number of trade irritants between Canada and the United States, Canadian Minister of International Trade wrote a letter to then Environment Minister Sergio Marchi expressing his concern about the reintroduction of Bill C-29, due to its potential as a serious trade issue and its lack of corresponding environmental benefits.[50]

In its efforts to convince the US government to take up its claim, Ethyl Corp. has argued that Bill C-29 violated NAFTA in two ways.[51] First, a ban in MMT would violate NAFTA's national treatment provisions, for the same reasons as outlined in the Chapter 11 claim.[52] Second, although NAFTA recognizes the freedom of parties to adopt measures relating to the protection of the environment, such measures cannot constitute an unnecessary obstacle to trade unless it can be shown that its purpose is to achieve a legitimate objective. The purpose of the legislation is to remove MMT from the Canadian market. The legislation fails to meet this objective, since MMT can still be produced and sold within Canada. Therefore, the argument was put forth that it could not be shown that the measure achieved the desired objective.[53] The failure of the US government thus far to take up Ethyl's Chapter 20 claim, and the unlikelihood that it will in the future, underlines how important the NAFTA right of direct access to dispute settlement for firms under Chapter 11 is for Ethyl's protecting its competitive position.

Canada's Agreement on Internal Trade (AIT)

At the time of the passage of the FTA, it became apparent that Canada needed the same liberalized movement of goods not just internationally but interprovincially as well. Free trade was required not just along the north–south axis, but east–west as well. The logic of globalization requires reduction of local and national barriers, and that firms operate at larger, more efficient, scales to become competitive. Thus, the Agreement on Internal Trade was born, with NAFTA functioning as the causal catalyst and the model for the agreement, particularly with respect to its dispute settlement mechanism and the exceptions it provided in the case of trade-restricting environmental regulation. The AIT thus helped to both avoid the regulatory fragmentation between provinces that threatened to undermine the gains from trade and to help Canadian firms to meet the challenges of the increasingly global market place.

Under the Chapter 17 dispute resolution provisions of the AIT, a challenge of the legality of the ban in MMT was launched by the Canadian provincial governments of Alberta (the home of Canada's oil industry), and backed by Quebec and Saskatchewan (McCarthy 1998a: B1). In July 1998 a panel ruled in favour of these provinces. The three provinces had requested that Ottawa repeal the ban, and to further work jointly with the provinces on the scientific uncertainty surrounding its safety (ibid.).

Much like NAFTA, the objectives of the AIT are to 'reduce and eliminate barriers to the free movement of goods, services, persons and investments within Canada' and 'to establish an open, efficient and stable domestic market'.[54] Similar to NAFTA, trade barriers can be established where it can be demonstrated that such barriers achieve a legitimate objective based on sound science and risk assessment without imposing an undue or disguised restriction on trade.[55] The three provinces challenged the bill on the basis that the legislation does not meet these requirements, as the intraprovincial ban is an example of federal favouritism of the auto industry over the refineries (McCarthy 1988a: B1).

All of these three challenging provinces have large refineries, whose interests are adversely affected by the regulation. In its submission to the panel, Alberta cited the expected injury to Alberta refineries alone of such a ban as amounting to $12 million in capital costs and $11 million annually in operating costs. About one-quarter of the operational costs of the ban, that is, the monitoring necessary to enforce the ban, would also be borne by the Alberta refineries. Additional costs would be imposed on those who wished to develop stockpiling facilities. Furthermore, the efficiency and convenience of current supply arrangements would be disrupted.

The reasons of Saskatchewan and Quebec in bringing the case were similar

154   *Case Studies*

to those of Alberta. However, in the case of Saskatchewan, its refinery had no suitable facilities for stockpiling MMT, and therefore ran out of MMT shortly after the legislation came into force. The Saskatchewan refinery had already undertaken the expense of adopting alternative additives and processes to boost its octane ratings at the time of the hearing. Thus, Saskatchewan's search for relief for the industry took on a somewhat different tone and status from that of Alberta.

An additional central argument of the provinces was that the federal government was trespassing in an area of provincial jurisdiction, thus damaging federal–provincial cooperation. In their submission to the Senate Standing Committee on Energy, the Environment and Natural Resources, the Alberta government argued that the ban in MMT was not consistent with the principles of sound regulation[56] for three reasons. First, where there are issues of overlapping jurisdiction, there should be federal–provincial consultation. Of particular concern is the need to work cooperatively to ensure a more consistent regulatory framework in the area of environmental harmonization.[57] Here, the federal government acted unilaterally, without taking provincial objections into account. Second, the provinces argued that regulations must be in pursuit of a clear public purpose and enacted in a way that is effective and efficient.[58] The ban in MMT does not meet this standard. Furthermore, the regulatory policy of the Treasury Board Secretariat was disregarded. This mandates public consultation, a clear justification for federal intervention, and respect for intergovernmental agreements. Third, the appropriateness of the instrument was brought into question. By enacting this legislation, the federal government brings its commitment to free trade into question. It further violates the principle of directness which states that the regulatory framework must apply directly to that which it regulates. A direct approach would be to place an outright ban on the substance, not just its movement.[59]

Chapter 11 and Complex Institutional Responsiveness

The MMT case illustrates the significance of granting firms direct access to NAFTA's dispute settlement mechanism. It allows foreign investors to challenge discriminatory environmental regulation without the political support previously necessary on the part of national governments. The success of this strategy will no doubt lead to additional firms bringing similar actions under the Chapter 11. The Ethyl case has given an indication that the Chapter 11 process may yet prove to be used as a vehicle to combat environmental and regulatory protectionism. Indeed, in the last year, three additional pending claims under Chapter 11 were initiated. All three of these cases have an environmental dimension and are currently at different stages of progress. Table 8.1 provides a list of the six Chapter 11 cases to date at their different levels of progress, four of which are environmentally related.

MMT and Investment Dispute Settlement 155

TABLE 8.1. *NAFTA Chapter 11 cases initiated*

Firm (nationality) and type of business	Country of regulation challenge	Level of progress
Hachette Distribution Service (US and Canadian) Airport shop concessions	Mexico	Not pursued beyond initial filing
Signa S.A. de C.V. (Mexican) Pharmaceuticals	Canada	Not pursued beyond initial filing
Ethyl Corp. (US) MMT fuel additive	Canada	Settled outside panel process
Metalclad (US) Hazardous waste disposal	Mexico	In progress
DESONA (US) Waste disposal	Mexico	In progress
USA Waste (US) Street cleaning and landfills	Mexico	Filed first brief

The first case with an environmental dimension involves a complaint filed with the Mexican government in October 1997 by Metalclad Inc., a hazardous waste disposal company based in Newport Beach, California. It claims that the state government of San Luis Potos prevented it from establishing a hazardous waste landfill and is seeking US $65 million for breach of contract. Another similar case is expected to be filed on behalf of the US-owned waste disposal company Desechos Solidos de Naucalpan de C.V. (DESONA). At a preliminary hearing on 25 September 1997, the owners of DESONA, who are seeking $17 million in damages, stated that their property was seized by armed agents of the government of the city of Naucalpan (Fleischer 1997). A third case also has an environmental dimension—it involves a Houston-based waste management company, USA Waste, which is seeking US $60 million in damages for the alleged breach of an agreement granting a street-cleaning concession in Acapulco and permission to develop a landfill. USA Waste's Mexican subsidiary is alleging that it performed the street cleaning but received no payment, forcing it to abandon its investment. The firm also claims that it was forced to abandon its investment of millions of dollars in the design and initial development of the landfill site (Americas Trade 1998: 3).

The increasing use of this mechanism illustrates that firms are slowly beginning to use the new political strategies of complex institutional responsiveness in the case of environmental protectionism, an element of all four of the Chapter 11 cases to date. The Chapter 11 process becomes particularly appealing as a firm strategy when considering the options. Ethyl Corp. had the option of the traditional strategy of lobbying its government to bring a case under the Chapter 20 state-to-state dispute settlement mechanism. This option was not successful because its home government would not take up the case. The fact that the company had direct access to the tribunal through the new institutional dispute settlement procedure was the key to its success. Likewise, domestically, the traditional strategy of challenging the regulation in the domestic courts has not been successful. But the Canadian ITA has given firms, through provincial governments, the option of challenging a trade-restricting environmental regulation under different provisions. Thus, the ITA reflects the same conditions of complex institutional responsiveness under NAFTA.

All four of the potential environmental dispute settlement cases have been US companies that are using NAFTA to combat discriminatory environmental regulation in Canada and Mexico, rather than vice versa. Yet this is very weak evidence that NAFTA is evolving as a hegemonic imposition of US interests over those of its weaker trading partners. Such a fear is not based on the institutional structure of Chapter 11 panels, since there is nothing unique in the dispute settlement mechanism to allow the United States to use it to the exclusion of Canada and Mexico.

The fuel additives issue has become a Byzantine structure of business interests, environmental coalitions, and political manoeuvring on a number of different levels. In this case, a complex 'Baptist–Bootlegger' coalition has been created. The environmental and consumer advocacy groups are working in the public interest, as they believe that MMT is harmful to the environment and human health. They are joined by essentially two 'bootleggers': the ethanol producers and the auto manufacturers. The ethanol producers are the more obvious bootleggers. This group has undertaken lobbying efforts to have MMT banned, are being heavily subsidized by the Canadian government, and, as a firm, have a wealth maximization agenda.[60] The ethanol producers, however, are minuscule compared to the size and power of the auto manufacturers, who stand to gain or lose a great deal depending on the outcome of the MMT dispute. It may be unfair, however, to cast the auto industry in the light of the bootlegger, as they are responding to the increasingly strict demands on the part of consumers and government to develop cleaner technologies. In this way, they are only partially 'cloaking' themselves in a public interest agenda, as that agenda has been imposed on them. The more subtle point is that the auto manufacturers are attempting to shift that burden to the oil producers through this regulation.

The outcome of this case will have far-reaching implications to the resolution of environmentally related trade and investment disputes. One major concern surrounds the environmental efficacy of the measure. This is difficult to judge without the full scientific data on MMT. Here the least trade-restrictive policy has not been used and the better alternative would have been to have banned MMT as a toxic substance under CEPA, pending further scientific evidence. Clearly there are trade-offs between the alternatives that need to be evaluated fully. The case that ethanol is the superior additive is far from clear from an environmental standpoint. Although ethanol emissions are arguably less polluting, more accurate would be a life-cycle analysis which assesses environmental impact from start to finish.

A related issue is the weight that should be accorded to the precautionary principle which states that when there is a small but serious risk posed by a potential toxin, regulators should err on the side of caution.[61] The conduct of a cost-benefit analysis becomes even more controversial where there is no agreement on the supporting science. The controversy surrounding the scientific evidence highlights the great difficulty facing trade policy today, that is, in a world of limited scientific knowledge, how can good policy decisions be made? Scientific data has the initial appeal of being completely objective, but in fact, scientific inquiry is riddled with value judgements. Scientific risk assessments are by nature uncertain and even the choice of methodology necessary to conduct a risk assessment requires to some degree a normative judgement (see Fralbery and Trebllcock 1998 and Wirth 1994).

An additional concern arises from the subsidy and protection given to the ethanol industry. Many economists view subsidies and protection as business environments where firm inefficiencies flourish. Such policies stand to allow a relatively small number of well-organized and well-financed individuals that represent specific industry interests to gain at the expense of the broader consumer welfare. What cost does this represent to the Canadian taxpayer? Could this be a farm welfare programme in disguise? To what extent have competitive distortions been introduced into the agricultural market place and its secondary markets such as feedgrains for livestock? These are the additional policy considerations that arise in the tension between trade and investment liberalization and environmental regulation.

NOTES

1. Bill C-29, The Manganese-Based Fuel Additives Act 1996. MMT is an acronym for methylcyclopentadienyl manganese tricarbonyl.
2. The Honourable Sergio Marchi, PC, MP, Minister of the Environment, *Statement to the Senate Standing Committee on Energy, Environment and Natural Resources on Bill C-29: The Manganese Based Fuel Additives Act*, delivered at Parliament Hill, Ottawa, 20 Feb. 1997.
3. Canadian Environmental Protection Act., RSC 1985, c. 16 (4th Supp.) (hereinafter CEPA).
4. The OECD has studied this issue. See OECD 1996; see also Sykes 1995.
5. The addition of octane enhancers to gasoline, such as MMT, allows gasoline refiners to increase fuel efficiency. Ethyl cites that MMT allows gasoline refiners to increase Research Octane Numbers up to approximately 1.5 to 2 units. According to the Canadian Petroleum Products Institute (CPPI), the amount of MMT in gasoline has ranged from 0 to 17.2 milligrams of manganese per litre. The Canadian General Standards Board has set a maximum allowable amount of 18 milligrams per litre. See Standing Committee 1997.
6. See Ethyl website <http://www.ethyl.com/mmt.html>.

158 *Case Studies*

7. Interview with the Honourable Ralph Ferguson, former Minister of Agriculture, 10 July 1997. Mr Ferguson was responsible for introducing a Private Members' Bill in the House of Commons to ban MMT.
8. For a comprehensive history of the disputes between EPA and Ethyl Corp., see Pocalyko 1995.
9. Ethyl Corporation, *MMT Timeline*, Ethyl Corporation website at <http://www.ethyl.com/mmt.html>.
10. Title II of the Act, 42 USC §§ 7521–7590 (1988 & Supp. V 1993). For a comprehensive evaluation of s. 211 of the Clean Air Act, see Reitze 1994.
11. Testimony of C. Hicks of Ethyl Corporation, 5 Feb. 1997, found in Standing Committee 1997.
12. United States Federal Register, Volume 58, No. 235, Thursday, 9 Dec. 1993, p. 64761.
13. United States Federal Register, Volume 60, No. 136, Monday, 17 July 1995, p. 36414.
14. *Ethyl Corporation v. Environmental Protection Agency et al.*, United States Court of Appeals for the District of Columbia Circuit, No. 94-1505.
15. Note 7 above.
16. The oil companies that have confirmed in letters to the Environmental Defense Fund that they are not presently using MMT are: Amoco, Anchor, ARCO, BP, Chevron, Conoco, Exxon, Hess, Marathon Oil, Mobil, Pennzoil, Phillips, Shell, Sun, and Texaco. The reasons that these companies are not using MMT was not stated in the newsletter. Apart from environmental concerns, it is possible that the companies do not want to undergo expensive capital changes to blending facilities in order to use MMT, which had been banned for the previous 17 years. It is also possible that they are waiting to see how this issue finally settles, given its current volatility.
17. Groups opposed to MMT in Canada are represented by the Coalition for Banning MMT and include: The Allergy/Asthma Information Association, Association of International Automobile Manufacturers in Canada, Canadian Automobile Association, Canadian Institute of Child Health, Council of Canadians, the Cities of North York and Toronto Public Health Departments, Environmental Defense Fund, Learning Disabilities Association of Canada, Motor Vehicle Manufacturers' Association of Canada, Ontario Public Health Association, Pollution Probe, and Sierra Club of Canada. See Canada NewsWire, 'Coalition Want MMT-Free Fuel for Canadians Now', 18 Sept. 1996, at <http://www.newswire.ca>. Groups opposed to MMT in the United States include: Environmental Defense Fund, Alliance to End Childhood Lead Poisoning, American Lung Association of Massachusetts, American Psychological Association, Boston Women's Health Book Collective, Centre for Auto Safety, Centre for Environmental Legal Studies, Clean Air Council, Coalition to End Childhood Lead Poisoning, Conservation Law Foundation, Consumer's Union, Environmental Advocates, Environmental Health Watch, Friends of the Earth, Harbour-UCLA Research and Education Institute, Intercommunity Centre for Justice and Peace, The Joseph P. Kennedy, Jr. Foundation, Kentucky Resources Council, Inc., Lead Safe California, League of Conservation Voters, Learning Disability Association, Montana Environmental Information Centre, National Parks and Conservation Assoc., National Wildlife

Federation, Natural Resources Council of Maine, Natural Resources Defense Council, New Jersey City Action, Parkinson's Action Network, Parkinson's Disease Foundation, Inc., Physicians for Social Responsibility, Population Action International, Sierra Club, Sierra Club Legal Defense Fund, Inc., Society for Developmental and Behavioural Pediatrics, United Methodist Board of Church and Society, US Public Interest Research Group, Zero Population Growth. See Environmental Defense Fund, Letter to Mr L. G. Rawl, Chairman and CEO, Exxon Corporation, 14 Feb. 1996 and Environmental Defense Fund 1996b.
18. Environmental Defense Fund, Letter to Mr L. G. Rawl, Chairman and CEO, Exxon Corporation, 14 Feb. 1996. See also Sierra Club 1996.
19. Ibid.
20. Gina Solomon MD, MPH, 'MMT Manganese in Gasoline: Potential Public Health Effects', a position paper of Greater Boston Physicians for Social Responsibility, <http://www.igc.apc.org/psr/index.html>.
21. Ibid.
22. Canada NewsWire, 'Coalition Want MMT-Free Fuel for Canadians Now', 18 Sept. 1996, at <http://www.newswire.ca>.
23. Ethyl Corporation, MMT Q&A, Ethyl Corporation website at <http://www.ethyl.com/mmt.html>.
24. Testimony of D. Krewski, Health Canada, 6 Feb. 1997, found in Standing Committee 1997.
25. This may soon change. A recent proposal to amend CEPA died in Parliament, but may be reintroduced. There were significant increases in the power of CEPA to enshrine pollution prevention as a national goal'. See Environment Canada 1995.
26. Interview with Frank Vena, Environment Canada, 8 July 1997.
27. Interview with Mark Nantais, President, Canadian Vehicle Manufacturing Association, 11 July 1997.
28. Interview with Mark Nantais. See also Sillars 1996.
29. Canada NewsWire, 'Province's Concern Over MMT Ban Confirmed By New Study Released Today', 29 October 1996 at <http://www.newswire.ca>.
30. Ibid.
31. Ibid.
32. Ibid.
33. The Clean Air Agenda contains five priorities as outlined by Minister Sergio Marchi at the Transportation, Air Quality, and Human Health Conference at York University, Toronto, 25 Apr. 1996: (1) The health of Canadians; (2) federal leadership on national environmental standards and the modernization of the Canadian Environmental Protection Act; (3) new car emission standards, new fuel efficiency rules, and new encouragement for alternative fuels; (4) building environmental citizenship and partnership across Canadian society; and (5) vigorous bilateral and multilateral action.
34. See 'Table of Health Benefits: Estimated Health Benefits (1997–2020) for Canada' (CCME 1995a).
35. Commercial Alcohol website at <www.comalc.com>. See also Renewable Fuels Association Homepage <www.ethanolrfa.org> and Canadian Renewable Fuels Association Homepage <www.greenfuels.org>. There is currently a strong and effective US ethanol lobby which has succeeded in securing tax incentives for the ethanol industry. See RFA 1997: 51.

160 *Case Studies*

36. Interview with Jim Johnson, President, Canadian Renewable Fuels Association, 10 July 1997.
37. Although MMT is distributed through its Canadian subsidiary, it is really a US product. See Rugman and Verbeke (1990).
38. Interview with Brendan Hawley, Vice-President, Government Relations, Canadian Petroleum Products Institute, Apr. 1996.
39. The *Financial Post* obtained copies of these reports that are not available to date (Geddes 1997: 10).
40. For the NAFTA Chapter 20 claim, see 'U.S. may Challenge Canada via NAFTA in MMT Case, Ex-Negotiator says', *Inside NAFTA*, 29 Nov. 1995 and 'Company may Press US for NAFTA Challenge on Canadian Fuel Bill', *Inside NAFTA*, 15 Nov. 1995. For the NAFTA Chapter 11 claim, see 'Canadian MMT Bill Heads to Senate, Closer to Chapter 11 Complaint', *Inside NAFTA*, 8 Jan. 1997.
41. The arbitral panel for the case is comprised of three members. Presiding over the case is Karl Heinz Bocksteigel, a German professor. The US member is Charles Brower, an international arbitration lawyer located in Washington, DC, and the Canadian member is Marc Lalonde, also an international arbitration lawyer and former bureaucrat. See Americas Trade (1997a: 9).
42. As the Chapter 11 case is currently pending, the submissions of the parties to the proceedings are not available. The argument outlined here is taken from the testimony of Ethyl's trade counsel, Barry Appleton, before the Standing Senate Committee on Energy, the Environment and Natural Resources, 19 Feb. 1997. Mr Appleton was asked to comment on the legality of Bill C-29 with respect to NAFTA.
43. NAFTA Article 1102.
44. NAFTA Article 1106.
45. NAFTA Article 1106.
46. Presentation by Ivan Feltham, QC to Senate Standing Committee, 19 Feb. 1997.
47. Ibid.
48. NAFTA Article 2006(1).
49. Interview with Alan Alexandroff, Special Counsel to Ethyl Corp., 9 July 1997.
50. Letter from Minister of International Trade, Art Eggleton, to Environment Minister, Sergio Marchi, on the illegality of Bill C-29. See Morton and Toulin 1997.
51. Ethyl Corp. relied on an analysis done by Gordon Ritchie, Former Deputy Chief Negotiator for the Canada–US Free Trade Agreement and current Chief Executive Officer of Strategico, Inc., a public policy consulting firm. See 'US may Challenge Canada via NAFTA in MMT Case, Ex-Negotiator says', *Inside NAFTA*, 29 Nov. 1995.
52. See analysis of Chapter 11 breach above. Gordon Ritchie wrote, 'We would argue that an outright prohibition against the importation of U.S. produced MMT, while allowing the continued production and sale of MMT within Canada, amounts to a violation of the national treatment obligation.' See ibid.
53. Ibid.
54. See Articles 101–103 of the ITA. For a more comprehensive analysis of this issue, see Lenihan 1995. See also CCME 1995c.
55. See Articles 210, 404, and Annex 405.1, 405.2 of the ITA.
56. Available at the Government of Alberta website: <http:\\www.gov.ab.ca/iaa-/html/billc29.html>.

57. Ibid.
58. Ibid.
59. Ibid.
60. Interview with Jim Johnson, President, Canadian Renewable Fuels Association, 10 July 1997.
61. For a concise formulation of the precautionary principle in the context of trade, see Blackhurst et al. 1994.

9
The Agriculture Disputes

Food safety, trade, and industry protection have evolved into a major issue on the trade policy agenda around the world. This is seen in the WTO Appellate Body's 1998 Beef Hormones decision. The dispute involved the use of growth hormones in the production of beef by both the United States and Canada. Long considered by the EU to be detrimental to human health, hormone-treated beef was thus excluded from the European market, costing North American beef producers hundreds of millions of dollars since 1989. This dispute provided the impetus to develop a detailed sanitary and phytosanitary (SPS) measures code under the auspices of the WTO legal framework, in order to specify what is permissible when countries regulate environmental health and safety standards differently.

In the case of Beef Hormones, both the WTO panel and the subsequent appeal body found that the EU's actions amounted to an unjustifiable restriction on trade and were therefore inconsistent with its trading obligations under the WTO. This decision is thus a victory for those who viewed the restriction on US and Canadian beef as little more than industry protection. Most significantly, this decision underscored for national policymakers that the trade implications of the decisions they make within their domestic sphere must be taken into account in formulating policy. It further underscored the importance of having measures based on sound science and risk assessment, and having some relation to internationally set standards.

From the advent of the WTO to 1998, there have been five cases concerning trade-restricting environmental standards. And within the WTO SPS Committee which attempts to handle such issues before they develop into full-scale disputes, it seems as if more are on the way. In 1998 Australia, Argentina, Brazil, Canada, Senegal, Malaysia, and the United States took issue with the EU's proposed maximum allowable levels of the micro-toxin aflatoxin in agriculture (BRIDGES 1998; Journal of Commerce 1998). The EU is seeking a much stricter standard than other countries, who argue that the health effects are not relevant in the present case. Other related issues concern cumbersome SPS rules in South Korea, and a Japanese ban on US apples (ibid.). And a number of Latin American countries appear to be fearful that new US SPS rules will have a trade-restricting effect on their fruit and vegetable exports, thereby providing protection to US producers (ibid.).

The key problem is that the domestic administration of SPS measures can be captured, or at least influenced, by domestic producers seeking shelter against more competitive foreign imports. Since fresh food products are highly sensitive to quality deterioration, and since the science of health codes and other environmental regulations is a national prerogative, it is relatively easy for domestic producer interests to raise fears against foreign products. This can create a barrier to entry, as the foreign producer is unlikely to receive due process or other aspects of fair treatment.

The following chapter explores this dynamic in terms of North American trade in agriculture. But the principles here are by no means limited to the North American experience. The opportunities for firms to respond to protection by using the strategies of complex institutional responsiveness are also applicable in some instances under the WTO, given its developing institutional structure for trade and the environment. They are relevant for firms that will be operating under the FTAA as well, since provisions similar to NAFTA are currently forming a basis for negotiations. Within APEC, to the extent that there are ad hoc legal and institutional arrangements to deal with trade-restricting standards, the strategies of complex institutional responsiveness are similarly relevant.

The Context of Agriculture

NAFTA represented a significant step forward in its rules governing trade in agriculture. Prior to the FTA and NAFTA, agricultural trade had been hindered by prohibitive import quotas and tariff rate quotas, high tariffs, and massive industry subsidies. Once these measures were substantially eliminated, a new group of barriers began to emerge. These barriers were harder to detect and much more costly. The use of sanitary and phytosanitary (SPS) measures—the rules governing the appropriate level of pesticides on apples or the health of the animals humans consume—became one of the most effective trade-restricting tools in recent years. A study conducted by the US Department of Agriculture identified more than 300 measures operating in 63 different foreign markets by the mid-1990s (Robert and De Remer 1997). These barriers threatened or constrained US $4.97 billion worth of US exports in 1996 (ibid.). At the time of the negotiation of the Uruguay Round and NAFTA, there was tremendous momentum to design a legal framework that could effectively discern between, on the one hand, SPS regulation that served a legitimate health concern, and on the other, SPS regulation used primarily to protect domestic industry.

The NAFTA rules governing SPS measures were negotiated at the same time as those of NAFTA and largely mirror those of the WTO. Similar texts are currently being negotiated among APEC economies and within the FTAA. All emphasize sound science and risk assessment as the basis for any SPS measure taken. They further adopt the 'sham principle', that is, they provide criteria which separates industry protection from legitimate regulation. Regulation must restrict trade to the least degree possible in order to be consistent with NAFTA. Where products are essentially equivalent in their degree of safety or protection, this must be recognized between countries. And the NAFTA places a premium on the standards set by private sector and intergovernmental international standardization organizations, such as the International Standardization Organization (ISO), the North American Plant Protection

164 *Case Studies*

Organization (NAPPO), or the Codex Alimentarius. If a country prohibits goods that adhere to such standards, they will be prima facie in violation of their trading obligations.

Therefore firms are no longer virtually powerless in penetrating export markets that have been closed by regulation. They can now encourage their national governments to bring actions under NAFTA's Chapter 20. They can take their concerns to their government representatives active in the NAFTA institutions, notably its SPS and Committee on Agricultural Trade (CAT) bodies. They can make the case that an SPS measure is in non-compliance with a specific and clearly defined set of rules and principles. Firms can also participate in the standards setting processes in an effort to become purveyors of the dominant standard.

Despite the economic significance of this issue, there has been during NAFTA's first five years very little actual dispute settlement in agriculture in the face of trade-restricting standards. Indeed there has been only one formal dispute settlement case, pursued under Chapter 20. This was a case between Canada and the United States, which concerned the tariffication of Canada's supply management system.

This lack of disputes can be explained by several factors. First, in the area of standards and agriculture, the NAFTA institutions have been relatively effective. Trilateral groups have met regularly to discuss privately the myriad of irritants that hinder the free flow of North American trade. NAFTA's CAT and its SPS Committee have been effective in preventing and managing disputes before they reach the critical level of political controversy that would justify formal dispute settlement at the national government level. This active political management of trade irritants in appropriate forums with experts has thus contained and dealt with issues before they become serious problems. Moreover, in some cases, the very intensity of domestic political controversy had led governments to prefer to manage issues politically through the senior NAFTA FTC institutions and processes rather than surrender control to panellists in a formal, legal dispute settlement process. In fact, if a case ever did actually reach a Chapter 20 panel, as did the UHT milk case under the FTA, it would be due to the failure of many layers of committees, working groups, and political consultations that NAFTA put in place to solve such issues. One particularly successful example is NAFTA's Technical Working Group on Pesticides (TWGP), a group which includes broad industry, NGO and government representation. It has sought to harmonize standards, contribute to international standard setting, share information, develop guidelines, and phase out harmful chemicals. Thus, the TWGP has diffused issues from erupting that had the potential to adversely affect trade.

Second, many of the agricultural disputes use SPS measures as one type of weapon among many. In many such disputes, threatened or actual antidumping action often accompanies the discriminatory application of SPS measures. The antidumping action offers firms quicker and more effective access to relief than can action in the area of SPS standards. Thus, the resolution of such disputes requires dealing with the temporary duties imposed by antidumping actions. This involves the complicated and difficult task of proving that an industry is not selling its product below its cost of production or that it has not caused injury to the protected market. More likely, a truce will be arrived at, that is, a private sector market-sharing agreement will be made by industries from the exporting and importing countries. Such agreements state that the offending country will suspend the 'harassment' through antidumping actions and bogus SPS challenges on the condition that the exporting country 'voluntarily' restrict exports, and/or export at a price no lower than an agreed upon minimum. Such arrangements have the peculiar effect of penalizing those producers most efficient and competitive within North America.

Third, agricultural disputes are distinguished by their size (small) and frequency (often). Like many small grains of sand in one's shoe, removing one probably will not make a difference. Although the industry taken as a whole is large, it is more often the case (save for a few exceptions) that the barrier does not warrant the kind of political muscle necessary for a national government to take the issue to a Chapter 20 dispute. A border inspector holding up meat is irritating, especially when it happens repeatedly. However, it is not necessarily worthy of a Chapter 20 challenge. And as one issue gets solved, another related but slightly different one may emerge. Retaliation may span different subsectors within agriculture.

A parallel dynamic which has intensified the political visibility of these issues, another component of the conditions of complex institutional responsiveness, is the recent rising concern with food health and safety. A central criticism of the anti-NAFTA debate has been that it effectively takes away domestic control over SPS standards, thereby subjecting the population at large to grave risk. In terms of NAFTA, this led to a very clearly stated freedom in the text of the preservation of a country's right to set standards as deemed appropriate. In comparison, the WTO disciplines afford slightly less freedom on the part of national governments to justify trade-restricting SPS regulation. But despite these NAFTA guaranteed rights, there exists a very strong and effective political lobby which views free trade as antithetical to consumer safety due to a perceived increase in unhealthy, adulterated, uninspected food finding its way onto 'America's dinner table'. And to a large extent, due to the political sensitivity of issues such as food safety, the Clinton administration has been responsive to these intense public concerns.

Nonetheless, despite environmental regulatory protection bred by such concern, North American trade in agriculture is on the increase, and has been steadily growing since NAFTA came into force. In 1995 Mexico exported to the United States over US $3 billion worth of produce. Mexico's exports of horticultural products alone amounted to $1.5 billion; this volume represented a full three-quarters of US vegetable imports. Between the years 1993 and 1996, US agricultural exports to Mexico and Canada rose from US $8.9 billion

166 *Case Studies*

to US $11.6 billion. During the same time, US agricultural imports from Mexico and Canada rose from US $7.3 billion to US $10.5 billion.

This chapter reviews fourteen major cases out of the more extensive set of twenty-four North American cases listed in Table 9.1. It does so to demonstrate the use of health and safety standards to protect industry from competition and show how exporting firms can and do respond to such protectionism.[1]

The cases in this chapter are divided into those which concern consumer health and safety and those which concern agricultural health and safety. Each are arranged roughly in chronological order, in an effort to illustrate the pre- and post-NAFTA pattern of dispute processing.

Many of the firms affected by the discriminatory application of SPS standards are small, home-based exporters. In each case the strategy of the affected firm is discussed in the context of the strategies of complex institutional responsiveness.

TABLE 9.1. *NAFTA agriculture cases*

Case	Regulatory initiator	Challenger (supporter)	Outcome closer to objectives of instrument	International institutional response
Apples, 1989–98	Mexico	US	Mexico	NAFTA 19
Avocados, 1914–97	US	Mexico	Equal	
Beef 1, 1991–8	US	Canada	Ongoing	NAFTA SPS
Beef 2, 1994–7	Mexico	US	Mexico	—
Blueberries, 1991–3	US	Canada	US	FTA
Christmas trees 1, 1994–8	Mexico	Canada	Ongoing	NAFTA SPS
Christmas trees 2, 1994–8	Mexico	US	Ongoing	NAFTA SPS
Citrus canker, 1991–7	Mexico	US	US	NAFTA SPS
Global wheat trade	All	All	Ongoing	NAFTA CAT
Mangoes, 1993–5	US	Mexico	US	NAFTA SPS
Pork, 1997	US	Mexico	Mexico	NAFTA SPS
Potatoes, 1995–6	US	Canada	Ongoing	
Poultry 1	US	Mexico	Ongoing	—
Poultry 2	Mexico	US	Ongoing	—
Seed potatoes	Mexico	Canada	—	NAFTA SPS
Sorghum, 1997–8	Mexico	US	Ongoing	NAFTA SPS
Strawberries, 1996	US	Mexico	US	—
Stone fruits, 1991–7	Mexico	US	US	NAFTA SPS
Supply management	Canada	US	Canada	NAFTA 20
Sweet cherries, 1991–7	Mexico	US	US	NAFTA
Tomatoes, 1937–8	US	Mexico	US	NAFTA 19
UHT milk, 1987–95	US	Canada	US	FTA 18
Wheat 1, 1995–8	Mexico	US	US	—
Wheat 2, 1995–7	US	Mexico	Mexico	NAFTA SPS

The use of the new corporate strategy of producing to the high environmental standards in the dominant export market is in evidence, as is the strategic response of private sector market sharing. The older political strategies have been extensively employed by firms: intense lobbying in the political system of the blocking party; coalition creation with suppliers and customers in the blocking country; bilateral diplomacy through home government; retaliation with reciprocal home government measures. Yet firms have also started to use the new political strategies: international institutional dispute settlement; international institutional dispute prevention and management; international institutional regulatory convergence and international private sector standardization. Each case will evaluate the use of and level of success firms experience in employing the various strategies.

The Agriculture Cases: Consumer Health and Safety

Mexican Tomatoes to the United States, 1937–1998

Trade in tomatoes between Mexico and the United States has had a difficult history. Yet in 1993, $300 million worth of tomatoes were imported into the United States from Mexico. The Culiacan Valley located in Mexico produces most Mexican tomatoes. It farms 250,000 acres of vegetables, more than five times as many as it did ten years ago. Ninety per cent of this acreage is in the hands of large-scale producers, who are predominantly home-based exporters.

US restrictive legislation dates back to 1937 when the US Agricultural Marketing Agreement Act allowed agricultural producers to establish marketing orders and agreements which define the terms and conditions under which a commodity may be marketed. The legislation provides the regulatory mechanism for agricultural producers to promote orderly marketing and, in many cases, stabilize and increase prices. In 1954 an important amendment subjected imports to the same regulations that were applied to domestic production.

The size of tomatoes has also been historically regulated. In 1969, the Florida Tomato Committee recommended that mature green tomatoes (produced primarily in Florida) had to be larger than $2^{9}/_{32}$ inches in diameter while vine-ripe tomatoes (produced primarily in Mexico) were required to be $2^{17}/_{32}$ inches or larger. This requirement would have significantly reduced exports to the United States. Several importers challenged this decision in the federal courts. Imports were supported by consumer groups who resented the efforts of the large producers who dominated the Florida winter vegetable industry from seeking higher prices through import restrictions. Moreover, they alleged that the quality of Florida tomatoes was poorer than that of Mexican tomatoes. In 1973 the USDA ruled that although imported tomatoes must have minimum grading and sizing, they did not have to be graded and sized equivalent to Florida tomatoes (Bredhal, Schmitz, and Hillman 1987).

Mexico subsequently proposed the establishment of an international marketing order for tomatoes. The proposal would have laid the groundwork for an import–export cartel, since Mexican producers offered to coordinate supply with demand and with supply from US producers. Mexican producers proposed identical regulations for vine-ripe and mature green tomatoes. These proposals regulated quality first and size second.

The Mexican government restricted the production and export of tomatoes after the dual restrictions were suspended (1971–2). In the following marketing year, they implemented a trigger price mechanism to limit export shipments. Mexico reasoned that if they indicated a willingness to limit exports, the United States would not impose an import quota and the two countries could reach a market-sharing agreement. Subsequently, policing the export limitations was left to Mexican producer groups.

However, as it became clear that the reduction in Mexican exports were met by increased Florida production, export restrictions were lessened. At the start of the marketing order dispute, Florida producers refused to negotiate the dual restriction provisions of the marketing order, meaning in effect, that the entire reduction in supply would be borne by Mexican producers. The marketing order may have been viewed by Florida producers as more restrictive—and certainly more controllable—than the voluntary export restriction. Mexican representatives proposed a marketing order which may have had a greater impact on Florida producers. However, the negotiations ended without an agreement (ibid.).

In February 1996, faced with complaints from Florida growers that Mexican imports were affecting sales of their winter crops, the United States moved to restrict Mexican imports by establishing weekly rather than quarterly quotas (Beachy 1996). Mexican importers now would be unable to send fewer tomatoes for a few weeks and then make up the difference later in the quarter. For their part, Florida officials promised to check every shipment of Mexican produce arriving by truck for possible diseases, chemical residues, and insects. These actions were strongly criticized by Mexico as inconsistent with US obligations under NAFTA. The US media began to raise concern about the danger to Mexican workers from exposure to the chemicals (such as toxic organophosphate) found on tomatoes (Schrader 1995). A 1992 Government Accounting Office study had revealed that Mexican growers use at least six pesticides that are illegal in the United States (ibid.).

Florida farmers sell roughly $700 million worth of tomatoes annually (Swisher, Bastidas, and Hochmuth 1995). Mexican tomatoes are primarily vine-ripened, red, small, and are preferred by 'homemakers' because they have a better flavour. Tomatoes from Florida are primarily large, green (subject to gassing in order to turn them red) and are preferred by institutional food service and fast food restaurants.[2] Mexican imports of tomatoes have steadily

The Agricultural Disputes 169

increased since 1992 for reasons such as a cheaper peso, lower labour costs, and better weather. Florida tomato producers, alleging that Mexican tomatoes have been imported in quantities large enough to cause injury to its market, initiated a number of antidumping petitions in 1995 and 1996. They have further argued for country-of-origin labelling and requirements that imported tomatoes be packaged according to US standards. The Florida producers have further argued that they are disadvantaged by the low environmental protection standards in Mexico, as workers apply pesticides with no body protection (Brananman 1996).

Mexican producers allege that the Florida producers' actions violate NAFTA and are an abuse of the system. They argue that they have developed valid competitive advantages in production technology, such as drip irrigation and plastic sheets, which reduce costs and make better tomatoes. The Mexican climate is also more suitable to growing tomatoes. They further argue that the ultimate costs of these tomato wars are borne by the consumer who must pay artificially high prices.

This issue was not solved under the auspices of the NAFTA institutional framework. However it had been subject to discussions at US–Mexico binational commission meetings. Eventually the issue was resolved outside of the NAFTA institutional context. A suspension agreement—The Suspension Agreement on Fresh Tomatoes from Mexico—was signed on 28 October 1996. The parties to the agreement were the Confederacion de Asociaciones del Estado de Sinaloa (CAADES) and the Confederacion de Nacional de Productores de Hortalizas (CNPH) and the US Department of Commerce. The CAADES and the CNPH represent members who operate in the Michoacan, Sinaloa, and Baja areas. To avoid any antidumping duties, Mexican growers were required under the terms of the agreement to sell into the United States at a minimum fixed price of $5.17 per 25 lb. (ibid.). This number was arrived at by averaging the import prices from 1992 to 1994 when there was no price suppression. The Mexican government stated its concern with the agreement, and the fact that it was not consistent with NAFTA disciplines. At a meeting of Commerce and Mexican industry representatives, one proposal included an increased minimum size requirement for both domestic and imported tomatoes for greater ease of handling.[3] Confirmation was given on the part of the US producers that if the Mexican producers complied with the suspension agreement, then they would not pursue any trade remedies or seek amendments to current packaging statutes.[4] The suspension agreement is slated to expire on 1 November 2001.

WTO regulations allow exporters affected by antidumping investigations to directly negotiate with the authorities of the country that is imposing antidumping duties.[5] The firm strategy in North America, however, has been to seek a private sector market sharing agreement which sets minimum prices and quotas, thereby limiting competition to Florida producers. The suspension agreement is harmful to consumers in that it prevents valid competition from

170   Case Studies

occurring within North America. There is currently no North American-wide regulation or regime to address such agreements which restrain competition. Such agreements are not legal within countries. For example, the California and Florida tomato industries would be prohibited from colluding on price, restricting production, and dividing up the market according to growing seasons. This international arrangement is at odds with the goals and intent of NAFTA, an agreement designed to foster and protect liberalized trade, rather than protect outdated or inefficient industries.

Mexican Inspection of US Meat, 1994–1997

According to the US Department of Agriculture, the United States sold more than $400 million worth of beef, pork, and lamb products and $240 million worth of poultry to Mexico in 1994.[6] Significant inspection issues arise in this trade. On 1 March 1995 the Secretaria de Agricultura, Ganaderia y Desarrollo Rural announced a plan to create new inspection requirements for all types of fresh, refrigerated, and frozen meat in order to ensure that meat products are of a high-level sanitary standard and quality for humans.[7] The proposed standard represents part of an ongoing effort by the Mexican government to design specifications for the thousands of goods and services produced or sold in the country every day.

The US meat industry has criticized the proposed new Mexican standard for the inspection and approval of imported meat as scientifically unjustified, overly bureaucratic, and likely to hurt US exporters.[8] The US industry claims that the proposed Mexican standard would impose unnecessary costs on importers, is redundant in light of high US standards, and would make it practically impossible to sell US meat products in Mexico. The industry further contends that the regulation would require that refrigerated and frozen meats cross the Mexican border within three and sixty days, respectively, after slaughter. The US Meat Export Federation (USMEF) claims that this time period is much too short. There is also concern about a lack of sufficient inspection points to process the large amount of meat imported into Mexico. Mexico requires the sampling of 25 per cent of all meat imports, rather than much lower sampling requirements of the United States. In addition, the only laboratory qualified to conduct the sampling tests is in Morelos. There is no current agreement that allows Mexican meat inspectors to enter the United States.

In 1997 the Mexican government again detained US meat at the US–Mexico border, as it had been added to a list of sensitive products, and thus required a special licence. This was done with little notice. The sudden enforcement of the new ruling imposed considerable costs on the US producers (US Foreign Agricultural Service 1997a). The four primary shippers of US beef are Excel, Montfort, ABP, and National (US Foreign Agricultural Service 1997b).

The Mexican action has been accompanied by the threat of antidumping actions from the Mexican Association of Cattle Feeders (AMEG). In 1997

AMEG claimed that US beef entered Mexico 25–90 per cent below market value and that over 98 per cent of all US beef entering the Mexican market is 'dumped'. In 1994 AMEG had brought a similar antidumping action that was later dropped because an agreement was reached between the US and Mexican cattlemen (ibid.).

The Mexican cattlemen have captured the administration of inspection processes as well as antidumping activity and have used these processes to prevent the US product from entering Mexico. The US firms have relied not on the NAFTA institutions, but on the new corporate strategy of private sector market-sharing agreements. The solution here lay not in the resolution of environmentally related issues, but in an agreement in which firms essentially bypassed the NAFTA institutions and agreed to restrain any such action (inspection or antidumping) as long as the products maintained an agreed upon base price.

US Inspection of Canadian Meat, 1991–1998

Inspection issues over trade in beef have been a long-time irritant between Canada and the United States. Canadian producers have complained of the 'strategic' use of inspection measures (Kerr 1997). Such issues have the potential to impose severe costs on meat producers. Because meat is a perishable product, if it is turned back from the border or delayed, both the quality and the price will diminish (ibid.). The producer is further jeopardized by delays when the consignee begins to question the reliability of its sources (ibid.).

There have been various attempts to overcome these border barriers. They have met with varied success. One incident occurred in 1991, when US consumer groups criticized the FTA for allowing meat that was unsafe for human consumption to enter the United States as a result of the streamlined meat inspection system established a month after the FTA went into effect (Dodge and Law 1991: A15). Under the new system, only one truck in fifteen is inspected. According to the consumer groups, this resulted in increased meat imports into the United States which were contaminated with various infections and foreign objects such as metal and glass (ibid.). US officials had claimed that the Canadian meat inspection system is equivalent to that of the United States. The American Food Safety Inspection Service informed Congress that it had confidence in the Canadian inspection system's ability to certify meat equivalent to the US standard.[9] Despite that, in 1991 the US Department of Agriculture agreed to withdraw a proposal to end all US meat inspections along the Canadian border.

At the time of NAFTA, the Canadian beef industry lobbied for a section of NAFTA to address this problem.[10] Article 708:3 attempts to further streamline the process by eliminating border inspection and replacing it by inspection at the final destination of the meat. This system, however, has been unsuccessful to date. Under the new US 'regionalization' rules, the United States adopts

172 *Case Studies*

measures that more accurately reflect the specific health conditions in the area where a product originates rather than its nationality. Thus, there may be improvements in the area of meat inspection under these rules.

For Canada, this means that the majority of cattle in Alberta should now be able to cross the border freely, despite problems that exist in other areas of the country. However, the gains made by these advances may be undercut by a proposed mandatory labelling of the country-of-origin on all meat and animals. This rule has been strongly supported by the US industry, led by the National Cattleman's Beef Association. The marking of country-of-origin adds expense and creates significant administrative problems for the movement of live cattle from Canada to United States (incidentally, often coming from the same herd). It will potentially encourage US buyers to 'buy American' rather than deal with such problems. There is no ostensible health or safety reason for such a marking, given that the Canadian beef has been granted equivalent status in terms of its safety.

Here firms engage in strategies to work with the relevant agencies to overcome these issues. They pursue the long run political strategies of international institutional regulatory convergence in groups such as NAFTA's SPS Committee, where the meat issue has been discussed. It is not clear if the issue has been addressed in CAT's subcomittees, namely the Committee on Agriculture and Livestock Trade and the Working Group on Technical Measures and Commercialization of Livestock and Agricultural Products. In the short term, however, they have little choice but to choose the traditional corporate strategy of 'paying' or enduring the harassment. Also noteworthy is the fact that the NAFTA institutions such as SPS Committee and the CAT are employed only after the myriad of lower level bureaucratic institutions have dealt with the problem, signalling again that the use of the NAFTA institutions signifies somewhat a failure on the part of others to solve the issue. Some commentators argue that dealing with the reduction of non-tariff barriers imposes much higher transaction costs than the straight negotiation of tariff reductions. But a weakness in the NAFTA institutional structure is not necessarily to blame. When protectionist intent drives the process, rather than just differences in regulation, there is a higher likelihood that issues will not get resolved until they reach the political level.

Strawberries from Mexico to the United States, 1996

In April 1996 over 100 schoolchildren in California became sick by consuming Mexican strawberries contaminated by Hepatitis A. The strawberries were served as part of a school lunch programme. The programme had certified them to be 100 per cent grown and packed in the United States, although they were not. This issue became a lightning rod in the NAFTA debate within the United States. It was a key motivator of President Clinton's push for legislation—the Safety of Imported Food Act—to ban the imports of fruits and vegetables that do not meet US standards. The strawberries incident supported the otherwise invalid arguments of protectionist coalitions in the United States who could argue that not only was NAFTA responsible in shifting jobs and investment in agriculture towards Mexico, but now NAFTA was making American schoolchildren sick as well. Consumer and labour groups expressed concern about not just Hepatitis A but also E.coli, cyclospora (in raspberries from Guatemala), and other diseases connected to unsanitary practices. In response, President Clinton announced an extra $74 million to be devoted to food safety issues within the US government, including $25 million to be devoted towards 250 new FDA fruit and vegetable inspectors.[11]

The Mexican Ministry of Agriculture (SAGAR) defended itself, stating that strawberry production followed strict sanitary and quality rules and that the contamination must have occurred in California, not Mexico. They viewed it as a protectionist campaign in the US media on the part of California strawberry producers. The economic impact on the Mexicans was severe and spanned its entire international market. Strawberry imports from Mexico came to an almost complete halt. US $5 million and 2,500 jobs were lost in Baja California. Harvesting came to a standstill within Mexico (US Foreign Agricultural Service 1997c). Cancelled shipments amounted to about 30,000 5 kg crates per day. The United States threatened a country-of-origin labelling regulation which would further discriminate against Mexican imports.

The implementation of this legislation has been high on the US trade agenda. It has been accompanied by a number of parallel policy initiatives. Here the NAFTA institutions such as the SPS Committee have been helpful in providing a more technical forum for discussion. But the more political initiatives have come from the long-standing US–Mexico binational commission. On 12 June 1998 US Secretary of Agriculture Dan Glickman and the Mexican Secretary of Agriculture, Livestock and Rural Development, Romarico Arroyo Morroquin, met and signed a joint statement enhancing food safety standards 'to the highest level to achieve the goals of President Clinton's Food Safety Initiative' under the auspices of the 15th meeting of the US–Mexico binational commission.[12] In the food safety agreement, both Mexico and the United States committed to working together to solve many of these irritants through greater consultation. For example, both countries pledged to make greater use of appropriate forums to achieve these goals, such as the NAFTA SPS Committee. They further agreed to share information in the scientific areas relating to food safety. The rules were focused on the draft guidelines for the safe production of fruits and vegetables pursuant to President Clinton's food safety initiative. The guidelines concern quality of water used for irrigation purposes and the sanitary issues relating to the field workers.

At this meeting, a number of 'deals' were announced to solve trade irritants. The United States announced its decision to allow Mexico to sell apples, oranges, peaches, and tangerines in the United States from selected Mexican

174 *Case Studies*

growing areas. Mexico promised to make its SPS rules concerning grain imports clearer.

The Agriculture Cases: Agricultural Health and Safety

Mexican Exports of Avocados to the United States, 1914–1997

Mexico is the world's largest producer of avocados. In 1994 it produced 718,000 metric tons, equal to the combined 1994 production of the next seven largest producers, including the United States. Mexican avocados are harvested year round but reach their peak productivity between October and February. Mexico is also the world's largest consumer of avocados, exporting only 2 per cent of its total production. California has roughly 6,000 avocado growers and 65,000 acres of avocados.[13]

The United States is the world's second largest avocado producer, harvesting 168,000 metric tons in 1994 (Darlin 1995). California is the primary growing area (86%), followed by Florida (14%) and Hawaii (less than 1%). In 1994 the United States imported 23,932 metric tons, or US $30.7 million worth of avocados, with Chile supplying 77 per cent of this total and Dominican Republic, 18 per cent. Previously, the only Mexican avocados allowed entry into the continental United States were those trans-shipped to Canada and Alaska in sealed containers.

Between 1914 and 1997, the United States had banned the import of avocados from Mexico.[14] This embargo had been aimed at preventing certain pests—the seed and stem weevil—found only in Mexico from invading California and Florida orchards. US officials have historically claimed that this ban is motivated only by sanitary considerations. The Mexican Ministry of Agriculture claimed that US fears were unwarranted. There is a low incidence of avocado pests in Mexico. They have developed a 'systems approach' for handling fruit that has been effective in eliminating pest infestations in exported fruit (Orden and Romano 1996). The systems approach consists of nine safeguard measures which substantially eliminate the risk of contamination to US agriculture.[15] And even if Mexican crops were infested, they are easily treatable with pesticides legally available in the United States.[16]

There are a number of economic considerations as well. Avocados from California are significantly higher in price than Mexican avocados. A box of US avocados sells for US $30, while a box of Mexican avocados sells for US $8 in Canada.[17] Therefore, opening the market to Mexican avocados would impose severe economic costs on California producers, allowing Mexican producers to potentially gain a US $60 million per year market.[18] In fact, the California producers have claimed that their industry will be destroyed if the ban is lifted (Orden and Romano 1996).

In March 1997 the US Department of Agriculture permitted Mexico to export avocados to most of the United States on a restricted basis. Mexican avocados now face strict inspection—which Mexico pays for—and can come only from a single district in Mexico's Michoacan state where the pests are not common. Moreover shipments to nineteen north-eastern US states can only take place between November and February (ibid.). All Mexican avocados require a country-of-origin label.

This new ruling has met with fierce opposition from shelter-seeking US avocado producers.[19] According to the California Avocado Commission, the US Department of Agriculture sold out the California producers and ignored scientific evidence in the name of free trade, threatening 6,000 businesses and 21,000 jobs in a billion-dollar US industry.

The lifting of the ban was motivated in part by the obligation under NAFTA to incorporate sound science when restricting international trade. The United States was further under pressure from other fruit industry groups in the United States, namely sweet cherries and stone fruits, who had had their access to the Mexican market restricted as retaliation for the avocado ban. The agreement later cleared the way for the subsequent resolution of these issues. The strategic response on the part of the Mexican avocado industry was to use the traditional political strategy of reciprocal retaliation with home government measures. This was used in conjunction with the corporate strategy of product adaptation—producing a product that fits the high standards of the dominant US market, that is, avocados that are free of pest infestations.

US Apples to Mexico, 1989–1998

Since 1991 US apples have faced difficulty in gaining market access to Mexico. Apples from Washington State, Idaho, and Oregon have faced very restricted access to the Mexcian market due to alleged SPS issues, such as pest infestations. Thus, US apples are required to be held in cold storage at a temperature of 0° C for a minimum of 40 days or alternatively at 3.3 ° C for a minimum of 90 days before being exported to Mexico. This gave Mexican producers a 40-day 'head start' at the time apples became ready for market. In addition, the North West Fruit Producers Association is required to pay for Mexican inspectors to permanently reside in the United States for the purpose of an ongoing inspection of apple orchards. Some US producers claim that this is done in an effort to mirror the provisions that the United States has imposed on Mexican mango groves, which similarly require payment for a permanent US official for inspection reasons. Whatever the reason, these requirements add significant production costs to the US producers.

Under NAFTA, US apples were subject to a 20 per cent tariff after their quota of 60,099 metric tons of apples was filled. The quota increases by 3 per cent annually and the tariff decreases at a rate of 2 per cent annually.[20] The United States in 1996 shipped 5.5 million boxes of apples in 1996, which amounted to US $41 million.

On 1 September 1997 Mexico's Ministry of Commerce and Industry

(SECOFI) imposed an antidumping duty of 101.1 per cent on US red and golden delicious apples. This effectively brought shipments of US apples to Mexico to a complete halt, and left large amounts of apples 'stranded' at the border. The antidumping petitioner who supplied the preliminary information for the case was the Chihuahua State Fruit Growers Association, whose members produce 65 per cent of the apples consumed in Mexico. The US producers argued that this was in complete violation of their rights under both NAFTA and the WTO.

In March 1998 a suspension agreement was signed between the SECOFI (although the Chihuahua producers were present at the negotiations) and the US industry. It was apparently modelled after the Suspension Agreement for tomatoes. The agreement allows producers to sell year round at a minimum FOB price of US $13.72 per standard 42-pound carton.[21] This minimum is significantly higher than the price of Mexican apples. US growers were encouraged to accept the deal under threats on the part of SECOFI that if they did not, additional duties would be imposed, over and above the 101 per cent preliminary duty in place at that time. Thus, the US industry accepted the agreement, although they strongly believed that the charges of selling at less than fair value, of causing or threatening material injury to the Mexican apple industry was entirely baseless. The reasons that the Mexican industry was in trouble was due, they believed, to lack of credit, poor weather conditions, and legitimate competition on the part of the US growers.

The US producers did not seek help from the NAFTA institutions to solve their dilemma. Even with respect to the antidumping action, they felt that the WTO gave them a stronger avenue of appeal than did NAFTA against the preliminary duty imposed by SECOFI. But such recourse was not practicable once the antidumping duty became effective. There was no reasonable alternative on the part of the US producer other than to accept the deal. If they had not, they could face possible extinction, as Mexico is their biggest export market. There was no time for legal recourse. Thus the tomato precedent is unsettling, as firms are able to bypass the agreement and impose on their competitors private sector market-sharing strategies which are in clear violation of NAFTA.

US Sweet Cherries to Mexico, 1991–1997; Citrus from Florida and Arizona to Mexico, 1991–1997; US Stone Fruit to Mexico, 1991–1997

US cherry growers and other stone-fruit growers (nectarines, peaches, plums) located in the Pacific North-west (Washington, Oregon, and Idaho) and California were denied market access to Mexico from 1991 to 1997, allegedly because of concerns regarding pest infestation (Oriental fly moth; plum curculio) that could spread to Mexican orchards. Mexican officials requested that sweet cherries be sprayed with methyl bromide, a chemical which causes rapid deterioration of the fruit. At the same time, citrus products from Arizona and Florida were denied access because of concerns with fruit flies and a disease called citrus canker. When the ban was introduced, there was very little transparency in the rules or any clear or consistent policy guidelines. The US producers of all of these products alleged that the ban was imposed in retaliation for the US ban on Mexican avocados. The solution to these issues occurred roughly simultaneously in 1997 when the US ban on Mexican avocados was lifted.

All of these issues were discussed in the NAFTA SPS Committee. It worked to solve these ongoing trade irritants, through the discussion of risk assessment methodologies and appropriate standard levels. The Agricultural Working Group of the Mexico–United States binational commission was also active in the solution to this issue. At the 14th meeting of the commission, US Secretary of Agriculture Dan Glickman and the Mexican Secretary of Agriculture, Livestock and Rural Development, Francisco Labastida Ochoa, announced that progress had been made on all of these issues. Specifically, they stated that US sweet cherries and stone fruit would be allowed into Mexico, along with citrus from Florida and Arizona. At this meeting, it was also announced that Mexican avocados would be now permitted entry into the United States. However, in the case of sweet cherries, a Mexican health official will be permanently responsible for inspecting orchards in order to ensure that the pest-control agreement will be adequately enforced. This will be paid for by the US cherry industry.

The economic consequences of the restrictive measures are significant. Sweet cherry exports from the United States to Mexico are valued at approximately US $7 million. After the ban was lifted, it was estimated that Florida grapefruit exports to Mexico could reach between US $1–2 million annually and that Arizona citrus, primarily oranges and lemons, could reach several million dollars annually.

In this case, the firms used the traditional political strategy of bilateral diplomacy through their home government. They also used the new strategies of international institutional dispute prevention and management through the NAFTA committees. But ultimately the solution to this issue was beyond their own industry. Rather it required the use of issue linkage—first a resolution of the avocado issue. Here the binational commission, with its broader agricultural mandate, was helpful.

Mexican Exports of Mangoes to the United States, 1993–1995

Mexico is the world's largest exporter of mangoes. Production is estimated at 1 million metric tons annually. The growing season lasts from April to September. Over the five years since 1994 exports to the United States had been increasing at an average rate of 20 per cent a year, reaching 108,385 metric tons (US $89.8 million) in 1994, double the volume in 1990. This represents 88 per cent of total US imports of this commodity. Mexico's produce

178   *Case Studies*

is generally shipped to the United States between March and September. US production of mangoes is centred in Puerto Rico, with some (2,500 metric ton) occurring in Florida as well. Mexican and South American mangoes shipped to the United States no longer require quality inspections at the border. Yet some importers still require that mangoes be checked before shipment or on arrival, and some exporters voluntarily carry out inspections before shipment.

In the 4,900 mango hectares in the Jalisco coast, seven diseases have been identified.[22] As a result, in 1994, the US APHIS (Animal and Plant Health Inspection Service) required that mangoes be treated with hot-water prior to their export, a process which kills all pests but seriously diminishes the quality of the mangoes. This changed again in 1995 when APHIS proposed a rule that would allow mangoes to have a longer shelf life. Under the new rules, the mangoes are placed in a chamber where high temperature forced air heats the fruit until its core reaches 118° Fahrenheit. This rule also negatively affects the product, but less so, and remains in effect today. A permanent APHIS inspector, paid for by the Mexican mango producers, is also required in order to maintain market access.

Christmas Tree Exports from Canada and the United States to Mexico, 1994–1998

In 1994 Mexican authorities decided not to honour the phytosanitary certificate issued by US and Canadian inspectors and accepted by many countries for Christmas trees.[23] In a bid to appeal the Mexican decision in time for the Christmas season, Canada's growers and government quickly paid to bring two mid-level Mexican plant quarantine officials to visit farms in three provinces to assess the crop and verify the absence of gypsy moth infestation. However, the Mexican officials were unmoved. According to both US and Canadian officials, while there was a potential problem related to gypsy moth infestation, it is peculiar to trees grown in parts of Wisconsin, Michigan, Ontario, Quebec and Nova Scotia.

Moreover, according to US and Canadian growers, treatment and inspection has made it possible to certify trees as being free from the gypsy moth as well as other pests and diseases. In addition, according to the growers, conifers are not among the tree types prone to infestation in any case; they claim the risk has been reduced virtually to zero for managed production areas, such as Christmas tree farms.[24] This problem appears to be due to the actions of border officials, as Mexico has no domestic tree industry to protect.

Mexican Wheat Exports to the United States, 1995–1997

The presence of the fungus karnal bunt has been a major issue restricting access of Mexican wheat to the United States. Despite pressure from over a dozen US Representatives from wheat-producing states to slow talks with

Mexico and keep the US market closed to its wheat, the United States certified that the Mexican Valley is free of fungus in 1997.[25] The US Agriculture Secretary announced that Mexico's Mexicali Valley was free of fungus at the US binational commission meeting in 1997. Here NAFTA's SPS Committee as well as the binational commission was helpful in solving this issue.

US Wheat Exports to Mexico, 1995–1998

US wheat destined for Mexico has been subjected to border harassment due to a fungus allegedly present in the wheat. In 1995 Mexican officials decided to deny 45 railcars full of US wheat entry into Mexico on the basis that it was contaminated with the fungus ergot, a toxin which can cause hallucinations.[26] Mexico made this decision based on an unratified rule which has a zero-tolerance level for ergot, a rare fungus in both United States and Mexico.[27]

The US industry argued that the fungus exists in Mexico, so it does not make sense to have a zero tolerance approach towards it. They further argued that the amount of fungus on the railcars in question amounted to no more than trace amounts in two cars—a rate of one 1/100 or less.[28]

Later shipments of US wheat were allowed into Mexico, due to pressure imposed on President Clinton by US Agricultural Committee Chairman Pat Roberts.[29] Thus, the traditional political strategy of bilateral diplomacy proved most effective. But this case also raises the importance that the NAFTA rules have had in requiring that measures be based on sound science and risk assessment. Under NAFTA, governments are required to justify their rules, which the Mexican government clearly was unable to do in this case. The regionalization rules do not allow for a zero tolerance approach to be imposed on an entire country. That would mean that if any pest is found anywhere in the country, the relevant good could be denied market access. Rather, tolerance levels and market access issues must be determined according to each particular region, rather than political boundaries.

US Sorghum to Mexico, 1997–1998

Excessive SPS requirements on US sorghum have been imposed by Mexico. Sorghum is used to feed animals, and Mexican farmers rely on US shipments of sorghum as critical inputs. The Mexican government fears that outbreaks of ergot in Texas will spread throughout Mexico. In May 1997 Sandiad Vegetal was considering whether to allow an 'acceptable' level of sorghum into Mexico. Mexico tried to impose restrictions on the US product by requiring a certificate that it was not infected with ergot and that it had not travelled through Texas.[30] The US government cited a complete lack of scientific knowledge on the part of Mexican officials. It further charged that the border restrictions are really an attempt at price protection for the upcoming Mexican sorghum production.[31]

Conclusions

Many of the agriculture cases that have arisen under NAFTA seem to be driven, at least in part, by a protectionist agenda. Such protectionism has led to substantial losses on the part of firms engaged in agricultural trade who had expected that NAFTA would, at least to some degree, increase their market access for the benefit of food processors and consumers throughout North America. At the same time however, there has been a high rate of resolution of agricultural issues in the post-NAFTA era. Long-standing issues such as avocados, stone fruit, and apples have been solved, demonstrating that NAFTA has had a positive influence on the most difficult and politicized trade issues. Although bilateral bodies such as the US–Mexican commission continue to be important, there is clear evidence of the liberalizing impact of NAFTA's institutions for dispute management and its rules for sound science as a basis for regulation.

The key response used by firms seeking to overcome protectionist agricultural trade barriers has been producing to the high environmental standards in the dominant export market. It is primarily Mexican firms that are capitalizing on their natural comparative advantages in agriculture and producing more and more products which meet the standards of the US and Canadian market. The NAFTA institutions have further encouraged the process of technological diffusion and have heightened awareness of SPS issues more broadly.

Between Canada and the United States, where standards are uniformly high, disputes have involved border inspection, and prospectively, labelling. The threat of country-of-origin labelling on the part of the United States has little substantive justification, as there is no rational scientific basis to differentiate between Canadian and US beef. This is especially true when considering that many of the cattle in dispute originate from the same herd. Thus the nuisance factor of border inspections and country-of-origin labelling may provide a fertile ground for disputes in the near future.

The key political strategy activated in the response to protectionist application of SPS rules is the traditional bilateral diplomacy through a firm's home government. This often occurs through trade associations, rather than from individual firms. Additional political strategies engaged are international institutional dispute settlement, in the case of antidumping, and international institutional dispute prevention and management through the work of the NAFTA institutions.

More disturbing for NAFTA's liberalization objectives is the new corporate strategy of private sector market sharing. It is increasingly in evidence, first in the tomatoes cases and second in the apples case. This strategy bypasses the carefully negotiated rules of the NAFTA and other trading arrangements to constrain competition between foreign and domestic producers and artificially maintain high prices. Such a strategy is allowed to flourish due to the lack of a regionally applicable set of competition rules or enforcement authority.

The conclusions of this analysis of the North American experience can be easily extended to other trading regimes, where the issues are quite similar. Indeed, as the agricultural barriers become resolved within North America, they are increasing between the NAFTA parties and their non-NAFTA trading partners. The era of transatlantic agricultural trade wars between North America and the EU has already arrived. And the issue of SPS rules as protection for shelter-seeking firms will become more acute as trade in agriculture increases worldwide.

The backbone of the NAFTA SPS regime, like the WTO SPS regime, is based on the principles of sound science, least trade-restrictive measures, the 'sham' principle, transparency of rule making, harmonization and mutual recognition. These rules need to operate through an institutional structure that interprets, expands, and develops these principles to the particular region or sector at issue. Thus, these principles should similarly form the foundation of any future trading regime within a strengthened WTO, the FTAA, or a deeper APEC regime. Only then can these small issues, not necessarily worthy (due to their size) of the political impetus necessary to bring a case before the WTO, be resolved to the benefit of consumers. And only then can firms maximize their use of the internationally based strategies of complex institutional responsiveness to deliver outcomes that benefit all.

NOTES

1. Twenty-four agricultural disputes are listed in Table 11.1. However, these fourteen were chosen on the basis of data availability and the fact that they were not discussed previously in this book.
2. Fresh Produce Association of the Americas, 'Post-Hearing Brief', The Impact of NAFTA and the Economy, Investigation 332-381, 16 May 1997.
3. 'Commerce Tomato Deal Remains Tenuous, Mexican Sources Warn', *Inside U.S. Trade*, 14/42, 18 Oct 1996.
4. Ibid.
5. Ibid.
6. 'A Meat Conflict', *International Trade Reporter*, 12 (1995), 770–1.
7. Ibid.
8. *El Diario Oficial*, 1 Mar. 1995.
9. US General Accounting Office, 6 July 1990.
10. Ibid.
11. 'Clinton Wants Ban on Unsafe Food Imports', *CNN WebNews*, 4 Mar. 1998.
12. 'U.S., Mexico Sign Food Safety Agreement at Binational Commission', *Inside U.S. Trade*, 16/23,12 June 1998.
13. 'Mexico–U.S. Avocado Dispute', TED Case Number 413. Available at <http://gurukul.ucc.american.edu/ted/avocado.htm>.
14. 'The Avocado Embargo', *Christian Science Monitor*, 13 Nov. 1991, p. 80.
15. 'Mexico–U.S. Avocado Dispute', TED Case Number 413. Available at <http://gurukul.ucc.american.edu/ted/avocado.htm>.
16. Ibid.

17. Ibid.
18. Ibid.
19. *El Universal*, 14 Feb. 1996.
20. 'U.S. Exporters Blast Methods Leading to Mexican AD Duties on Apples', *Inside U.S. Trade*, 15/36, 5 Sept. 1997.
21. Ibid.
22. Siglo 21 de Jalisco, C.D. Press, 1993.
23. 'Canada and the U.S. vs. Mexico', *Washington Post*, Dec. 1994.
24. Ibid.
25. 'Legislators Seek to Slow U.S.–Mexico Talks on Pest-Free Wheat', *Inside NAFTA*, 27 Dec. 1995, 1,18.
26. 'House Panel Chairman Calls on Clinton to Pressure Mexico on Wheat', *Inside U.S. Trade*, 24 Nov. 1995.
27. Ibid.
28. Ibid.
29. Ibid.
30. 'Mexican Sorghum Situation Still Unsettled', US Foreign Agricultural Service, 28 May 1997.
31. Ibid.

10

Trade and Environment Regimes in Operation: The North American Auto Industry

Beyond the realms of dispute settlement, management, and prevention lie the instruments for regulatory communication, capacity building, convergence, and coalition building offered by the new NAFTA regime. As the centre of the new era of complex institutional responsiveness, it offers improved mechanisms to combat environmental regulatory protectionism when conflicts erupt between firms, governments, and environmental non-government organizations (ENGOs). Equally importantly, the NAFTA regime provides instruments of proactive cooperation, aimed at reducing regulatory barriers before conflicts arise. These create a wider regulatory regime that directly strengthens firms' competitiveness through international commerce, while simultaneously protecting and enhancing the natural environment.

The activities of firms and governments in the North American automotive industry in the lead-up to, and during the first five years of operation of, NAFTA show many of these new cooperative instruments being created and employed. The variety and vigour with which automotive firms are mobilizing these instruments reflect the fact that the conditions of complex institutional responsiveness are most advanced in this sector. The 'big three' North American assemblers built on the highly integrated regional production system they first constructed in the 1960s across the US–Canadian border, to move towards partnerships on a global scale, as the 1998 Chrysler–Daimler Benz merger shows. It is in this industry that many of the new techniques of just-in-time inventory and lean production were first pioneered.

Automobiles, and their impacts on the atmosphere through emissions from their operation, have long been at the forefront of the move to more stringent environmental regulation in North America, Europe, and Asia (Vogel 1995). As the dominant industry sector in the North American manufacturing economy, the automotive industry is the subject of many of the most important changes in the new NAFTA regime.

The firms in the North American automotive industry have focused their energies in the post-NAFTA era on the highly cooperative end of the array of instruments that complex institutional responsiveness allows. Firms have not primarily looked to national governments to settle, manage, or prevent their international disputes, nor even to NAFTA's intergovernmental institutions to assist in this process or lead the way in regulatory convergence. Rather, the firms have preferred anticipatory private sector action, notably in Mexico, to adjust in advance to NAFTA's environmental requirements, and manage the continuing political debate over NAFTA in subsequent years. They have relied on private sector processes for transborder environmental regulatory convergence, both within individual MNEs operating throughout the region, and on an industry-wide basis across the Canada–US border. Finally they have emphasized high-level regulatory convergence aimed at pollution prevention and total systems integration rather than reactive environmental control or remediation on an uncoordinated basis within segmented industry sectors. Moreover, despite NAFTA's protectionist rules of origin for automotive production, and the resulting fear that industry would create a 'fortress North America' behind these barriers, the thrust towards high-level environmental regulatory convergence has been outward looking. The high and rapidly increasing degree of North American industry integration has been used as a platform to seek broader multilateral standards.

Despite fears that NAFTA would generate a regulatory race to the bottom, the automobile firms have not moved to Mexico to produce and operate cars with lower environmental standards. Nor has producing throughout a seamless North America to meet the existing, highest level California environmental standards been their core strategy. Rather they have supported the flexible, comprehensive, and integrated, environmental standards that complement the multilateral standards of the fully global market place. The North American automotive industry is thus moving to pioneer, in their corporate and political actions, strategies that take account of the realities of a world of complex institutional responsiveness.

The North American automotive industry also provides clear evidence that these new instruments are not only available to firms but that their use can produce successful, competitiveness-enhancing outcomes. An industry once faced with the bankruptcy of major firms such as Chrysler, and antiquated production techniques as overseas rivals raised the prospect of global overcapacity, had by the late 1990s met the challenge of Japanese imports and produced a vibrant sales performance within North America and abroad. They did so notwithstanding the fact that environmental equipment, largely mandated by regulations, cost an estimated average of US $2,000 per vehicle.

In the realm of environmental regulations the US-owned automobile firms have encouraged the Mexican government since 1993 to adopt vehicle emission and ambient air quality standards closely modelled on those of the United States. They pushed the Canadian government in 1997 to announce new regulations to match the US standards for emissions and on-board diagnostics. They have thus far contained the potential fragmentation of the market arising from a proliferation of diverse subnational state and provincial emission standards. As discussed in Chapter 8, they have encouraged the Canadian government to ban MMT, to have the Mexican government initiate studies of its harmful effects, and to prevent the US oil industry from using the additive, even though US judicial action has once again made it legal.

Despite this success in the practice of complex institutional responsiveness, firms in the North American automotive industry have yet to fully exploit the opportunities provided by the NAFTA regime. In particular, the firms have been slow to mobilize the power of the NAFTA institutions to enhance their global competitive position. This reluctance to regard governments as partners rather than antagonists, or to form Japanese-style or European-type alliances with governments, has impeded the ability of automobile firms to develop flagship relationships across five partner networks (Rugman and D'Cruz 1996). The new era of global competition requires a more comprehensive response. Governmentally secured regulatory convergence, even as a codification of regimes pioneered by private sector processes, offers the certainty and sanctions that come with the full force of law. Inter-governmentally agreed regulations through the NAFTA institutions would provide firms with a stronger, region-wide home base from which to compete globally. And a NAFTA-based, governmentally backed coalition would strengthen the hand of North American firms in the looming multilateral debates to define the regulations for the world cars of the future.

Introduction

This chapter examines how environmental policy and regulation, as shaped by the NAFTA regime of rules and institutions, is affecting automotive trade, investment, and production in North America and having broad economic implications for the North American automotive industry, including its consumers and other stakeholders.[1] This chapter argues that there are three broad forces affecting the environmental regulation and performance of the North American automotive industry in the NAFTA era.[2]

The first is an intensification of the move towards a full-scale rationalization and integration of the industry on a regional rather than national basis, with a corresponding production incentive to have a uniform set of relevant environmental standards in all three countries and across all their subfederal jurisdictions. The second is a new wave of high-level regulatory harmonization as NAFTA's consciousness-raising, institutions, dispute settlement mechanisms, and incentives have prevented any regulatory 'race to the bottom' but instead inspired a 'push to the top', driven and guided largely by the anticipatory and voluntary efforts of industry and its stakeholders. The third is the rapid spread of this push to high-level harmonization from the assembly to the original equipment manufacture (OEM) parts and then aftermarket sectors, and from manufacturing standards, to fuel standards, and then inspection, maintenance, and other operating standards.

In the first instance, NAFTA is leading to the full integration and rationalization of the North American auto industry on a regional rather than national basis, by absorbing the historically protected Mexican market into the long integrated US–Canada production system, and by drawing the latter ever more tightly together. As one leading analyst put it: 'It is now appropriate to talk of a North American auto market' (Weintraub 1997: 41).[3] Although delayed by the 1995 peso crisis in Mexico and the paucity of new big three investment in Mexico in NAFTA's first four years, this process of full rationalization is clearly proceeding. With it, and the move to just-in-time inventory and the tiering of the parts chain, comes an increasing interconnection and rationalization that will lead industry to seek and secure from governments tighter regionally harmonized environmental standards.[4]

Second, the environmental consciousness unleashed by NAFTA is leading to a new wave of high-level harmonization of environmental and safety regulations. There is an emerging North American community beyond industry whose citizens in the partner countries are calling for more open, environmentally responsible practices on the part of actors in all three countries. Canada as well as Mexico is rapidly moving up to the US-wide and even pathfinder Californian level. In contrast to those who feared that NAFTA would lower standards, there are demands for the latest generation of automotive emission, fuel technology, and inspection and maintenance standards.

Third, this high-level environmental harmonization is extending from original equipment manufacturer (OEM) assemblers and parts producers to the fuels and aftermarket sectors. Thus, there is a slowly emerging total systems approach to environmental protection with action on fuels, inspection and maintenance, pollution prevention, and international cooperation.

The centrality of the automotive industry to the core environmental challenges of NAFTA are clear. Cars and trucks are the single leading source of air pollution on the North American continent (Marchi 1997). In highly populated and industrialized areas such as southern Ontario, Canada's heartland, auto emissions account for up to 80 per cent of benzene, 60 per cent of nitrogen oxides, 55 per cent of volatile organic compounds, and 4 per cent of sulphur oxides released into the air. In Canada as a whole, a full 80 per cent of this automotive pollution comes from only 20 per cent of the vehicles—the older, poorly maintained ones, as each such car or truck produces the same amount of pollution as 25 new vehicles.

The National Automotive Environmental Regulatory Systems before NAFTA

Prior to NAFTA, the United States, Canada, and Mexico possessed a largely integrated automotive industry (for assemblers and OEM parts producers) but a substantially varying set of environmental regulations and enforcement patterns. The result was that larger, US-based and owned manufacturers generally applied higher US-level standards in Canada and Mexico in their ongoing industrial practices, and sought and often secured from these governments a common set of standards based on those prevailing in the much larger US market. However the different standards setting systems in the three countries, production in Mexico for the domestic Mexican market, separate high California standards in the United States, and the move towards more specific state and provincial systems, created an inconvenient and prospectively expanding, more costly differentiation.

The Foundation of Regulatory Uniformity

Prior to NAFTA, there was a substantial foundation of regulatory uniformity across the United States, Canada, and Mexico. Proximity, openness, a common geography (relative to Europe and other regions), the sheer size of the US market, and policy instruments such as the 1965 Canada–US automotive pact, the 1982 US–Mexico La Paz Agreement, and the 1990 Canada–US Air Quality Agreement, had produced a substantial degree of environmental convergence relevant to the automotive industry. While most advanced in the case of the highly contiguous and long highly integrated Canada–US relationship, this process developed quickly between the United States and Mexico as the latter country opened to trade during the 1980s and saw automotive products replace oil as its dominant trade item with the United States.

In practice, the sheer size and integrated nature of the automotive industry led to a high degree of environmental management and international convergence on the part of the major assemblers and parts manufacturers. In both their demands on government, and their adoption of internal environmental management systems, pollution control equipment, and technology, these large firms sought (and largely secured) uniform and high-level standards. They did so not only as a matter of corporate conviction, but also in response to: customer demands; concerns about corporate reputation; insurance and liability considerations, public pressures, and anticipated regulatory developments in all three countries. This was especially true in Canada, which, led by Ontario, sent 85 per cent of its automotive production to the United States and hosted almost 20 per cent of continental automotive assembly activity.[5] Because the auto industry also dominated the three trading and transborder investment relationships in the region, and because these links were growing prior to NAFTA, the pressures for regulatory convergence in policy and practice steadily strengthened. This process was reinforced as parts of Canada (in the lower Fraser Valley and Southern Ontario) began to acquire visible environmental problems similar to those in demographically and industrially dense parts of the United States.[6]

Differing Systems and Standards

Yet there remained important differences, not only in regulatory levels and particular standards, but more importantly in constitutional and legal approaches to regulation, federal–subfederal divisions of responsibility, and testing and certification procedures. In Mexico, power for environmental regulation was heavily concentrated in the federal government, based on a statist regulatory model often applied to national monopoly industry suppliers producing only for a highly protected national market, and unalleviated by voluntary, private sector driven, standards setting involving environmental NGOs and other stakeholders. In the United States there prevailed a litigation-based regulatory-enforcement approach, with power shared between federal and state governments, and a heavy reliance on voluntary standards setting by thousands of associations outside government (such as the American National Standards Institute). In Canada, where an estimated 70 per cent of responsibility for environmental regulation lay with provincial governments, there flourished an administrative consensus approach with minimum litigation, based in part on multistakeholder, consensus-oriented standards setting, centred in the five major quasi-public umbrella standards setting organizations (operating under the auspices of the Standards Council of Canada).

Beyond difference in government systems, there were three broad economy-based exceptions to the prevailing pattern of high-level, harmonized industry performance. The first was in still substantially protected Mexican industry, and among the smaller parts and aftermarket producers who faced the additional challenge of integrating into increasingly outsourced but multi-tiered supplier systems. The second came from the fuels sector, whose products were increasingly consequential for the ability of assemblers with fuel-sensitive electronic diagnostic systems to meet higher emissions standards, but who wielded greater relative size and influence, regional power, monopoly claims, and less modern capacity in Canada and Mexico than in the United States. The third came in operating rather than manufacturing standards, where local differences and responsibilities were greater, and the temptation to make ad hoc adjustments for protectionist and political purposes more intense.

The Separated Mexican Parts Sector

The largest initial challenge came in the parts and aftermarket sector. Here the unbalanced capabilities across the three countries made it difficult for many firms, especially in Mexico, to match the rising levels of expected environmental performance, even with assistance from the larger firms they supplied.[7] In particular, Mexican parts producers, which represented almost half the Mexican auto industry, were relatively small in size and lagging in technology.[8]

To survive in an era of NAFTA-intensified regionalization and increasingly globalized production, these Mexican auto parts firms needed economies of scale, technological infusions, and total quality and environmental management systems. As NAFTA started they were moving to get them. Many received government credits and sought to forge strategic alliances with foreign firms.

Particularly among the 100 largest and most dynamic Mexican firms, the process of NAFTA-inspired modernization began in earnest. Led by the export-oriented engine plants largely established by the Big Five assemblers in northern Mexico in the early 1980s, the parts industry became more export-oriented. The 750 maquiladoras producing auto parts in Mexico, many US-owned and associated with assemblers, expanded their operations. In 1993 there were about 100 international joint ventures in auto parts, bringing in badly need foreign capital and technology.[9] In the four years to 1993, many Mexican suppliers received awards for reaching international quality standards.[10] There remained much room for this segment of the auto industry to increase its exports to, and thus competitively move the environmental standards prevailing and coming in, the US market. Only 10 per cent of Mexican parts production in 1992 was exported, primarily to the United States.

The Economic Impact of NAFTA on Auto Trade

The integration of the North American automotive industry has increased in the four years since NAFTA has taken effect. Total vehicle and parts trade between the United States and Mexico doubled from 1991 to reach $25 billion in 1995. From 1993 to 1996 US exports of vehicles and parts to Mexico increased 11 per cent. US exports of vehicles alone increased more than 500 per cent. As the President's July 1997 report on NAFTA's impact concluded: 'with the growth in US-made vehicle sales to Mexico, the opportunities for sales of US aftermarket parts in Mexico should rise' (USTR 1997: 48). Consistent with this view is the fact that US exports of parts themselves were 25 per cent higher in the first quarter of 1997 than in the first quarter of 1993. The US share of Mexico's parts imports rose steadily, from 66.3 per cent in 1993 to 71.7 per cent in 1996.

During the same period, US imports of vehicles and parts from Mexico doubled.[11] Because US imports of Mexican-assembled vehicles contain more than 50 per cent US-made parts, a figure which is rising under NAFTA, there is clearly a trade-induced integration taking place, which will intensify as NAFTA eliminates the previous requirement to use Mexican-made parts. US imports of Mexican parts directly rose 58.4 per cent from 1993 to 1996. The result is a strong NAFTA-produced incentive for parts manufacturers in both the United States and Mexico to meet the highest environmental standards demanded by their customers.

Trade specialization has not yet extended in a major way to increased foreign direct investment. There has thus far been a paucity of new foreign direct investment into Mexico, in part because major companies have been wary of providing evidence to support the 'giant sucking sound' argument featured so prominently in the initial US NAFTA debate. In the first three years after NAFTA came into force, the big three invested US $39.1 billion in plant and equipment in the United States but less than one-tenth of that amount ($3 billion) in Mexico. However, even this increased US investment is assisting the process of rationalization and region-wide uniformity in environmental performance.[12]

The Post-NAFTA Regime

During its first four years, the NAFTA regime has experienced a rapid upward Canadian and Mexican environmental harmonization based on US standards

190   *Case Studies*

for automotive emissions and fuel use, the adoption of US-like inspection and maintenance programmes at the subfederal level, and the spread of US-pioneered pollution prevention programmes to the NAFTA neighbours.[13] This process is most readily apparent in the case of the already highly integrated but uniquely interdependent United States–Canadian relationship, but is also evident in the United States–Mexican case. Yet there has to date been very limited moves towards direct Canada–Mexico harmonization or fully trilateral (as opposed to US-centric hub-and-spoke) convergence or harmonization. Moreover the role of the NAFTA institutions and dispute settlement mechanism in the convergence process has thus far been secondary in the core manufacturing and fuels areas of central interest to the automotive industry.

The United States

Air pollution and quality is central to the environmental performance of the North American automotive industry. In the United States, the primary relevant regulatory framework is set by the US Clean Air Act which specifically regulates six elements central to atmospheric pollution—ozone, particulate matter, nitrogen dioxide, carbon monoxide, sulphur dioxide, and lead.[14] Revisions to the standards take place every five years to account for evolving scientific information. The next revision is due in 1999.

Despite the enhanced competitive pressures brought by NAFTA, and the advent of a Republican majority opposed to stringent environmental regulations in the 1994 mid-term elections, the United States has continued to increase its environmental standards.[15] In November 1996 the US Environmental Protection Agency (US EPA) proposed new National Ambient Air Quality Standards (NAAQS) for ground-level ozone and particulate matter, based on epidemiological and human toxicological data. Despite considerable criticism, they were adopted in June 1997. The ozone standard will thus rise from .12 ppm measured over one hour to .08 ppm measured over eight hours in 2000 with full compliance coming several years after.[16] Particulate matter standards will remain for larger particles (PM-10) and be imposed on smaller particles (2.5 microns or smaller), with plans to meet such standards required by 2002. The new standards will push the number of non-attainment areas in the United States from 106 to about 250 counties, with many of the additions coming along the Canada–US Great Lakes border.[17]

Increasing US air quality standards are also affecting the US automotive industry more directly. The EPA will move in 1998 to Tier 2 emission and diagnostic standards and then define the next level to be in force by 2003. Massachusetts and New York states have been before the courts seeking to join California in having the right to set their own, higher vehicle emission standards.

The move to an integrated, total systems approach has also led to impetus for an increase in fuel standards. One sign of the upward trend is the unwillingness of fifteen US petroleum producers and the State of California to take advantage of a recent administrative law ruling allowing the use of gas additive MMT, which US EPA banned 17 years ago and which California still outlaws. US petroleum producers representing over 80 per cent of the market are refusing to use it while US EPA tests its health affects.

While rollback has been avoided in fuel standards, forward movement has been more difficult. The US automotive and petroleum industries have combined in a joint study to assess standards for low sulphur gasoline, which (like MMT) threatens major damage to on-board diagnostic systems and thus emissions on vehicles. The automotive industry is calling for a low sulphur fuel standard it knows is compatible with the diagnostic and emissions technology it currently has, with the standards it must meet, and with the capacity of petroleum refiners. It has agreed to the petroleum industries' request to determine if new automotive technologies might permit a less stringent low sulphur standard to be imposed.

The integrated approach to pollution control is also propelling a spread and rise in automotive inspections and maintenance systems, pioneered by California several years ago. In the face of rising frustration from motorists facing the 'yo-yo' of being forced back and forth between state inspection stations who find them non-compliant and service centres who conduct inadequate repairs, a consensus has emerged that the solution lies in enhanced certification and training among those conducting the repairs. The primary bottleneck at present is the lack of well-trained and well paid technicians, amidst the booming California economy (Moore 1997). Yet the spread of such systems to other states also raises costs to consumers and some aftermarket producers.[18]

If an integrated approach to automotive emission control requires a lateral link to fuel standards and a forward link to inspection and maintenance, it has also inspired a backward link to pollution prevention in the plants and processes that assemble the vehicles and produce their parts. In September 1991 US EPA, the US Motor Vehicle Manufacturers Association (MVMA), and the State of Michigan initiated the Auto Industry Pollution Prevention Project (Auto Project) which led to a programme to reduce the release of persistent toxic substances into the Great Lakes. This effort built on the work of individual companies following the pollution prevention strategy prepared by the US President's Commission on Environmental Quality.[19]

Canada

As NAFTA took effect, Canada also moved to higher level environmental standards and a tighter integration with the US policy, regulatory, and industry system. Since 1993 Canada has raised its automotive emissions and a few fuel standards to US levels, by explicitly adopting evolving US regulations as the new Canadian standards. It has also assisted the spread of US pioneered inspection and maintenance and pollution prevention programmes.

In spring 1996 Sergio Marchi, Canada's environment minister (and

192 *Case Studies*

subsequently, from 1997, trade minister), announced that a priority for his portfolio was the introduction of 'new car emission standards, new fuel efficiency rules and new encouragement for alternative fuels' (Marchi 1996).[20] He also promised to follow the Canadian Council of Ministers of the Environment's (CCME) call for Canada to harmonize with anticipated US standards for low emission vehicles or for moving independently if the United States did not proceed. On 3 March 1997 Marchi announced that the federal government was tightening emission standards for cars and trucks, by harmonizing in 1998 its regulations with those of the federal government in the United States. This would reduce emissions of hydrocarbons by 30 per cent and of nitrogen oxide by 60 per cent.[21] Canada would also require manufacturers to equip new vehicles in the 1998 model year with diagnostic systems that can monitor emissions, and bring emissions regulations to new types of vehicles (such as motorcycles), fuels (such as methanol, liquefied petroleum gas, and natural gas), and processes (including exhaust, evaporative, and refuelling emissions).

Marchi further urged the provinces, who have responsibility for cars once they are on the road, to follow British Columbia's 'Aircare' programme of mandatory car and truck inspection and repair. Such a move would reduce by half the pollutants emitted into congested southern Ontario. Finally, Marchi pointed to one of the inescapable physical incentives for environmental regulatory harmonization, by noting that half the smog in Canada's core, the Windsor–Quebec corridor, is produced in the United States.[22] He thus called for the 1990 Canada–US Air Quality Agreement on acid rain to be expanded to regulate smog, air toxins, and inhalable particulate matter, with a goal of reducing imported pollution by 50 per cent by the year 2010.[23]

Because high-level controls on auto emissions require similar controls on fuel quality, Canadian action on high-level harmonization moved seamlessly to fuel standards and thus to the petroleum industry. Here, however, even compared to the United States, progress has been slower, industry resistance greater, and NAFTA, through its investment provisions, a prospective initial obstacle rather than an aid to forward movement. Yet the functional need for a total systems approach to meet the higher emission control standards should soon lead to continental and ultimate regional harmonization here as well.

The first post-NAFTA case of Canadian harmonization on prevailing US fuel standards was the Canadian federal government's move in 1996 to ban international and interprovincial trade in MMT.[24] This substance was first introduced in 1977 to replace lead as an octane-enhancer in gasoline (Vogel and Rugman 1997). In an early sign that pressures for convergence are arising in the third, Canada–Mexico, leg of the NAFTA triangle, the Canadian move led Mexico, where MMT is still legal, to initiate an evaluation of its effects.

The ban on MMT is being followed by a similar move to reduce or remove the level of sulphur in Canadian gasoline.[25] In early 1997 Cabinet passed new Diesel Fuel regulations requiring, as of 1 January 1998, all on-road vehicles to use diesel fuel no more than .05 per cent by weight of sulphur (the current

Mexican standard).[26] Marchi also said he planned to come forward with a plan and a timetable to reduce the sulphur content of gasoline.[27]

The emerging total systems approach to automotive environmentalism involves, as its third component, enhanced mandatory inspection and maintenance programmes. Here the impact of NAFTA's informal pressures towards high-level harmonization are also evident. States and provinces have begun to cooperate to adopt similar programmes, and create transnational, subgovernmental coalitions for more advanced measures such as quotas for zero-emission vehicles. The available evidence indicates that the immediate pre- and post-NAFTA period has seen extensive US–Canada/state–provincial cooperation on environmental, emissions, and automotive standards (including cooperation relating to the introduction of zero-emission vehicles). In contrast, trilateral, subfederal cooperation has been slower to develop and strongest in operating transportation standards (Munton and Kirton 1995; 1996a, b; Kirton and Munton 1996).

The movement is clearly evident in Ontario, where the government of Premier Michael Harris is generally averse to environmental regulation, but was considering in 1998 a plan to adopt a variant of the 'Aircare programme' pioneered in British Columbia.[28] The Canadian assembly industry prefers a uniform system across Canada and the continent; one with a central repository for test data that the assemblers can challenge in regard to warranty claims. Such a system (INM 240) could steer the bulk of the work to the OEM dealerships.[29] The Ontario government was inclined to adopt a more decentralized, 'repair grade' model, under which any properly licensed, equipped, and trained service station could perform the inspection.

Canada has also moved to implement pollution prevention. The Canadian effort on pollution prevention, paralleling that of the United States, began in May 1992, when an agreement among the federal and provincial governments and the Canadian Motor Vehicle Manufacturers Association (MVMA) (creating the Canadian Automotive Pollution Prevention Project) made the automotive industry the first to enter a voluntary pollution prevention agreement.[30] Virtually from its inception, discussions were held with its US counterpart.[31] The two task forces quickly committed to biannual meetings to coordinate their activities and formalize communication. In December 1994 they hosted a joint suppliers' forum, the North American Auto Supplier Environmental Workshop. The joint programme, which reinforced the significant achievements secured in each country, was re-examined in the summer of 1996. Neither the CEC nor other NAFTA institutions were involved in the venture. Nor was there any move to extend the cooperative activity to include Mexico.

Mexico

The pattern of upward high-level harmonization is also visible in Mexico. In Mexico, transportation is the leading cause of CO_2 emissions from fossil fuel consumption, (accounting for 37 per cent of the total), and a major contributor of atmospheric pollution overall. Current projections indicate that Mexican CO_2 emissions in the year 2005 will be 40 per cent higher than their 1990 level (Sheinbaum and Rodriguez Viqueria 1996). Tentative evidence further suggests that the acidity (pH) of rain in Mexico City from mobile and stationary emissions has been rising from 1987 to 1993.

Mexico acquired its first federal laws and regulations governing emissions of atmospheric, fluid and solid wastes, and noise in 1972. In 1993 it set standards (NOM-CCA-001-ECOL/193 (DOF 1993)) regulating water quality, including wastewater discharges from industrial facilities such as automotive plants. As of 1997 it had not established any standards for maximum levels of soil pollutants, but informally followed international (largely European) standards covering organic compounds such as hydrocarbons and inorganic compounds such as mercury and lead.

In contrast, Mexico has moved rapidly to set and raise standards for air quality. At the outset of 1994 its Ministry of Health published air quality standards relating to concentrations of atmospheric pollutants. By 1998 eight Mexican cities beyond Mexico City had air quality monitoring programmes, which focus on total suspended particulates and (in the case of Mexico City and Tijuana) ozone.[33] The primary ozone precursors are car exhausts, industrial smoke stacks, and electrical generating facilities.

In 1994 Mexico set its first standard on fossil fuel quality used by mobile and stationary sources to enhance the environment. In December 1994 its National Ecology Institute (INE) published NOM-ECOL-086-1994 on maximum emission levels for SOx and NOx from fuels. These covered the maximum levels of lead, vapour, sulphur, benzine, olefin, and ash in gasoline, diesel, natural gas, and fuel oil. Improved fuels, such as the super unleaded gasoline premium, were quickly introduced into various regional markets. Driven by such policies, and by the Ministry of Energy's Integrated Fuels Policy, unleaded gasoline jumped from 10 per cent of total gas consumption in 1991 to 58 per cent in 1997. High sulphur diesel fuel, which represented 79 per cent of consumption in 1991, was eliminated in 1993. Low sulphur diesel (0.05 per cent) currently represents 76 per cent of consumption. The Integrated Fuels Policy seeks further investment in desulphurization and the establishment of environmental standards in other critical zones and areas of the country.

Mexico has also moved to cooperate with the United States for monitoring and controlling air emission standards at the border. In May 1996 the two countries' foreign ministers extended the 1982 La Paz Agreement to designate the El Paso–Juarez Valley as a common airshed for International Air Quality Management Basin (IAQMD). While respecting each countries' existing legal and regulatory regimes, such an agreement envisages the integration of air quality monitoring networks and reporting of air quality pollution indices, the exchange of information, training and technology, public education and outreach, modelling to identify abatement strategies, and emissions trading programmes. In addition, the US–Mexico Border 11 Program, with nine working groups, is seeking to reduce emissions from vehicles idling at border crossings, tracking transboundary hazardous wastes, reducing risks of chemical accidents, and reducing solid wastes from maquiladoras.

The Role of the NAFTA Institutions

Thus far these moves to high-level harmonization have come largely from industry and national political pressure, rather than the direct work of NAFTA's institutions.[34] This is somewhat of a puzzle, given the explicit responsibilities assigned the ASC in the NAFTA text to move rapidly to stringent region-wide automotive emissions standards. Slow progress here is further highlighted by the progress of the ASC's sister body, the LTSS (or LTS), regarding the transportation of dangerous goods.

The LTS has done much to promote high-level trilateral harmonization of regulations for the transportation of dangerous goods. It has already produced a single Emergency Response Guide giving the three NAFTA countries identical procedures to deal with emergencies caused by an accident during the transport of a dangerous substance. It has assisted Mexico in upgrading its relevant standards. And it is moving rapidly to address such difficult issues as bulk packaging, halogenated organic chlorides (HOCs), and manifests for hazardous waste. With a mandate to make the parties' standards for the transportation of dangerous goods compatible by the year 2000, based on broader UN standards, it has taken as its vision the development of single North American Dangerous Goods Code. Elsewhere the LTS has been less effective. It has done very little to meet its NAFTA obligation to implement a work programme, within three years of NAFTA coming into effect, to render compatible the parties' vehicle standards, including emissions, environmental and pollution standards not covered by the work programme of the ASC.

Nor has its sister body the ASC, which lacks any NAFTA-imposed deadline for action, done much more.[35] The ASC also has not taken up its NAFTA authority to address emissions from on-road and non-road mobile sources, even though off-road vehicles may account for up to 30 per cent of all transportation emissions. Yet the ASC's initial consultations with industry identified a list of 17 priority issues that included the full array of emissions, fuels, pollution prevention, and operating standards. The list of such issues, which involved all three NAFTA countries, included: emission and emission test procedures (especially California emission regulations adopted by British Columbia, and prospectively New England states); alleged Mexican non-enforcement of emission regulations; the safety of MMT in gasoline; the non-availability of low sulphur fuel in Canada; and different noise standards in the three countries. None of these problems, however, appeared to have a clear, trade-inhibiting effect.

196   *Case Studies*

Compliance and Enforcement in Principle and Practice

Higher level environmental action and international cooperation and convergence is also evident in the area of compliance, inspection, and enforcement. Here again it is the broader NAFTA regime rather than the NAFTA institutions or dispute settlement mechanisms directly that are propelling the process. The pre- and post-NAFTA need to demonstrate NAFTA's environmental effectiveness to the US public has led to a major increase in inspection and enforcement action in Mexico, while the larger need to secure and maintain the open NAFTA market has led the larger firms to readily comply, often on a voluntary and anticipatory basis.

The NAFTA's Dispute Settlement Mechanisms in Action

One striking trend during NAFTA's first three and a half years is the exceptional record of compliance with NAFTA's environmental and overall obligations. There have been relatively few cases taken to NAFTA's three trade and investment dispute settlement panels, as the very credibility of the NAFTA dispute settlement process appears to have deterred unfair actions from occurring in the first place. Moreover, the wider array of NAFTA institutions have avoided, managed or politically settled disputes before they have had to go to the 'NAFTA court'.[36] Of the 30 or more cases thus far before the Chapter 19 mechanism, none has involved the auto industry. Automotive-related disputes have been similarly absent from Chapter 20 cases. They are tangentially involved through the Chapter 11 case on MMT. Nor have any of the 10 cases taken to the CEC under NAAEC's Article 14–15 process, or either of the 2 cases under Article 13, involved the automotive industry.[37] Given the industry's dominant size and share within North America in both economic and environmental terms, this is a striking finding. The one automotive-related dispute of some significance is the Chapter 11 case on MMT (discussed in detail in Chapter 8 above).

Patterns of National-Level Inspection and Enforcement

In all three countries, the resources available for environmental inspection and enforcement at the national and subfederal level have been challenged by severe budgetary cutbacks to environmental agencies, as governments have moved aggressively to address serious fiscal deficits. Such moves have curtailed the available capacity in Canada and the United States. Yet in Mexico, despite the particularly severe shocks brought by the 1994 peso crisis, the record of environmental inspection and enforcement and compliance has improved markedly.

Since NAFTA took effect, Mexico has done much to augment its capacity for environmental enforcement.[38] It has created an environmental crime unit in its Attorney General's office. It has increased the number and quality of its environmental inspectors, especially in important areas such as the transboundary shipment of hazardous waste. Since 1992 over 660 Mexican environmental inspectors have been trained, including 460 from border states. US EPA trained 230 inspectors in 1995 and 220 in 1996 from the US and Mexico.[39] Mexico has also expanded the number of enforcement actions (Steinberg 1997).

The results of these actions are evident in the record of the maquiladoras, where many automotive parts operations are clustered. From 1992 to 1996 Mexico conducted 12,347 inspections and compliance verifications visits in the border, fined 9,884 facilities and partially or completely closed 548 facilities. From 1993 to 1996 there has been a 43 per cent increase in the number of maquiladoras in complete environmental compliance, and a 72 per cent reduction in serious environmental violations in the maquiladoras.[40]

In addition to government enforcement, Mexico, starting in 1992, has promoted voluntary compliance through a new environmental auditing programme. In 1996, 274 operations joined the programme. By April 1997, 617 facilities had completed environmental audits. Over 400 had adopted compliance Action Plans generating more than $800 million in new environmental investments.

To these trends can be added the absence of any known cases of industries migrating to Mexico in order to take advantage of Mexico's allegedly weak pattern of environmental enforcement.[41] Together they suggest that, with continued US assistance, there are adequate technical and financial resources for enforcement, especially as Mexican growth is now being vibrantly restored. The record further suggests that Mexico's initial pre-NAFTA increase in environmental inspection, fines, and shutdown as part of the NAFTA debate, has been joined by a deep-seated and sustained desire to maintain a high level of environmental enforcement as a matter of national policy. It is also possible that NAAEC's ultimate power to re-impose tariffs in the event of a persistent pattern of environmental non-enforcement, and the increasing value of liberalized NAFTA trade to Mexico's economy has conditioned its authorities into maintaining high standards or economy-wide environmental enforcement, especially in the visible border area.

Nor do the costs of compliance appear to have placed an undue burden on Mexican or foreign owned firms in Mexico. The Mexican government gave smaller firms a grace period for compliance when the 1994–5 peso crisis left them unable to meet their legal obligations for environmental improvements. The relatively small amount (3 per cent) that pollution control equipment commands in the overall costs of US industry has been overwhelmed as a cost factor by massive exchange rate, interest rate, and inflation rate changes in the Mexican economy. The general trend towards greater environmental regulation in the United States temporarily abated after the mid-term Congressional elections in 1994. The absence of large-scale US automotive investment in

Mexico since 1993 is consistent with this pattern of higher Mexican enforcement and a reduced increase in US costs, but the causes of the investment trend lie primarily in calculations of broad politics rather than specific environmentally related costs.

Economic Implications of Environmental Policy for the Auto Industry

Although NAFTA's automotive institutions have begun work relating to manufacturing emissions standards, fuel standards, operating standards, and enforcement as potential agenda items, it is industry forums for international dialogue and pressure on national governments, together with strong public environmental consciousness, that are driving the process of higher level, region-wide harmonization. There have thus been minimal costs and substantial benefits to industry in the area of manufacturing standards, as they have largely shaped the regulatory process and reaped the rewards of rapid and pioneering pollution prevention action. Nor has compliance and enforcement provided a major burden to most firms. The major challenges and potential costs to the industry come from the prospective proliferation of different standards in increasingly smaller state and provincial jurisdictions, in the difficulty of reaching consensus with the petroleum industry on US (and thus Canadian and eventually Mexican) fuel standards, and in the diversity of subfederal inspection and maintenance systems.

The Benefits of a Single Regional Regulatory System

In general, the prevailing trends of regional integration and rationalization, and high level, continental, and eventual region-wide environmental regulatory harmonization are of major benefit to the industry. They make all three NAFTA markets more open to the products and services of the other country.[42] Region-wide uniformity in industry practice and government regulation is of particular advantage to those smaller and weaker domestic producers and home-based exporters who lack the capacity to absorb the transaction costs to produce separate products and services for segmented markets.[43] The move to harmonize Canadian emissions and diagnostic standards with those of the United States in 1998 has thus been strongly and wisely supported by an integrated automotive industry in both countries, who have long recognized the value of 'one standard, one test, one mark'.[44]

Despite this ideal, there are some remaining consequential challenges across the US–Canadian border. While Canada adopted the US 1998 emissions standards, effective September 1997, the industry in both countries is being harmed by the current uncertainty about the US (and thus the Canadian) regulations for the year 2001. The confidence that the projected 2001 standards would go forward in the United States and thus Canada has largely evaporated, given a dispute over whether the 2001 standards should include a mandatory fuel requirement for sulphur levels of 30 ppm on average and 80 ppm maximum. The auto industry favours such a standard but is participating in a joint auto–oil study to determine what the appropriate level might be if new technologies for catalysts that are more tolerant of sulphur come on stream. Current technologies are known to work at 30/80 and the refining technology has long been available to take the sulphur out.[45]

Similar issues arise with regard to the dispute over MMT, which some regard as a precursor of the larger political struggle to come over sulphur and other fuel standards. The MMT issue raises the important question of whether the required technology will become available to allow the continued use of MMT, and who will incur the costs of developing the technology required for enhanced pollution control. Will it be the refiners or the OEMs or parts makers or governments?[46] Will it require aftermarket parts producers to engage in equally expensive product upgrades, or open new markets for their advanced products?

This uncertainty points to the advantages which government regulation can have over the voluntary standardization that is generally preferred and strongly relied on by industry. Despite its success in the New Low Emission Vehicle (NLEV) and pollution prevention programmes, and in maintaining the floor in the case of MMT, voluntary regimes are always subject to the danger of defection, and thus offer less certainty, especially in focusing on future targets and timetables, than mandatory government regulation. The prospects of defection are increased when solutions involve not only the highly concentrated automotive industry, but the more diffuse set of actors from the petroleum industry who may seek allies (the Pemex monopoly in Mexico, and the relatively powerful petroleum industry in Canada) in NAFTA partner countries.[47]

The Challenge of Subfederal Differentiation

The greatest challenge and potential cost, however, flows from the threat of further subfederal differentiation and the adoption of different and higher standards in increasingly smaller jurisdictions and markets. This trend threatens to impose significant additional costs on the automotive industry (already incorporating about US $2,000 worth of environmental equipment into each car) and weakens its ability to compete internationally (especially with European Union rivals) in the rapidly emerging era of the global car. Even in the core area of automotive manufacturing emissions standards, Massachusetts and New York have gone before the courts seeking permission to follow California in setting their own local standards. Any success would destroy a system in which the United States maintained only two standards (federal and California ones). It would encourage the legally more powerful Canadian provinces led by British Columbia to reproduce this proliferation in Canada as well. An increasing array of subjects, such as requirements for a minimum percentage of zero-emission vehicles, could become the subject of such subfederal regulatory proliferation.

Such a trend, if allowed to develop, could impose major costs on industry. The additional, state and provincial jurisdictions lack the market size of California. Moreover, the smaller Canadian and Mexican vehicle and parts producers lack the ability to economically produce for these segmented markets. Thus far, the industry response has been to initiate voluntary, preventative action, through its NLEV. In the usual pattern, the US auto industry developed the programme, its Canadian counterpart joined, and is urging its government to harmonize on the EPA's US-wide 1998 level. Such continental collaboration, and related work to develop pre-competitive technology for a new generation of vehicles has not as yet fully involved Mexican industry, nor made use of the resources of the NAFTA regime and the CEC.

The threat of subfederal regulatory proliferation is also acute in regard to inspection and maintenance programmes, especially as the trend-setting California model is encountering problems and is in a state of flux. It is important for the aftermarket industry to ensure that the North American norm for such programmes emphasizes replacement and upgrade, with appropriate warranty programmes, rather than the early scrapping of vehicles. Scrapping programmes should be combined with a move to the disposable-reusable vehicle, to open up a major new segment of the aftermarket industry, as it has in Europe.

The case of industry would be strengthened, and its economic and environmental strength enhanced, with further moves to expand the well-developed pattern of US–Canadian collaboration to Mexico. The low level of US and Canadian foreign direct investment in the Mexican automotive industry in the post-NAFTA period has meant a restricted flow of new environmental technology and management systems through corporate practices and industry diffusion. There is a particular need in Mexico, especially in the wake of the peso crisis and its temporary regulatory relaxation, to diffuse environmentally state-of-the-art practices and technology downward from the largest assemblers into the smallest tier of Mexican parts and aftermarket firms. Nor has industry itself moved to deal on a trilateral basis, in an anticipatory and preventative fashion, with issues such as pollution prevention, NLEV, fuels standards, and next-generation vehicles.

Conclusions

Thus far NAFTA has imposed few environmental burdens on the automotive industry, while opening important new economic opportunities for it. NAFTA has brought no discernable additional environmental costs to the automotive industry. Yet its economic provisions have led to region-wide integration and rationalization, and an upward-level harmonization of environmental practices and standards that have benefited producers and citizens in all three countries. The policy challenge of the present and future is thus to build on this foundation. More precisely, it is to harness the NAFTA regime to prevent emerging environmental regulatory backsliding (as with MMT), uncertainty (as with 2001 emissions and sulphur fuel standards), and differentiation (with emissions, and inspection and maintenance programmes) within and between the United States and Canada. Mexico and the NAFTA institutions need to be involved more directly in the largely informal US–Canada processes that have prevailed to date. This challenge has acquired some urgency with Canada and Mexico already enjoying free trade agreements with promising South America partners, with the FTAA deadline of hemispheric free trade by 2005 and the APEC process of free trade by 2010/2020 promising to begin liberalization in environmental products and services.

Region-wide automotive industry integration and rationalization, higher level harmonization of environmental regulation, and public pressure for higher environmental standards and performance are the dominant trends of the NAFTA era. But the process remains uneven. Within the United States and Canada, regulatory proliferation is strengthening at the subfederal level, even though there is a place for states and provinces within NAFTA's environmental institutions and regime. As the case of MMT shows, there is the threat of an economically and environmentally costly backsliding with seventeen-year-old fuel standards, with NAFTA's dispute settlement mechanism a potential accomplice in the unravelling. Even in the United States and thus Canada, where industry cooperation and regulatory harmonization comes easily, there is uncertainty over emission and fuel standards, even though the NAFTA text instructed its premier automotive institutions, the ASC and LTSS, to have in place by the start of 1997 a work plan to harmonize automotive emissions standards. And in ongoing industry processes such as the diffusion of technology through foreign direct investment and multi-stakeholder pollution prevention programmes, Mexico often remains outside the Canada–US network.

It is thus clear that the intergovernmental, trilateral institutions and processes created by NAFTA are not performing up to their potential, and thus not adequately assisting the automotive industry with the environmental regulatory challenges it faces. In broad terms, the directions the NAFTA regime should follow to support the needs of the industry are clear. The first is the prevention of a further differentiation of regulations among the NAFTA countries and their subfederal jurisdiction, so that the common upward progression can be maintained, and the costs of a regulatory patchwork avoided. The second is to legitimize an integrated, total systems based approach to environmental regulation, so that the costly conflicts between the automotive and petroleum industries can be minimized. The third is to foster a truly trilateral process that engages Mexico as a full equal. The fourth is to strengthen the role of science, technical cooperation, and policy advice to governments seeking harmonized regulations, in ways that broaden the base of involved stakeholders and thus the legitimacy the NAFTA regime

202   Case Studies

commands. And the fifth is to equip North American industry to prevail in the competition for the markets of the hemisphere and beyond.

Chapter 10 has examined how environmental policy and regulation, as shaped by the NAFTA regime of rules and institutions, is affecting automotive trade, investment, and production in North America and having broad economic implications for the North American automotive industry, its consumers, and other stakeholders. It has argued that three broad forces are affecting the environmental regulation and performance of the North American automotive industry in the NAFTA era.

The first is an intensification of the move towards a full-scale rationalization and integration of the industry on a regional rather than national basis, with a corresponding production incentive to have a uniform set of relevant environmental standards in all three countries and across all their subfederal jurisdictions. The second is a new wave of high-level regulatory harmonization as NAFTA's consciousness-raising, institutions, dispute settlement mechanisms, and incentives have prevented any regulatory 'race to the bottom' but inspired a 'push to the top', driven and guided largely by the anticipatory and voluntary efforts of industry and its stakeholders. The third is the rapid spread of this push to high-level harmonization, from the assembly to the OEM parts and then aftermarket sectors, and from manufacturing standards to fuel standards, inspection and maintenance, pollution prevention, and other operating standards.

Prior to NAFTA, the United States, Canada, and Mexico possessed a substantially integrated automotive industry (for assemblers and OEM parts producers) but, especially outside the US–Canada relationship, a widely varying set of environmental regulations and enforcement patterns. The result was that US-based and owned larger manufacturers generally applied higher US-level standards in their operations in Canada and Mexico. However production in Mexico by smaller firms for the domestic Mexican market, separate California standards in the US, and the spread of such subfederal distinctiveness across the United States and Canada created an inconvenient differentiation that was threatening to expand. At the same time, the move to an integrated total systems approach to environmental control in the automotive industry increased the pressure for uniform standards over a wider range of industries and jurisdictions.

The advent of NAFTA brought a strong move towards more stringent and expanded environmental regulation, enforcement, and regulatory convergence. These factors have led to explicit upward environmental harmonization on US standards for emissions, and the use of US-pioneered pollution prevention programmes. The process has extended, with greater difficulty, into fuel use, the adoption of US-like inspection and maintenance programmes at the subfederal level, and other operating standards. There has also been a notable improvement in compliance with environmental regulations, despite the severe reductions in public sector resources for environmental protection, inspection, and enforcement in all three NAFTA countries. In their first four years of operation NAFTA's economic and environmental dispute settlement mechanisms have received no automotive related cases (with the exception of the MMT dispute), suggesting that the NAFTA rules and the regime's deterrent effect are operating effectively to encourage effective government enforcement and industry performance. There has been a major increase in inspection and enforcement action in Mexico, where the larger firms readily comply, often on a voluntary and anticipatory basis.

Thus, NAFTA has imposed few environmental burdens on, but opened important new opportunities for, the automotive industry. Taking advantage of these opportunities will largely require action by national and subfederal governments in all three countries. Intensified moves towards high-level harmonization should be focused on the region-wide adoption of a total systems approach to environmental regulation (embracing manufacturing, fuel, and operating standards and pollution prevention action), the reduction of different subfederal regimes, and increasing region-wide capacity for compliance. This will improve the competitiveness of North American producers in global markets.

Further research should concentrate on how current and prospective high-level harmonized North American environmental regulations compare with those faced by Japanese and German producers in their home markets, with those in the Chilean and other South American markets, and with the distinctive, geographically based environmental requirements of North America and the Western hemisphere. It is important to consider how North American producers, the US Government, and the Canadian and Mexican governments (through their existing bilateral free trade agreements in the hemisphere) can best extend the existing and developing NAFTA environmental and regulatory regime to the hemisphere as the deadline of hemispheric free trade by 2005 approaches.

NOTES

1. The North American automotive industry is taken to mean primarily the original equipment assemblers and parts manufacturers producing in the United States, Canada, and Mexico. Yet given the pervasive economic and environmental interdependencies, attention extends where necessary to the automotive aftermarket and fuel suppliers. The aftermarket includes 'that part of the industry concerned with the manufacturing, re-manufacturing, distribution and retailing of all vehicle parts, tools, equipment, accessories and services, except those products that are used as original equipment to manufacture new vehicles' (AIAC 1993).
2. In assessing NAFTA's effects on the automotive industry and relevant environmental regulations, it is important to recall that NAFTA is but one of many forces shaping the regulatory environment for the industry, that there was extensive preexisting integration and harmonization, that it is in many cases still too soon to assess NAFTA's effect, and that most change at the moment is being felt in the economically smaller and less integrated Mexican partner.
3. He continues: 'Integration with Mexico is still not an overwhelming factor in the US automotive industry. But it may well be one day, just as integration with

204 *Case Studies*

Canada is today.' This view that NAFTA will lead in the long term to complete trilateral regional integration to a level enjoyed by the United States and Canada today is accepted by Studer (1994).

4. While this process has been delayed somewhat by the peso crisis and lack of new large-scale US automotive investment in Mexico, the additional profitability which integration brings will increase the affordability of high-level environmental performance, while the transfer of technology and training through integrated production systems provides an additional incentive.

5. The Mexican industry was also substantially integrated with that of the United States. The automotive industry was and is the single most important sector in two-way US–Mexican trade. Indeed, most of overall US–Mexican trade comes from intra-corporate shipments by the big three (General Motors, Ford, and Chrysler) and US parts producers. In 1995 the United States exported $394 million in vehicles and $6.7 billion in parts to Mexico, while importing $7.8 billion in vehicles and $10.5 billion in parts (US Department of Commerce 1995; USTR 1997: 48).

6. On the deep and pervasive consensus behind high environmental performance in Canada, see Kirton (1994).

7. The United States began the NAFTA era with 30,000 auto parts producers, with $100 billion in annual sales, servicing 15 million vehicles. Canadian firms produced $12 billion worth of parts for about 2 million vehicles. In contrast, Mexico had only 680 parts manufacturers selling $6.5 billion worth of parts for 1 million vehicles (Studer 1994: 45).

8. They accounted for 48% of the sector's GDP. About 500 were majority Mexican-owned, producing, in family-controlled, labour-intensive firms, low value added and low technology parts largely for the local market and particularly the after-market. These firms accounted for 40% of Mexican autoparts production and 60% of employment in the industry (Studer 1994: 25).

9. These enjoyed high technology, high value added, and economies of scale. They accounted for 40% of auto industry employment and over half of auto parts exports from Mexico. With Mexico's 1994 removal of all remaining FDI restrictions in the industry, their ranks were clear to expand.

10. 20 received Chrysler's Penstar award, 37 more Nissan's Hyoka award from 1991 to 1992, and 77 Ford's Quality Q-1 certification (Studer 1994: 55).

11. This was from US $11.1 to US $22.9, in part due to US tariff reductions on light truck imports from Mexico.

12. There has been some rationalization. For example, Ford has stopped producing Thunderbirds and Cougars in Mexico and concentrated their production at Lorain, Ohio.

13. The 1997 generation of studies on NAFTA effects, centred on the President's report of July 1997, point to extensive economic benefits and environmental disappointments, but generally do not address the impact of regulatory changes and convergence. For the main studies, see USTR (1997), the Heritage Foundation (Sweeney 1997), the Center for Strategic and International Studies (Weintraub 1997), the Federal Reserve Bank of Chicago (Kouparitsas 1996), the Brookings Institution (Lustig 1997), the Economist (1997). Those critical of the Agreement include the Council on Hemispheric Affairs (1997), and the Economic Policy Institute (1997). The environmental disappointments relate to the absence of a NAFTA development fund to support needed scientific research and environmental enhancement, the

The North American Auto Industry   205

low level of environmental enforcement action, and the limited access environmental groups have to the environmental dispute settlement system, rather than the alleged downward harmonization of environmental rules or pollution haven seeking industry migration that featured so prominently in the initial NAFTA debate.

14. For a full account of the relevant pre-NAFTA US regulatory framework affecting automotive industry, see Gayle (1993). For a comprehensive and detailed review of US and Canadian air and other environmental quality levels and pressures, see DeWiel et al. (1997).
15. This is in part because many freshmen Republican Congresspeople soon discovered that their electors were strongly committed to high levels of environmental protection.
16. The equivalent 1994 Mexican standard is .11 ppm over one hour per year.
17. Municipal authorities in Detroit in particular are claiming they are unable to meet such standards without severe economic cost.
18. For example, the regulatory climate and environmental issues were two factors which led Sears to abandon full service automotive operations in favour of a concentration on tyres and batteries only (Baffico 1997).
19. Andrew Neblett, 'Eleven Major Companies Take Quality Environmental Management Initiatives within President's Commission', *Total Quality Environmental Management*, 2 (Autumn 1992): 17–25, and 'Total Quality Management: A Framework for Pollution Prevention', Washington, DC, January 1993.
20. The CCME estimated that cleaner air from cleaner vehicles and fuels would produce health benefits of up to Can. $31 billion or one billion per year (Marchi 1997). Marchi was not alone, for his provincial counterparts, who control an estimated three-quarters of the jurisdiction for environmental protection in Canada have also been moving. British Columbia had introduced its Aircare programme, and joined a network of states and provinces exploring the advent of zero-emission vehicles (Munton and Kirton 1996).
21. According to the minister, each of the more than 14 million automobiles on the road in Canada generates four to five tonnes of pollutants every year.
22. Canada thus has a clear interest in having US national environmental regulations move strongly and rapidly upward. Canada shares this ecological interdependence with distant Mexico, whose airborne pesticides and pollutants are, for example, arriving in the Great Lakes.
23. In April 1996 the current American standard of 120 ppbillion for ozone was well above Canada's objective of 82 ppbillion (Marchi 1996). Marchi also sought to amend the US Clean Air Act, up for review in 1999.
24. For a discussion of the MMT case, see Chapter 8.
25. At present, Canada's average level of sulphur content of gasoline is 360 parts per million (ppm) compared to the proposed European level of 150 ppm, a slightly lower level than that expected in the United States, and a current standard of 30 in California (the trend setter for automotive emission regulations). In 1996 the Canadian government created a committee of federal, provincial, and industry officials to examine emissions of sulphur, a natural component of crude oil. Representatives from industry, government, and the environmental community have begun to meet to consider reducing or removing gasoline sulphur emissions.

26. Sulphur generates particulate matters and ground-level ozone precursors leading to smog. While diesel trucks are only 10% of vehicles on the road, they produce a large share of vehicular emissions. The new regulations would reduce emissions of affected vehicles by 23% for particulates, 30% for sulphur dioxide, 10% for volatile organic compounds, and 10% for carbon monoxide. The health benefits were estimated at Can. $4–11 billion by the year 2020.
27. The Committee's draft reports of April 1997 indicated that reducing to the California level would save 118 lives a year by 2001 (if the rule were imposed that year) and 192 by 2020, and prevent thousands of respiratory illnesses. However 16 of Canada's 17 refineries would have to spend nearly $1.8 billion to upgrade and incur annual operating costs of Can. $119 million to meet the California standard. Adding a reduction in diesel fuel (a less likely step) would require another Can. $1.2 billion in capital costs. Final reports were expected at the end of May. The auto industry prefers a regulatory rather than voluntary approach, recalling an earlier case where a voluntary approach allowed the oil industry to defect, in ways that imperilled the sales of three truck manufacturers. CCME ministers also sought a national regulation to curb benzine in gasoline, a known human carcinogen, declared toxic under the Canadian Environmental Protection Act (CEPA). Marchi promised to produce in spring 1997 a regulation to halve the benzine content of gasoline to 1% by volume, one of the most stringent levels in the world, and one that would reduce annual benzine emissions by 3,000 tonnes by 1999. An estimated 56% of Canadian benzine emissions come from gas-powered vehicles, with a higher figure in urban areas.
28. British Columbia's Aircare programme of mandatory inspection and maintenance, introduced into Vancouver and the Lower Fraser Valley in 1992, tests over one million cars and light trucks for emissions every year and requires repairs to pollution control equipment to meet emission requirements.
29. Existing OEM warranties already accept US EPA's test results, and the manufacturers have extended this acceptance to BC's Aircare programme, which is deemed to meet EPA levels.
30. Task Force of the Canadian Automotive Manufacturing Pollution Prevention Project (MVMA Project). *Fourth Progress Report*, June 1996.
31. Canada also has its equivalent of the US Car programme to develop pre-competitive technology that would generate a threefold increase in fuel efficiency to 80 mpg, through the use of advanced materials that may not be recyclable and perhaps hydrogen fuel cells that may threaten the existing oil industry.
32. The standards, published by the DOF on 18 January 1994 covered ozone, carbon monoxide, nitrogen dioxide, sulphur dioxide, total suspended particulates, PM10, and lead. These cover the same six substances specified in the US Clean Air Act, and add carbon monoxide.
33. The cities are Mexico, D. F., Monterrey, Guadalajara, Minatitlan, Ciudad Juarez, Chihuahua, Tijuana, Mexicali, and Torreon. Data from 1991 and 1992 indicate the maximum ozone levels effective in 1994 were exceeded in Mexico City by a wide margin for almost half the year.
34. The relevant activity has come from NAFTA's economic institutions. The CEC has not dealt directly with the automotive industry, although it has developed projects on such related areas as environmental laboratories' standards, transportation and standards, climate change, ISO 14000, pollution prevention, voluntary compliance, and air monitoring.

35. The ASC is assisted in Canada by an industry advisory group, the Automotive Advisory Committee (AAC). Industry is now aiming at standards that are not necessarily harmonized or identical but consistent, accommodating, and that allow functional equivalency. It also wants standards that are not regionally specific but globally compatible.
36. The one major case of US non-compliance has come over safety concerns in the trucking industry—its December 1995 decision to postpone indefinitely the implementation of a NAFTA deadline to allow Mexican trucks to circulate in the US south-west. While safety was the issue, the President was driven by pressure from the unions, environmental groups, and anti-drug crusaders.
37. During its first three years, one of the two Article 13 cases concerned Continental Pollutant Pathways for air pollutants.
38. Data provided from USTR (1997: 112, 125). Although these data apply to all firms, the large share of automotive plants in the Mexican economy and particularly in the border regions means they provide an accurate if rough reflection of patterns prevailing in this industry.
39. The CEC itself has been active in the area of enforcement, as its Secretariat has mounted a major programme of cooperation for officials from the three countries.
40. Because NAFTA gives to all of Mexico the trade policy advantages historically enjoyed by the maquiladoras, its long-term effect is to lessen the concentration of industry at the border, and the environmental stresses that stem from such concentration.
41. The failures or weaknesses of Mexico's environmental enforcement were largely absent from the 1997 studies reviewing and criticizing NAFTA's effects, a notable contrast with the prominence this issue possessed in the initial NAFTA debate. The few cases cited did not involve the auto industry, and represented a temporary response to the peso crisis rather than a persistent pattern of non-enforcement. See Public Citizen's contribution to Economic Policy Institute (1997).
42. While currently of greatest value to the smaller NAFTA partners this will become of increasing benefit to the United States. The percentage of US GDP accounted for by trade is rising from 10% in 1970 to 25% at present to an estimated 33% by 2010. In the first five months of 1997, Canada and Mexico alone accounted for over half (53%) of the increase in US exports. The 1993–6 increase in US trade with its NAFTA partners is more than the level of US trade with all countries except Canada, Mexico, and Japan, making the NAFTA increase alone America's fourth largest trading partner.
43. While such environmental standards should respect local peculiarities in geography, and environmental stresses, supports, and absorptive capacity, common standards can be constructed in such a way as to make allowance for such variations, for example by specifying varying allowable emissions levels measured at different altitudes throughout the NAFTA region, or requiring more stringent inspection and maintenance in local hot spots. The classic sovereignty-based demand for the right to regulatory localism in response to distinct political preferences should dissipate as knowledge of health effects becomes more widely known and the sense of a common North American community develops (through, for example, expanded flows of people).
44. Even though existing pollution control equipment adds an estimated US $2,000 to the cost of each car, the real issue is less the level or even type of standard than its

application in law and practice across the entire region, in ways that all players, from North America and outside, are obliged to respect.
45. For example, in Canada, Shell already provides such low sulphur fuel.
46. The auto industry has the option of forcing the issue and the adjustment onto fuel makers by moving from advisory to mandatory its warning in existing warranties that the use of MMT-free fuel is advised.
47. Canada's recent experience with low sulphur diesel standards provides an example as the petroleum industry's defection from an auto–oil consensus threatened the bankruptcy of some Canadian truck firms, and forced the auto industry to seek and secure regulatory relief from the new standards from government.

Part IV
Conclusions

11

Implications for Firm Strategy and Public Policy

The new conditions of complex institutional responsiveness are now the dominant reality for firms doing business in and from North America. These conditions require a major adjustment in the corporate and political strategies upon which firms have long relied to gain entry to the foreign markets now essential to ensuring their competitiveness in an increasingly global economy. These new conditions can appear to be obstacles to firms used to operating successfully within a North American market insulated from global competition. Yet these new conditions of complex institutional responsiveness, created by NAFTA, offer North American firms major new opportunities, at both the corporate and political level, to compete in the rapidly opening global market place.

The New Era of Environmental Regulatory Protectionism

The new conditions of complex institutional responsiveness have now become a dominant feature of the business environment for firms in North America. They have created a major new challenge for even the largest firms seeking to do business across international boundaries. During the 1990s they have made environmental regulatory protectionism more frequent, widespread, entrenched, complex, and costly.

In the first instance, the new politically grounded conditions of complex institutional responsiveness have led to an upsurge in the frequency and range of environmental regulatory protection. Those hoping that NAFTA would usher in a new era of transborder commercial and environmental harmony, have grounds to be disappointed with the record of its first five years. As Table 11.1 indicates, there have been substantially more trade–environment issues involving at least two North American countries that have arisen in the five years since NAFTA took formal effect, than in the five years when the FTA operated (1989–1993), and in the preceding five years when the three countries of North America could look only to the distant GATT for international relief.

The widespread nature of environmental regulatory protection in the NAFTA era is further seen in the broad range of sectors that have been affected by it. Such issues abound in the automotive sector (at the heart of the North American manufacturing economy), in the environmentally rich natural resource sectors of agriculture, fisheries, and forestry, in other manufacturing

212 *Conclusions*

TABLE 11.1. *Cases of North American environmental regulatory protection*

Case	Regulatory initiator	Challenger (supporter)	Outcome closer to objectives of instrument	International institutional
A. Environmentally-related trade issues (60)				
Automotive emissions (6)				
SOx	US	(Mexico)	US	
NOx	US	(Mexico)	US	
Ozone	US	(Canada, Mexico)	US	
Particulates	US	(Canada, Mexico)	US	
OBD systems	US	(Canada, Mexico)	US	
INM	US	(Canada)	US	
Automotive fuels (4)				
Lead*	US	(Mexico)	US	
MMT	Canada	US (Ethyl)	US (Eythl)	NAFTA 11
Sulphur	US	(Canada)	US	
Benzene	US	(Canada)	Ongoing	
Agriculture inspections (24)				
Apples, 1989–98	Mexico	US	Mexico	NAFTA 19
Avocados, 1914–97	US	Mexico	Equal	
Beef 1, 1991–8	US	Canada	Ongoing	NAFTA SPS
Beef 2, 1994–7	Mexico	US	Mexico	—
Blueberries, 1991–3	US	Canada	US	FTA
Christmas trees 1, 1994–8	Mexico	Canada	Ongoing	NAFTA SPS
Christmas trees 2, 1994–8	Mexico	US	Ongoing	NAFTA SPS
Citrus canker, 1991–7	Mexico	US	US	NAFTA SPS
Global wheat trade	All	All	Ongoing	NAFTA CAT
Mangoes, 1993–5	US	Mexico	US	NAFTA SPS
Pork, 1997	US	Mexico	Mexico	NAFTA SPS
Potatoes, 1995–6	US	Canada	Ongoing	
Poultry 1	US	Mexico	Ongoing	—
Poultry 2	Mexico	US	Ongoing	—
Seed potatoes	Mexico	Canada	—	NAFTA SPS
Sorghum, 1997–8	Mexico	US	Ongoing	NAFTA SPS
Strawberries, 1996	US	Mexico	US	—
Stone fruits, 1991–7	Mexico	US	US	NAFTA SPS
Supply management	Canada	US	Canada	NAFTA 20
Sweet cherries, 1991–7	Mexico	US	US	NAFTA
Tomatoes, 1937–98	US	Mexico	US	NAFTA 19
UHT milk, 1987–95	US	Canada	US	FTA 18

Implications for Firm Strategy 213

Case	Regulatory initiator	Challenger (supporter)	Outcome closer to objectives of instrument	International institutional
Wheat 1, 1995–8	Mexico	US	US	—
Wheat 2, 1995–7	US	Mexico	Mexico	NAFTA SPS
Manufacturing recycling (4)				
Newsprint, 1995	US	Canada	US	—
Beer cans 1*, 1988	Canada	US + EU	US	GATT
Beer cans 2*, 1992	Canada	US	US	GATT
Beer cans 3, 1992	Canada	US	Equal	—
Fisheries conservation (6)				
Lobsters*, 1989–	US	Canada	US	FTA
Tuna*, 1979–82	US	Canada	Canada	GATT
Herring/salmon 1*, 1988	Canada	US	US	GATT
Herring/salmon 2*, 1989	Canada	US	US	FTA
Pacific salmon, 1998	Both	Canada	US	—
Tuna–dolphin, 1993	US	Mexico	Mexico	GATT
Forestry conservation (4)				
Lumber 1*, 1986	US	Canada	US	
Lumber 2*, 1992	US	Canada	Canada	FTA
Lumber 3, 1998	US	Canada	Ongoing	—
BC forestry, 1998	EU	Canada	Equal	—
Environmental services (4)				
PCB exports, 1995	Canada	US	Equal	
Metalclad	US	Mexico	Ongoing	NAFTA 11
DeSona	US	Mexico	Ongoing	NAFTA 11
USA Waste	US	Mexico	Ongoing	NAFTA 11
Dangerous goods transportation (5)				
Small packages	All	(All)	Equal	NAFTA CSRM
Large containers	All	—	Ongoing	NAFTA CSRM
HOC	All	—	Ongoing	NAFTA CSRM
Truck spills (ERG)	All	(All)	Equal	NAFTA CSRM
Rail cars	All	—	Ongoing	NAFTA CSRM
Other (2)				
Asbestos*	US	Canada	US	—
Trucking	US	Mexico	Canada	NAFTA FTCC

214 *Conclusions*

TABLE 11.1. (*Continued*)

Case	Regulatory initiator	Challenger (supporter)	Outcome closer to objectives of instrument	International institutional
B. Trade-related environmental issues (25)				
Pesticides (4)				
PCBs	All	All	All	CEC TWGP
DDT	US (Canada)	Mexico	US (Canada)	CEC TWGP
Chlordane	Canada (US)	Mexico	Canada (US)	CEC TWGP
Mercury	All	All	Canda (Mexico)	CEC TWGP
Environmental information (1)				
NAPRI, 1997	CEC	All	Mexico	CEC
Environmental science (3)				
Silva Reservoir	CEC	Mexico	Mexico	CEC 13
LRTAP	CEC	All	Equal	CEC 13
San Pedro	CEC	US–Mexico	Ongoing	CEC 13
Environmental enforcement (17)				
Biodiversity, 1995	US	US	Terminated	CEC 14–15
Sierra Club, 1995	US	US	Terminated	CEC 14–15
CPPRN, 1966	Mexico	Mexico	Can/US	CEC 14–15
Tottrup, 1996	Canada	Canada	Terminated	CEC 14–15
Oldman River, 1996	Canada	Canada	Terminated	CEC 14–15
SW Biodiversity, 1996	US	US	Terminated	CEC 14–15
BC Fisheries, 1997	Canada	Canada	Proceeding	CEC 14–15
Rio 1997	Mexico	Mexico	Proceeding	CEC 14–15
CQDE, 1997	Canada	Canada	Proceeding	CEC 14–15
CEDF, 1997	Canada	Canada	Terminated	CEC 14–15
Animal Alliance, 1997	Canada	Canada	Terminated	CEC 14–15
Oldman River, 1997	Canada	Canada	Proceeding	CEC 14–15
IDA, 1997	Mexico	Mexico	Proceeding	CEC 14–15
IDA, 1998	Mexico	Mexico	Proceeding	CEC 14–15
Martinez, 1998	Mexico	Mexico	Terminated	CEC 14–15
Planet Earth, 1998	Canada/US	US	Proceeding	CEC 14–15
Sierra Club, 1998	Canada	Canada	Proceeding	CEC 14–15

Note: *denotes non-NAFTA cases, defined as those effectively resolved prior to NAFTA and whose resolution was unaffected by calculations about the onset of NAFTA.

industries and service industries such as trucking and, paradoxically, in the new sector of environmental services. Indeed, no sector of a modern, internationally engaged economy is likely to escape the impact of environmental regulatory protectionism in its future operations.

Nor is a home-base location in a highly developed, long internationally integrated country with high degrees of environmental consciousness and regulations likely to allow firms to escape facing the impact of environmental regulatory protection from abroad. For the issues have arisen not only, as the US debate over NAFTA assumed, across the US–Mexican border, but equally voraciously along the rhetorically 'undefended' Canada–US border as well. Indeed, there are good reasons for expecting that even in such relationships, characterized by high degrees of intra-industry trade, trade liberalization will lead individual firms to seek protection ever more strongly (Cilligan 1997). And the early disputes over agriculture suggest that environmental regulatory protectionism will proliferate in the rapidly growing Canada–Mexican relationship as well.

This upsurge in the frequency and range of environmental regulatory protectionism can be traced to three particular conditions of complex institutional responsiveness. First, the spread of mass public environmental concern in the three NAFTA countries has generated a demand for and thus a governmental supply of such regulations. Second, as Table 3.2 indicated, both subfederal and international governmental bodies have joined national governments in meeting this demand. And third, the advent of NAFTA itself changed environmental issues from being considered fully domestic to a matter of international concern.

Second, environmental regulatory protectionism has now become much more entrenched. As is evident in the cases of herring/salmon and softwood lumber, several of these issues go through multiple stages, with outcomes at a particular moment leading not to enduring solutions but only to temporary respites before an offspring of the dispute erupts to impede or close the border again. Moreover, such disputes, once centred in the traditional trade domain of antidumping and countervailing duties have now spread to involve general trade disputes, foreign direct investment disputes, and issues involving the domestic enforcement of federal and subfederal environmental regulations.

The new tenacity of environmental regulatory protectionism has its origins in three particular conditions of complex institutional responsiveness. The rise of mass public environmental concern has enormously increased the number, resources, and political influence of environmental NGOs, not only in the United States, but also in Canada and now Mexico. The new generation of environmental regulations, with provisions for expanded public participation, and the activism of subfederal governments, have increased the access and power which such groups wield. It has also increased their opportunities to identify compatible or common industries with industries seeking protection, and to forge active alliance of green and greedy coalitions to secure such

216 *Conclusions*

outcomes. Governments seeking to keep their border open must now face not only the self-interested claims of a particular firm or industry promising jobs but the often nationwide, highly attractive pleas of not-for-profit groups claiming to represent the public good.

As Chapter 4 shows, such green and greedy coalitions exist in abundance in North America. Indeed, in nine of the ten major cases examined in Chapter 4, such coalitions can be identified as a force that has held the trade-restricting regulation in place. Moreover, such coalitions exist, operate, and prevail not only in the United States. As the agriculture cases confirm, they have also arisen in Canada and Mexico as well.

Also of note is the broad array of groups that have joined such coalitions. Industry groups and their environmental allies are now often joined by the subfederal governments where an industry is concentrated, consumer groups, and, as in the MMT case, religious groups as well. When, as in the MMT case, they are supported by subfederal governments, they have the full resources of government, and constitutional law in federal systems, behind them. It is the very diversity of groups and motives that often makes such coalitions, once formed, difficult to counter and dislodge.

Third, environmental regulatory protectionism is now more complex in the content and character of the regulations that industry must face. Regulations address, and industry must now be concerned about, not merely the nature of their product, but also their after sales services (as the case of California Recycling and Ontario Beer show), their harvesting production processes (as with the herring/salmon, lumber, and eco-labelling cases), and with the components of the materials used by consumers to operate their products (as with the MMT and other automotive fuel-additive cases). The scientific evidence required to challenge regulations is becoming more subtle and complex, as the MMT case indicates. And regulatory politics now confront major issues of coordination and burden sharing between powerful industries such as automobiles and petroleum in the case of automotive emissions, and between the chemicals and railroad industry in the case of halogenated organic chlorides.

Such complexity is a direct result of a further condition of complex institutional responsiveness—the new generation of environmental regulation. In particular, regulations now often express the environmentalists' core values of full life-cycle environmentalism and the precautionary principle. This has increased the backward and forward linkages that regulations embrace, and made the task of using sound science to challenge regulations more difficult. Moreover, the move to a 'total systems' approach to environmental control raises major issues of inter-industry and economy-wide coordination.

Finally, environmental regulatory protectionism is now more costly for the firms that face it. As the experience of Lactel in the case of UHT milk shows, the cost and time of process protectionism can impose major competitive costs—destroying a firm's entire export market—even when its claims are ultimately accepted as legally valid by a foreign government. As the experience of British Columbia in the California newsprint recycling case demonstrates, small regulatory changes can put major export markets at risk, even for some of the world's major multinational enterprises (notably, MacMillan Bloedel). Such was also the case for Ethyl Corporation, which faced the complete termination of its ability to export to Canada as a result of one regulatory change.

While not all or even most of this new environmental regulatory protection and the aims of the coalition partners behind it is consciously protectionist in intent, it is protectionist in impact. Regardless of the motives of its originators, it severely compromises the competitiveness of most firms having to operate under new business conditions.

Several conditions of complex institutional responsiveness have generated these increased costs. Most generally, trade and investment liberalization have made domestic firms and home-based exporters vulnerable to competitors from abroad and raised the protectionist impact of regulatory arbitrage (Leyshon 1992). As the automotive industry shows, the spread and speed of new technology, and the move to integrated production and the just-in-time inventory which it allows, makes it necessary to have rapid, unimpeded, and costless access to foreign markets. The emergence of international business alliances, as in the automotive industry, reinforces the need for integrated international production. Meanwhile the move to global markets and competition means even large firms from large countries, such as the big three of the North American automobile industry, need a seamless regional home base on which to build the scale required to compete in world markets.

Efficiency Aspects of Compliance Strategies

In terms of the literature of strategic management, it should be noted that in this book no attempt is made to develop a 'resource-based view' (RBV) of the firm's corporate strategy. The strategies discussed here are all based on compliance with environmental regulations; there is no consideration of the firm developing 'green capabilities'. Such work has been explored elsewhere, for example by Rugman and Verbeke (1998). In that paper a clear distinction is drawn between the bulk of the strategic management literature in which issues of compliance (and avoidance) of environmental regulations is considered and the RBV whereby firms could invest in developing capabilities such that they could beat the average competitor by this green strategy alone.

The nature of the NAFTA regime and the NAFTA cases considered here, especially those in agriculture and auto-related areas, are classic examples of shelter-based strategies of firms seeking protection from efficient rivals through government-imposed entry barriers. Few, if any, of the cases could lead to the development of RBV capabilities, so the analytical framework adopted here can be simplified to ignore such considerations. Instead, the main contribution of this book is to embed political strategies explicitly into the traditional corporate strategy framework of mainstream management literature.

In the mainstream management literature, the work of Michael Porter (1980) is definitive. He argues that there are three types of generic strategies for firms: low-cost production; differentiation by branded products or services; and focus by finding niches. In the NAFTA cases of this book most attention relates to Porter's first generic strategy of low-cost and related price competition. The corporate strategies of firms discussed here are usually variations of cost savings. Compliance with environmental regulations can have adverse cost impacts, indeed it is usually assumed by economists that a tariff-like regulation simply increases the price of imports. This can then lead the firm to considering switching from exporting to foreign direct investment to access the protected foreign market (Rugman 1981).

All three of Porter's generic strategies are efficiency based. Most of the NAFTA cases which impose entry barriers create relative inefficiencies and are thereby welfare reducing. In addition, some of the cases seek to redistribute profits and rents and are thereby equity/distributionally based. Here the concepts of political science are useful to complement economic efficiency considerations. When a domestic firm gains protection it can nudge the government into redistribution of rents in its favour at the expense of the foreign producers affected by the environmental barriers to trade. In this concluding chapter, we distinguish between such efficiency and distributional actions in our review of the NAFTA cases.

The new conditions for complex institutional responsiveness offer an opportunity for NAFTA-based firms to overcome the inefficiency of discriminatory environmental regulations. With use of the appropriate political and bureaucratic channels, firms can seek to offset or mitigate expenses involved in protectionist-inspired environmental regulations. The new corporate strategy responses to environmental regulations discussed here are all examples of rational efficiency-driven and compliance-based actions. Firms act to minimize the adverse impacts on their cost structure. In the following section a further set of compliance-based political strategies of firms is considered.

New Compliance Strategies

With environmental regulatory protectionism being so frequent, widespread, entrenched, and complex in the new era, it is difficult to dislodge it by incremental adjustments in corporate strategy, and through a reliance on the proven corporate and political instruments of old. New responses are required.

They are also available in abundance. For as part of these new conditions have come new opportunities and instruments for firms to act in competitiveness-enhancing ways. Moreover, in response to these changed conditions, North American firms have begun to activate the full array of instruments now available to them, as part of their core corporate strategies.

Implications for Firm Strategy 219

The most striking pattern is how infrequently firms have attempted to modify their traditional corporate strategy of price competition in the face of environmental regulatory protectionism in North America. Perhaps this is because many of the industries are mature, commodity-type businesses, such as in natural resources (lumber, fish) and agriculture. Similarly, the MMT producer was not exactly high tech and marketing-type strategies are rarely evident in these cases. Exemptionalism was used by Lactel in the UHT case. Canadian blueberry producers paid the higher price of meeting the US regulation as a cost of maintaining access to a US market in which they hoped to expand ('pay and expand'). The strategy of altered production was used by these same producers (through the substitute of a higher cost pesticide) and, in a different form, by Saskatchewan gas refiners in the MMT case (who turned to a substitute for the banned substance). Development of new core competencies shifts to alternative products, innovation and new technology, and export diversification were not in evidence.

The absence of alternative strategies reflects the highly developed presence within North America of the business conditions of complex institutional responsiveness. The rapidly growing importance of the regional market to Mexican, Canadian, and increasingly US firms makes loss of exports a major problem. This is especially the case for Mexican and Canadian firms. The December 1994 peso crisis in Mexico and the slow growth in Canada in NAFTA's first few years (where exports accounted for most of the growth in the Canadian economy) made access to the US market essential. With a booming US economy in the seven years to 1998, the share of exports and imports in US GDP is steadily increasing (USTR 1997). The high degree of intra-industry trade within the integrated North American market makes it difficult to penetrate new market segments, as such entry would face stiff competition from entrenched producers. And the raw growth in the US market, where 80 per cent of Canadian and Mexican exports are destined, makes world export diversification unattractive.

It is useful to distinguish between small and medium-sized business, whose instruments of corporate strategy are limited (such as the Saskatchewan refinery faced with the regulatory removal of a valued input) and small home-based exporters (Quebec's Lactel and Maritime blueberry producers) and multinational enterprises. For such companies with multinational investment and operations, a more complex business logic prevailed.

Multinationals were more prone to employ the new instruments of corporate strategy to combat environmental regulatory protectionism. Here the instruments of choice were production to the standards of the major export market (Vogel production), border production, and above all foreign direct investment. Production by firms to meet foreign regulations was evident in the case of the Ford Motor company in Mexico, which produced according to company-wide standards and thus ones that met the US regulations (Ramírez de la O 1996). US-owned multinationals operating in Mexico also displayed a political variant of Vogel production, for they visibly increased their level of corporate environmental standards and practices in order to influence the political debate in the United States in a pro-NAFTA and thus trade-liberalization direction. Border production was evident in the rise in post-NAFTA activity in Mexico's maquiladora industries, as border production makes it easier to comply with US laws demanding that hazardous wastes be returned to the United States for treatment.

The most widespread, however, is the instrument of jumping border regulatory barriers through direct foreign investment in partner countries and producing there in ways that meet that country's domestic standards. The popularity of this strategy is evident in the overall increase of stocks and flows of FDI among the three NAFTA countries since 1993 (Kirton 1998). Such flows are motivated by considerations other than environmental regulatory barrier jumping, particularly among large transnationals, as in the automotive industry, where environmental regulations are not a leading corporate concern (Eden and Molot 1994). Yet through the embedded transfer of technology and management skills that FDI brings, they make it easier to support environmental regulatory convergence, at higher levels, within corporations and industries and eventually by their member governments. What is clear through the relatively balanced growth in stocks and flows of FDI among the three bilateral relationships in North American is that investment is not moving in a pollution-haven seeking way to jurisdictions in which environmental regulations or enforcement is lower. In short, NAFTA's trade and investment liberalization is producing an environmental regulatory push to the top rather than race to the bottom.

Absent from the array of new corporate strategies firms have employed during NAFTA's first five years are those of demanding higher standards at home to prepare for export markets abroad (Porter-type production capabilities), and a move to supplying domestic input to unregulated export products rather than direct exports. The absence of the former reflects the fact that the Canadian and Mexican markets are too small to support such a strategy, and that US multinationals, with extensive operations in Canada and the United States, find it more efficient to produce to a similar standard there from the start rather than anticipate the foreign governments' moving to demand such high standards. The rapidly integrating production systems in most industries in North America explain why a move to domestic input supply rather than direct exporting is unpopular.

The corporate strategic response of private sector market sharing was evident throughout the agricultural sector. Agreements between industry associations with regard to minimum prices and the withdrawal of antidumping actions are made, often in contravention of NAFTA, when other solutions are not practicable. Such agreements are easily explainable—firms work out and agree on the specific issues that affect them, rather than wait for the often long and protracted government negotiations to further their interests.

The New Political Strategy Response

North American firms have been more active in coping with environmental regulatory protectionism by pursuing the full array of political instruments made available by the conditions of complex institutional responsiveness. Indeed, at times, the force of environmental regulatory protectionism and the public pressures and industry NGO coalitions behind it render any corporate responses unavailable, and make a purely political strategy necessary. The prevalence of green and greedy coalitions means that firms will find it difficult to solve their access problems by relying on corporate instruments alone. Political strategies of considerable magnitude are now required.

Such was the situation in the case of MMT, where Ethyl, faced with a full import ban, was unable to rely on any of the available corporate strategies, old or new. Ad hoc exemptionalism, pay and expand, product alteration or alternative products were not available in the face of a full ban directed at the proprietary product of a single firm. Domestic withdrawal was not an option for a product banned in the United States and which most refiners continued to refuse to use. And export market diversification was unappealing, given Mexico's move towards studying the harmful effects of MMT and the likelihood that US and Canadian prohibitions would become the global norm.

Nor were the new corporate strategies useful. As the sole manufacturer of a patented product, faced with the elimination of its core, technology-based firm-specific advantage, Ethyl was unable to adjust through altering production to meet the new standards in the home US market or the foreign Canadian market, by border production or by using MMT as an input into US gasoline exported to Canada. Nor was further FDI a viable option, given the cost of creating fully integrated production facilities to serve each, now segregated Canadian provincial market. With only political instruments available, Ethyl moved aggressively to activate them.

North American firms faced with environmental regulatory protectionism have made abundant use of political strategies, of both traditional and new varieties. The traditional instrument of litigation in the national trade law system or courts of the regulating country is a standard, first-order response that is frequently employed. In the MMT case, for example, Ethyl went to the Canadian federal courts, and the new, NAFTA-inspired tribunal created under the AIT to press its case.

Lobbying in the political system of the regulating country is also frequent. It was evident in the MMT case, with Ethyl's intervention before Canadian parliamentary committees and publicity campaign. It was also evident among those trying to shape and secure the regulations that benefited them, with the automotive industry attempting to displace compliance costs onto the oil industry and, in the case of HOC, the chemical industry attempting to have the railroads bear the costs.

In the open, participatory political systems of North America, lobbying often extends to the creation of broad multistakeholder coalitions. In the Ontario beer can case, for example, Anheuser Busch and Heilmanns recruited as an ally the Canadian multinational, Alcan, that supplied them with their now provincially banned aluminium cans, and that operated plants in Ontario. In the case of PCB exports, the aggrieved US firms mobilized the Ontario government and Ontario industry (their customers) and supported the latter in their litigation in the regulators' jurisdiction. In the MMT case, Ethyl quickly formed a coalition with its major customer, the Canadian petroleum industry, which backed the case, less for its attachment to the economic merits of MMT for its corporate fortunes, than for its fear that the MMT issue was a precursor for the far more costly battles on sulphur and other fuel additives about to come.

One of the most frequently employed of the traditional political instruments is bilateral diplomacy through the home government. These have involved a wide range of diplomatic techniques, as developed during the 'special relationship' between Canada and the United States and predicted by the model of special partnership as the optimum way of managing that relationship (Kirton 1993). These techniques were in evidence in the cases of UHT; tuna 1979–82 (where a bilateral treaty was used); herring/salmon 2, 1989 (through bilateral consultations); softwood lumber 1, 1986 (through a memorandum of understanding); softwood lumber 2, 1992–4 (through a bilateral agreement); Ontario beer 3 (through a bilateral understanding in anticipation of NAFTA); automotive emissions (through a bilateral 1990 Canada–US Air Quality Accord and a US–Mexico Border 11 Program on automotive idling at the border).

When bilateral diplomacy looks unlikely to succeed, firms at times seek to adjust to the new foreign regulations by seeking offsetting subsidization from their home government to help them bear the additional costs they face. Such an instrument was employed by Mexican automotive parts producers in the lead up to NAFTA, as they geared up to produce to US-level standards for their soon to be integrated industry. The technique of offsetting subsidization, however, is rarely practised, in part because it is ineffective against regulations which close an entire market, and perhaps in part because of the strengthened disciplines against subsidies under the FTA and NAFTA. For example, offsetting subsidization was not in evidence in the MMT case as an instrument which the targeted firm, Ethyl employed. Indeed, subsidies to competing ethanol producers in Canada and the United States that would benefit from a ban on MMT were part of the difficulties that Ethyl faced. However, subsidies did constitute part of a potential solution, either in financing more reliable scientific studies of MMT's effects or more broadly in determining who—the automotive industry, oil industry, or government—would bear the cost of moving towards the higher regulations of the future.

Reciprocal retaliation is a somewhat more frequently employed strategy. Firms succeeded in having their governments retaliate with largely mirror-image measures in the cases of tuna in 1979–82 (where the United States

Implications for Firm Strategy 223

retaliated), potatoes in 1995–6, and Ontario beer, phase 3. There are, however, severe limits on its use from the prevailing rational calculations and ideology of special partnership held by government managers of the bilateral Canada–US relationship. The vast disparity in size and market of the two countries makes retaliation a difficult strategy to employ by Canada and Mexico against the United States. It carries the danger that the target country may link issues, thus mobilizing the superior overall capability of the United States against Canada and Mexico and poisoning overall relations. However there is some evidence that such a politicization of relations may work to the benefit of the smaller country (Nye 1974). Moreover in the NAFTA era, such reciprocal retaliation may be a useful interim step designed to induce an otherwise recalcitrant partner to come to a bilateral accommodation or seek a NAFTA-incubated and conditioned settlement.

Perhaps the most often employed of the traditional political strategies is convergent national adjustment, where firms urge their governments to adjust national regulations to meet those prevailing in the foreign, often much larger export market. Its use created the MMT case, as Canadian automotive manufacturers successfully lobbied their government to adopt a ban on the use of MMT similar to that prevailing in the United States. Here the US EPA's progressive banning of MMT, culminating in 1995 was followed by the Canadian government moving in the same year to ban the movement of the substance into and within Canada. It also dominated the other issues of automotive emissions and fuel standards, such as Mexican and Canadian emissions and ambient air quality standards, Canadian on-board diagnostic standards, Canadian diesel sulphur standards, and Mexican lead standards. It was also evident in softwood lumber 1 in 1989 over the issue of stumpage fees.

Convergent national adjustment is the preferred strategy of home based and transnational multinationals, such as those prevailing in the automobile and forest products industries. Here these firms rationally ask the governments of the smaller jurisdictions in which they operate to change to converge on the standards prevailing in their larger market. For such firms the transaction costs of regulatory diversity, and the prospect of having to change production processes and products to tailor them to the unique demands of increasingly small markets outweighs whatever advantage might be obtained from producing in jurisdictions with lower standards to serve open markets. This is particularly so as integrated production increases transaction costs and the new generation of environmental regulation creates compounding doubts about international market access.

Notwithstanding its prevalence, convergent national adjustment is a hegemonic process, of smaller countries with smaller markets and other forms of power moving unilaterally to meet the regulations prevailing at the moment in a larger export market. Those regulations may be the result of green and greedy coalitions or of other domestic political struggles, rather than scientific judgements of the optimum measures required to protect human and ecological health and safety. Such regulations, when adopted in smaller countries, may be even less appropriate to the ecological conditions prevailing there. Moreover, when delivered through a hegemonic process, political forces in the smaller country may resist the straightforward adoption of the foreign regime. Thus convergent national adjustment, as with the other traditional political instrument, requires time-consuming, costly, often conflict-ridden processes that impose mounting costs on firms engaged in intensifying global competition.

The new political instruments made available under complex institutional responsiveness offer a solution. They replace hegemonic adoption with negotiated mutual adjustment. They do so under permanent rules and institutions, in which both trade and environmental values are expressed. They assist in lowering transaction costs. And they help multilaterally oriented North American firms and regulatory regimes towards the large challenges that await in the world beyond. It is thus hardly surprising that with the advent of first the US–Canada FTA, and then NAFTA itself, these new political instruments have become the strategies of choice for firms in North America.

The most striking trend is the use of regional international institutions, under the FTA and NAFTA, to settle, manage, or prevent disputes arising over environmental regulatory protection and to foster communication and capacity building, regulatory convergence, and multilateral cooperation. Indeed, as Table 11.1 indicates, of the 84 cases of environmental regulatory protectionism examined in this study, at least 54 have involved the use of such institutions at the bilateral or regional level. A further 5 have witnessed the use of the multilateral GATT or WTO. In total, then, 70 per cent of these issues are dealt with by and through international institutions.

The use of regional institutions has risen sharply since NAFTA took effect in 1994. Of the 22 issues dealt with prior to 1994, 5 involved the use of regional institutions and a further 4 the use of multilateral ones. In the five years of NAFTA's operation, of the 62 cases, 49 have involved regional institutions and only 1 multilateral ones.

There is also a clear shift from the FTA to the NAFTA era, with the NAFTA institutions being much more frequently employed than their FTA predecessors. The advent of the NAFTA institutions has also meant a reduced reliance on the distant, less environmentally friendly institutions of the WTO. One of the most prevalent of these new instruments is the use of international institutional dispute settlement.

Of the 5 under NAFTA, 4 have come under Chapter 11, 1 under Chapter 20, and none under Chapter 19. There is an environmental component to all of the cases thus far that have proceeded under Chapter 11. In addition, the NAAEC's Article 13 has conducted 3 investigations and its Article 14–15 taken up 16 cases, even though its government-to-government Part V has remained unused.

The ease and frequency of use of international institutional dispute settlement is further seen in particular cases. In the case of MMT, Ethyl activated both the Chapter 20 and the Chapter 11 mechanism of the NAFTA regime. In many of the Chapter 11 cases, the ease of filing in the initial stage—a declaration of intent—has made this a useful tactic for companies in their ongoing struggle with governments, hoping to use it to prompt an out-of-court settlement.

It is apparent from the widespread use of international institutional dispute settlement that they are an instrument readily available and rational to use for a wide variety of firms. Domestic producers in the US fisheries industry found them attractive in the herring/salmon cases, in an effort to retain access to a critical raw material input they needed which their potential Canadian competitors had access to as a country-specific advantage. Home-based exporters used it in the UHT, blueberries, lobster, supply management, and beer cans cases. Home-based multinationals used it, through the new Chapter 11 mechanism, in the Metalclad, DESONA, and US Waste cases. And transnational MNEs activated this instrument in the MMT and lumber cases.

Another frequently employed instrument is dispute management and prevention. It was used regularly under the FTA, notably in the UHT case through the Working Group on Dairy Fruits and Vegetables and the 1995 Joint Study, in herring/salmon 2 through a bilateral allocation of the catch, and in Beer 3 through a similar out-of-court accommodation. Its use has risen sharply under NAFTA, with most of the agricultural inspection cases being dealt with through this technique. Indeed, with only one agricultural case going to formal dispute settlement (Supply Management), dispute management and prevention has been the instrument of choice in the agricultural domain.

In part, this reflects the fact that NAFTA has produced a robust set of institutions that make the management and prevention of such disputes easier. While many of the Working Groups existed on a bilateral basis under the FTA, under NAFTA almost all have been rapidly transformed into trilateral bodies and begun to benefit from the same scientifically-based problem-solving spirit that has long characterized the Canadian–US special relationship. Moreover, NAFTA has created a high-level, politically oriented set of trade institutions—the annual Free Trade Commission meeting of ministers, the ongoing consultation among NAFTA coordinators, and the NAFTA trade deputies forum established in 1998—where broader political judgement can be brought to bear. One example of such judgement, and the conflict dampening impact of NAFTA comes from the Ontario beer case, where a desire not to disturb the delicate political balance leading to the conclusion of NAFTA led Canada and the United States to arrive at an out-of-court settlement of the third stage of their dispute over aluminium beer cans.

The popularity of dispute management and prevention in the agricultural cases can be explained by the fact that many of the firms involved in generating protectionist action—such as Florida tomato growers—are small domestic producers resisting the new import competition generated by NAFTA. Even though their domestic trade policy processes give them access to launch actions, the pro-NAFTA policy of their government provides an incentive for the latter to politically manage the dispute in more certain, liberalizing ways. Many of the firms challenging such restrictions are small home-based exporters, who lack the influence with their government to have the latter initiate formal dispute settlement proceedings under Chapters 19 and 20. Yet because such agricultural producers, along with those on both sides of the border have disproportionate political influence and visibility (given widespread consumer concerns about the integrity of the food supply), they induce governments to take up and deal with their concerns on a political level.

The new political instrument of communication and capacity building is also widely used. It was evident in the UHT joint study that led to a certificate of equivalency being granted. Under NAFTA it has been seen in the work of the LTSS 1 which has discussed the different methods of testing automotive emissions in Mexico and the United States, and in the provision of assistance by the United States to train Mexican environmental inspectors who deal, *inter alia*, with automotive emissions. In most cases the NAFTA institutions have been the vehicle through which this process has been undertaken. By providing a regular, trilateral forum for dialogue they have created the communication that fosters transparency and, over time, trust. Capacity building, while a rational response to the difficulties industry faces in coping with a poorly developed Mexican regulatory system, breeds further trust. Over time, communication and capacity building engender a new conception of interests on the part of participating North American governments and firms, and an emergent sense of identity as members of a North American community. Such a process, most apparent in regard to smaller export-oriented firms without broad multinational involvement, makes it easier to move to region-wide regulatory convergence through negotiated mutual adjustment and from there to regional cooperation in multilateral forums.

Regulatory convergence through negotiated, rules-governed mutual adjustment is a defining and increasingly prevalent feature of the NAFTA era. It has been used in small packages and trucking labels, manifests and emergency response guides in the area of dangerous goods transportation. And it is at the centre of activity in the four cases of pesticides, where industry is a direct participant. Its popularity in areas where the chemicals industry is centrally engaged reflects the fact that this industry moved at an earlier stage towards rationalization on a region-wide North American basis (Rugman and D'Cruz 1999). More generally, it flows from the incentive such transnational MNEs have to secure a single set of stable rules over a broad territorial area of their operation.

The instrument of transnational coalition formation is apparent in several cases. These include MMT (where the automotive industry formed a coalition with ENGOs in Canada and the United States); and in European Eco-labelling,

Implications for Firm Strategy 227

1998 (where industry multinationals such as MacMillan Bloedel and the environmental group Greenpeace came to an accommodation over the forest industry's clear-cutting and forestry management practices). Not surprisingly, such transnational coalitions arise most easily in the case of multinational corporations involved in many large national markets, and with equally broadly engaged ENGOs who can harm or facilitate their commercial prospects in all such markets.

A similar logic applies in regard to the creation of regional coalitions for multilateral standards setting activity. Such coalitions are active on the issue of wheat exports and on other issues dealt with by the Committee on Agricultural Trade, in the case of automotive emissions where efforts at standardization are fully oriented towards the work of the UN ECE Working Party 24, and in the cases of dangerous goods transportation where the UN ECE is also an important focus. The home-based exporters in the wheat industry, and especially the transnational MNEs that dominate the automotive and chemicals industry fuel this focus towards a common broadly multilateral regime designed in ways that meet particular North American economic and ecological interests.

The final new political instrument of private standardization is often a preferred choice. It was used in the area of automotive emissions, in the cases of US–Canada pollution prevention programmes and the NLEV programme, and over BC forestry practices, 1998.

In both cases it was forwarded by the transnational MNEs in the automotive and forest products industries. It is such firms which have an incentive to standardize as rapidly and broadly as possible, and which have the size, resources, and influence to undertake the task on their own, with minimum government involvement. The emergence of integrated global production in these industries provides an added incentive for the leading firms to act in this way, rather than rely on intergovernmental processes which are likely to be slower and to accord greater weight to the preference of companies from the many small, less developed countries outside.

It is apparent from this analysis of the frequency of use of the various instruments of corporate and political strategies that firms are employing those most rationally appropriate to their stage of internationalization.

Thus, as Table 11.2 indicates, domestic firms, whose primary concern is import competition, rely on altered production, but largely look to their home governments for bilateral diplomacy, offsetting subsidies, reciprocal retaliation, and, especially with NAFTA, dispute settlement. Home-based exporters, for whom access to the US market is essential, have available to them the additional traditional corporate instruments of exemptionalism, and pay and expand, and the additional political instruments of coalition creation, communication, and multilateralism. For home-based multinationals, the distinctive instrument is regional convergence through negotiated, rules based, mutual adjustment, a strategy appropriate for the high importance of the North American market place to them and the need for a single set of rules govern-

228 *Conclusions*

TABLE 11.2. *Preferred corporate and political strategies by level of internationalization of firm*

Domestic	Home-based exporter	Home-based multinational	Transnational multinational
Corporate instruments			
Altered production	Exemptionalism		Vogel production
	Pay and expand		Border production
	Altered production		FDI
	Private sector		
	market sharing		
Political instruments			
			Litigation
			Lobbying
	Coalition creation	coalition creation	Coalition creation
Bilateral diplomacy	Bilateral diplomacy	Bilateral diplomacy	Bilateral diplomacy
Offsetting subsidies	Offsetting subsidies		
Reciprocal retaliation	Reciprocal retaliation	Reciprocal retaliation	
			National adjustment
Dispute settlement	Dispute settlement	Dispute settlement	Dispute settlement
Dispute management	Dispute management		
	Communication		Communication
		Convergence	Convergence
			Transnationalism
	Multilateralism		Multilateralism
			Standardization

ing it in an age of regionally integrated production. Transnational MNEs, operating on a global scale, have available and actively use a broader array of instruments, especially from the political domain. But they display a distinctive aversion to offsetting subsidies and reciprocal retaliation, due to a distaste for the intergovernmental political conflict it can breed. Their distinctive preference is for transnational coalitions to reduce national regulatory barriers, and for private sector standardization, both instruments they are uniquely able to afford.

Sources of Strategic Success

Identifying successful uses of the instruments of complex institutional responsiveness, and explaining why specific instruments are successfully employed under different conditions is a difficult exercise. The NAFTA regime has been in operation for only a short period of time. Many of the issues dealt with under it are still in progress. Some of the issues resolved immediately prior to NAFTA taking formal effect were done so in anticipation of and thus under the influence of the NAFTA, as a calculated consequence of how countries and firms would be better off by moving to particular solutions. Most importantly,

Implications for Firm Strategy 229

in many of these cases several instruments worked together to produce an outcome, making it somewhat artificial to single out and score each in operation alone. Nonetheless, after a half decade of operation of the NAFTA regime itself, there is a sufficiently strong empirical foundation for confident judgements about the emerging patterns to be made.

As Table 11.3 indicates, 50 of the 84 cases have come to an effective resolution. Ten have done so in the pre-NAFTA period, and 40 have done so in the post-NAFTA period or in the immediate lead-up to and under the conscious anticipation of NAFTA.

One of the most striking findings is how the outcome of issues over environmental regulatory protectionism have benefited the United States and its firms. Of the 50 cases effectively resolved, the United States has won 29, Canada 8, and Mexico 7, while 8 have been resolved to the mutual benefit of two or three of the North American partners. Such a pattern, with the United States prevailing in 58 per cent of the cases, would appear to be a further testament to the realist presupposition that in this bargaining domain as in so many others, the United States with its overwhelmingly superior power, is bound to prevail.

However this first order conclusion needs immediate qualification, for the impact of complex institutional responsiveness is to equalize outcomes in a trade liberalizing and environmentally enhancing manner. On a GNP basis,

TABLE 11.3. *Outcomes of North American regulatory protectionism by country and issue (post-NAFTA resolved cases)*

Case	Cases	US	Canada	Mexico	Equal/All
Trade cases	42 (32)	27 (18)	4 (2)	5 (5)	6 (6)
Automotive emissions	6 (6)	6 (6)	—	—	—
Automotive fuels	3 (2)	3 (2)	—	—	—
Agriculture inspections	15 (5)	9 (9)	1 (1)	4 (4)	1 (1)
Manufacturing recycling	4 (2)	3 (1)	—	—	—
Fisheries conservation	6 (2)	4 (1)	1 (0)	1 (1)	—
Forestry conservation	3 (1)	1 (0)	1 (0)	—	1 (1)
Environmental services	1 (1)	—	—	—	1 (1)
Dangerous goods	2 (2)	—	—	—	2 (2)
Other	2 (1)	1 (0)	1 (1)	—	—
Environment cases	8 (8)	2* (2)	3* (3)	2 (2)	2 (2)
Pesticides	4 (4)	1 (1)	2 (2)	—	1 (1)
Environmental information	1 (1)	—	—	1 (1)	—
Environmental science	2 (2)	—	—	1 (1)	1 (1)
Environmental enforcement	1 (1)	1* (1)	1* (1)	—	—

*Both the US and Canada scored as successful in the CPPRN (Cozumel) case.

230 Conclusions

the United States commands at least 87 per cent of the overall economic capability within the North American region, far more than its 58 per cent success rate actually delivered. Second, in keeping with an issue-structure model, the degree of US success varies widely across issue area, in keeping with the relative size of the home-based firms which dominate each (Keohane and Nye 1977). Thus, the United States enjoys complete success (prevailing in nine of the nine cases) in the area of automotive emissions and fuels, an area dominated by the US-owned big three assemblers and US-owned parts suppliers. It has a success rate of 75 per cent in manufacturing recycling, and 67 per cent in fisheries conservation, but only 60 per cent in agricultural inspection, where the Canadian and especially Mexican industries (based on home-based exporters) loom relatively large. Moreover, the United States has a success rate of only 33 per cent in forestry conservation, an area where Canadian companies are particularly strong.

Third, in many of the cases, notably in the areas of automotive emissions, US dominance arises because it is the first to recognize an environmental problem and take regulatory action. Canadian and Mexican compliance with these regulations is not a case of acquiescence after significant resistance but a case of these two partner countries coming to support the initial US action to produce an environmentally superior result. While this process, often involving convergent national adjustment, does involve the exercise of structural and other forms of power, it is best seen as a form of beneficent rather than coercive hegemony, based in part on the superior scientific resources of the United States. In some cases, it is a matter of NAFTA operating in a world where states do not have fixed preferences but acquire their interests through the process of NAFTA-inspired and guided interaction. Propelling this process is the dominance of US-owned transnational MNEs, and an empowered North American public demanding better environmental solutions.

Fourth, in the domain of trade-related environmental cases there is an almost perfect equality of outcome, and a complete absence of US dominance. In contrast to the environmentally related trade issues, where the United States is successful in 64 per cent (27 of 42) of the cases, in the domain of trade-related environmental cases it prevails in only 25 per cent of the cases. In this latter realm, success is shared equally among the US with 25 per cent, Canada with 38 per cent, Mexico with 25 per cent, and all three with 25 per cent. This sharp shift towards balanced outcomes can be attributed to two factors. The first is the superior ecological capability of Mexico and especially Canada, manifested in a vulnerability for the United States that has been expanded by NAFTA economic liberalizations. To contain this new vulnerability, the United States is forced to cooperate and accept balanced outcomes, as the cases of pesticides and environmental information suggest. The second is the presence in the trade-related environmental area of a strong international institution—the CEC—which unlike those in the trade area possesses an international organization with a single Secretariat, substantial budget and staff, and considerable powers of autonomous investigation.

Implications for Firm Strategy 231

The autonomous power of international institutions is further seen by examining the outcome of the cases according to their non-NAFTA or NAFTA-affected resolution. As Table 11.4 displays, in the 10 resolved pre-NAFTA cases (with the US directly involved in all), the United States prevailed in 8 cases or 80 per cent of the time. Canada, directly involved in 10, won in 2, for a success rate of 20 per cent overall and 20 per cent in the issues of direct engagement. Mexico was not directly involved in any of the resolves pre- and post-NAFTA cases of direct engagement. This distribution is very close to the overall distribution of economic capability in the region, with Canada's somewhat larger-than-predicted score (20 per cent rather than 10 per cent) traceable to the presence of the bilateral FTA. Mexico's zero per cent score in issues of direct engagement reflects a relatively autarkic Mexico, carefully choosing the issues on which it ventured to confront the United States. Equally striking, in this pre-NAFTA era none of the cases resulted in an equal outcome.

In sharp contrast, in the much larger set of 40 cases in the NAFTA era, the distributions are dramatically different. The rate of success for the United States, directly involved in all 40 cases, has dropped from 80 to 50 per cent. Canada's has remained relatively constant, moving from 20 to 13 per cent in all cases and 19 per cent in the 26 cases in which it is directly involved (as a disputant or through the NAFTA trilateral institutions). Mexico's has strongly increased to 18 per cent over all cases and risen to 23 per cent in the 30 issues in which it is directly involved. And outcomes that benefit both or all of the countries and their firms involved have risen from 0 to 20 per cent. Indeed, 57 per cent or over half of the cases involving all three NAFTA countries are resolved according to the preferences of all three.

From these figures it is clear that the NAFTA era works for the United States, in that it still wins over half (50 per cent) of the issues in the region. It further shares in the additional 20 per cent of joint gains, to produce an overall success rate of 70 per cent. The NAFTA era also works for Canada, as its

TABLE 11.4. *Outcomes of resolved cases of North American environmental regulatory protection* (pre- and post-NAFTA)

Winner	Overall	Pre-NAFTA All	Pre-NAFTA Direct	Post-NAFTA All	Post-NAFTA Direct
US	29	8 80%	(8) 80%	20 50%	(20) 50%
Canada	7	2 20%	(2) 20%	5 13%	(5) 19%
Mexico	7	0 0%	(0) 0%	7 18%	(7) 23%
Both/Equal	8	— —	— —	8 20%	— —

(Number of cases of direct involvement)

232 *Conclusions*

success rate holds at 19 per cent in the issues in which it is directly involved, and it records an overall success rate of 39 per cent. The greatest beneficiary of the NAFTA era, however, is the region's weakest member, Mexico, whose success rate rises to the encouraging level of 38 per cent overall. Over the dramatically expanded number of issues in which it is directly involved, relative to the pre-NAFTA period, it records a success rate of 23 per cent against a still much stronger United States, with which it is now much more intensely involved. Above all, the NAFTA area works for the common North American Community, as all three members benefit equally in 20 per cent of the issues, and do so in 50 per cent of those in which all three are directly involved. The world of three competitors struggling for relative gains is clearly giving way to a single integrated community in which all members equally participate and profit.

The importance of the NAFTA era can be further seen by examining the outcomes of those resolved cases in the post-NAFTA era which have been importantly dealt with through the NAFTA institutions, from either its trade or environmental domain.

As the data in Table 11.5 show, of the 40 resolved cases in the post-NAFTA era, 19 or 48 per cent were resolved through the NAFTA institutions (even if other instruments of firm strategy ultimately proved decisive in securing particular outcomes). Of these 19 cases, the United States prevailed in 47 per cent (7), Canada in 22 per cent, Mexico in 21 per cent and all three countries equally in 21 per cent. These are still clearly the United States' NAFTA's institutions, as it is the sole beneficiary of their use to a greater degree than the other partner countries. Indeed, taking its individual and collective gains together, the United States wins through the NAFTA institutions 68 per cent of the time. However, the autonomous impact of international institutions is evident in the greater equality of outcomes when issues are processed through the NAFTA bodies, as Canada's success rate rises from 19 to 32 per cent and Mexico's from 18 to 21 per cent. Most strikingly, when individual and common gains are taken together, the NAFTA institutions deliver a distribution of outcomes that is vastly more equal than power ratios among countries in North America: United States 68 per cent, Canada 53 per cent, Mexico 42 per cent.

The continued imbalance points both to the legacy of US power and highly active environmental movement, but also to Canada's particular historic skill at diplomacy through international institutions. However, the autonomous importance of international organization, and the environmental intervulnerabilities which underlie it are again apparent. For in the 11 cases where NAFTA's trade institutions served as a nest for resolution, the outcomes were distributed: United States 55 per cent; Canada 18 per cent; Mexico 27 per cent; and all 18 per cent. In the 8 cases where NAFTA's environmental institution—the CEC—served as the nest, the outcomes were Canada 50 per cent, the United States 30 per cent, Mexico 38 per cent, and all 25 per cent.

TABLE 11.5. *Resolved cases of post-NAFTA North American environmental regulatory protection dealt with through the NAFTA institutions*

Case	Regulatory initiator	Challenger (supporter)	Outcome closer to objectives of instrument	International institutional
A. Environmentally-related trade issues (59)				
Automotive fuels				
MMT	Canada	US (Ethyl)	US (Ethyl)	NAFTA 11
Agriculture inspections				
Tomatoes, 1992–7	US	Mexico	US	NAFTA 19
Stone fruits, 1997	Mexico	US	US	NAFTA SPS
Sweet cherries	Mexico	US	US	NAFTA
Pork, 1997	US	Mexico	Mexico	NAFTA SPS
Citrus canker	Mexico	US	US	NAFTA SPS
Mangoes	US	Mexico	US	NAFTA SPS
Supply management	Canada	US	Canada	NAFTA 20
Dangerous goods transportation (5)				
Small packages	All	(All)	Equal	NAFTA CRSM
Truck spills (ERG)	All	(All)	Equal	NAFTA CSRM
Other (2)				
Trucking	US	Mexico	Canada	NAFTA FTCC
B. Trade-related environmental issues (24)				
Pesticides (4)				
PCBs	All	All	All	CEC TWGP
DDT	US (Canada)	Mexico	US (Canada)	CEC TWGP
Chlordane	Canada (US)	Mexico	Canada (US)	CEC TWGP
Mercury	All	All	Canada (Mexico)	CEC TWGP
Environmental information (1)				
NAPRI, 1997	CEC	All	Mexico	CEC
Environmental science (3)				
Silva Reservoir	CEC	Mexico	Mexico	CEC 13
LRTAP	CEC	All	Equal	CEC 13
Environmental enforcement (17)				
Cozumel Pier, 1996	All	Mexico	Canada/US	CEC 14–15

At the level of the firm, the importance of effective international institutions is again seen in the particular form in which the NAFTA bodies were fashioned. Of particular importance is their open architecture, allowing firms to have direct access to, and involvement in, the work of these institutions. Firms are involved in the CEC through the JPAC, and many of its working groups. This direct industry involvement was a critical element in producing the mutually beneficial outcomes through regulatory convergence in the TWGP. Within the NAFTA trade institutions, industry involvement is less

234 Conclusions

direct. The mechanism for industry involvement, through the joint meetings of the CSRM with trilateral industry bodies, is a facilitator of success.

Perhaps of greatest importance is the right provided by NAFTA for firms to directly catalyse processes of enforcement-surveillance and dispute settlement, without having to face the barrier of first securing often unavailable or unenthusiastic home government support. Although firms have not yet moved to employ the NAAEC's Article 14–15 process, the importance of this right of direct access is readily apparent in NAFTA's new provisions for investment dispute settlement in Chapter 11.

Indeed, one of the most important elements of complex institutional responsiveness in generating successful, competitive-enhancing outcomes for firms is the direct access NAFTA gives them to international dispute settlement mechanisms. For example, faced with a Canadian government ban on the transborder movement of MMT, Ethyl took its case to both the general dispute settlement mechanism of NAFTA's Chapter 20, modelled closely on its predecessor under the FTA, and NAFTA's Chapter 11, which, unlike the FTA, dealt with investment and allowed firms to activate the mechanism even without the support of their home governments. Ethyl's Chapter 20 action was unsuccessful, as its home US government, having already banned MMT, refused to take up its case. However despite this refusal, Ethyl was able to proceed to secure the first panel ever under NAFTA's Chapter 11. This was also seen in NAAEC with the societally activated Article 14–15 taking up 11 cases and the government-to-government Part V initiating none during the Agreement's first four and a half years.

A second, more broadly operating element of complex institutional responsiveness in generating the use and success of new instruments is the role of the NAFTA institutions in moving actors' conceptions of their interests from the local to ever larger territorial scales. The NAFTA institutions help show how environmental problems once considered local—pesticides in the Great Lakes—have origins and solutions that are regional. They similarly educate firms as to how they can benefit from moving to operate in, and further open, the full North American market place.

One aspect of this move is the shift from fragmented, subfederal regulation to the single national systems that meet the need for a larger home base from which to engage in more global competition. In the MMT case, Ethyl was confronted with the use of a federal trade regulation—a ban on interprovincial movement—that met the needs of an integrated North American automotive industry. But it was able to activate a NAFTA-catalysed and inspired IAT tribunal created to ensure that the internal Canadian market was kept open. And while Ethyl's actions before the Canadian federal courts were unsuccessful, its appeal to the AIT was far more productive. A final decision that the interprovincial movement of MMT was legal opened up for Ethyl a second-best corporate strategy of further FDI—producing rather than just mixing.

New Opportunities for Managers and Policymakers under Complex Institutional Responsiveness

The conditions of complex institutional responsiveness, and the experience of firms and governments in the NAFTA era thus far offer both managers and policymakers clear guidance as to how their operations under and the content of the North American regulatory and institutional framework could be strengthened. Managers, most generally, can use their NAFTA instruments to aggressively develop, through cross-border alliances and other means, the integrated production platforms they need to conquer the global market place beyond and shape the rules that govern it in ways that reward the distinctive interests and values that flourish in their home region. While the particular corporate and political strategies employed must be tailored to the specific stage of internationalization of each firm, virtually all should recognize and plan to capture the rapidly coming regional and global market of the future. In this market, a regionally integrated supply and sales base offers major advantages. Forging transborder business alliances, especially under a five partners flagship model (Rugman and D'Cruz 1996) offers low-cost ways to secure such systems and to combat the national and local regulations that impede their effective operation.

It is evident that firms need stronger NAFTA institutions than they have at present if they are to further open North America and meet intensifying competition in the global market place. The proven performance of the CEC in combating regulatory environmental protection with a protectionist impact highlights the beneficial role which improved regional institutions can have. This strengthening of NAFTA's institutional capacity could take place in several ways.

In the first instance, it is useful to bring into being a single Secretariat for NAFTA's Free Trade Commission, and endow it with powers and resources comparable to that of the Secretariat of the CEC. Such a body could support the NAFTA ministers and deputies in their important work, initiated in 1998, to revitalize and extend the NAFTA trade institutions. It could liaise with the CEC Secretariat to further the largely unaccomplished trade–environment agenda of the CEC and identify joint gains for the trade and environment community through further liberalization. It could identify the pace of, and useful opportunities for, regulatory convergence. As an umbrella rather than sector-specific body, it could identify opportunities for inter-sectoral coordination, as in auto–oil and chemicals–railroads, to speed the pace of regulatory convergence and with it market access with environmental protection. Moreover, it could systematically identify the interests of North America industry and countries in the broader processes of multilateral regulatory convergence. It could thereby mobilize North American firms to engage as a regional grouping to shape the development of those regimes in competitiveness-enhancing ways. Indeed, it would be useful to have ministers beyond those of trade and environment, for example ministers responsible for industry, small business, and natural resource sectors, meet regularly on a trilateral basis to identify common regional interests in the larger multilateral negotiations now underway.

As a second step, it is important to ensure that all NAFTA institutions are functioning on a trilateral basis, with vigorous work programmes to meet their NAFTA mandates. Trilateralizing the remaining working groups of the SPS Committee, and the working groups of the ASC should be the start of such a process. Such intense trilateral interaction fosters the communication, capacity building, and changing conceptions of interests and identity from which regulatory convergence and multilateral cooperation flow. Although private sector standardization is often the preferable alternative, the current regulatory incoherence in the automotive sector points to the need for the certainty that only government regulation can bring. As part of this process, it is important to give practical expression to the many trade–environment powers vested in the CEC, including those for dispute management and prevention.

A third step is to build bodies in new areas where the current regime was silent or where regulatory barriers are looming. One such field is energy. NAFTA could profit from a mechanism for bringing together the North American oil industry, to join with the automotive industry in dealing with the new generation of fuel standards and in mobilizing cooperative regional opportunities on global issues such as climate change. The current rapid restructuring of the electricity industry in North America points to other energy-related opportunities, for example, the establishment of a regional labelling regime for the energy efficiency of appliances and a broad range of consumer goods. More generally, there is a pressing need to have the NAFTA institutions pioneer a new generation of environmental regulations that are both trade liberalizing and environmentally enhancing. The local and national regulations that have long divided communities, are now increasingly inappropriate for the integrated industry and ecology of North America and for the new world of global competition.

A fourth step is to further the opportunities for firms to participate in the work of the NAFTA institutions. At the most general level, the new FTC Secretariat should have mechanisms for ongoing liaison with industry. In a broader modernization of the NAFTA agreements, it would be important to construct a mechanism, modelled on the CEC's JPAC, to ensure that industry and other stakeholders are equally involved in the work of the NAFTA trade institutions.

A fifth step is to strengthen the ability of both the CEC and FTC bodies to engage in independent scientific studies to provide science-based grounds for resolving costly disputes—such as those over MMT, UHT milk, blueberry pesticides, and many others. It is necessary to define regional standards that provide the highest levels of market access and environmental protection. Such a move need not involve the creation of a large supranational bureaucracy on the EU model. Rather it would give the NAFTA institutions the ability to proactively assemble the best scientific talent from around the world to address critical concerns.

A sixth step is to provide a common North American Development Fund to support needed scientific research and develop critical capacity throughout North America, including financing consortia for the development of pre-competitive environmental technologies. NAFTA's existing development mechanisms—the US–Mexican bilateral BECC and NADBank and the tiny CEC—mistakenly assume that North America's environmental challenges lie only within 100 miles of the US–Mexican border. The solutions are not the provision of nineteenth-century-like infrastructure, nor more small community projects. They are both inappropriate to meeting the current environmental challenges. The operation of a fund, directed at consortia of firms from the three NAFTA countries could directly foster the business alliances required to meet the new larger global competition.

A final step is to broaden, as well as deepen, the NAFTA institutions by expanding them to embrace the new free trade communities the United States, Canada, and Mexico are constructing with partners through the FTAA and APEC. As a regime with advanced trade–environment provisions appropriate to countries of widely different levels of development, the NAFTA architecture serves as a model of environmentally enhancing provisions for these new communities. Applying the NAFTA provisions to these new areas would ensure that their trade liberalizing thrust is neither threatened by lack of national regulatory capacity, nor by the green and greedy coalitions that can deny them access to the developed market they seek. Finally, such an extension would enlarge the market for North American firms, better enabling them to meet the intensifying competition faced on a global scale.

Trade and Environment Disputes Beyond North America

The themes discussed in the present case in the context of North America have similarities to cases in the European Union and the WTO. Table 11.6 lists some of the major trade and environment disputes that have occurred within the European Union and Table 11.7 lists the major trade and environment disputes that have occurred between the United States and the European Union (Vogel 1997; Esty 1994). The dynamics of these cases are similar to the cases reviewed in this book within North America. As traditional border barriers decline and the range of environmental, health, and safety regulation increases, opportunities to enact regulations which shelter industry become more appealing to governments. In a rapidly globalizing world economy this threatens the competitiveness of firms of all sizes and degree of internationalization. Within the European Union and throughout the world, there are instances of environmental regulatory protection that has harmed or impeded the activities of firms at all levels, ranging from small home-based exporters to transnational MNEs.

238 *Conclusions*

Thus, the conditions of complex institutional responsiveness are in evidence not just in North America, but in the European Union and the rest of the world as well. Some firms have to some degree begun to engage the tools of complex institutional responsiveness as they exist in their respective regimes. An analysis of the firms who have used such tools could yield valuable new research. A brief review of the major cases illustrates some of the parallel points. For example, within the European Union, the Treaty of Rome contains provisions which balance the goals of trade liberalization with environmental protection, seemingly discouraging the advent of discriminatory environmental regulation. The landmark case—'Cassis de Dijon'—established the 'rule of reason' which opened the door to allow the pursuit of environmental protection to be a justifiable limit to unrestricted inter-Community trade (Gerardin and Stewardson 1995). In the much discussed 'Danish Bottles' case, Denmark enacted a restrictive deposit-return scheme on beer and soft drink containers which placed a heavier burden on foreign producers than Danish producers. This regulation was only partially rescinded by the European Court of Justice (ECJ). For the most part, the ECJ allowed Denmark to pursue the higher level of environmental protection that it deemed necessary, despite its impact on commerce.

Between the United States and the European Union, there has been a

TABLE 11.6. *Major EU trade and environment disputes*

Name	Issue	Date/resolution
Cassis de Dijon	German trading firm challenged trade-restrictive German regulation on French liqueur	1979 landmark case before ECJ overturned German regulation
German beer	German regulation on beer purity standards challenged by French beer firm	ECJ ruled in French firm's favour in 1984
Danish bottles	Trade-restrictive recycling regulations imposed on Danish beer and soft drink containers	In 1988 the ECJ ruled that the regulations were a legitimate trade restriction
French HCFCs	French chemical firms challenging the EU regulations for the planned elimination of HCFSs	Regulation adopted in 1992/93 (no ECJ case to date)
Walloon waste (Belgium)	1985 decree of the Walloon government prohibited the import and discharge of waste from other states	1992 ECJ decision upheld the ban

Implications for Firm Strategy 239

TABLE 11.7. *Major US–EU trade and environment disputes*

Name	Issue	Date/resolution
Tuna–dolphin	EU challenged secondary embargo on tuna caught in a dolphin unfriendly manner	1994—GATT Panel found secondary embargo to be inconsistent with GATT
Beef hormones	US challenged EU ban on hormone treated beef	1998—WTO Appeal Body found EU ban to be inconsistent with GATT
Leghold traps	EU ban on fur caught in leghold traps	1991–present Ban on steel-jawed traps currently in place
CAFE and auto taxes	EU argued that burden of specific environmentally related auto taxes fell disproportionately on EU exports	1975–1994 In 1994, GATT panel found the taxes to be consistent with the US's obligations under the GATT
Eco-labelling	US alleges that EU eco-labelling is discriminatory	1995–present On agenda of WTO's Trade and Environment Committee
Genetically modified Organisms (GMO)	US alleged that EU trade restrictions and labelling requirements on GMOs is discriminatory	1997–present Negotiations ongoing between governments

number of cases heard before the WTO dispute settlement mechanism and the WTO Appellate Body respectively, illustrating that firms increasingly view the WTO as a useful tool of complex institutional responsiveness. Cases increasingly involve a challenge of trade-restricting environmental regulations. Results have been mixed to date. The beef hormones case found the EU ban on hormone-treated US beef to be inconsistent with the provisions of the GATT/WTO. But in 1994 when the EU challenged as discriminatory the US environmental taxes on autos, they were found to be consistent with the US obligations under the GATT. Today, the EU restrictions on genetically modified agricultural products, eco-labelling, and fur caught with leghold traps remain outstanding issues on the US–EU trade agenda (Vogel 1997).

Conclusion

After its first five years, the NAFTA regime works. It is enhancing competitiveness in environmentally enhancing ways. It assures access to the North

American market and helps firms capture global markets by opening regulations that help raise access to the global market place. We can see this by looking at firms using these instruments successfully. Individual firms within North America have an unrecognized benefit in the environmental regime of NAFTA, which provides a successful architecture for future expansion in global markets.

References

ABBOTT, F. (1996). 'From Theory to Practice: The Second Phase of the NAFTA Environmental Regime', in R. Wolfrum (ed.), *Enforcing Environmental Standards*. Berlin: Springer, 451–78.

ABRAHAM, B., and LAWLESS, J. F. (1995). *Analysis of 1988 and 1992–93 Ethyl Corporation Test Fleet HC and NOx Emissions*. Institute for Improvement in Quality and Productivity, University of Waterloo.

AGGARWAL, V. (1983). 'The Unravelling of the Multi-Fibre Agreement, 1981: An Examination of International Regime Change'. *International Organizations*, 37: 617–45.

AIAC (Automotive Industries Association of Canada) (1993). *Automotive Aftermarket Industry: Outlook Study*. Ottawa.

ALCERRECA-JOAQUIN, C. (1997). 'Free Trade and Human Resources in North America: Theory and Practice'. *North American Outlook*, 6: 52–63.

Americas Trade (1997*a*). 'Court Ruling Limits Role of Third Parties in Canada MMT Case'. *Americas Trade*, 4/23 (13 November): 9–11.

—— (1997*b*). 'NAFTA Institutions Should Go Further on Green Issues, Report Says'. *Americas Trade*, 4 (11 December): 11–13.

—— (1998). 'New NAFTA Investor–State Case Against Mexico to be Filed'. *Americas Trade*, 5/12 (11 June): 3.

ANDERSON, A. D. M. (1995). *Seeking Common Ground: Canada–U.S. Trade Dispute Settlement Policies in the Nineties*. Boulder, Colo.: Westview Press.

AUDLEY, J. (1997). *Green Politics and Global Trade: NAFTA and the Future of Environmental Politics*. Washington, DC: Georgetown University Press.

BAFFICO, P. (1997). 'A Retailer's Perspective on the Changing Aftermarket'. Address to the 23rd Annual Strategic Automotive Aftermarket Conference, Chicago, July.

BARRY, D. (1980). 'The Politics of Exceptionalism: Canada and the United States as a Distinctive International Relationship'. *Dalhousie Review*, 60: 114–37.

BARTLETT, C., and Ghoshal, S. (1989). *Managing Across Borders: The Transnational Solution*. Boston: Harvard Business School Press.

BEACHY, D. (1996). 'U.S.–Mexico Backing Away from NAFTA Deal'. *Gazette*, 9 February.

'Beer Blast' (1992). *Wall Street Journal*, 4 August.

BENDESKY, L., BRAMBLE, B., and OWEN, S. (1998). *Four-Year Review of the North American Agreement on Environmental Cooperation: Report of the Independent Review Committee*. Montreal: Commission for Environmental Cooperation.

BHAGWATI, J. N., and HUDEC, R. E. (eds.) (1996). *Fair Trade and Harmonization: Prerequisites for Free Trade?*. Cambridge, Mass.: MIT Press.

BLACKHURST, R., FERRETTI, JANINE, HANSON, ARTHUR J., ISLAM, NURAL, VON MOLTKE, KONRAD, RUBENS RICUPERO, H. E., RUNNALLS, DAVID, MOHAMED SAHNOUN, H. E., and WITOELAR, ERNA (1994). *Trade and Sustainable Development: Principles*. Winnipeg: International Institute for Sustainable Development.

BOUGIE, J. (1993). 'Ontario's Misguided Game of Kick the Can'. *Globe and Mail*, 15 March.

BOVARD, J. (1995). 'Corporate Welfare Fueled by Political Contributions'. *Business and Society Review*, 94: 24–8.

BRADSHER, K. (1993). 'U.S. and Canada Make Deal on Beer Amid Trade Talks'. *New York Times*, 6 August.

BRANANMAN, B. (1996). 'Tomato Imports: Pros and Cons of US Protection Measures'. CRS Report for Congress 96-97, ENR.

BREDHAL, M., SCHMITZ, A., and HILLMAN, J. S. (1987). 'Rent Seeking in International Trade: The Great Tomato War'. *American Journal of Agricultural Economics*, February: 4–8.

BRIDGES (1998). 'SPS Agreement Needs More Clarity to Protect Against Trade Barriers'. *BRIDGES Weekly Trade News Digest*, 2/5, 7 July.

Canada (1992). *North American Free Trade Agreement: Canadian Environmental Review*. Ottawa: Government of Canada.

—— (1993). *North American Agreement on Environmental Co-operation between the Government of Canada, the Government of the United Mexican States, and the Government of the United States of America*. Ottawa: Government of Canada.

—— (1997). *NAFTA: A Partnership at Work*. Ottawa: Department of Foreign Affairs and International Trade.

CCME (Canadian Council of Ministers of the Environment Task Force on Cleaner Vehicles and Fuels) (1995a). *Report to the Canadian Council of Ministers of the Environment*, 23 October.

—— (1995b). *Communiqué: Environment Ministers Endorse Tougher Standards for Vehicles and Fuels*, Whitehorse, Yukon, 24 October.

—— (1995c). *Environmental Protection Measures and the Agreement on Internal Trade: A Practical Manual*. Winnipeg: Manitoba Statutory Publications.

CEC *see* Commission for Environmental Cooperation

CHARNOVITZ, S. (1992). 'GATT and the Environment: Examining the Issues'. *International Environmental Affairs*, 4/3: 203–33.

—— (1997). 'NAFTA and the Expansion of Free Trade: Current Issues and Future Prospects'. *Arizona Journal of International and Comparative Law*, 14/2: 341–79.

COLE, E., and ENSIGN, P. (1997). 'An Examination of United States Foreign Direct Investment into Mexico and its Relation to the North American Free Trade Agreement: Towards a Balanced Understanding of the Effects of Environmental Regulation and the Factor Endowments that Affect the Location Decision', Paper presented at the Annual Meeting of the Academy of International Business, Monterrey, Mexico, 8–12 October 1997.

Commission for Environmental Cooperation (1996a). 'Dispute Avoidance: Weighing the Values of Trade and the Environment under the NAFTA and the NAAEC'. *Environment and Trade Series*, 3. Montreal: Commission for Environmental Cooperation.

—— (1996b). 'Final Communique: North American Environmental Ministers Accelerate Environmental Protection Efforts'. Toronto, 2 August.

—— (1997a). *Independent Review of the North American Agreement for Environmental Cooperation*. Montreal: Commission for Environmental Cooperation.

—— (1997b). *Annual Program and Budget 1997*. Montreal: Commission for Environmental Cooperation.

—— (1997c). *Taking Stock: North American Pollutant Releases and Transfers*. Montreal: Commission for Environmental Cooperation.

—— (1997d). 'Final Communique of the NAFTA Environment Commission's 4th Annual Session'. Pittsburgh, 13 June.

—— (1997e). *Continental Pathways*. Montreal: Commission for Environmental Cooperation.

CONDON, B. (1994). 'NAFTA and the Environment: A Trade-Friendly Approach'. *Northwestern Journal of International Law and Business*, 14: 528–44.

CORCORAN, T. (1996a). 'Marchi Sets a Messy Precedent'. *Globe and Mail*, 11 April.

—— (1996b). 'End the PCB Protection Game'. *Globe and Mail*, 23 August.

—— (1996c). 'Introducing Sheila Marchi'. *Globe and Mail*, 27 September.

Council on Hemispheric Affairs (1997). *NAFTA's Failure to Deliver*. Washington, DC: Council on Hemispheric Affairs.

CUFF, R. D., and GRANATSTEIN, J. L. (1972). 'Canada and the Perils of Exemptionalism'. *Queen's Quarterly*, 79: 473–81.

DARLIN, D. (1995). *Forbes*, 4 December.

DAVEY, W. J. (1996). *Pine & Swine: Canada–United States Trade Dispute Settlement: The FTA Experience and NAFTA Prospects*. Ottawa: Centre for Trade Policy and Law.

DEPALMA, A. (1997). 'NAFTA Environmental Lags May Delay Free Trade Expansion', *New York Times*, 21 May.

DE SOMBRE, E. (1995). 'Baptists and Bootleggers for the Environment: The Origins of United States Unilateral Sanctions'. *Journal of Environment and Development*, 4: 53–75.

DEWIEL, B., HAYWARD, S., JONES, L., and SMITH, M. D. (1997). *Environmental Indicators for Canada and the United States*. Fraser Forum, March. Vancouver: Fraser Institute.

DODGE, D., and LAW, C. (1991). 'Poisoned Meat from Canada'. *New York Times*, 31 May.

DORAN, C. (1984). *Forgotten Partnership: U.S.–Canada Relations Today*. Baltimore: Johns Hopkins Press.

—— and SOKOLSKY, J. (1984). *Canada and Congress: Lobbying in Washington*. Washington, DC: Johns Hopkins University, Strategic and International Studies, Centre for Canadian Studies.

DROHAN, M., (1989). 'Canada Agrees to Allow Fish to be Sold Directly for Export'. *Globe and Mail*, 7 November.

DUNNE, N., and SIMON, B. (1992). 'Canada–U.S. Beer War Gets Green Tinge'. *Financial Times*, 31 July.

DUNNING, J. H. (1993). *Multinational Enterprises and the Global Economy*. New York: Addison-Wesley.

Economic Policy Institute (1997). *The Failed Experiment: NAFTA at Three Years*. Washington, DC: Economic Policy Institute.

Economist (1997). 'When Neighbours Embrace'. *The Economist*, 5 July.

EDEN, L., and MOLOT, M. A. (1994), 'The Challenge of NAFTA: Canada's Role in the North American Auto Industry'. *North American Outlook*, 5 (November): 56–92.

EKLUND, C. D. (1992). 'A Primer on the Arbitration of NAFTA Chapter Eleven Investor–State Disputes'. *Journal of International Arbitration*, 11/6: 135–71.

Environmental Defense Fund (1996a). 'Makers of Over 70% of US Gasoline Reject MMT Use'. *EDF Letter*, 27/3, May.

—— (1996b). 'Consumers Union Says "No" to MMT'. *EDF News Letter*, 27/4, July.

—— (1996c). 'Environmental Defense Fund Urges Oil Firms to Take a Strong "No MMT" Pledge'. *EDF Press Release*, 30 July.

244 References

Environment Canada (1995). 'Environmental Protection Legislation Designed for the Future—A Renewed CEPA', Response to the Recommendations of the Standing Committee on Environment and Sustainable Development outlined in its Fifth Report.

—— (1996a). *News Release and Backgrounder to the Press Release: Government Reintroduces MMT Bill C-94*. Ottawa, 18 April.

—— (1996b). *Government Reintroduces MMT Bill C-29*. Ottawa, 19 April.

ESTY, D. (1994). *Greening the GATT*. Washington, DC: Institute for International Economics.

—— and GERADIN, D. (1997). 'Market Access, Competitiveness, and Harmonization: Environmental Protection in Regional Trade Agreements'. *Harvard Environmental Law Review*, 21/2: 265–336.

FAETH, P., and MCGINNIS, P. (1997). *Estimates of Industrial Pollution Related to Total and Export Production in Latin America*. Washington, DC: World Resources Institute.

FLEISCHER, M. (1997). 'International', *American Lawyer*.

—— (1998). 'New NAFTA Investor–State Case Against Mexico to be Filed'. *Americas Trade*, 5/12 (11 June): 3.

FOX, A. B., HERO, A., and NYE, J. (eds.) (1976). *Canada and the United States: Transnational and Transgovernmental Relations*. New York: Columbia University Press.

FRAIBERG, J., and TREBILCOCK, M. J. (1998). 'Risk Regulation: Technocratic and Democratic Tools for Regulatory Reform'. *McGill Law Journal* (forthcoming).

FREEMAN, A. (1995). 'Companies Fight PCB Export Ban'. *Globe and Mail*, 21 December.

FRENCH, H. F. (1993). 'Battle Over a Bottle'. *World Watch*, March–April: 32–3.

FRY, E. (1997). 'NAFTA and the Expanding Role of Non-Central Governments in North America', Paper presented at the Joint Conference of the Asociacion Mexicana de Estudios Internacionales and the International Studies Association, Manzanillo, Mexico, 11–13 December 1997.

GATT (1992). *International Trade 1990–91*, Volume I.

GATT Panel Report (1993). 'Canada, Import, Distribution and Sale of Certain Alcoholic Drinks by Provincial Marketing Authorities'. *Report of the Panel adopted on February 18, 1992*, BISD 39S (GATT Doc. DS17/R,16 October 1991).

GAYLE, D. (1993). 'Regulating the American Automobile Industry: Sources and Consequences of U.S. Automobile Air Pollution Standards', in Molot (1993), 181–208.

GEDDES, J. (1997). 'Refiners Facing Heavy Costs'. *The Financial Post*, 10 April.

GERARDIN, D., and STEWARDSON, R. (1995). 'Trade and Environment: Some Lessons from Castlemaine Tooheys (Australia) and Danish Bottles (European Community)'. *International and Comparative Law Quarterly*, 44: 41–71.

GILLIGAN, M. (1997). 'Lobbying as a Private Good with Intra-Industry Trade'. *International Studies Quarterly*, 41/3: 455–74.

GLOBERMAN, S. (1993). 'Trade Liberalization and the Environment', in S. Globerman and M. Walker (eds.), *Assessing NAFTA: A Trinational Analysis*. Vancouver: Fraser Institute, 293–314.

GOTLIEB, A. (1984). 'Canadian Business Representation in the U.S.', *Behind the Headlines*, 42.

—— (1991). *I'll be with you in a minute, Mr. Ambassador*. Toronto: University of Toronto Press.

Greenpeace (1998). 'Greenpeace Intensifies Campaign against Western Forest Products to Stop Clearcutting of Ancient Rainforest'. Greenpeace Media Release, 11 June, at <www.greenpeacecanada.org>.

HAAS, P., KEOHANE, R., and LEVY, M. (eds.) (1993). *Institutions for the Earth: Sources of Effective International Environmental Protection*. Cambridge, Mass.: MIT Press.

HART, M. (1994). *What Next? Canada, the Global Economy and the New Trade Policy*. Ottawa: Centre for Trade Policy and Law.

—— DYMOND, B., and ROBERTSON, C. (1995). *Decision at Midnight: Inside the Canada–U.S. Free Trade Negotiations*. Vancouver: University of British Columbia Press.

HARVEY, J., and WEIDENBAUM, M. (1993). *When Businesses Cross International Borders: Strategic Alliance and their Alternatives*. Westport, Conn. and London: Praeger.

HOUSMAN, R. (1994). 'The North American Free Trade Agreement's Lessons for Reconciling Trade and the Environment'. *Stanford Journal of International Law*, 30: 379–422.

Inside U.S. Trade (1998). 'U.S. Lumber Firms Call for Arbitration in Wake of Canadian Fee Change'. *Inside U.S. Trade*, 16/21, 29 May 1998.

JAMES, H., and WEIDENBAUM, M. (1993). *When Businesses Cross International Borders: Strategic Alliances and their Alternatives*. Westport, Conn.: Praeger.

JOHNSON, P. M., and BEAULIEU, A. (1996). *The Environment and NAFTA: Understanding and Implementing the New Continental Law*. Washington, DC: Island Press.

Journal of Commerce (1998). 'WTO Pact Won't Curb Health, Safety Rules'. *Journal of Commerce*, 30 June.

KAWASAKI, T. (1998). 'Managing Macroeconomic Relations with the United States: Japanese and Canadian Experiences', in M. Fry, J. Kirton, and M. Kurosawa (eds.), *The North Pacific Triangle: The United States, Japan and Canada at Century's End*. Toronto: University of Toronto Press.

KEENAN, G. (1996). 'Car Dealers Join Fight to Ban Gas Additive MMT'. *Globe and Mail*, 27 September.

KEOHANE, R. (1984). *After Hegemony: Cooperation and Discord in the World Political Economy*, Princeton: Princeton University Press.

—— and Levy, M. (eds.) (1996). *Institutions for Environmental Aid: Pitfalls and Promise*. Cambridge, Mass.: MIT Press.

—— and Nye, Jr., J. S. (1977). *Power and Interdependence: World Politics in Transition*. Boston: Little, Brown.

—— (1989). *Power and Interdependence*. Glenview, Ill.: Scott, Foresman & Company.

KERR, W. A. (1997). 'Removing Health, Sanitary and Technical Non-Tariff Barriers in NAFTA—A New Institutional Economics Paradigm'. *Journal of World Trade*, 31/5: 57–74.

KIRTON, J. (1993). 'Building a Global Partnership: Canadian–American Relations in the 1990s'. *Canadian–American Public Policy*, 15: 1–46.

—— (1994). 'Promoting Plurilateral Partnership: Managing United States–Canadian Relations in the Post Cold War Period'. *The American Review of Canadian Studies*, 24/X (Winter): 453–72.

—— (1997a). 'NAFTA's Commission for Environmental Co-operation and Canada–US Environmental Relations'. *American Review of Canadian Studies*, 27/4: 459–86.

—— (1997b). 'NAFTA's Future Implications for the Automotive Industry'. *Automotive Aftermarket Business*, November.

—— and FERNANDEZ DE CASTRO, R. (1997). 'NAFTA's Institutions: Their Environmental

Impacts and Potential'. *Environment and Trade Series*, 5. Montreal: Commission for Environmental Cooperation.

KIRTON, J. and MUNTON, D. (1996). 'Subfederal Linkages and the NAFTA Community: The Societal Dimension', Paper prepared for a Conference of the Association of Canadian Studies in the United States, Toronto, 8–9 November.

—— and RICHARDSON, S. (eds.) (1992). *Trade, Environment and Competitiveness: Sustaining Canada's Prosperity*. Ottawa: National Round Table on the Environment and the Economy.

—— —— (1995). 'Advancing Sustainable Development at the Summit of the Americas', in R. Rosenberg and S. Stein (eds.), *Advancing the Miami Process: Civil Society and the Summit of the Americas*. Miami: North South Center Press, 309–40.

—— and SOLOWAY, J. (1996). 'Assessing NAFTA's Environmental Effects: Dimensions of a Framework and the NAFTA Regime'. *NAFTA Environmental Effects Working Paper No. 1*. Montreal: Commission for Environmental Cooperation.

—— WEINTRAUB, SIDNEY, GILBRAETH, JAN, RAMÍREZ DE LA O, ROGELIO, MACLAREN, VIRGINIA, MASERA, OMAR, WILK GRABER, DAVID, and BARRIOS, RAÚL GARCÍA (1996). 'Building a Framework for Assessing NAFTA Effects'. *Environment and Trade Series*, 4. Montreal: Commission for Environmental Cooperation.

KOUPARITSAS, M. (1996). 'A Dynamic Macroeconomic Analysis of NAFTA'. *Economic Perspectives*, Federal Reserve Bank of Chicago.

KRASNER, S. (ed.) (1983). *International Regimes*. Ithaca, NY: Cornell University Press.

LENIHAN, D. (1995). 'When a Legitimate Objective Hits an Unnecessary Obstacle: Harmonizing Regulations and Standards in the Agreement on Internal Trade', in M. Trebilcock and D. Schwanen (eds.), *Getting There: An Assessment of the Agreement on Internal Trade*, C. D. Howe Institute Policy Study 26. Toronto.

LEWINGTON, J. (1989). 'Trade Mechanism Little Help in U.S. Fish Dispute.' *The Globe and Mail*, 10 November.

LEYSHON, A. (1992). 'The Transformation of Regulatory Order: Regulating the Global Economy and Environment'. *Geoforum*, 23: 249–67.

LEYTON-BROWN, D. (1974). 'The Multinational Enterprise and Conflict in Canadian–American Relations'. *International Organization*, 28/4: 733–54.

LUSH, P. (1996). 'Softwood Headaches Loom'. *Globe and Mail*, 20 February.

LUSTIG, N. (1997). 'Setting the Record Straight'. *Policy Brief 20*. Washington, DC: Brookings Institution.

MCCARTHY, S. (1998a). 'Provinces Attack MMT Ban: Alberta Leads Charge in First Case under Internal Trade Pact'. *Globe and Mail*, 16 April.

—— (1998b). 'Failed Ban Becomes Selling Point for MMT'. *Globe and Mail*, 21 July.

MCKENNA, B. (1996a). 'Fuel-additive Bill Expected to Stay Dead'. *Globe and Mail*, 8 February.

—— (1996b). 'Fuel Additive Debate Recharged'. *Globe and Mail*, 25 March.

—— (1996c). 'Canada Warned about PCB Rules: U.S. Waste Management Firm Says Restricting Exports of Some PCBs Violates NAFTA'. *Globe and Mail*, 27 September.

—— (1997). 'Alberta Vows to Challenge Federal Ban on Gas Additive'. *Globe and Mail*, 31 January.

—— and FESCHUK, S. (1996). 'Ottawa to Lift Ban on PCB Exports to US'. *Globe and Mail*, 12 September.

—— FAGAN, D., and LUSH, P. (1996). 'Softwood Tax is Best Deal in a Bad Situation'. *Globe and Mail*, 3 April.

MANARD, Jr., J. (1992). 'GATT and the Environment: The Friction between International Trade and the World's Environment—The Dolphin and Tuna Dispute'. *Tulane Environmental Law Journal*, 5/2: 400–4.
MARCHI, S. (1996). 'Speech to the Transportation, Air Quality and Human Health Conference'. York University, Toronto, 25 April.
—— (1997). 'A Speech to the Pollution Probe National Workshop on Vehicle Inspection and Maintenance'. Toronto, 3 March, Environment Canada.
MATAS, R., and LUSH, P. (1998). 'How a Forestry Giant Went Green'. *Globe and Mail*, 13 June, A1, A10.
MITCHELL, R. (1994). *Intentional Oil Pollution at Sea: Environmental Policy and Treaty Compliance*. Cambridge, Mass.: MIT Press.
MOLOT, M. (ed.) (1993). *Driving Continentally: National Policies and the North American Auto Industry*. Ottawa: Carleton University Press.
MOORE, T. (1997). 'California's Environmental Frustrations', Paper prepared for the 23rd Annual Strategic Automotive Aftermarket Conference, Frost and Sullivan, Chicago, July.
MORTON, P., and TOULIN, A. (1997). 'Eggleton Picks Trade Battles'. *Financial Post*, January.
MUMME, S., and DUNCAN, P. (1996). 'The Commission on Environmental Co-operation and the U.S.–Mexico Border Environment', *Journal of Environment and Development*, 5: 197–215.
—— —— (undated). 'The Commission on Environmental Cooperation and Environmental Management in the Americas', unpublished paper, Department of Political Science, Colorado State University, Fort Collins.
MUNTON, D., and KIRTON, J. (1994). 'Environmental Cooperation: Bilateral, Trilateral, Multilateral'. *North American Outlook*, 4: 59–87.
—— —— (1995). 'Province–State Interaction in the NAFTA Era: A Preliminary Report', Paper prepared for the Commission for Environmental Cooperation, December.
—— —— (1996*a*). 'Province–State Interactions in the 1990's: A Preliminary Report', Report prepared for the Department of Foreign Affairs and International Trade, March.
—— (1996*b*). 'Beyond and Beneath the Nation-State: Province–State Interactions and NAFTA', Paper presented at the International Studies Association Annual Meeting, San Diego, California, 17 April.
MVMA (Motor Vehicles Manufacturing Association and the Association of International Automobile Manufacturers of Canada) (1995). 'The Impact of Manganese Based Fuel Additives on Vehicle Emission Control Technology In Canada'. A report for submission to the Standing Committee on Environment and Sustainable Development, 24 October.
NYE, Jr., J. S. (1974). 'Transnational Relations and Interstate Conflicts'. *International Organization*, 28/4: 961–98.
OECD (1996). *Regulatory Reform and International Market Oppenness*. Paris: OECD.
O'NEILL, K. (1997). 'Regulations as Arbiters of Risk: Great Britain, Germany, and the Hazardous Waste Trade in Western Europe'. *International Studies Quarterly*, 41/4: 687–718.
ORBUCH, P., and SINGER, T. (1995). 'International Trade, the Environment and the States: An Evolving State–Federal Relationship'. *Journal of Environment and Development*, 4: 121–44.

ORDEN, D., and ROMANO, E. (1996). 'The Avocado Dispute and Other Technical Barriers to Agricultural Trade under NAFTA', Paper presented at the conference NAFTA and Agriculture: Is the Experiment Working?, San Antonio, November.

ORME, Jr., W. A. (1996). *Understanding NAFTA: Mexico, Free Trade and the New North America*. Austin: University of Texas Press.

OYE, K., and MAXWELL, J. (1994). 'Self-interest and Environmental Management'. *Journal of Theoretical Politics*, 6/4: 593–624.

POCALYKO, S. (1995). 'Note: Ethyl Corp. v. Environmental Protection Agency: Circuit Court Limits EPA Administrator's Discretion under Waiver Provisions of the Clean Air Act'. *Tulane Environmental Law Journal*, 9: 183–94.

PORTER, M. E. (1990). *The Competitive Advantage of Nations*. New York: Free Press/Macmillan.

—— and VAN DER LINDE, C. (1995). 'Toward a New Conception of the Environment-Competitiveness Relationship'. *Journal of Economic Perspectives*, 9/4: 97–118.

PORTER, M. G. (1980). *Competitive Strategy*. New York: Free Press/Macmillan.

Public Citizen (1995). *NAFTA's Broken Promises*. Washington, DC: Public Citizen.

RAMÍREZ DE LA O, R. (1996). 'North American Investment under NAFTA', NAFTA Effects Working Paper Series No. 3. Montreal: Commission for Environmental Cooperation.

REITZE, Jr., A. W. (1994). 'The Regulation of Fuels and Fuel Additives Under Section 211 of the Clean Air Act'. *Tulsa Law Journal*, 29: 485–540.

RFA (Renewable Fuels Association) (1997). *Ethanol Report*.

RICHARDSON, S. (ed.) (1992). *The North American Free Trade Agreement and the North American Commission on the Environment*. Ottawa: National Round Table on the Environment and Economy.

—— (ed.) (1993). *Shaping Consensus: The North American Commission on the Environment and NAFTA*. Ottawa: National Round Table on the Environment and Economy.

ROBERT, D., and DeREMER, K. (1997). 'Overview of Foreign Technical Barriers to US Agricultural Exports'. ERS Staff Paper ERS-AGES-9705, US Department of Agriculture.

ROHT-ARRIAZA, N. (1992). 'Precaution, Participation and the "Greening" of International Trade Law'. *Journal of Environmental Law and Litigation*, 7: 57–98.

ROMAIN, J. (1993). 'U.S. Recycled-Content Newsprint Legislation: Environmental Regulation or Trade Barrier?'. *Research Note by the Canadian Forest Service*, November.

RUBIN, S. J., and ALEXANDER, D. C. (1996). *NAFTA and the Environment*. The Hague: Kluwer Law International.

RUGMAN, A. M. (1981). *Inside the Multinationals: The Economics of Internal Markets*. New York: Columbia University Press.

—— (1988). 'The Multinational Enterprise', in I. Walter (ed.), *Handbook of International Management*. New York: Wiley, 1–18.

—— (1990). *Multinationals and Canada–United States Free Trade*. Columbia: University of South Carolina Press.

—— (1994). *Foreign Investment and NAFTA*. Columbia: University of South Carolina Press.

—— (1995). 'Environmental Regulations and International Competitiveness: Strategies for Canada's West Coast Forest Products Industry'. *The International Executive*, 37/5: 451–65.

—— (1996). *Multinational Enterprises and Trade Policy*. Cheltenham: Elgar.
—— and ANDERSON, A. D. M. (1987). *Administered Protection in America*. London: Routledge.
—— and D'CRUZ, J. R. (1996). 'Partners across Borders: The Five Partners Business Network Model'. *Management International*, 1: 15–26.
—— —— (forthcoming). *Multinationals as Flagships: A Theory of Regional Business Networks*. Oxford: Oxford University Press.
—— and HODGETTS, R. (1995). *International Business: A Strategic Management Approach*. New York: McGraw-Hill.
—— and KIRTON, J. (1999). 'Multinational Enterprise Strategy and the NAFTA Trade and Environment Regime'. *Journal of World Business*, 33/4: 438–54.
—— and SOLOWAY, J. A. (1997). 'An Environmental Agenda for APEC: Lessons from NAFTA'. *International Executive*, 39/6: 735–44.
—— —— (1998). 'Corporate Strategy and NAFTA when Environmental Regulations are Barriers to Trade'. *Journal of Transnational Management Development*, 3/4: 231–51.
—— and VERBEKE, A. (1990). *Global Corporate Strategy and Trade Policy*. London and New York: Routledge.
—— —— (1994). 'Foreign Direct Investment and NAFTA: A Conceptual Framework', in A. M. Rugman (ed.), *Foreign Investment and NAFTA*. Columbia: University of South Carolina Press, 80–104.
—— —— (1998). 'Corporate Strategies and Environmental Regulations: An Organizing Framework'. *Strategic Management Journal*, 19/3: 363–75.
—— KIRTON, J., and SOLOWAY, J. A. (1997a). 'Canadian Corporate Strategy in a North American Region'. *American Review of Canadian Studies*, 27/3: 199–219.
—— —— —— (1997b). 'NAFTA, Environmental Regulations and Canadian Competitiveness'. *Journal of World Trade*, 31/4: 129–44.
—— —— (eds.) with SOLOWAY, J. A. (1998). *Trade and Environment: Economic, Legal, and Policy Perspectives*. Cheltenham: Edward Elgar.
RUNGE, C. F. (1990). 'Trade Protectionism and Environmental Regulations: The New Nontariff Barriers'. *Northwestern Journal of International Law & Business*, 11/1: 47–61.
—— et al. (1997). *Sustainable Trade Expansion in Latin America and the Caribbean: Analysis and Assessment*. Washington, DC: World Resources Institute.
RUSK, J. (1992). 'Green Concerns Color Trade Disputes in the '90s'. *Globe and Mail*, 10 August.
SAKURADA, D. (1998). 'The "Nixon Shokku" Revisited: Japanese and Canadian Foreign Economic Policies Compared', in M. Fry, J. Kirton, and M. Kurosawa (eds.), *The North Pacific Triangle: The United States, Japan and Canada at Century's End*. Toronto: University of Toronto Press, 17–35.
SCHRADER, E. (1995). *Mother Jones*, January–February: 33–7, 72–3.
SFORZA, M., and VALLIANTOS, M. (1997). 'The Case with Ethyl—MAI Coming Attractions'. *Preamble Center for Public Policy Briefing Paper*, Washington, DC.
SHEINBAUM, C., and RODRIQUEZ VIQUEIRA, L. (1996). 'Inventory of Greenhouse Gas Emissions Associated with Eenergy Use in Mexico'. Instituto de Ingenieria–UNAM, May.
SCHWANEN, D. (1995). 'When Push Comes to Shove: Quantifying the Continuing Use of Trade Remedy Laws between Canada and the United States', in B. Leycegui, W. B. P. Robson, and S. D. Stein (eds.), *Trading Punches: Trade Remedy Law and Disputes under NAFTA*. Toronto: C. D. Howe, 161–82.

SHRYBMAN, S. (1991). *Selling the Environment Short*. Toronto: Canadian Environmental Law Association.

Sierra Club (1996). 'Environmentalists Hail Minister's Decision to Ban MMT'. *Sierra Club Press Release*, Ottawa, 19 April.

SILLARS, L. (1996). 'High-octane Regionalism'. *Western Report*, 18 November.

SOLOWAY, J. A. (1997). 'NAFTA and SPS Standards: The Case of UHT Milk'. Unpublished Mimeo, available from author at Centre for International Studies, University of Toronto, 252 Bloor Street West, 8/F, Toronto, Ontario, M5S 1V6.

—— (1999). 'Environmental Trade Barriers in NAFTA: The MMT Fuel Additives Controversy', *Minnesota Journal of Global Trade*, 8/1: 55–95.

SPENCER, R., KIRTON, J., and NOSSAL, K. R. (eds.) (1982). *The International Joint Commission Seventy Years On*, Toronto: Centre for International Studies, University of Toronto.

Standing Committee on Energy, the Environment and Natural Resources (1987). *Interim Report Concerning Bill C-29, An Act to Regulate Intraprovincial Trade in and Importation for Commercial Purposes of Certain Manganese-Based Substances*, 4 March.

STEINBERG, R. (1997). 'Trade–Environment Negotiations in the EU, NAFTA and WTO: Regional Trajectories of Rule Development'. *American Journal of International Law*, 91/2: 231–67.

STOPFORD, J. M., STRANGE, S., with HENLEY, J. S. (1992). *Rival States, Rival Firms: Competition for World Market Shares*. Cambridge: Cambridge University Press.

STRANGE, S. (1996). *The Retreat of the State: The Diffusion of Power in the World Economy*. Cambridge: Cambridge University Press.

STUDER, I. (1994). 'The Impact of NAFTA on the Mexican Auto Industry'. *North American Outlook*, 5: 20–55.

SUTTON, H. J. (1993). 'The Sweet Lowbush Blueberry (*Vaccinium angustifolium*) in International Trade: Technical Standards as Agricultural Trade Barriers in the Canada–United States Context', *Dalhousie Journal of Legal Studies*, 2: 310–25.

SWANSON, R. F. (1978). *Intergovernmental Perspectives on the Canada–U.S. Relationship*. New York, NY: New York University Press.

SWEENEY, J. (1997). 'NAFTA's Three Year Report Card: An "A" for North America's Economy'. *Roe Backgrounder No. 1117*. Washington, DC: Heritage Foundation.

SWISHER, M. E., BASTIDAS, E. and HOCHMUTH, G. J. (1995). 'Florida's Tomato Producers Adopt Sustainable Practices'. Institute of Food and Agricultural Sciences, University of Florida, Document SS-SA-4.

SYKES, A. O. (1995). *Product Standards for Internationally Integrated Goods Markets*. Washington, DC: Brookings Institution Press.

TED (Trade and Environment Database) (1996). At <http://gurukul.ucc.american.-edu/TED/super.htm#a4>.

THOMAS, J. C. (1992). 'The Future: The Impact of Environmental Regulations on Trade'. *Canada–United States Law Journal*, 18: 383–93.

TREBILCOCK, M. J., and HOWSE, R. (1995). *The Regulation of International Trade*. London and New York: Routledge.

—— —— (1998). *The Regulation of International Trade*, 2nd edn. London: Routledge.

—— PRICHARD, R. S., HARTLE, D. G., DEWEES, D. N. (1982). *The Choice of Governing Instrument*. Ottawa: Minister of Supply and Services.

US Congress, Office of Technology Assessment (1994). *Trade and Environment: Conflicts and Opportunities*, OTA-BP-ITE-94. Washington, DC: US Government Printing Office.

US Foreign Agricultural Service (1997a). 'US Meat Exports Stopped at Mexican Border, Categorized as Sensitive'. *Agricultural News from Mexico*, 10 March.

—— (1997b). 'Another Anti-Dumping Move Against US Beef?'. *Mexican Weekly Highlights and Hot Bites*, 27 March.

—— (1997c). 'The Mexican Strawberry Debacle Continues'. *Mexican Weekly Highlights and Hot Bites*, 14 April.

US Department of Commerce (1995). *Impact of the North American Free Trade Agreement on U.S. Automotive Exports to Mexico*. A report to Congress prepared by the US Department of Commerce International Trade Administration.

US General Accounting Office (1994). *North American Free Trade Agreement: Structure and Status of Implementing Organizations*. Washington, DC: US General Accounting Office.

USTR (US Trade Representative) (1997). *Study on the Operation and Effect of the North American Free Trade Agreement*. Washington, DC: US Trade Representative.

VALIANTE, M., and MULDOON, P. (1990). 'Annual Review of Canada U.S. Environmental Relations—1989'. *International Environmental Affairs*, 2/3: 253–4.

VOGEL, D. (1995). *Trading Up: Consumer and Environmental Regulations in a Global Economy*. Cambridge, Mass.: Harvard University Press.

—— (1997a). 'Trouble for Us and Trouble for Them: Social Regulations as Trade Barriers', in P. S. Nivola (ed.), *Comparative Disadvantages? Social Regulations and the Global Economy*. Washington, DC: Brookings Institution Press.

—— (1997b). *Barriers or Benefits?: Regulation in Transatlantic Trade*. Washington, DC: Brookings Institution Press.

—— and RUGMAN, A. M. (1997). 'Environmentally-Related Trade Disputes between the United States and Canada', *American Review of Canadian Studies*, 27/2: 271–92.

—— —— and SCHETTINO, M. (1997). 'Environmentally Related Trade Disputes in North America'. Montreal: Commission for Environmental Cooperation, unpublished report.

VON MOLTKE, K. (1993). 'Dispute Resolution and Transparency', in *The Greening of World Trade: A Report to EPA from the Trade and Environment Committee of the National Advisory Council for Environmental Policy and Technology*, 112–35.

WALKER, S. (1993). *Environmental Protection versus Trade Liberalization: Finding the Balance*. Brussels: Universitaire Saint-Louis.

WEINTRAUB, S. (1994). 'Current State of U.S.–Canada Economic Relations'. *American Review of Canadian Studies*, 24: 473–88.

—— 1997). *NAFTA at Three: A Progress Report*. Washington, DC: Center for Strategic and International Studies.

—— and GILBREATH, J. (1996). 'North American Trade under NAFTA'. *NAFTA Environmental Effects Working Paper No. 2*. Montreal: Commission for Environmental Cooperation.

WINHAM, G. (1994). 'Enforcement of Environmental Measures: Negotiating the NAFTA Environmental Side Agreement'. *Journal of Environment and Development*, 3/1: 29–42.

WIRTH, D. A. (1994). 'The Role of Science in the Uruguay Round and NAFTA Trade Disciplines'. *Cornell Int'l L.J.* 27: 817–59.

YOUNG, O. (1994). *International Governance: Protecting the Environment in a Stateless Society*. Ithaca, NY: Cornell University Press.

Index

Abbott, F. 75, 77, 80, 92
Abraham, B. 146
Aggarwal, V. 85
Agricultural Working Group 177
agriculture 26, 40–1, 45–7, 51, 81, 121, 130, 149, 162–81, 211, 215, 217, 219, 230
air quality 142–4, 147–8, 150, 190–5, 223
Alberta 48, 66, 68, 86, 109, 124, 150, 153–4
Alcan 43, 123, 222
American Food Safety Inspection Service (AFSIS) 171
American National Standards Institute 188
Anderson, A. D. M. 26, 40, 61, 123–4
Anheuser-Busch 42, 222
anti-dumping 26, 29, 82, 121, 126, 164–5, 169, 220
apples 175–6
Arizona 112
asbestos 24
Asia 127
Asia-Pacific Economic Cooperation (APEC) 76, 80, 85, 109, 134, 162, 181, 201, 237
Audley, J. 77, 80
Australia 162
Auto Industry Pollution prevention Project (Auto Project) 191, 193
automobile industry 24, 48, 51, 85–8, 116, 125, 139–40, 142, 146, 183–203, 211, 216–17, 230, 235–6
Automotive Advisory Council (AAC) 85
Automotive Standards Council 81–2, 84, 134, 195, 201
avocados 174–5

Bacchus, Senator 28
'baptist–bootlegger' 50, 53–4, 65, 67, 129, 131, 156
Barry, D. 123
Bartlett, C. 28
Basel Convention on Hazardous Waste Movement 95
Bastidas, E. 168
Beachy, D. 168
Beaulieu, A. 23, 32, 77, 92
beer 40–2, 53, 63–4, 67–8, 118, 121, 123, 216, 222–3, 225
Border Environment Cooperation Commission (BECC) 91, 237
Bougie, J. 64

Bovar Inc. 48, 67
Bovard, J. 150
Bradsher, K. 64
Brananman, B. 169
Brazil 162
Bredhal, M. 168
Brewers Retail Inc. 42
BRIDGES 162
British Columbia (BC) 28, 39, 46–7, 56, 60, 102, 109, 119, 130, 192, 195, 199, 217, 227
Browner, Carol 101

California 24, 39–40, 47, 50, 53, 119, 121, 130, 142, 150, 172–4, 176, 184, 186, 190–1, 195, 199, 202, 216–17
California Avocado Commission 175
California Farm Bureau Federation (CFBF) 47
Canada–US Air Quality Agreement 187, 192, 222
Canadian Council of Ministers of the Environment (CCME) 148, 192
Canadian Department of International Trade, Fisheries, and Oceans 57
Canadian Environmental Law Association 64
Canadian Environmental Protection Act (CEPA) 48–9, 66, 141, 146
Canadian Petroleum Producers Institute (CPPI) 46, 65, 147, 149
Canadian Vehicle Manufacturers Association (CVMA) 146–7
capacity building 126, 183, 224, 226
capture 38, 52, 105–6
Carabias, Julia 101
CCME Task Force on Cleaner Vehicles and Fuels 148
CEC General Standing Committee 104
Charnovitz, S. 64, 75, 90
chemical 63, 80, 104, 112, 148, 162, 216, 235
Chemsecurity Inc. 48, 67
Chihuahua State Fruit Growers Association 176
Chile 76, 94, 101, 108, 111, 132, 203
Christmas trees 178
Chrysler-Daimler Benz 183–4
Cintec Ltd. 48, 67
Clean Air Agenda 148, 150
Clinton, Bill, US President 95, 108, 110, 113, 152, 172, 179
Cobi Foods 46
Commercial Alcohol 149

Commission for Environmental Cooperation (CEC) 23–6, 28–9, 36, 77, 82, 91–2, 94, 96–113, 126, 128–9, 232
Commission for Labor Cooperation (CLC) 103, 107, 134
Committee for Trade and the Environment (CTE) 75
Committee for Wildlife and Ecosystem Conservation and Management 104
Committee on Agricultural Trade (CAT) 81, 84, 134, 164, 172, 227
Committee on Agriculture and Livestock Trade 172
Committee on Sanitary and Phytosanitary Standards 81, 84
Committee on Standards 81
Committee on Standards-Related Measures (CSRM) 87, 134
competitiveness 23–4, 26–30, 114–15, 117, 128, 133, 237
Condon, B. 32–3
Confederacion de Asociaciones del Estado de Sinaloa (CAADES) 169
Confederacion de National de productores de Hortalizas (CNPH) 169
Conference Board of Canada 61
Convention on Trade in Endangered Species 95
convergence 76, 80–1, 87–9, 91, 122, 127–9, 133–4, 167, 183–5, 220, 223–4, 226–7, 230, 233, 235
Copps, Sheila 47–8, 66, 143
Corcoran, T. 66, 149
Council on Hemispheric Affairs 92
countervailing duties 26, 28–9, 40, 53, 82, 124, 126
Cozumel 101–2, 111
Cuff. R. D. 123

Darlin, D. 174
Davey, W. J. 35
D'Cruz, J. R. 27, 185, 226, 235
Denmark 69, 238
De Palma, A. 102
DeRemer, K. 163
De Sombre, E. 87, 131
DESONA (Desechos Solidos de Naucalpan de C. V.) 155, 225
discriminatory regulation 23, 30–4, 36, 38, 41, 43, 45, 48, 50, 52, 54, 56–9, 61, 67, 69, 114
    see also countervailing duties
dispute settlement 26, 31, 37, 40, 45, 75–6, 82–3, 89, 98, 122, 125–6, 139, 152, 156, 167, 183, 196, 201, 224–5, 231–2, 234
Dodge, E. 171
dolphins 33, 40

Dominican Republic 174
Doran, C. 28, 85
Drohan, M. 57
Duncan, P. 77, 92
Dunne, N. 63
Dunning, J. H. 117
Dymond, B. 60

Economic Policy Institute 92
Eden, L. 220
Eklund, C. D. 150
electricity 236
emissions 48–9, 81, 86, 130, 147, 184, 190–5, 222, 226
Environment Canada 48–9, 103, 140, 146, 148–9
environmental non-governmental organization 24, 36, 62, 76, 79, 85, 91–3, 95, 98, 100, 102–3, 106, 113, 127, 129, 134, 145, 148, 183, 226–7
environmental regulation 23–7, 29–30, 32, 36–9, 43, 50, 53–4, 77, 81–3, 87, 96, 114–17, 120–1, 124, 129, 134, 183, 186–9
    see also capture; discriminatory regulation; labelling; municipal level rules; national level rules; packaging; sub-national level rules
equivalency 34–6, 44–5, 59–60, 117, 123
Esty, D. 75, 83, 127
Ethyl Corporation 50, 52, 54, 65, 139, 141, 143–4, 150–2, 217, 220–2, 225, 234
European Commission 69
European Court of Justice (ECJ) 69, 75, 238
European Union (EU) 26–7, 29, 39, 69–70, 75, 79, 83, 89, 134, 162, 199, 237–9
Extraordinary Challenge Committees 124

Fagan, D. 61
Fernandez de Castro, R. 31, 40, 44, 77, 81, 93, 106
Feschuk, S. 66
Fishery 24, 53, 211, 219, 225, 230
    see also lobster; herring/salmon; dolphins; tuna
Fishery Conservation and Management Act 55
Fleischer, M. 155
Florida 122, 167–8, 176, 178, 225
Ford Motor Company 219
foreign direct investment (FDI) 27, 38, 220–1, 234
forest products 30, 39
    see also forestry; softwood lumber
forestry 26, 28, 53, 60–1, 211, 227, 230
Fox, A. B. 92
Fraiberg, J. 157
Free Trade Commission (FTC) 25, 98, 100, 106–8, 111, 225, 235–6

Freeman, A. 67
French, H. F. 42–3
Fry, E. 85

General Agreement on Tariffs and Trade (GATT) 26–8, 30–5, 42, 55–8, 62, 64, 80, 134, 211, 224, 239
Gerardin, D. 75, 85, 127, 238
Germany 69, 120, 203
Glickman, Dan 173, 177
Globe and Mail 69
Globerman, S. 23
Goodale, Ralph 45
Goshal, S. 28
Gotlieb, A. 28, 123
Government Advisory Committee (GAC) 99, 106
Granatstein, J. L. 123
'green and greedy' 87, 133, 237
Greenpeace 69, 227
Guatemala 173

Haas, P. 77–8
harmonization 23, 25, 47, 49, 85–6, 95, 127, 130, 140, 142, 147–8, 180, 185–6, 189, 192, 198–200
Hart, M. 60
Hatfield, Senator 28
Hawaii 174
Health Canada 146
Heilemann's 41, 222
Hero, A. 92
herring/salmon 24, 32, 55–8, 67–8, 215, 222, 225
Hillman, J. S. 168
Hodgetts, R. 28
Houseman, R. 24, 80, 94
Houston 155
Howse, R. 32–3, 69

Idaho 175–6
institutional responsiveness 135, 139–40, 166
Integrated Fuels Policy 194
Internal Trade Agreement (ITA) 66, 142, 150, 153–4, 156
International Air Quality Management Basins 194
International Dispute Settlement 125
International Joint Commission (IJC) 99
International Standards Organization 163

Johnson, P. M. 23, 32, 77, 92
Joint Public Advisory Committee (JPAC) 91, 93, 99, 101–2, 105–6, 110–11, 233, 236

Kawasaki, T. 123
Keenan, G. 65

Keohane, R. 28, 77–8, 230
Kerr, W. A. 171
Kirton, J. J. 23–4, 26–7, 31, 40, 44, 76–7, 80–2, 92–4, 106, 109, 130, 152, 193, 220, 222
Krasner, S. 78

Labatt 41
labelling 38, 40, 52, 69, 127, 172–3, 180, 226
Lactel 34–6, 44, 53–60, 118, 122–3, 216, 219
Land Transportation Subcommittee 81, 182
Law, C. 171
Lawless, J. E. 146
Levy, M. 77–8
Lewington, J. 57
Leyshon, A. 217
Leyton-Brown, D. 28
lobster 40, 58–9, 67–8, 225
Lush, P. 61, 69
Lustig, N. 92

McCarthy, S. 152–3
McKenna, B. 61, 65–7, 150
MacMillan Bloedel 69, 217, 227
Magnuson Act 58–9
Maine 45, 47, 124
Malaysia 182
Manard, J. 58
mangoes 177–8
Manitoba 109, 149
maquilladoras 94, 121, 188, 197
Marchi, Sergio 47, 64–6, 101, 143, 152, 191–3
market access 32, 39
Massachusetts 190, 199
Matas, R. 69
Maxwell, J. 79
meat 170–2
Metalclad 83, 155, 225
Mexican Association of Cattle Feeders (AMEG) 170
Mexican Ministry of Agriculture (SAGAR) 173–4
Mexican Ministry of Commerce and Industry (SECOFI) 175
Mexican National Ecology Institute (INE) 194
Michigan 178, 191
Mitchell, R. 78
MMT 40, 48–54, 64–8, 83, 125, 130, 139–57, 184, 191–2, 199, 201, 203, 216, 219–23, 225–6, 234, 236
Molot, M. A. 220
Molson 41
Montreal 99, 102
Montreal Protocol on Ozone Depletion 95
Moore, L. 191

Morroquin, Romarico 173
Motor Vehicle Manufacturers Association (MVMA) 49, 65, 146, 191, 193
Muldoon, P. 56
multinational corporation (MNC) 89, 125
  see also multinational enterprises (MNE)
multinational enterprises (MNE) 27–30, 37, 86, 88, 123, 128, 130, 132, 139, 184, 225–8, 230, 238
Mumme, S. 77, 92
municipal level rules 26
Munton, D. 23, 27, 77, 80, 93, 109, 193

NAFTA's Environmental Effects 102
National Advisory Committee (NAC) 99, 106
National Ambient Air Quality Standards (NAAQS) 190
National Cattleman's Beef Association 172
National Consultative Committee for Sustainable Development 106
national level rules 26, 50, 54, 82, 129
national treatment 23, 25, 30–2, 42, 50, 53–4, 65, 151
New Brunswick 45–7, 119, 124
Newfoundland 46–7
New Low Emissions Vehicle (NLEV) 199–200, 227
New York 190, 199
non-governmental organization 79, 92, 101–2, 105–6, 118–19, 142, 144, 187, 215–16, 220
North American Aerospace Defence Command 102
North American Agreement on Environmental Cooperation (NAEEC) 77, 79, 91–2, 96, 98–9, 101, 106, 108–10, 112, 126, 131, 234
North American Auto Supplier Environmental Workshop 193
North American Commission on the Environment 95
North American Dangerous Goods Code 195
North American Development Bank (NADBANK) 91, 237
North American Fund for Environmental Cooperation 103
North American Plant Protection Organization (NAPPO) 163–4
North American Pollutant's Release Inventory 109–11
North American Trilateral Standardization Forum 87
North American Wildlife Federation 95
North West Fruit Producers Association 175
Nossal, K. R. 77, 92
Nova Scotia 46–7, 109, 178
Nye, J. 28, 78, 92, 123, 230

Oaxaca 100
Ochoa, Francisco Labastida 177
Ontario 24, 28, 40–2, 48, 63–4, 66, 70, 104, 109, 118, 121, 123, 178, 186, 192–3, 216, 222
Orbuch, P. 82, 130
Orden, D. 174
Oregon 46, 175–6
Organisation for Economic Cooperation and Development (OECD) 76, 85
Orme, W. A. 23
Oxford Frozen Foods Limited 46
Oye, K. 79
ozone 80

Pacific Salmon Treaty 68
packaging 122
Packwood, Senator 28
PCB 24, 40, 47–8, 51, 66–8, 222
Pemex 199
pesticides 46, 84–7, 94, 104, 112, 119, 164, 168, 230, 234, 236
petroleum industry 48, 86, 116, 140, 142, 191, 216, 235–6
Pittsburgh 100
Porter, M. 29, 120, 124, 218, 220
Prince Edward Island 45, 47
proportionality test 57
protectionist policies 23, 30, 32, 37, 42, 53, 69, 75–6, 79, 82–4, 89, 122, 129–30, 133, 141, 162, 166, 172, 180, 183, 211–15, 217–18, 220, 229
Puerto Rico 34–5, 43–4, 59–60, 68, 178

Quebec 34–5, 59–60, 66–8, 109, 150, 153, 178, 219

Ramirez de la O, R. 219
Reagan, Ronald, US President 101
recycle 41–2, 61–3, 121, 216–17, 230
regimes 23, 53, 120, 124, 183
Richardson, S. 23–4, 27, 94
Rio Conference 96, 110
Roberts, Pat 179
Robertson, C. 60
Rodriguez Vigueria, L. 194
Romain, J. 62
Romano, E. 174
Rugman, A. 23, 25–30, 39–41, 45, 48, 50, 55, 61, 67, 76–7, 79–80, 83, 87, 94, 117, 120, 123–4, 130, 185, 217–18, 226, 235
Rusk, J. 63–4
Russia 127

Safety of Imported Food Act 172
Sakurada, D. 124

Index   257

sanctions 131–2, 222–3, 228
Sandiad Vegetal 179
Sarnia 141
Saskatchewan 149–50, 153–4, 219
Schettino, M. 25, 40
Schmitz, A. 168
Schrader, E. 168
Schwanen, D. 26
S. D. Myers 48, 66
Senate Standing Committee on Energy, Environment, and Natural Resources 64, 143, 146–7, 151, 154
Senegal 162
Sforza, M. 151
Sheinbaum, C. 194
shelter 23, 29, 39, 48, 50–2, 67, 180
Shrybman, S. 58, 61
Silva Reservoir 102, 111
Simon, B. 63
Singer, T. 82, 130
softwood lumber 28, 53, 60–1, 67, 119, 123–4, 219, 222–3
Softwood Lumber Agreement 124
Sokolsky, J. 28
Soloway, J. A. 26, 31, 40, 47, 49, 76–7, 80, 83, 94, 152
sorghum 179
South Korea 162
Spencer, R. 77, 92
standards 27, 30–3, 48, 54, 84–5, 88, 115, 127, 132, 147, 170, 173, 177, 186–8, 190–1, 196–203, 228, 236
  environmental 30, 33, 81, 97–8, 130, 139
  health and safety 43–5, 52, 59–60, 166
  sanitary and phytosanitary 34, 76, 81, 84, 95, 134, 162–3
Standards Council of Canada 188
steel 26, 127
Steinberg, R. 75–6, 78–9
Stewardson, R. 238
Stockholm Conference 96
Strange, S. 78, 104
strategies 115–35, 167, 177, 211
strawberries 172–4
Stroh 41–2
sub-national level rules 26, 41, 50, 82, 86, 129
subsidies 53, 82, 124, 163, 228
subsidization 122, 124, 222
Suspension Agreement on Fresh Tomatoes from Mexico 169, 176
sustainable development 80, 100–1
Sutton, H. J. 46
Swanson, R. F. 77, 92
Sweeney, J. 93
sweet cherries 176–7
Swisher, M. E. 168

tariff 163, 175
Technical Working Group on Dairy, Fruit, Vegetable, and Egg Inspection 44, 59, 225
Technical Working Group on Pesticides 84–5, 104, 164, 233
Tennessee 104
Texas 85, 104, 179
tomatoes 167–70, 225
Toronto 100–2
Toronto Star 64
trade:
  and the environment 23, 26, 28, 36, 40, 79, 88, 100–2, 104, 106–7, 111–12, 236–7
  and investment 29, 96
  liberalization 35, 109, 114, 115, 128, 9, 134, 215
Treasury Board Secretariat 154
Treaty of Rome 69, 238
Trebilcock, M. J. 32–3, 69, 157
trilateral 101–2, 104, 108
trilateralism 100
Trilateral Working Group on Pesticides 81
tuna 33, 40, 55, 222

UHT 24, 34–7, 40–1, 44, 51, 53, 59–60, 67–8, 114, 118, 122–3, 164, 216, 219, 222, 225–6, 236
UN Commission for International Trade (UNCITRAL) 151
UN Conference on Environment and Development (UNCED) 94
UN Economic Commission for Europe 85, 227
Uruguay round 163
US Agricultural Marketing Agreement Act 167
US Animal and Plant Health Inspection Service (APHIS) 178
US Clean Air Act 144, 190
US Coalition for Fair Lumber Imports (COFLI) 61
US Commerce Department 39, 60–1, 169
US Department of Agriculture (USDA) 45–6, 163, 167, 170–1, 174–5
US Environment Protection Agency (EPA) 47, 62, 66, 100, 144, 152, 190–1, 200, 223
US Food and Drug Administration (USFDA) 44, 59
US Home Builder's Association 123
US International Trade Commission (ITC) 39, 61
US Meat Export Federation (USMEF) 170
US–Mexico La Paz Agreement 187, 194
US National Academy of Sciences 149

258 *Index*

US Trade Representative (USTR) 152
USA Waste 83, 155, 225

Valiante, M. 56
Valliantos, M. 151
Van der Linde, C. 29, 120
Verbeke, A. 26, 29, 39, 50, 67, 217
Vogel, D. 25, 29, 32, 39–41, 45, 48, 50, 52, 54, 76, 79, 87, 114, 120, 124, 130–1, 141, 149–50, 183, 219–20, 237, 239
voluntary export restrictions 165, 168
von Moltke, K. 58

Walker, S. 69
Washington 100
Washington State 175–6

Waste Management 48, 66
Weintraub, S. 77, 93, 106, 185
wheat 178–9
Winham, G. 23, 96
Wirth, D. A. 157
Wisconsin 178
Working Group on Technical Measures and Commercialization of Livestock and Agricultural Products 172
Working Group on the Transportation of Dangerous Goods 81, 84
Working Group on Vehicle Standards 84
World Trade Organisation (WTO) 26–8, 75, 79–80, 85, 101, 124, 134, 162–3, 165, 169, 181, 224, 237, 239